English-Turkish
Turkish-English

Word to Word®
Bilingual Dictionary

Compiled by:
C. Sesma, M.A.

Translated & Edited by:
Nagme Yazgin
Özer S...

D1254132

Bilingual Dictionaries, Inc.

Turkish Word to Word® Bilingual Dictionary
2nd Edition © Copyright 2012

Published in the United States by:

Bilingual Dictionaries, Inc.
PO Box 1154
Murrieta, CA 92564
T: (951) 296-2445 • F: (951) 296-9911
www.BilingualDictionaries.com

ISBN13: 978-0-933146-95-2
ISBN: 0-933146-95-7

Table of Contents

Preface

Bilingual Dictionaries, Inc. is committed to providing schools, libraries and educators with a great selection of bilingual materials for students. Along with bilingual dictionaries we also provide ESL materials, children's bilingual stories and children's bilingual picture dictionaries.

Sesma's Turkish Word to Word® Bilingual Dictionary was created specifically with students in mind to be used for reference and testing. This dictionary contains approximately 19,500 entries targeting common words used in the English language.

Word to Word®

Bilingual Dictionaries, Inc. is the publisher of the Word to Word® bilingual dictionary series with over 30 languages that are 100% Word to Word®. The Word to Word® series provides ELL students with standardized bilingual dictionaries approved for state testing. Students with different backgrounds can now use dictionaries from the same series that are specifically designed to create an equal resource that strictly adheres to the guidelines set by districts and states.

entry: our selection of English vocabulary includes common words found in school usage and everyday conversation.

part of speech: part of speech is necessary to ensure the translation is appropriate. Entries can be spelled the same but have different translations and meanings depending on the part of speech.

translation: our translation is Word to Word® meaning no definitions or explanations. Purely the most simple common accurate translation.

List of Irregular Verbs

present - past - past participle

arise - arose - arisen
awake - awoke - awoken, awaked
be - was - been
bear - bore - borne
beat - beat - beaten
become - became - become
begin - began - begun
behold - beheld - beheld
bend - bent - bent
beseech - besought - besought
bet - bet - betted
bid - bade (bid) - bidden (bid)
bind - bound - bound
bite - bit - bitten
bleed - bled - bled
blow - blew - blown
break - broke - broken
breed - bred - bred
bring - brought - brought
build - built - built
burn - burnt - burnt *
burst - burst - burst
buy - bought - bought
cast - cast - cast
catch - caught - caught
choose - chose - chosen
cling - clung - clung
come - came - come
cost - cost - cost
creep - crept - crept
cut - cut - cut
deal - dealt - dealt

dig - dug - dug
do - did - done
draw - drew - drawn
dream - dreamt - dreamed
drink - drank - drunk
drive - drove - driven
dwell - dwelt - dwelt
eat - ate - eaten
fall - fell - fallen
feed - fed - fed
feel - felt - felt
fight - fought - fought
find - found - found
flee - fled - fled
fling - flung - flung
fly - flew - flown
forebear - forbore - forborne
forbid - forbade - forbidden
forecast - forecast - forecast
forget - forgot - forgotten
forgive - forgave - forgiven
forego - forewent - foregone
foresee - foresaw - foreseen
foretell - foretold - foretold
forget - forgot - forgotten
forsake - forsook - forsaken
freeze - froze - frozen
get - got - gotten
give - gave - given
go - went - gone
grind - ground - ground
grow - grew - grown
hang - hung * - hung *
have - had - had

hear - heard - heard	**ring** - rang - rung
hide - hid - hidden	**rise** - rose - risen
hit - hit - hit	**run** - ran - run
hold - held - held	**saw** - sawed - sawn
hurt - hurt - hurt	**say** - said - said
hit - hit - hit	**see** - saw - seen
hold - held - held	**seek** - sought - sought
keep - kept - kept	**sell** - sold - sold
kneel - knelt * - knelt *	**send** - sent - sent
know - knew - known	**set** - set - set
lay - laid - laid	**sew** - sewed - sewn
lead - led - led	**shake** - shook - shaken
lean - leant * - leant *	**shear** - sheared - shorn
leap - lept * - lept *	**shed** - shed - shed
learn - learnt * - learnt *	**shine** - shone - shone
leave - left - left	**shoot** - shot - shot
lend - lent - lent	**show** - showed - shown
let - let - let	**shrink** - shrank - shrunk
lie - lay - lain	**shut** - shut - shut
light - lit * - lit *	**sing** - sang - sung
lose - lost - lost	**sink** - sank - sunk
make - made - made	**sit** - sat - sat
mean - meant - meant	**slay** - slew - slain
meet - met - met	**sleep** - sleep - slept
mistake - mistook - mistaken	**slide** - slid - slid
must - had to - had to	**sling** - slung - slung
pay - paid - paid	**smell** - smelt * - smelt *
plead - pleaded - pled	**sow** - sowed - sown *
prove - proved - proven	**speak** - spoke - spoken
put - put - put	**speed** - sped * - sped *
quit - quit * - quit *	**spell** - spelt * - spelt *
read - read - read	**spend** - spent - spent
rid - rid - rid	**spill** - spilt * - spilt *
ride - rode - ridden	**spin** - spun - spun

spit - spat - spat
split - split - split
spread - spread - spread
spring - sprang - sprung
stand - stood - stood
steal - stole - stolen
stick - stuck - stuck
sting - stung - stung
stink - stank - stunk
stride - strode - stridden
strike - struck - struck (stricken)
strive - strove - striven
swear - swore - sworn
sweep - swept - swept
swell - swelled - swollen *
swim - swam - swum
take - took - taken
teach - taught - taught
tear - tore - torn

tell - told - told
think - thought - thought
throw - threw - thrown
thrust - thrust - thrust
tread - trod - trodden
wake - woke - woken
wear - wore - worn
weave - wove * - woven *
wed - wed * - wed *
weep - wept - wept
win - won - won
wind - wound - wound
wring - wrung - wrung
write - wrote - written

Those tenses with an * also have regular forms.

English-Turkish

Bilingual Dictionaries, Inc.

Abbreviations

a - article
n - noun
e - exclamation
pro - pronoun
adj - adjective
adv - adverb
v - verb
iv - irregular verb
pre - preposition
c - conjunction

a *a* bir
abandon *v* terketmek
abandonment *n* terk
abbey *n* manastır
abbot *n* başrahip
abbreviate *v* kısaltmak
abbreviation *n* kısaltma
abdicate *v* çekilmek
abdication *n* çekilme
abdomen *n* karın
abduct *v* kaçırmak
abduction *n* kaçırma
aberration *n* sapma
abhor *v* iğrenmek
abide by *v* itaat
ability *n* yetenek
ablaze *adj* ışıltılı
able *adj* muktedir
abnormal *adj* anormal
abnormality *n* anormallik
aboard *adv* içinde
abolish *v* feshetmek
abort *v* durdurmak
abortion *n* kürtaj
abound *v* bol olmak
about *pre* civarında
about *adv* hakkında
above *pre* üstünde
abreast *adv* yanyana

abridge *v* özetlemek
abroad *adv* yurtdışında
abrogate *v* feshetmek
abruptly *adv* birdenbire
absence *n* eksiklik
absent *adj* eksik
absolute *adj* tam
absolution *n* af
absolve *v* bağışlamak
absorb *v* emmek
absorbent *adj* emici
abstain *v* kaçınmak
abstinence *n* kaçınmak
abstract *adj* soyut
absurd *adj* saçma
abundance *n* bolluk
abundant *adj* bol
abuse *v* kötüye kullanmak
abuse *n* suistimal
abusive *adj* kötüleyici
abysmal *adj* berbat
abyss *n* uçurum
academic *adj* akademik
academy *n* akademi
accelerate *v* hızlandırmak
accelerator *n* hızlandırıcı
accent *n* aksan
accept *v* kabul etmek
acceptable *adj* kabul edilebilir
acceptance *n* kabul
access *n* erişim
accessible *adj* erişilebilir

accident *n* kaza
accidental *adj* yanlışlıkla
acclaim *v* övmek
acclimatize *v* alıştırmak
accommodate *v* yerleştirmek
accompany *v* eşlik etmek
accomplice *n* suç ortağı
accomplish *v* başarmak
accomplishment *n* başarı
accord *n* muvafakat
according to *pre* e göre
accordion *n* akordeon
account *n* hesap
account for *v* hesap vermek
accountable *adj* sorumlu
accountant *n* muhasebeci
accumulate *v* biriktirmek
accuracy *n* doğruluk
accurate *adj* doğru
accusation *n* suçlama
accuse *v* suçlamak
accustom *v* alıştırmak
ace *n* as
ache *n* ağrı
achieve *v* başarmak
achievement *n* başarı
acid *n* asit
acidity *n* asitlik
acknowledge *v* kabul etmek
acorn *n* meşe palamudu
acoustic *adj* akustik
acquaint *v* haberdar olmak

acquaintance *n* tanıdık
acquire *v* elde etmek
acquisition *n* kazanım
acquit *v* aklamak
acquittal *n* beraat
acre *n* dönüm
acrobat *n* akrobat
across *pre* öbür tarafına
act *n* kanun; oyun
act *v* davranmak
action *n* eylem
activate *v* etkinleştirmek
activation *n* etkinleştirme
active *adj* faal
activity *n* faaliyet
actor *n* aktör
actress *n* aktris
actual *adj* asıl
actually *adv* aslında
acute *adj* keskin; akut
adamant *adj* kararlı
adapt *v* uyarlamak
adaptable *adj* uyarlanabilen
adaptation *n* adaptasyon,uyum
adapter *n* adaptör
add *v* eklemek
addicted *adj* bağımlı
addiction *n* bağımlılık
addictive *adj* bağımlılık yapan
addition *n* ekleme
additional *adj* ek
address *n* adres

address *v* hitap etmek
addressee *n* muhatap
adequate *adj* yeterli
adhere *v* e yapışmak
adhesive *adj* yapışkan
adjacent *adj* bitişik
adjective *n* sıfat
adjoin *v* bitiştirmek
adjoining *adj* yanyana
adjourn *v* sona ermek
adjust *v* düzenlemek
adjustable *adj* düzenlenebilir
adjustment *n* düzenleme
administer *v* yönetmek
admirable *adj* takdire değer
admiral *n* amiral
admiration *n* takdir
admire *v* beğenmek
admirer *n* hayran
admissible *adj* makbul
admission *n* kabul; itiraf
admit *v* kabul etmek
admittance *n* kabul
admonish *v* tembih etmek
admonition *n* tembih
adolescence *n* ergenlik
adolescent *n* ergen
adopt *v* evlat edinmek
adoption *n* evlat edinme
adoptive *adj* üvey
adorable *adj* tapılası
adoration *n* tapınma

adore *v* tapmak
adorn *v* süslemek
adrift *adv* sürüklenmiş
adulation *n* dalkavukluk
adult *n* yetişkin
adulterate *v* karıştırmak
adultery *n* zina
advance *v* ilerlemek
advance *n* ilerleme
advantage *n* avantaj
Advent *n* Advent
adventure *n* macera
adverb *n* belirteç, zarf
adversary *n* düşman
adverse *adj* karşıt
adversity *n* zorluk
advertise *v* reklam yapmak
advertising *n* tanıtım
advice *n* nasihat
advisable *adj* makul
advise *v* tavsiye etmek
adviser *n* danışman
advocate *v* savunmak
aesthetic *adj* estetik
afar *adv* uzakta
affable *adj* cana yakın
affair *n* iş; aşk ilişkisi
affect *v* etkilemek
affection *n* düşkünlük
affectionate *adj* düşkün
affiliate *v* birleştirmek
affiliation *n* yakın ilişki

affinity *n* benzerlik
affirm *v* doğrulamak
affirmative *adj* olumlu
affix *v* sonek; önek
afflict *v* acı vermek
affliction *n* dert
affluence *n* refah
affluent *adj* zengin
afford *v* karşılamak
affordable *adj* karşılanabilir
affront *v* hakaret etmek
affront *n* hakaret
afloat *adv* yüzen
afraid *adj* korkmuş
afresh *adv* yeniden
after *pre* sonra
afternoon *n* öğleden sonra
afterwards *adv* daha sonra
again *adv* tekrar
against *pre* karşı
age *n* yaş
agency *n* ajans
agenda *n* ajanda
agent *n* ajan; acenta
agglomerate *v* yığışmak
aggravate *v* kötüleştirmek
aggravation *n* kötüleştirme
aggregate *v* toplamak
aggression *n* saldırı
aggressive *adj* saldırgan, kavgacı
aggressor *n* saldırgan
aghast *adj* donakalmış

agile *adj* çevik
agitator *n* kışkırtıcı
agnostic *n* bilinemezci, agnostik
agonize *v* ızdırap çekmek
agonizing *adj* ızdırap verici
agony *n* ızdırap
agree *v* anlaşmak
agreeable *adj* uygun
agreement *n* anlaşma
agricultural *adj* tarımsal
agriculture *n* tarım
ahead *pre* ileride
aid *n* yardım
aid *v* yardımcı olmak
aide *n* yardımcı
ailing *adj* rahatsız
ailment *n* hastalık
aim *v* amaçlamak
aimless *adj* amaçsız
air *n* hava
air *v* havalandırmak
aircraft *n* uçak
airfare *n* uçuş ücreti
airfield *n* havaalanı
airline *n* havayolu
airliner *n* yolcu uçağı
airmail *n* uçak postası
airplane *n* uçak
airport *n* havalimanı, havaalanı
airspace *n* hava boşluğu
airstrip *n* uçak pisti
airtight *adj* hava geçirmez

aisle *n* koridor
ajar *adj* aralık
akin *adj* benzer
alarm *n* alarm
alarm clock *n* çalar saat
alarming *adj* endişe verici
alcoholic *adj* alkolik
alcoholism *n* alkolizm
alert *n* uyarı
alert *v* uyarmak
algebra *n* cebir
alien *n* yabancı
alight *adv* yanan
align *v* hizaya getirmek
alignment *n* hiza
alike *adj* benzer
alive *adj* canlı
all *adj* hepsi
allegation *n* iddia
allege *v* iddia etmek
allegedly *adv* sözde
allegiance *n* sadakat
allegory *n* kinaye
allergic *adj* alerjik
allergy *n* alerji
alleviate *v* azaltmak
alley *n* patika
alliance *n* ittifak
allied *adj* müttefik
alligator *n* timsah
allocate *v* ayırmak
allot *v* pay etmek

allotment *n* hisse
allow *v* izin vermek
allowance *n* harçlık
alloy *n* alaşım
allure *n* cazibe
alluring *adj* cazibeli
allusion *n* ima
ally *n* müttefik
ally *v* ittifak etmek
almanac *n* almanak
almighty *adj* ulu
almond *n* badem
almost *adv* neredeyse
alms *n* sadaka
alone *adj* yalnız
along *pre* boyunca
alongside *pre* yanında
aloof *adj* ilgisiz; soğuk
aloud *adv* yüksek ses
alphabet *n* alfabe
already *adv* zaten
alright *adv* peki
also *adv* ayrıca
altar *n* sunak
alter *v* değiştirmek
alteration *n* değişim
altercation *n* çekişme
alternate *v* sırayla yapmak
alternate *adj* karşılıklı
alternative *n* alternatif
although *c* rağmen
altitude *n* yükseklik

altogether *adj* hep beraber
aluminum *n* alüminyum
always *adv* her zaman
amass *v* yığmak
amateur *adj* amatör
amaze *v* şaşırtmak
amazement *n* hayret
amazing *adj* şaşırtıcı
ambassador *n* büyükelçi
ambiguous *adj* belirsiz
ambition *n* hırs
ambitious *adj* hırslı
ambivalent *adj* kararsız
ambulance *n* ambulans
ambush *v* pusuya düşürmek
amenable *adj* uysal
amend *v* düzeltmek
amendment *n* düzeltme
amenities *n* rahatlıklar, kolaylıklar
American *adj* Amerikan, Amerikalı
amiable *adj* sevimli
amicable *adj* dostane
amid *pre* ortasına
ammonia *n* amonyak
ammunition *n* cephane
amnesia *n* hafıza kaybı
amnesty *n* genel af
among *pre* arasında
amoral *adj* ahlak dışı
amorphous *adj* şekilsiz
amortize *v* amorti etmek

amount *n* miktar
amount to *v* kadar etmek
amphibious *adj* amfibi
amphitheater *n* amfiteatr
ample *adj* bol
amplifier *n* yükselteç
amplify *v* yükseltmek
amputate *v* ampute etmek
amputation *n* ampütasyon
amuse *v* eğlendirmek
amusement *n* eğlence
amusing *adj* eğlenceli
an *a* bir
analogy *n* analoji
analysis *n* analiz
analyze *v* analiz etmek
anarchist *n* anarşist
anarchy *n* anarşi
anatomy *n* anatomi
ancestor *n* ata
ancestry *n* soy
anchor *n* çapa
anchovy *n* ancüez
ancient *adj* antik
and *c* ve
anecdote *n* anekdot
anemia *n* anemi
anemic *adj* anemik
anesthesia *n* anestezi
anew *adv* yeniden
angel *n* melek
angelic *adj* meleksi

anger *v* sinirlenmek
anger *n* sinir
angina *n* anjin
angle *n* açı
angle *v* açı vermek
Anglican *adj* Anglikan
angry *adj* sinirli
anguish *n* ıstırap
animal *n* hayvan
animate *v* canlandırmak
animation *n* animasyon
animosity *n* husumet
ankle *n* ayak bileği
annex *n* ilhak
annexation *n* istila
annihilate *v* imha etmek
annihilation *n* imha
anniversary *n* yıldönümü
annotate *v* not eklemek
annotation *n* açıklayıcı not
announce *v* duyurmak
announcement *n* duyuru
announcer *n* sunucu
annoy *v* kızdırmak
annoying *adj* sinir bozucu
annual *adj* yıllık
annul *v* feshetmek
annulment *n* fesih
anoint *v* yağlamak
anonymity *n* anonimlik
anonymous *adj* anonim
another *adj* başka

answer *n* cevap, yanıt
answer *v* cevaplamak
ant *n* karınca
antagonize *v* düşman etmek
antecedent *n* önce gelen
antecedents *n* atalar
antelope *n* antilop
antenna *n* anten
anthem *n* marş
antibiotic *n* antibiyotik
anticipate *v* ummak
anticipation *n* beklenti
antidote *n* panzehir; antidot
antipathy *n* antipati
antiquated *adj* çağdışı
antiquity *n* antikite
anvil *n* örs
anxiety *n* endişe
anxious *adj* endişeli
any *adj* herhangi bir
anybody *pro* kimse
anyhow *pro* bir şekilde
anyone *pro* hiç biri
anything *pro* herhangi bir şey
apart *adv* ayrı
apartment *n* apartman; daire
apathy *n* ilgisizlik
ape *n* maymun
aperitif *n* aperitif
apex *n* zirve
aphrodisiac *adj* afrodizyak
apiece *adv* parça başına

apocalypse *n* kıyamet
apologize *v* özür dilemek
apology *n* özür
apostle *n* havari
apostolic *adj* papaya ait
apostrophe *n* kesme işareti
appall *v* dehşete düşmek
appalling *adj* dehşet verici
apparel *n* giyim kuşam
apparent *adj* belli
apparently *adv* belli ki
apparition *n* olay; hayalet
appeal *n* temyiz; cazibe
appeal *v* temyiz etmek
appealing *adj* cazip
appear *v* görünmek
appearance *n* görünüm
appease *v* yatıştırmak
appeasement *n* yatıştırma
appendicitis *n* apandisit
appendix *n* ek; apandis
appetite *n* iştah
appetizer *n* meze
applaud *v* alkışlamak
applause *n* alkış
apple *n* elma
appliance *n* cihaz
applicable *adj* uygulanabilir
applicant *n* aday
application *n* başvuru; uygulama
apply *v* uygulamak
apply for *v* müracaat etmek

appoint *v* tayin etmek
appointment *n* atama; randevu
appraisal *n* kıymet tahmini
appraise *v* değer biçmek
appreciate *v* takdir etmek
appreciation *n* takdir etmek
apprehend *v* idrak etmek
apprehensive *adj* evhamlı
apprentice *n* çırak
approach *v* yakınlaşmak
approach *n* yakınlaşma
approachable *adj* yaklaşılabilir
approbation *n* tasvip
appropriate *adj* uygun
approval *n* onay
approve *v* onaylamak
approximate *adj* yaklaşık
apricot *n* kayısı
April *n* Nisan
apron *n* önlük
aptitude *n* kabiliyet
aquarium *n* akvaryum
aquatic *adj* suda yaşayan
aqueduct *n* sukemeri
Arabic *adj* Arap
arable *adj* tarıma elverişli
arbiter *n* arabulucu
arbitrary *adj* keyfi
arbitrate *v* aracılık yapmak
arbitration *n* hakemlik
arc *n* yay
arch *n* kemer

archaeology *n* arkeoloji
archaic *adj* arkaik
archbishop *n* başpiskopos
architect *n* mimar
architecture *n* mimari
archive *n* arşiv
arctic *adj* arktik
ardent *adj* gayretli
ardor *n* gayret
arduous *adj* güç
area *n* alan
arena *n* arena; saha
argue *v* tartışmak
argument *n* tartışma
arid *adj* kuru
arise *iv* ortaya çıkmak
aristocracy *n* aristokrasi
aristocrat *n* aristokrat
arithmetic *n* aritmetik
ark *n* sandık
arm *n* kol; silah
arm *v* silahlanmak
armaments *n* silahlanma
armchair *n* koltuk
armed *adj* silahlı
armistice *n* ateşkes
armor *n* zırh
armpit *n* koltukaltı
army *n* ordu
aromatic *adj* aromatik
around *pre* etrafında
arouse *v* canlandırmak

arrange *v* düzenlemek
arrangement *n* düzenleme
array *n* düzen
arrest *v* tutuklamak
arrest *n* tutuklama
arrival *n* varış
arrive *v* varmak
arrogance *n* kibir
arrogant *adj* kibirli
arrow *n* ok
arsenal *n* cephanelik
arsenic *n* arsenik
arson *n* kundakçılık
arsonist *n* kundakçı
art *n* sanat
artery *n* atardamar
arthritis *n* artrit
artichoke *n* enginar
article *n* nesne; makale
articulate *v* ifade etmek
articulation *n* telaffuz,
    artikülasyon
artificial *adj* yapay
artillery *n* ağır silah
artisan *n* artizan
artist *n* sanatçı
artistic *adj* artistik
artwork *n* sanat çalışması
as *c* olarak
as *adv* gibi
ascend *v* yukarı çıkmak
ascendancy *n* hüküm

ascertain *v* keşfetmek
ascetic *adj* sofu
ash *n* kül; dilbudak ağacı
ashamed *adj* mahcup
ashore *adv* kıyıda
ashtray *n* küllük; tabla
aside *adv* kenara
aside from *adv* dışında
ask *v* sormak; istemek
asleep *adj* uykuda
asparagus *n* kuşkonmaz
aspect *n* görünüş
asphalt *n* asfalt
asphyxiate *v* boğmak
asphyxiation *n* boğulma
aspiration *n* nefes almak
aspire *v* talip olmak
aspirin *n* aspirin
assail *v* saldırmak
assailant *n* saldırgan
assassin *n* suikastçı
assassinate *v* öldürmek
assassination *n* suikast
assault *n* saldırı
assault *v* saldırmak
assemble *v* toplanmak
assembly *n* toplantı; montaj
assent *v* razı olmak
assert *v* öne sürmek
assertion *n* iddia
assess *v* talep etmek
assessment *n* değerlendirme

asset *n* mal
assets *n* mal varlıkları
assign *v* tayin etmek
assignment *n* tayin
assimilate *v* asimile etmek
assimilation *n* asimilasyon
assist *v* yardım etmek
assistance *n* yardım
associate *v* ilişkilendirmek
association *n* ilişki; dernek
assorted *adj* çeşitli
assortment *n* karışım
assume *v* varsaymak
assumption *n* varsayım
assurance *n* güvence
assure *v* temin etmek
asterisk *n* yıldız imi
asteroid *n* asteroit
asthma *n* astım
asthmatic *adj* astımlı
astonish *v* şaşırtmak
astonishing *adj* şaşırtıcı
astound *v* şoke etmek
astounding *adj* hayret verici
astray *v* doğru yoldan sapmış
astrologer *n* astrolog
astrology *n* astroloji
astronaut *n* astronot
astronomer *n* astronom
astronomic *adj* astronomik
astronomy *n* astronomi
astute *adj* kurnaz

asunder *adv* parçalar halinde
asylum *n* akıl hastanesi
at *pre* de
atheism *n* ateizm
atheist *n* ateist
athlete *n* atlet
athletic *adj* atletik
atmosphere *n* atmosfer
atmospheric *adj* atmosferik
atom *n* atom
atomic *adj* atomik
atone *v* kefaret etmek
atonement *n* kefaret
atrocious *adj* zalim
atrocity *n* vahşet
atrophy *v* körelmek
attach *v* iliştirmek
attached *adj* ilişik
attachment *n* ek; bağlılık
attack *n* saldırı
attack *v* saldırmak
attacker *n* saldırgan
attain *v* ulaşmak
attainable *adj* ulaşılır
attainment *n* ulaşma
attempt *v* teşebbüs etmek
attempt *n* teşebbüs
attend *v* katılmak
attendance *n* katılım
attendant *n* görevli
attention *n* uyarı
attentive *adj* dikkatli

attenuate *v* hafifletmek
attenuating *adj* hafifletici
attest *v* doğrulamak
attic *n* tavanarası
attitude *n* tutum
attorney *n* avukat
attract *v* cezbetmek
attraction *n* cazibe
attractive *adj* çekici
attribute *v* vasıf
auction *v* müzayedeyle satmak
auction *n* müzayede
auctioneer *n* mezatçi
audacious *adj* yürekli
audacity *n* cesaret
audible *adj* duyulur
audience *n* seyirci
audit *v* denetlemek
auditorium *n* toplantı salonu
augment *v* ilave
August *n* Ağustos
aunt *n* hala; teyze
auspicious *adj* hayırlı
austere *adj* sade
austerity *n* sadelik
authentic *adj* otantik
authenticate *v* belgelemek
authenticity *n* otantiklik
author *n* yazar
authoritarian *adj* otoriter
authority *n* otorite
authorization *n* yetki; izin

authorize *v* yetkilendirmek
auto *n* araba; oto-
autograph *n* imza
automatic *adj* otomatik
automobile *n* otomobil
autonomous *adj* otonom
autonomy *n* otonomi
autopsy *n* otopsi
autumn *n* sonbahar
auxiliary *adj* yardımcı
avail *v* fayda
availability *n* müsait olma
available *adj* mevcut
avalanche *n* heyelan
avarice *n* para hırsı
avaricious *adj* tamahkar
avenge *v* intikam almak
avenue *n* cadde
average *n* ortalama
averse *adj* isteksiz
aversion *n* isteksizlik
avert *v* yön değiştirmek
aviation *n* havacılık
aviator *n* havacı
avid *adj* coşkun
avoid *v* kaçınmak
avoidable *adj* kaçınılabilir
avoidance *n* kaçınma
avowed *adj* tasdikli
await *v* gözlemek
awake *iv* uyandırmak
awake *adj* uyanık

awakening *n* uyanış
award *v* ödüllendirmek
award *n* ödül
aware *adj* farkında
awareness *n* farkındalık
away *adv* uzakta
awe *n* huşu
awesome *adj* korkunç
awful *adj* berbat
awkward *adj* uygunsuz
awning *n* tente
ax *n* balta
axiom *n* belit, aksiyom
axis *n* eksen
axle *n* dingil

babble *v* gevezelik etmek
baby *n* bebek
babysitter *n* çocuk bakıcısı
bachelor *n* bekar
back *n* arka
back *adv* arkasında
back *v* desteklemek
back down *v* boyun eğmek
back up *v* desteklemek
backbone *n* omurga

backdoor *n* arka kapı; yasadışı
backfire *v* geri tepmek
background *n* arkaplan
backing *n* destek
backlash *n* geri tepme
backlog *n* birikim
backpack *n* sırt çantası
backup *n* yedek
backward *adj* çekingen
backwards *adv* arkaya doğru
backyard *n* avlu
bacon *n* domuz pastırması
bacteria *n* bakteri
bad *adj* kötü
badge *n* rozet
badly *adv* kötü bir şekilde
baffle *v* şaşırtmak
bag *v* çantaya koymak
bag *n* çanta
baggage *n* bagaj
baggy *adj* bol; sarkık
baguette *n* baget
bail *n* kefalet
bail out *v* kefaletle kurtarmak
bailiff *n* mübaşir
bait *n* yem
bake *v* fırında pişirmek
baker *n* fırıncı
bakery *n* fırın
balance *v* dengelemek
balance *n* denge; bakiye
balcony *n* balkon

bald *adj* kel
bale *n* balya; denek
ball *n* top; balo
balloon *n* balon
ballot *n* oy pusulası
ballroom *n* balo salonu
balm *n* merhem
balmy *adj* yumuşak; iyileştirici
bamboo *n* bambu
ban *n* yasak
ban *v* yasaklamak
banality *n* bayağı
banana *n* muz
band *n* band; müzik grubu
bandage *n* bandaj
bandage *v* bandajlamak
bandit *n* haydut
bang *v* vurmak
bangs *n* kâkül, perçem
banish *v* sürgüne yollamak
banishment *n* sürgün
bank *n* bank; banka
bankrupt *v* iflas etmek
bankrupt *adj* iflas etmiş
bankruptcy *n* iflas
banner *n* ilan; bayrak
banquet *n* ziyafet
baptism *n* vaftiz
baptize *v* vaftiz etmek
bar *n* bar; çubuk
bar *v* sokmamak
barbarian *n* barbar

B

barbaric *adj* barbarca
barbarism *n* barbarlık
barbecue *n* mangal
barber *n* berber
bare *adj* çıplak; açık
barefoot *adj* çıplak ayak
barely *adv* güç bela
bargain *n* pazarlık
bargain *v* pazarlık etmek
bargaining *n* pazarlık etme
barge *n* mavna
bark *v* havlamak
bark *n* hav hav; çığırtkanlık
barley *n* arpa
barmaid *n* bayan barmen
barman *n* barmen
barn *n* ahır
barometer *n* barometre
barracks *n* kışla; baraka
barrage *n* baraj
barrel *n* fıçı
barren *adj* meyvesiz; çorak
barricade *n* barikat
barrier *n* bariyer
barring *pre* haricinde
bartender *n* barmen
barter *v* takas yapmak
base *n* temel; üs
base *v* dayanmak
baseball *n* beyzbol
baseless *adj* asılsız; temelsiz
basement *n* bodrum; zemin

bashful *adj* utangaç
basic *adj* temel
basics *n* temel bilgiler
basin *n* leğen
basis *n* kaynak
bask *v* güneşlenmek
basket *n* sepet
basketball *n* basketbol
bass *n* bas; levrek
bastard *n* piç
bat *n* yarasa; sopa
batch *n* yığın
bath *n* banyo
bathe *v* banyo yapmak
bathrobe *n* bornoz
bathroom *n* banyo
bathtub *n* banyo küveti
baton *n* değnek; baton
battalion *n* tabur
batter *v* dövmek
battery *n* pil
battle *n* savaş
battle *v* savaşmak
battleship *n* savaş gemisi
bay *n* körfez
bayonet *n* süngü
bazaar *n* pazar
be *iv* olmak
be born *v* doğmak
beach *n* plaj
beacon *n* fener
beak *n* gaga

beam *n* ışın
bean *n* fasulye
bear *n* ayı
bear *iv* dayanmak; taşımak
bearable *adj* dayanılır
beard *n* sakal
bearded *adj* sakallı
bearer *n* taşıyıcı
beast *n* canavar
beat *iv* dövmek; yenmek
beat *n* vuruş; ritm
beaten *adj* mağlup
beating *n* yenilgi; mağlubiyet
beautiful *adj* güzel
beautify *v* güzelleştirmek
beauty *n* güzellik
beaver *n* kunduz
because *c* çünkü
because of *pre* nedeniyle,
　sebebiyle
beckon *v* işaretle çağırmak
become *iv* olmak
bed *n* yatak; nehir yatağı
bedding *n* yatak takımı
bedroom *n* yatak odası
bedspread *n* yatak örtüsü
bee *n* arı
beef *n* sığır eti
beef up *v* yakınmak
beehive *n* arı kovanı
beer *n* bira
beet *n* pancar

beetle *n* böcek
before *adv* önceki
before *pre* önce
beforehand *adv* önceden
befriend *v* arkadaş olmak
beg *v* yalvarmak
beggar *n* dilenci
begin *iv* başlamak
beginner *n* acemi
beginning *n* başlangıç
beguile *v* aklını çelmek
behalf (on) *adv* birinin namına
behave *v* davranmak
behavior *n* davranış
behead *v* başını kesmek
behind *pre* arkasında
behold *iv* dikkatle bakmak
being *n* varlık
belated *adj* geç kalmış
belch *v* geğirmek
belch *n* geğirti
belfry *n* çan kulesi
Belgian *adj* Belçikalı
Belgium *n* Belçika
belief *n* inanç
believable *adj* inanılır
believe *v* inanmak
believer *n* inanan; mümin
belittle *v* küçümsemek
bell *n* zil; çan
bell pepper *n* dolmalık biber
belligerent *adj* kavgacı

B

belly *n* göbek
belly button *n* göbek deliği
belong *v* ait olmak
belongings *n* kişisel eşyalar
beloved *adj* sevgili; aziz
below *adv* altında
below *pre* aşağısında
belt *n* kemer
bench *n* bank; benç
bend *iv* eğmek
bend down *v* aşağıya eğilmek
beneath *pre* altında; sonda
benediction *n* kutsama
benefactor *n* bağışçı
beneficial *adj* yararlı
beneficiary *n* faydalanan kişi
benefit *n* fayda
benefit *v* faydası olmak
benevolence *n* iyi niyet
benevolent *adj* iyi niyetli
benign *adj* iyi kalpli
bequeath *v* vasiyet etmek
bereaved *adj* matemli
bereavement *n* matem
beret *n* bere
berserk *adv* çılgına dönmüş
berth *n* ranza
beseech *iv* yalvarmak
beset *iv* etrafını sarmak
beside *pre* yanında
besides *pre* bunun yanında
besiege *iv* kuşatmak

best *adj* en iyi
best man *n* sağdıç
bestial *adj* hayvani
bestiality *n* canavarlık
bestow *v* armağan etmek
bet *iv* bahse girmek
bet *n* bahis
betray *v* aldatmak
betrayal *n* ihanet
better *adj* daha iyi
between *pre* arasında
beverage *n* içecek
beware *v* sakınmak
bewilder *v* şaşırtmak
bewitch *v* büyü yapmak
beyond *adv* ardında
bias *n* önyargı
bible *n* incil
biblical *adj* incilden
bibliography *n* kaynakça
bicycle *n* bisiklet
bid *iv* teklif vermek; emretmek
bid *n* fiyat teklifi
big *adj* büyük
bigamy *n* ikieşlilik
bigot *adj* bağnaz; yobaz
bigotry *n* yobazlık
bike *n* bisiklet
bile *n* garaz
bilingual *adj* iki dilli
bill *n* fatura; gaga
billiards *n* bilardo

B

billion *n* milyar
billionaire *n* milyarder
bimonthly *adj* iki ayda bir
bin *n* çöp
bind *iv* bağlamak
binding *adj* zorlayıcı; geçerli
binoculars *n* dürbün
biography *n* biyografi
biological *adj* biyolojik
biology *n* biyoloji
bird *n* kuş
birth *n* doğum
birthday *n* doğum günü
biscuit *n* bisküvi
bishop *n* piskopos
bison *n* bizon
bit *n* parça; küçük kısım
bite *iv* ısırmak
bite *n* ısırık; lokma
bitter *adj* acı
bitterly *adv* acı; keskin
bitterness *n* acılık
bizarre *adj* acayip
black *adj* siyah
blackberry *n* böğürtlen
blackboard *n* karatahta
blackmail *n* şantaj
blackmail *v* şantaj yapmak
blackness *n* karalık
blackout *n* elektrik kesintisi
blacksmith *n* demirci
bladder *n* mesane

blade *n* kılıç
blame *n* kınama
blame *v* suçlamak
blameless *adj* suçsuz
bland *adj* mülayim
blank *adj* boş
blanket *n* battaniye
blaspheme *v* küfretmek
blasphemy *n* tanrıya küfür
blast *n* infilak
blaze *v* parlamak
bleach *v* ağartmak
bleach *n* beyazlatıcı
bleak *adj* kasvetli
bleed *iv* kanamak
bleeding *n* kanayan
blemish *n* kusur
blemish *v* lekelemek
blend *n* harman
blend *v* harmanlamak
blender *n* mikser
bless *v* kutsamak
blessed *adj* kutsanmış
blessing *n* kutsama
blind *adj* kör, âmâ
blind *v* göz kamaştırmak
blindfold *v* gözlerini bağlamak
blindfold *n* gözleri bağlı
blindly *adv* kör gibi
blindness *n* körlük, âmâlık
blink *v* göz kırpmak
bliss *n* neşe

blissful *adj* neşeli
blister *n* kabarcık
blizzard *n* tipi
bloat *v* şişirmek
bloated *adj* şiş
block *n* büyük parça; blok
block *v* bloke etmek
blockade *v* abluka etmek
blockade *n* abluka
blockage *n* tıkanma
blond *adj* sarışın
blood *n* kan
bloodthirsty *adj* kana susamış
bloody *adj* kanlı
bloom *v* çiçek açmak
blossom *v* çiçeklenmek
blot *n* kusur
blot *v* lekelemek
blouse *n* bluz
blow *n* esinti
blow *iv* esmek; üflemek
blow out *iv* üfleyip söndürmek
blow up *iv* patlatmak
blowout *n* lastik patlaması
bludgeon *v* coplamak
blue *adj* mavi; hüzünlü
blueprint *n* mavi kopya
bluff *n* blöf
bluff *v* blöf yapmak
blunder *n* gaf
blunt *adj* körelmiş; dobra
bluntness *n* körlük; pervasız

blur *v* bulanıklaştırmak
blurred *adj* bulanık
blush *v* yüzü kızarmak
blush *n* pembeleşmiş
boar *n* yaban domuzu
board *n* tahta; yönetim kurulu
board *v* yemek vermek; binmek
boast *v* böbürlenmek
boat *n* gemi, bot
bodily *adj* maddi
body *n* beden; kütle
bog *n* bataklık
bog down *v* çıkmaza girmek
boil *v* kaynamak
boil down to *v* anlamına gelmek
boil over *v* taşmak
boiler *n* kazan
boisterous *adj* gürültülü
bold *adj* koyu; cesur
boldness *n* koyuluk; cüret
bolster *v* minder
bolt *n* sürgü; cıvata
bolt *v* sürgülemek
bomb *n* bomba
bomb *v* bombalamak
bombing *n* bombalama
bombshell *n* bomba mermisi
bond *n* senet; bono
bondage *n* kölelik
bone *n* kemik
bone marrow *n* kemik iliği
bonfire *n* şenlik ateşi

bonus _n_ bonus
book _n_ kitap
bookcase _n_ kitaplık
bookkeeper _n_ muhasebeci
bookkeeping _n_ muhasebe
booklet _n_ kitapçık
bookseller _n_ kitapçı
bookstore _n_ kitap evi
boom _n_ gümbürtü; çıkış
boom _v_ gümbürdemek
boost _v_ güçlendirmek
boost _n_ kuvvet
boot _n_ çizme
booth _n_ çadır; kabin
booty _n_ ganimet
booze _n_ içki
border _n_ hudut; kenar
border on _v_ ulaşmak
borderline _adj_ sınır
bore _v_ usandırmak
bored _adj_ bıkkın
boredom _n_ bıkkınlık
boring _adj_ sıkıcı
born _adj_ doğmuş
borough _n_ kasaba
borrow _v_ ödünç almak
bosom _n_ bağır
boss _n_ patron
boss around _v_ patronluk
  taslamak
bossy _adj_ amirane
botany _n_ botanik

botch _v_ berbat etmek
both _adj_ her ikisi de
bother _v_ uğraşmak
bothersome _adj_ uğraştırıcı
bottle _n_ şişe
bottle _v_ şişelemek
bottleneck _n_ dar geçit
bottom _n_ alt
bottomless _adj_ dipsiz
bough _n_ dal
boulder _n_ kaya
boulevard _n_ bulvar
bounce _v_ yansıma
bounce _n_ sıçramak
bound _v_ sınırlamak
bound _adj_ gidici
bound for _adj_ gitmek üzere
boundary _n_ sınır
boundless _adj_ sınırsız
bounty _n_ cömertlik
bourgeois _adj_ burjuva
bow _n_ reverans; yay
bow _v_ reverans yapmak
bow out _v_ başından savmak
bowels _n_ bağırsaklar
bowl _n_ kase, tas
box _v_ boks yapmak; kutulamak
box _n_ kutu
box office _n_ gişe
boxer _n_ boksör; şort kilot
boxing _n_ boks
boy _n_ oğlan

B

boycott v boykot etmek
boyfriend n erkek arkadaş
boyhood n erkeklik
bra n sütyen
brace for v sağlamlaştırmak
bracelet n bilezik
bracket n ayraç
brag v yüksekten atmak
braid n kordon
brain n beyin
brainwash v beyin yıkamak
brake n fren
brake v frenlemek
branch n dal
branch office n şube
branch out v dal salmak
brand v markalamak
brand n marka
brand-new adj yepyeni
brandy n konyak
brat n afacan
brave adj cesur
bravely adv cesurca
bravery n yiğitlik
brawl n arbede
breach n ihlal; yarık
bread n ekmek
breadth n genişlik
break n aralık; şans
break iv kırmak
break away v ayrılmak
break down v bozulmak

break free v kaçmak
break in v hırsızlık yapmak
break off v bozmak; kesmek
break open v kırıp açmak
break out v patlak vermek
break up v ayrılmak
breakable adj kırılır
breakdown n sinir bozukluğu
breakfast n kahvaltı
breakthrough n büyük buluş; atılım
breast n göğüs
breath n nefes
breathe v nefes almak
breathing n nefes alma
breathtaking adj nefes kesici
breed iv üremek; yol açmak
breed n cins; damızlık
breeze n meltem
brethren n din kardeşi
brevity n kısalık; özlük
brew v demlemek
brewery n birahane
bribe v rüşvet vermek
bribe n rüşvet
bribery n rüşvetçilik
brick n tuğla
bricklayer n duvarcı
bridal adj düğüne ait
bride n gelin
bridegroom n damat
bridesmaid n nedime

B

bridge *n* köprü
bridle *n* at başlığı
brief *adj* özlü
brief *v* özetlemek
briefcase *n* evrak çantası
briefing *n* brifing
briefly *adv* kısaca
briefs *n* özet
brigade *n* tugay
bright *adj* parlak; zeki
brighten *v* parlatmak
brightness *n* parlaklık
brilliant *adj* mükemmel
brim *n* bardak ağzı
bring *iv* getirmek
bring back *v* geri getirmek
bring down *v* aşağı indirmek
bring up *v* yetiştirmek
brink *n* eşik
brisk *adj* hareketli
Britain *n* Britanya
British *adj* Britanyalı
brittle *adj* kırılgan
broad *adj* engin
broadcast *v* yayımlamak
broadcast *n* yayın
broadcaster *n* yayımcı
broaden *v* genişletmek
broadly *adv* genişçe
broadminded *adj* geniş görüşlü
brochure *n* broşür
broil *v* ızgara yapmak

broiler *n* ızgara
broke *adj* beş parasız
broken *adj* kırık
bronchitis *n* bronşit
bronze *n* bronz
broom *n* süpürge
broth *n* etsuyu
brothel *n* genelev
brother *n* kardeş; ağabey
brotherhood *n* kardeşlik
brother-in-law *n* kayınbirader; enişte
brotherly *adj* kardeşçe
brow *n* kaş
brown *adj* kahverengi
browse *v* göz atmak
browser *n* listeleyici
bruise *n* bere; ezik
bruise *v* berelemek
brunch *n* geç kahvaltı, branç
brunette *adj* kumral
brush *n* fırça
brush *v* fırçalamak
brush aside *v* önemsememek
brush up *v* tazelemek
brusque *adj* düşüncesiz
brutal *adj* zorba
brutality *n* zorbalık
brutalize *v* zorbalık etmek
brute *adj* hayvan
bubble *n* kabarcık
bubble gum *n* sakız

B

buck *v* sıçramak
buck *n* antilop
bucket *n* kova
buckle *n* toka
buckle up *v* bağlamak
bud *n* tomurcuk; varlık
buddy *n* ahbap
budge *v* kımıldamak
budget *n* bütçe
buffalo *n* bufalo
bug *n* böcek
bug *v* can sıkmak
build *iv* inşaa etmek
builder *n* inşaat işçisi
building *n* inşaat
buildup *n* büyüme
built-in *adj* yerleşik
bulb *n* ampul; çiçek soğanı
bulge *n* bel vermek
bulk *n* yığın; hacim
bulky *adj* hacimli
bull *n* boğa
bull fight *n* boğa güreşi
bull fighter *n* boğa güreşçisi, matador
bulldoze *v* bulldozerle düzenlemek
bullet *n* kurşun
bulletin *n* tebliğ; bildiri
bully *adj* zorba
bulwark *n* siper
bum *n* kıç; serseri

bump *n* şiş; darbe
bump into *v* karşılaşmak
bumper *n* tampon
bumpy *adj* tümsekli
bun *n* sıkıntı; çörek
bunch *n* salkım
bundle *n* bohça
bundle *v* bohçalamak
bunk bed *n* ranza
bunker *n* yeraltı sığınağı
buoy *n* şamandıra
burden *n* yük
burden *v* yüklemek
burdensome *adj* yüklü
bureau *n* büro
bureaucracy *n* bürokrasi
bureaucrat *n* bürokrat
burger *n* hamburger
burglar *n* hırsız
burglarize *v* hırsızlık yapmak
burglary *n* hırsızlık
burial *n* cenaze töreni
burly *adj* iriyarı
burn *iv* yanmak
burn *n* yanık
burp *v* geğirmek
burp *n* geğirti
burrow *n* oyuk
burst *iv* patlamak
burst into *v* aceleyle girmek
bury *v* gömmek
bus *n* otobüs

bus *v* otobüsle götürmek
bush *n* çalı
busily *adv* faal olarak
business *n* iş
businessman *n* iş adamı
bust *n* büst
bustling *adj* telaşlı
busy *adj* meşgul
but *c* ama
butcher *n* kasap
butchery *n* mezbaha
butler *n* kilerci
butt *n* popo; kurban
butter *n* tereyağı
butterfly *n* kelebek
button *n* düğme
buttonhole *n* düğme iliği
buy *iv* satın almak
buy off *v* para yedirmek
buyer *n* müşteri
buzz *n* vızıltı
buzz *v* vızıldamak
buzzard *n* akbaba; şahin
buzzer *n* vızıldayan alet
by *pre* yanında; yakın
bye *e* eyvallah
bypass *n* güle güle
bypass *v* atlamak
by-product *n* yan ürün
bystander *n* seyirci kalan

cab *n* taksi
cabbage *n* lahana
cabin *n* kabin
cabinet *n* dolap; kabine
cable *n* kablo
cafeteria *n* kafeterya
caffeine *n* kafein
cage *n* kafes
cake *n* kek; pasta
calamity *n* felaket
calculate *v* hesaplamak
calculation *n* hesaplama
calculator *n* hesap makinesi
calendar *n* takvim
calf *n* dana; baldır
caliber *n* kalibre
calibrate *v* ayarlamak
call *n* çağrı; meslek
call *v* aramak; istemek
call off *v* iptal etmek
call on *v* uğramak
call out *v* devreye sokmak
calling *n* lüzum; davet
callous *adj* hissiz
calm *adj* sakin
calm *n* sakin
calm down *v* sakinleşmek
calorie *n* kalori
calumny *n* iftira**

camel *n* deve
camera *n* fotoğraf makinesi
camouflage *v* kamufle etmek
camouflage *n* kamuflaj
camp *n* kamp
camp *v* kamp yapmak
campaign *v* kampanya yapmak
campaign *n* kampanya
campfire *n* kamp ateşi
can *iv* yapabilmek; konservesini yapmak
can *n* teneke kutu
can opener *n* konserve açacağı
canal *n* kanal
canary *n* kanarya
cancel *v* iptal etmek
cancellation *n* iptal
cancer *n* kanser
cancerous *adj* kanserli
candid *adj* dürüst
candidacy *n* adaylık
candidate *n* aday
candle *n* mum
candlestick *n* mum
candor *n* tarafsızlık
candy *n* şekerleme
cane *n* baston; silah
canister *n* teneke kuru
canned *adj* konserve
cannibal *n* yamyam
cannon *n* toplu silah
canoe *n* kano

canonize *v* aziz saymak
cantaloupe *n* kavun
canteen *n* kantin
canvas *v* brandayla örtmek
canvas *n* çadır bezi; tuval
canyon *n* kanyon
cap *v* örtmek
cap *n* kapak; doruk
capability *n* yetenek
capable *adj* yetenekli
capacity *n* kapasite
cape *n* pelerin; burun
capital *n* başkent; sermaye
capital letter *n* büyük harf
capitalism *n* kapitalizm
capitalize *v* çıkar sağlamak
capitulate *v* teslim olmak
capsize *v* alabora olmak
capsule *n* kapsül
captain *n* kaptan
captivate *v* tutsak etmek
captive *n* tutsak
captivity *n* tutsaklık
capture *v* ele geçirmek
capture *n* yakalamak
car *n* araba
carat *n* karat
caravan *n* karavan
carburetor *n* karbüratör
carcass *n* ceset
card *n* kart; kartvizit
cardboard *n* mukavva

cardiac *adj* kalbe ait
cardiac arrest *n* kalp krizi
cardiology *n* kardiyoloji
care *n* dert
care *v* umrunda olmak
care about *v* merak etmek
care for *v* hoşlanmak
career *n* kariyer
carefree *adj* tasasız
careful *adj* dikkatli
careless *adj* dikkatsiz
carelessness *n* dikkatsizlik
caress *n* okşama
caress *v* okşamak
caretaker *n* bakıcı
cargo *n* kargo
caricature *n* karikatür
caring *adj* yardımsever
carnage *n* katliam
carnal *adj* cinsel
carnation *n* karanfil
carol *n* Noel ilahisi
carpenter *n* marangoz
carpentry *n* marangozluk
carpet *n* halı
carriage *n* at arabası
carrot *n* havuç
carry *v* taşımak
carry on *v* devam etmek
carry out *v* uygulamak
cart *n* el arabası
cart *v* taşımak

cartoon *n* çizgi film
cartridge *n* kutucuk
carve *v* uymak
cascade *n* basamaklamak
case *n* çanta; dava
cash *n* nakit para
cashier *n* kasiyer
casino *n* gazino
casket *n* tabut; küçük kutu
casserole *n* güveç
cassock *n* cübbe
cast *n* oynayanlar, rol alanlar
cast *iv* fırlatmak
castaway *n* kazazede
caste *n* kast, sınıf
castle *n* kale
casual *adj* tesadüfen
casualty *n* kazazede
cat *n* kedi
cataclysm *n* tufan
catacomb *n* katakomb
catalog *n* katalog
catalog *v* katalog yapmak
cataract *n* şelale; katarakt
catastrophe *n* afet
catch *iv* yakalamak
catch up *v* yetişmek
catching *adj* nefesini tutmak
catchword *n* slogan
catechism *n* ilmihal
category *n* kategori
cater to *v* ihtiyacı karşılamak

caterpillar *n* tırtıl
cathedral *n* katedral
catholic *adj* katolik
Catholicism *n* Katolik
cattle *n* sığır
cauliflower *n* karnabahar
cause *n* neden
cause *v* yol açmak
caution *n* uyarı
cautious *adj* ihtiyatlı
cavalry *n* süvari
cave *n* mağara
cave in *v* çökmek
cavern *n* mağara
cavity *n* çürük
cease *v* durdurmak
cease-fire *n* ateşkes
ceaselessly *adv* durmadan
ceiling *n* tavan
celebrate *v* kutlamak
celebration *n* kutlama
celebrity *n* ünlü
celery *n* kereviz
celestial *adj* kutsal
celibacy *n* bekarlık
celibate *adj* bekar
cell phone *n* cep telefonu
cellar *n* bodrum
cellphone *n* cep telefonu
cement *n* çimento
cemetery *n* mezarlık
censorship *n* sansür

censure *v* kınamak
census *n* nüfus sayımı
cent *n* sent
centenary *n* yüzüncü yıl dönümü
center *n* merkez
center *v* ortalamak
centimeter *n* santimetre
central *adj* merkezi
centralize *v* merkezleştirmek
century *n* yüzyıl
ceramic *n* seramik
cereal *n* gevrek
cerebral *adj* beyinsel
ceremony *n* seremoni
certain *adj* kesin
certainty *n* kesinlik
certificate *n* sertifika
certify *v* tasdik etmek
chagrin *n* utanç
chain *n* zincir
chain *v* zincirlemek
chainsaw *n* zincirli testere
chair *v* başkanlık etmek
chair *n* sandalye
chairman *n* kurul başkanı
chalet *n* küçük köşk
chalice *n* kadeh
chalk *n* tebeşir
chalkboard *n* karatahta
challenge *v* meydan okumak
challenge *n* meydan okuma
challenging *adj* mücadeleci

chamber *n* meclis
champ *n* şampiyon
champion *n* şampiyon
champion *v* savunmak
chance *n* şans; olasılık
chancellor *n* rektör
chandelier *n* avize
change *v* değiştirmek
change *n* değişim
channel *v* yönlendirmek
channel *n* kanal; su yolu
chant *n* ilahi
chaos *n* kaos
chaotic *adj* karmakarışık
chapel *n* şapel
chaplain *n* vaiz
chapter *n* bölüm
character *n* karakter; kişilik
characteristic *adj* karakteristik
charade *n* maskaralık
charbroil *v* ızgara yapmak
charbroiled *adj* ızgaralanmış
charcoal *n* mangal kömürü
charge *v* şarj etmek;
  görevlendirmek
charge *n* şarj; görev
charisma *n* karizma
charismatic *adj* karizmatik
charitable *adj* hayırsever
charity *n* hayırseverlik
charm *v* büyülemek
charm *n* cazibe

charming *adj* cazibeli
chart *n* grafik; çizelge
charter *n* dolmuş uçak
charter *v* kiralamak
chase *n* av
chase *v* kovalamak
chase away *v* peşine düşmek
chasm *n* kanyon
chaste *adj* namuslu
chastise *v* cezalandırmak
chastisement *n* ceza
chastity *n* iffet
chat *v* sohbet etmek
chauffeur *n* özel şoför
cheap *adj* ucuz
cheat *v* dolandırmak; aldatmak
cheater *n* hilekar
check *n* denetim; adisyon
check *v* kontrol etmek
check in *v* kaydını yaptırmak
check up *n* muayene
checkbook *n* çek defteri
cheek *n* yanak
cheekbone *n* elmacık kemiği
cheeky *adj* yüzsüz
cheer *v* tezahürat yapmak
cheer up *v* neşelendirmek
cheerful *adj* neşeli
cheers *n* şerefe
cheese *n* peynir
chef *n* şef
chemical *adj* kimyasal

chemist *n* kimyager

chemistry *n* kimya

cherish *v* üzerine titremek

cherry *n* kiraz

chess *n* satranç

chest *n* göğüs; sandık

chestnut *n* kestane

chew *v* çiğnemek

chick *n* civciv; genç kız

chicken *n* tavuk

chicken out *v* tırsmak

chicken pox *n* su çiçeği

chide *v* kusur bulmak

chief *n* şef

chiefly *adv* başlıca

child *n* çocuk

childhood *n* çocukluk

childish *adj* çocukça

childless *adj* çocuksuz

children *n* çocuklar

chill *n* soğuk; ürperti

chill *v* soğutmak

chill out *v* rahatlamak

chilly *adj* serin

chimney *n* baca

chimpanzee *n* şempanze

chin *n* çene

chip *n* yonga; çip

chisel *n* keski

chocolate *n* çikolata

choice *n* seçim

choir *n* koro

choke *v* boğmak

cholera *n* kolera

cholesterol *n* kolestorol

choose *iv* seçmek

choosy *adj* müşkülpesent

chop *v* doğramak

chop *n* pirzola

chopper *n* helikopter

chore *n* küçük iş

chorus *n* koro

christen *v* vaftiz etmek

christening *n* vaftiz

Christian *adj* Hristiyan

Christianity *n* Hristiyanlık

Christmas *n* Noel

chronic *adj* müzmin

chronicle *n* kronik

chronology *n* kronoloji

chubby *adj* tombul

chuckle *v* kıkırdamak

chunk *n* külçe

church *n* kilise

chute *n* paraşüt

cider *n* elma şarabı

cigar *n* puro

cigarette *n* sigara

cinder *n* kül

cinema *n* sinema

cinnamon *n* tarçın

circle *n* yuvarlak

circle *v* kuşatmak

circuit *n* devre

circular *adj* yuvarlak
circulate *v* havanın akması
circulation *n* hava akımı
circumcise *v* sünnet etmek
circumcision *n* sünnet
circumstance *n* durum
circumstantial *adj* tesadüfi
circus *n* sirk
cistern *n* sarnıç
citizen *n* vatandaş
citizenship *n* vatandaşlık
city *n* şehir, il
city hall *n* belediye
civic *adj* şehirli
civil *adj* medeni
civilization *n* medeniyet
civilize *v* medenileştirmek
claim *v* talep etmek
claim *n* talep; iddia
clam *n* deniztarağı
clamor *v* yaygara
clamp *n* kıskaç
clan *n* kabile
clandestine *adj* el altından
clap *v* el çırpmak
clarification *n* açıklama
clarify *v* açıklama getirmek
clarinet *n* klarnet
clarity *n* netlik
clash *v* çarpmak
clash *n* çarpış
class *n* sınıf; zümre

classic *adj* klasik
classify *v* sınıflandırmak
classmate *n* sınıf arkadaşı
classroom *n* sınıf
classy *adj* klas
clause *n* yan tümce, cümlecik
claw *n* pençe
claw *v* tırmalamak
clay *n* kil
clean *adj* temiz
clean *v* temizlemek
cleaner *n* temizlikçi
cleanliness *n* temizlik
cleanse *v* temizlemek
cleanser *n* temizleyici madde
clear *adj* şeffaf; temiz
clear *v* temizlemek
clearance *n* temizlik
clear-cut *adj* kesin
clearly *adv* açıkça; net
clearness *n* açıklık; netlik
cleft *n* yarık
clemency *n* merhamet
clench *v* sıkmak
clergy *n* ruhban
clergyman *n* papaz
clerical *adj* yazıcıya ait
clerk *n* katip
clever *adj* akıllı; zeki
click *v* tıklamak
client *n* müşteri
clientele *n* müvekkiller

C

C

cliff *n* uçurum; falez
climate *n* iklim
climatic *adj* iklimsel
climax *n* zirve
climb *v* tırmanmak
climbing *n* tırmanma
clinch *v* perçinlemek
cling *iv* tutunmak
clinic *n* klinik
clip *n* raptiye
clip *v* kırpmak
clipping *n* kırpma; kesme
cloak *n* pelerin
clock *n* saat
clog *v* tıkamak
cloister *n* manastır
clone *v* klonlamak
cloning *n* klonlama
close *v* kapatmak
close *adj* kapalı
close to *pre* yakın
closed *adj* kapalı
closely *adv* yakından
closet *n* klozet
closure *n* kapanış
clot *n* pıhtı
cloth *n* kumaş parçası; bez
clothe *v* giydirmek
clothes *n* giysi, giysiler
clothing *n* kıyafet
cloud *n* bulut
cloudless *adj* bulutsuz

cloudy *adj* bulutlu
clown *n* palyaço
club *n* kulüp; disko
club *v* dövmek
clue *n* ipucu
clumsiness *n* beceriksizlik
clumsy *adj* beceriksiz
cluster *n* küme
cluster *v* kümelenmek
clutch *n* debriyaj
coach *v* çalıştırmak
coach *n* antrenör
coaching *n* antrenörlük etmek
coagulate *v* pıhtılaşmak
coagulation *n* pıhtılaşma
coal *n* kömür
coalition *n* koalisyon
coarse *adj* kaba; görgüsüz
coast *v* yanaşmak
coast *n* sahil
coastal *adj* kıyı boyunca
coastline *n* kıyı
coat *n* palto; tabaka
coax *v* dil dökmek
cob *n* mısır koçanı
cobblestone *n* parke taşı
cobweb *n* örümcek ağı
cocaine *n* kokain
cock *n* horoz
cockpit *n* kokpit
cockroach *n* hamamböceği
cocktail *n* kokteyl

cocky *adj* kibirli
cocoa *n* kakao
coconut *n* hindistan cevizi
cod *n* morina
code *n* kod; kanun
codify *v* kodlamak
coefficient *n* katsayı
coerce *v* zorlamak
coercion *n* baskı; zorlama
coexist *v* birlikte varolmak
coffee *n* kahve
coffin *n* tabut
cohabit *v* nikahsız yaşamak
coherent *adj* mantıklı
cohesion *n* uyum
coin *n* madeni para
coincide *v* tesadüf etmek
coincidence *n* tesadüf
coincidental *adj* tesadüfen
cold *adj* soğuk
coldness *n* soğukluk
colic *n* kolik
collaborate *v* işbirliği yapmak
collaboration *n* işbirliği
collaborator *n* işbirlikçi
collapse *v* yıkılmak
collapse *n* çöküş
collar *n* yaka
collarbone *n* köprücük kemiği
collateral *adj* kollateral
colleague *n* iş arkadaşı
collect *v* toplamak

collection *n* koleksiyon
collector *n* koleksiyoncu
college *n* kolej
collide *v* çarpmak
collision *n* çarpışma
cologne *n* kolonya
colon *n* kolon
colonel *n* albay
colonial *adj* sömürgeci
colonization *n* sömürgeleştirme
colonize *v* sömürge kurmak
colony *n* sömürge
color *n* renk
color *v* renklendirmek
colorful *adj* renkli
colossal *adj* muazzam
colt *n* tay
column *n* sütun
coma *n* koma
comb *n* tarak
comb *v* taramak
combat *n* mücadele
combat *v* mücadele etmek
combatant *n* dövüşçü
combination *n* birleşim
combine *v* birleştirmek
combustible *n* yanıcı
combustion *n* tutuşma
come *iv* gelmek
come about *v* doğmak
come across *v* karşılaşmak
come apart *v* kopuvermek

come back *v* geri gelmek
come down *v* aşağı inmek
come forward *v* ilerlemek
come from *v* bir yerden gelmek
come in *v* içeri girmek
come out *v* dışarı çıkmak
come over *v* ulaşmak
come up *v* ortaya çıkmak
comeback *n* dönüş
comedian *n* komedyen
comedy *n* komedi
comet *n* kuyruklu yıldız
comfort *n* konfor
comfortable *adj* konforlu
comforter *n* yorgan
comical *adj* komik
coming *n* varış
coming *adj* gelen
comma *n* virgül
command *v* emir
commander *n* kumandan
commandment *n* emir; buyruk
commemorate *v* anmak
commence *v* başlamak
commend *v* tavsiye etmek
commendation *n* övgü
comment *v* yorum yapmak
comment *n* yorum
commerce *n* ticaret
commercial *adj* ticari
commission *n* komisyon
commit *v* adamak

commitment *n* vaat
committed *adj* söz vermiş
committee *n* komite
common *adj* ortak; genel
commotion *n* şamata
communicate *v* iletişim kurmak
communication *n* iletişim
communion *n* paylaşma
communism *n* komünizm
communist *adj* komünist
community *n* toplum
commute *v* seyahat etmek
compact *adj* kompakt
compact *v* sıkıştırmak
companion *n* yoldaş
companionship *n* yoldaşlık
company *n* şirket; arkadaşlık
comparable *adj* karşılanabilir
comparative *adj* karşılaştırmalı
compare *v* karşılaştırmak
comparison *n* karşılaştırma
compartment *n* bölme; kompartıman
compass *n* pusula
compassion *n* şefkat
compassionate *adj* şefkatli
compatibility *n* uygun
compatible *adj* uyumlu
compatriot *n* vatandaş
compel *v* zorlamak
compelling *adj* zorlayıcı
compendium *n* hülasa; özet

compensate *v* telafi etmek
compensation *n* tazminat
compete *v* rekabet etmek
competence *n* kabiliyet
competent *adj* ehil; yeterli
competition *n* yarışıma
competitive *adj* rakip
competitor *n* rakip; yarışmacı
compile *v* derlemek
complain *v* şikayet etmek
complaint *n* şikayet
complement *n* tümleyici
complete *adj* tam
complete *v* tamamlamak
completely *adv* tamamen
completion *n* tamamlama
complex *adj* karmaşık
complexion *n* ten rengi
complexity *n* karmaşıklık
compliance *n* itaat
compliant *adj* uysal
complicate *v* zorlaştırmak
complication *n* komplikasyon
complicity *n* suç ortaklığı
compliment *n* iltifat
complimentary *adj* övgü dolu
comply *v* razı olmak
component *n* bileşen
compose *v* bestelemek
composed *adj* oluşmuş
composer *n* besteci
composition *n* kompozisyon

compost *n* komposto
composure *n* kendine hakimiyet
compound *n* bileşik
compound *v* halletmek
comprehend *v* kavramak
comprehensive *adj* kapsamlı
compress *v* sıkıştırmak
compression *n* kompresyon
comprise *v* ihtiva etmek
compromise *n* uzlaşma
compromise *v* uzlaşmak
compulsion *n* baskı
compulsive *adj* kompülsif
compulsory *adj* mecburi
compute *v* hesaplamak
computer *n* bilgisayar
comrade *n* komrad
con man *n* hilekar
conceal *v* gizlemek
concede *v* teslim etmek
conceited *adj* kibir
conceive *v* gebe kalmak
concentrate *v* konsantre olmak
concentration *n* konsantrasyon
concentric *adj* ortak merkezli
concept *n* konsept
conception *n* gebe kalma
concern *v* endişe
concern *n* ilgilendiren şey
concerning *pre* alaka
concert *n* konser
concession *n* kabul; teslim

conciliate *v* gönlünü almak
conciliatory *adj* yatıştırıcı
concise *adj* özlü
conclude *v* sonuç çıkarmak
conclusion *n* sonuç; son kısım
conclusive *adj* kesin
concoct *v* tertip etmek
concoction *n* karışım; tertip
concrete *n* somut; beton
concrete *adj* somut
concur *v* uyuşmak
concurrent *adj* eş zamanlı
concussion *n* şiddetli sarsıntı
condemn *v* kınamak
condemnation *n* kınama
condensation *n* buğu
condense *v* yoğunlaştırmak
condescend *v* tenezzül etmek
condiment *n* baharat
condition *n* koşul
conditional *adj* koşullu
conditioner *n* artırıcı; düzeltici
condo *n* mülk
condolences *n* başsağlığı
condone *v* göz yummak
conducive *adj* yardımcı
conduct *n* idare
conduct *v* idare etmek
conductor *n* iletken; lider
cone *n* koni
confer *v* müzakere etmek
conference *n* konferans

confess *v* itiraf etmek
confession *n* itiraf
confessional *n* günah çıkarma odası
confessor *n* günah çıkartan papaz; itirafçı
confidant *n* sırdaş
confide *v* sırrını söylemek
confidence *n* itimat; güven
confident *adj* kendinden emin
confidential *adj* gizli
confine *v* hapsetmek
confinement *n* hapis
confirm *v* onaylamak
confirmation *n* onay
confiscate *v* el koymak
confiscation *n* haczetmek
conflict *n* itilaf; uyuşmazlık
conflict *v* uyuşmamak
conflicting *adj* çelişkili
conform *v* itaat etmek
conformist *adj* konformist
conformity *n* uygunluk
confound *v* şaşırtmak
confront *v* yüz yüze gelmek
confrontation *n* yüzleşme
confuse *v* kafasını karıştırmak
confusing *adj* kafa karıştıran
confusion *n* karışıklık
congenial *adj* sempatik
congested *adj* tıklım tıklım
congestion *n* tıkanıklık; izdiham

congratulate *v* tebrik etmek
congratulations *n* tebrikler
congregate *v* toplamak
congregation *n* toplama
congress *n* kongre
conjecture *n* varsayım
conjugal *adj* evlilikle ilgili
conjugate *v* birleşmek
conjunction *n* bağlaç; birleşme
conjure up *v* anımsatmak
connect *v* bağlamak
connection *n* bağ
connive *v* gizlice işbirliği yapmak
connote *v* akla getirmek
conquer *v* fethetmek
conqueror *n* fatih
conquest *n* fetih
conscience *n* vicdan
conscious *adj* vicdanlı
consciousness *n* bilinçlilik
conscript *n* askere alınmış
consecrate *v* kutsamak
consecration *n* kutsama
consecutive *adj* ardıl
consensus *n* fikir birliği
consent *v* rızasını almak
consent *n* rıza
consequence *n* sonuç
consequent *adj* netice
conservation *n* konuşma
conservative *adj* tutucu
conserve *n* muhafaza; konserve

conserve *v* muhafaza etmek
consider *v* dikkate almak
considerable *adj* önemli oranda
considerate *adj* düşünceli
consideration *n* düşünce
consignment *n* sevkiyat
consist *v* meydana gelmek
consistency *n* tutarlılık
consistent *adj* tutarlı; istikrarlı
consolation *n* teselli
console *v* teselli etmek
consolidate *v* pekiştirmek
consonant *n* ünsüz
conspicuous *adj* göstermelik
conspiracy *n* komplo
conspirator *n* komplocu
conspire *v* komplo kurmak
constancy *n* vefa
constant *adj* sabit
constellation *n* takımyıldız
consternation *n* dehşet
constipate *v* kabızlık vermek
constipated *adj* kabız
constipation *n* kabızlık
constitute *v* teşkil etmek
constitution *n* anayasa; yapı
constrain *v* sınırlamak
constraint *n* kısıtlama; baskı
construct *v* inşa etmek
construction *n* inşaat
constructive *adj* yapıcı
consul *n* konsolos

consulate *n* konsolosluk
consult *v* danışmak
consultation *n* danışma
consume *v* tüketmek
consumer *n* tüketici
consumption *n* tüketim
contact *v* temas etmek
contact *n* temas
contagious *adj* bulaşıcı
contain *v* içermek
container *n* konteyner
contaminate *v* bulaştırmak
contamination *n* pislik
contemplate *v* düşünmek
contemporary *adj* geçici
contempt *n* hor görme
contend *v* çekişmek
contender *n* yarışmacı
content *v* memnun etmek
content *adj* içerik
contentious *adj* kavgacı
contents *n* memnuniyet
contest *n* mücadele; itiraz
contestant *n* yarışmacı
context *n* bağlam
continent *n* kıta
continental *adj* kıtasal
contingency *n* durumsallık
contingent *adj* olası
continuation *n* devam etme
continue *v* devam etmek
continuity *n* süreklilik

continuous *adj* sürekli
contour *n* dış hatlar; kontur
contraband *n* kaçak
contract *v* sözleşmek
contract *n* sözleşme
contraction *n* kasılma
contradict *v* çelişmek
contradiction *n* çelişki
contrary *adj* karşıt
contrast *v* karşılaştırma
contrast *n* karşıtlık
contribute *v* katkıda bulunmak
contribution *n* katkı; makale
contributor *n* yardımcı
contrition *n* pişmanlık
control *n* kontrol
control *v* kontrol etmek
controversial *adj* tartışmalı
controversy *n* tartışma
convalescent *adj* iyileşen
convene *v* toplanmak
convenience *n* elverişlilik
convenient *adj* elverişli
convent *n* rahibe manastırı
convention *n* toplantı
conventional *adj* geleneksel
converge *v* yakınsamak
conversation *n* muhabbet
converse *v* konuşmak
conversely *adv* tersine
conversion *n* dönüşüm
convert *n* dönme

convert *v* dönüştürmek
convey *v* taşımak; nakletmek
convict *v* mahkum etmek
conviction *n* mahkumiyet; inanç
convince *v* ikna etmek
convincing *adj* ikna edici
convoluted *adj* sarılmış
convoy *n* konvoy
convulse *v* sarsmak
convulsion *n* sarsıntı
cook *v* pişirmek
cook *n* aşçı
cookie *n* kurabiye
cooking *n* yemek yapma
cool *adj* serin; serinkanlı
cool *v* soğutmak
cool down *v* soğumak; sakinleşmek
cooling *adj* soğutucu
coolness *n* soğukluk
cooperate *v* işbirliği yapmak
cooperation *n* işbirliği
cooperative *adj* yardımcı
coordinate *v* eşgüdümlemek
coordination *n* koordinasyon
coordinator *n* koordinatör
cop *n* polis
cope *v* uğraşmak
copier *n* fotokopi makinası
copper *n* bakır
copy *v* kopyalamak
copy *n* kopya

copyright *n* telif hakkı
cord *n* kablo; kordon
cordial *adj* samimi
cordless *adj* kablosuz
cordon *n* kordon
cordon off *v* kuşatmak
core *n* öz
cork *n* tapa
corn *n* mısır; nasır
corner *v* ele geçirmek
corner *n* köşe; korner
cornerstone *n* köşe taşı
cornet *n* kornet
corollary *n* doğal sonuç
coronary *adj* kalple ilgili
coronation *n* taç giyme töreni
corporal *adj* bedeni
corporal *n* onbaşı
corporation *n* anonim şirket
corpse *n* ceset
corpulent *adj* şişman
corpuscle *n* anat
correct *v* doğrulamak
correct *adj* doğru
correction *n* doğrulama
correlate *v* bağdaştırmak
correspond *v* mektuplaşmak
correspondent *n* muhabir
corresponding *adj* mutabık
corridor *n* koridor
corroborate *v* pekiştirmek
corrode *v* aşındırmak

C

corrupt *v* yozlaşmış
corrupt *adj* yoz; namussuz
corruption *n* yozlaşma
cosmetic *n* kozmetik
cosmic *adj* kozmik
cosmonaut *n* kozmonot
cost *iv* mal olmak; para etmek
cost *n* masraf
costly *adj* pahalı
costume *n* kostüm
cottage *n* kulübe
cotton *n* pamuk
couch *n* kanepe
cough *n* öksürük
cough *v* öksürmek
council *n* konsey; meclis
counsel *v* öğüt vermek
counsel *n* tavsiye; avukat
counselor *n* danışman; avukat
count *v* saymak
count *n* madde; sayma
countdown *n* geriye sayım
countenance *n* çehre
counter *n* sayaç; tezgah
counter *v* uymamak
counteract *v* karşı koymak
counterfeit *v* taklit etmek
counterfeit *adj* taklit; sahte
counterpart *n* mukabil
countess *n* kontes
countless *adj* sayısız
country *adj* kırsal

country *n* ülke
countryman *n* taşralı
countryside *n* kırsal bölge
county *n* ilçe
coup *n* darbe
couple *n* çift; iki tane
coupon *n* kupon
courage *n* cesaret
courageous *adj* cesaretli
courier *n* kurye
course *n* ders; süreç
court *n* avlu; saray
court *v* fayda sağlamak
courteous *adj* nazik
courtesy *n* kibarlık
courthouse *n* adliye sarayı
courtship *n* iltifat
courtyard *n* iç bahçe
cousin *n* kuzen; yeğen
cove *n* körfez
covenant *n* mukavele
cover *n* kapsam; örtü
cover *v* kapsamak
cover up *v* üstünü örtmek
coverage *n* kapsam
covert *adj* gizli
cover-up *n* gizleme
covet *v* imrenmek
cow *n* inek
coward *n* korkak
cowardice *n* korkaklık
cowardly *adv* korkakça

cowboy *n* kovboy
cozy *adj* rahat
crab *n* yengeç
crack *n* çatlak
crack *v* çatlamak
cradle *n* beşik
craft *n* zanaat; hile
craftsman *n* zanaatkar
cram *v* tıkıştırmak
cramp *n* kramp
cramped *adj* kramp girmiş
crane *n* vinç
crank *n* manivela; krank
cranky *adj* tuhaf
crap *n* bok; değersiz eşya
crappy *adj* boktan; zırva
crash *n* kırılma
crash *v* kaza yapmak
crass *adj* kaba
crater *n* krater
crave *v* arzulamak
craving *n* aşerme
crawl *v* sürünmek
crayon *n* pastel
craziness *n* çılgınlık
crazy *adj* çılgın
creak *v* gıcırdamak
creak *n* gıcırtı
cream *n* krem
creamy *adj* kremalı
crease *n* kırma; buruşuk
crease *v* buruştırmak

create *v* yaratmak
creation *n* yaratım, kreasyon
creative *adj* yaratıcı
creativity *n* yaratıcılık
creator *n* yaratıcı
creature *n* yaratık
credibility *n* güvenilirlik
credible *adj* güvenilir
credit *v* itibar etmek
credit *n* kredi
creditor *n* alacaklı
creed *n* iman
creek *n* dere
creep *v* emeklemek
creepy *adj* korkunç
cremate *v* kremasyon
crematorium *n* krematoryum
crest *n* tepelik
crevice *n* yarık
crew *n* ekip
crib *n* yemlik
cricket *n* kriket
crime *n* suç
criminal *adj* suçlu
cripple *adj* sakat
cripple *v* sakat etmek
crisis *n* kriz
crisp *adj* gevrek
crispy *adj* çıtır
crisscross *v* çaprazlama
criterion *n* kriter
critical *adj* kritik; eleştirel

C

criticism *n* eleştiri; tenkit
criticize *v* eleştirmek
critique *n* eleştiri
crockery *n* çanak çömlek
crocodile *n* timsah
crony *n* kafadar
crook *n* dönemeç
crooked *adj* virajlı
crop *v* otlamak
crop *n* ekin
cross *n* çarpı
cross *adj* çarpılı
cross *v* karşıya geçmek
cross out *v* üstünü çizmek
crossfire *n* çapraz ateş
crossing *n* geçit
crossroads *n* dörtyol; kavşak
crosswalk *n* yaya geçidi
crossword *n* çapraz bulmaca
crouch *v* çömelmek
crow *v* böbürlenmek
crow *n* karga
crowbar *n* kaldıraç
crowd *n* topluluk
crowd *v* doluşmak
crowded *adj* kalabalık
crown *n* taç; hükümdarlık
crown *v* taç giymek
crowning *n* taç giyme
crucial *adj* can alıcı
crucifix *n* çarmıh
crucifixion *n* çarmıha germe

crucify *v* çarmıha germek
crude *adj* ham; kaba
cruel *adj* acımasız
cruelty *n* acımasızlık
cruise *v* gemi yolculuğu
crumb *n* kırıntı
crumble *v* ufalamak
crunchy *adj* çıtır
crusade *n* haçlı seferi
crusader *n* Haçlı
crush *v* ezmek
crushing *adj* izdiham
crust *n* kabuk
crusty *adj* kabuklu
crutch *n* destek
cry *n* feryat
cry *v* ağlamak
cry out *v* haykırmak
crying *n* çığlık
crystal *n* kristal
cub *n* acemi
cube *n* küp
cubic *adj* kübik
cubicle *n* küçük bölme
cucumber *n* salatalık; hıyar
cuddle *v* kucaklamak
cuff *n* kolluk; manşet
cuisine *n* mutfak
culminate *v* son bulmak
culpability *n* kabahatli
culprit *n* suçlu
cult *n* kült; mezhep

cultivate *v* yetiştirmek
cultivation *n* ekip biçme
cultural *adj* kültürel
culture *n* kültür
cumbersome *adj* elverişsiz
cunning *adj* kurnaz
cup *n* fincan
cupboard *n* dolap
curable *adj* tedavisi mümkün
curator *n* küratör
curb *v* engellemek
curb *n* engel
curdle *v* pıhtılaşmak
cure *n* çare
cure *v* tedavi etmek
curfew *n* sokağa çıkma yasağı
curiosity *n* merak
curious *adj* meraklı
curl *v* dolamak; sarmak
curl *n* büklüm; lüle
curly *adj* bukle
currency *n* döviz
current *n* akım; akıntı
current *adj* şu anki
currently *adv* şu anda
curse *v* lanetlemek
curtail *v* kısa kesmek
curtain *n* perde
curve *n* kıvrım
curve *v* kıvırmak
cushion *n* minder
cushion *v* hafifletmek

cuss *v* küfür
custard *n* muhallebi
custodian *n* muhafız
custody *n* muhafaza
custom *n* gelenek
customary *adj* geleneksel
customer *n* müşteri
custom-made *adj* ısmarlama
customs *n* gümrük
cut *n* kesik
cut *iv* kesmek
cut back *v* kısaltmak
cut down *v* azaltmak
cut off *v* kesmek
cut out *v* kesmek; biçmek
cute *adj* sevimli
cutlery *n* çatal-bıçak takımı
cutter *n* kesici; filika
cyanide *n* siyanür
cycle *v* bisiklete binmek
cycle *n* dönüş; devir
cyclist *n* bisikletçi
cyclone *n* siklon; kasırga
cylinder *n* silindir
cynic *adj* kinik
cynicism *n* kinizm
cypress *n* servi
cyst *n* kist
czar *n* çar

D

D

dad *n* baba
dagger *n* hançer
daily *adv* günlük
dairy farm *n* mandıra
daisy *n* papatya
dam *n* baraj
damage *n* zarar
damage *v* zarar vermek
damaging *adj* zarar veren
damn *v* kahretmek
damnation *n* lanet
damp *adj* nem
dampen *v* nemlendirmek
dance *n* dans
dance *v* dans etmek
dancing *n* dans
dandruff *n* saç kepeği
danger *n* tehlike
dangerous *adj* tehlikeli
dangle *v* sarkmak
dare *v* cesaret etmek
dare *n* cüret
daring *adj* yiğit
dark *adj* koyu
darken *v* karartmak
darkness *n* karanlık
darling *adj* sevgili
darn *v* yamamak
dart *v* fırlamak; atılmak

dart *n* dart
dash *v* hızlı koşmak
dashing *adj* atılgan
data *n* veri
database *n* veritabanı
date *n* tarih; buluşma
date *v* tarih koymak
daughter *n* kız çocuk
daughter-in-law *n* gelin
daunt *v* yıldırmak
daunting *adj* gözüpek
dawn *n* seher
day *n* gün
daydream *v* hayal kurmak
daze *v* sersemletmek
dazed *adj* sersem
dazzle *v* göz kamaştırmak
dazzling *adj* göz kamaştıran
deacon *n* diyakoz
dead *adj* ölü
dead end *n* çıkmaz sokak
deaden *v* hafifletmek
deadline *n* son tarih
deadlock *adj* çıkmaz
deadly *adj* ölümcül
deaf *adj* sağır
deafen *v* sağır etmek
deafening *adj* sağır edici
deafness *n* sağırlık
deal *iv* anlaşmak
deal *n* anlaşma
dealer *n* dağıtımcı

dealings *n* muamele
dean *n* dekan
dear *adj* sevgili
dearly *adv* pahalıya
death *n* ölüm
death toll *n* ölü sayısı
death trap *n* ölüm tuzağı
deathbed *n* ölüm yatağı
debase *v* değerini düşürmek
debatable *adj* tartışılabilir
debate *v* tartışmak
debate *n* tartışma
debit *n* borç
debrief *v* sorguya çekmek
debris *n* döküntü
debt *n* borç
debtor *n* borçlu
debunk *v* çürütmek
debut *n* başlangıç
decade *n* on yıl
decadence *n* zeval
decaf *adj* kafeinsiz
decapitate *v* başını kesmek
decay *v* çürümek
decay *n* çürük
deceased *adj* merhum
deceit *n* hile
deceitful *adj* hilekar
deceive *v* kandırmak
December *n* Aralık
decency *n* edep
decent *adj* edepli

deception *n* aldatma
deceptive *adj* yanıltıcı
decide *v* karar vermek
deciding *adj* kesin
decimal *adj* ondalık sayı
decimate *v* kırıp geçirmek
decipher *v* şifre çözmek
decision *n* karar
decisive *adj* kararlı
deck *v* bezemek
deck *n* deste
declaration *n* bildiri
declare *v* bildirmek
declension *n* gerileme
decline *v* reddetmek
decline *n* meyil; düşüş
decompose *v* ayrıştırmak
décor *n* dekor
decorate *v* dekore etmek
decorative *adj* dekoratif
decorum *n* uygun davranış
decrease *v* azalmak
decrease *n* düşüş
decree *n* kararname
decree *v* buyurmak
decrepit *adj* yıpranmış
dedicate *v* adamak
dedication *n* adak
deduce *v* ithaf
deduct *v* hesaptan düşmek
deductible *adj* indirimli
deduction *n* indirim

deed

deed *n* iş; eylem
deem *v* saymak; farzetmek
deep *adj* derin
deepen *v* derinleştirmek
deer *n* geyik
deface *v* çirkinleştirmek
defame *v* kara çalmak
defeat *v* yenmek
defeat *n* yenilgi
defect *n* kusur
defect *v* iltica etmek
defection *n* iltica
defective *adj* kusurlu
defend *v* savunmak
defendant *n* davalı; sanık
defender *n* savunucu
defense *n* savunma
defenseless *adj* savunmasız
defer *v* ertelemek
defiance *n* muhalefet
defiant *adj* muhalif
deficiency *n* eksiklik
deficient *adj* eksik
deficit *n* zarar
defile *v* bozmak
define *v* tanımlamak
definite *adj* kesin
definition *n* tanım
definitive *adj* kati
deflate *v* söndürmek
deform *v* biçimsizleştirmek
deformity *n* biçimsizlik

defraud *v* dolandırmak
defray *v* ödemek
defrost *v* buzlarını çözmek
deft *adj* becerikli
defuse *v* yatıştırmak
defy *v* kafa tutmak
degenerate *v* yozlaşmak
degenerate *adj* dejenere
degeneration *n* dejenerasyon
degradation *n* itibarsızlık
degrade *v* rütbesini indirmek
degrading *adj* alçaltıcı
degree *n* derece; rütbe
dehydrate *v* su kaybetmek
deign *v* tenezzül etmek
deity *n* ilah
dejected *adj* kederli
delay *v* ertelemek
delay *n* gecikme
delegate *v* yetki aktarmak
delegate *n* delege
delegation *n* delegasyon
delete *v* silmek
deliberate *v* müzakere etmek
deliberate *adj* temkinli
delicacy *n* kibarlık
delicate *adj* narin
delicious *adj* lezzetli
delight *n* tat
delight *v* sevindirmek
delightful *adj* hoş
delinquency *n* suçluluk

delinquent *adj* suçlu
deliver *v* teslim etmek
delivery *n* teslimat; doğum
delude *v* aldatmak
deluge *n* tufan
delusion *n* hayal; hile
deluxe *adj* lüks
demand *v* talep etmek
demand *n* talep
demanding *adj* ısrarcı
demean *v* alçaltmak
demeaning *adj* alçaltılmış
demeanor *n* tavır
demented *adj* kaçık
demise *n* vefat
democracy *n* demokrasi
democratic *adj* demokratik
demolish *v* yıkmak
demolition *n* yıkım
demon *n* şeytan
demonstrate *v* ispat etmek
demonstrative *adj* kanıtlayan
demoralize *v* moralini bozmak
demote *v* indirgemek
den *n* mağara
denial *n* inkar
denigrate *v* iftira etmek
Denmark *n* Danimarka
denominator *n* payda
denote *v* belirtmek
denounce *v* ihbar etmek
dense *adj* yoğun

density *n* yoğunluk
dent *v* yamultmak
dent *n* girinti
dental *adj* dişsel
dentist *n* diş doktoru
dentures *n* takma diş
deny *v* inkar etmek
deodorant *n* deodorant
depart *v* yola çıkmak
department *n* departman, şube
departure *n* ayrılış
depend *v* bağlı olmak; güvenmek
dependable *adj* güvenilir
dependence *n* bağlılık
dependent *adj* muhtaç
depict *v* betimlemek
deplete *v* tüketmek
deplorable *adj* içler acısı
deplore *v* acı duymak
deploy *v* konuşlanmak
deployment *n* konuşlandırma
deport *v* sınırdışı etmek
deportation *n* sınırdışı
depose *v* görevden almak
deposit *n* emanet; depozit
depot *n* depo
deprave *adj* ayartıcı
depravity *n* ahlak bozukluğu
depreciate *v* ucuzlatmak
depreciation *n* yıpranma payı
depress *v* canını sıkmak
depressing *adj* can sıkıcı

D

depression *n* depresyon; ekonomik kriz

deprivation *n* mahrumiyet

deprive *v* yoksun bırakmak

deprived *adj* yoksun

depth *n* derinlik

derail *v* raydan çıkmak

derailment *n* raydan çıkma

deranged *adj* deli

derelict *adj* sahipsiz

deride *v* alay etmek

derivative *adj* türev

derive *v* türetmek

derogatory *adj* onur kırıcı

descend *v* inmek

descendant *n* torun

descent *n* iniş

describe *v* tarif etmek

description *n* tarif

descriptive *adj* tanımlayıcı

desecrate *v* saygısızlık etmek

desegregate *v* ırk ayrımına son vermek

desert *n* çöl

desert *v* sahra; terkedilmiş

deserted *adj* ıssız

deserter *n* kaçak

deserve *v* hak etmek

deserving *adj* layık

design *n* tasarım; amaç

designate *v* işaret etmek

desirable *adj* çekici

desire *n* arzu

desire *v* arzulamak

desist *v* vazgeçmek

desk *n* masa; resepsiyon

desolate *adj* kimsesiz

desolation *n* haraplık

despair *n* umutsuzluk

desperate *adj* umutsuz

despicable *adj* adi

despise *v* hor görmek

despite *c* rağmen

despondent *adj* meyus

despot *n* despot

despotic *adj* despotça

dessert *n* tatlı

destination *n* hedef

destiny *n* kader

destitute *adj* yoksul

destroy *v* harap etmek

destroyer *n* yok edici

destruction *n* yıkım

destructive *adj* yıkıcı

detach *v* ayırmak

detachable *adj* ayrılabilir

detail *n* detay

detail *v* ayrıntıya inmek

detain *v* alıkoymak

detect *v* meydana çıkarmak

detective *n* detektif

detector *n* detektör

detention *n* alıkoyma

deter *v* caydırmak

detergent *n* deterjan
deteriorate *v* kötüleştirmek
deterioration *n* kötüleşme
determination *n* kararlılık
determine *v* karar vermek
deterrence *n* caydırma
detest *v* nefret etmek
detestable *adj* tiksindirici
detonate *v* patlatmak
detonation *n* patlama
detonator *n* patlatıcı
detour *n* dolambaçlı yol
detriment *n* ziyan
detrimental *adj* zararlı
devaluation *n* devaluasyon
devalue *v* devalüe etmek
devastate *v* harap etmek
devastating *adj* harap edici
devastation *n* tahribat
develop *v* geliştirmek
development *n* kalkınma
deviation *n* sapma
device *n* aygıt
devil *n* şeytan
devious *adj* şeytanca
devise *v* tasarlamak
devoid *adj* mahrum
devote *v* adamak
devotion *n* sadakat
devour *v* yiyip yutmak
devout *adj* dindar
dew *n* çiy

diabetes *n* diyabet
diabetic *adj* diyabetik
diabolical *adj* zalim
diagnose *v* teşhis koymak
diagnosis *n* teşhis
diagonal *adj* köşegen
diagram *n* diyagram
dial *n* kadran
dial *v* çevirmek
dial tone *n* çevir sesi
dialect *n* lehçe
dialogue *n* diyalog
diameter *n* çap
diamond *n* elmas
diaper *n* bez
diarrhea *n* ishal
diary *n* günce
dice *v* küp küp kesmek
dice *n* oyun zarları
dictate *v* yazdırmak
dictator *n* diktatör
dictatorial *adj* diktatörce
dictatorship *n* diktatörlük
dictionary *n* sözlük
die *v* ölmek
die out *v* nesli tükenmek
diet *n* diyet
diet *v* diyet yapmak
differ *v* başka olmak
difference *n* fark
different *adj* farklı
difficult *adj* zor

D

difficulty *n* zorluk
diffuse *v* dağıtmak
dig *iv* kazmak
digest *v* sindirmek
digestion *n* sindirim
digestive *adj* dijestif
digit *n* basamak
dignify *v* ondurlandırmak
dignitary *n* rütbe
dignity *n* asalet
digress *v* konudan ayrılmak
dike *n* toprak duvar
dilapidated *adj* harap
dilemma *n* ikilem
diligence *n* özen
diligent *adj* gayretli
dilute *v* sulandırmak
dim *adj* loş
dim *v* azaltmak
dime *n* on sent
dimension *n* boyut
diminish *v* azaltmak
dine *v* akşam yemeği yemek
diner *n* restoran
dining room *n* yemek odası
dinner *n* akşam yemeği
dinosaur *n* dinazor
diocese *n* piskoposluk bölgesi
diphthong *n* diftong
diploma *n* diploma
diplomacy *n* diplomasi
diplomat *n* diplomat

diplomatic *adj* diplomatik
dire *adj* korkunç
direct *adj* doğrudan
direct *v* emretmek
direction *n* yön; talimat
director *n* yönetici
directory *n* dizin
dirt *n* kir
dirty *adj* kirli
disability *n* özür
disabled *adj* sakatlık
disadvantage *n* dezavantaj
disagree *v* anlaşmamak
disagreeable *adj* nahoş
disagreement *n* anlaşmazlık
disappear *v* kaybolmak
disappearance *n* kaybolma
disappoint *v* hayal kırıklığına
uğratmak
disappointing *adj* umut kırıcı
disappointment *n* hayal kırıklığı
disapproval *n* onaylamama
disapprove *v* onaylamamak
disarm *v* silahsızlandırmak
disarmament *n* silahsızlanma
disaster *n* felaket
disastrous *adj* feci
disband *v* dağılmak
disbelief *n* inanmama
disburse *v* para harcamak
discard *v* atmak
discern *v* ayırt etmek

discharge v ödemek; boşaltmak
discharge n ödeme; boşaltma
disciple n havari; çömez
discipline n disiplin
disclaim v yadsımak
disclose v açığa vurmak
discomfort n rahatsızlık
disconnect v bağlantıyı kesmek
discontent adj hoşnutsuzluk
discontinue v durdurmak
discord n uyuşmazlık
discordant adj uyumsuz
discount n indirim
discount v indirim yapmak
discourage v cesaretini kırmak
discouragement n cesaretsizlik
discouraging adj şevk kırıcı
discourtesy n nezaketsizlik
discover v keşfetmek
discovery n keşif
discredit v gözden düşürmek
discreet adj tedbirli
discrepancy n uyuşmazlık
discretion n sağduyu
discriminate v fark gözetmek
discrimination n ayrım
discuss v tartışmak
discussion n tartışma
disdain n tepeden bakma
disease n hastalık
disembark v karaya çıkarmak
disenchanted adj inancını yitirmiş

disentangle v çözmek
disfigure v biçimsizleştirmek
disgrace n yüzkarası
disgrace v gözden düşmek
disgraceful adj utanç verici
disgruntled adj küskün
disguise v kılık değiştirmek
disguise n kılık değiştirmiş
disgust n iğrenmek
disgusting adj iğrenç
dish n yemek; yemek tabağı
dishearten v umudunu kırmak
dishonest adj sahtekar
dishonesty n sahtekarlık
dishonor n alçaklık
dishonorable adj alçak
dishwasher n bulaşık makinası
disillusion n hayal kırıklığı
disinfect v dezenfekte etmek
disinfectant n dezenfektan
disinherit v evlatlıktan
  reddetmek
disintegrate v parçalamak
disintegration n bölünme
disinterested adj tarafsızlık
disk n disk
dislike v hoşlanmamak
dislike n hoşlanmama
dislocate v yerinden çıkarmak
dislodge v yerinden oynatmak
disloyal adj vefasız
disloyalty n vefasızlık

D

dismal *adj* keferli
dismantle *v* parçalara ayırmak
dismay *n* umutsuzluk
dismay *v* dehşete düşürmek
dismiss *v* kovmak
dismissal *n* işten çıkarma
dismount *v* kaldırmak; indirmek
disobedience *n* itaatsizlik
disobedient *adj* itaatsiz
disobey *v* itaat etmemek
disorder *n* kargaşa
disorganized *adj* düzensiz
disoriented *adj* kafası karışmış
disown *v* yadsımak
disparity *n* farklı
dispatch *v* dağıtmak
dispel *v* defetmek
dispensation *n* dağıtma
dispense *v* dağıtmak
dispersal *n* dağılım
disperse *v* dağıtmak
displace *v* yerini değiştirmek
display *n* görüntü; sergi
display *v* görüntülemek
displease *v* sinirlendirmek
displeasing *adj* nahoş
displeasure *n* hoşnutsuzluk
disposable *adj* bir kullanımlık
disposal *n* elden çıkarma
dispose *v* elden çıkarmak
disprove *v* aksini kanıtlamak
dispute *n* münakaşa

dispute *v* anlaşmazlık
disqualify *v* diskalifiye etmek
disregard *v* önemsememek
disrepair *n* bakımsızlık
disrespect *n* saygısızlık
disrespectful *adj* saygısız
disrupt *v* bozmak
disruption *n* bozma
dissatisfied *adj* tatmin olmamış
disseminate *v* saçmak
dissent *v* kabul etmemek
dissident *adj* muhalif
dissimilar *adj* farklı
dissipate *v* dağıtmak
dissolute *adj* çapkın; rezil
dissolution *n* erime
dissolve *v* eritmek
dissonant *adj* ahenksiz
dissuade *v* caydırmak
distance *n* uzaklık
distant *adj* uzak
distaste *n* beğenmeme
distasteful *adj* tatsız
distill *v* damıtmak
distinct *adj* farklı
distinction *n* üstün
distinctive *adj* kendine özgü
distinguish *v* ayırt etmek
distort *v* biçimini bozmak
distortion *n* çarpıtma
distract *v* dikkatini dağıtmak
distraction *n* dikkat dağınıklığı

distraught *adj* çılgına dönmüş
distress *n* üzüntü
distress *v* endişelenmek
distressing *adj* endişe verici
distribute *v* dağıtmak
distribution *n* dağıtım
district *n* mahalle
distrust *n* itaatsizlik
distrust *v* itimat etmemek
distrustful *adj* itimatsız
disturb *v* rahatsız etmek
disturbance *n* rahatsızlık
disturbing *adj* rahatsız edici
disunity *n* kopukluk
disuse *n* kullanılmazlık
ditch *n* hendek; çukur
dive *v* dalmak
diver *n* dalgıç
diverse *adj* çeşit
diversify *v* çeşitlendirmek
diversion *n* eğlence
diversity *n* çeşitlilik
divert *v* yönlendirmek
divide *v* bölmek
dividend *n* bölünen; pay
divine *adj* ilahi
diving *n* dalış
divinity *n* ilahilik
divisible *adj* bölünebilir
division *n* bölme; kısım
divorce *n* boşanma
divorce *v* boşanmak

divorcee *n* boşanan
divulge *v* ifşa etmek
dizziness *n* başı dönen
dizzy *adj* sersem
do *iv* yapmak, etmek
docile *adj* uysal
docility *n* uysallık
dock *n* tersane; rıhtım
dock *v* yanaşmak
doctor *n* doktor
doctrine *n* öğreti
document *n* doküman
documentary *n* belgesel
documentation *n* belgeleme
dodge *v* fırlamak
dog *n* köpek
dogmatic *adj* dogmatik
dole out *v* sadaka vermek
doll *n* oyuncak bebek
dollar *n* dolar
dolphin *n* yunus
dome *n* kubbe
domestic *adj* aile içi; yerel
domesticate *v* evcilleştirmek
dominate *v* egemen olmak
domination *n* hakimiyet
domineering *adj* mütehakkim
dominion *n* egemenlik
donate *v* bağış yapmak
donation *n* bağış
donkey *n* eşek
donor *n* bağışçı

D

D

doom *n* korkunç son
doomed *adj* mahkumiyet
door *n* kapı
doorbell *n* kapı zili
doorstep *n* kapı girişi
doorway *n* kapı aralığı
dope *n* malumat
dope *v* uyuşturucu vermek
dormitory *n* yatakhane
dosage *n* dozaj
dossier *n* dosya
dot *n* nokta
double *adj* çift
double *v* iki katına çıkarmak
double-check *v* kontrol etmek
double-cross *v* kazık atmak
doubt *n* şüphe
doubt *v* şüphelenmek
doubtful *adl* şüpheli
dough *n* hamur
dove *n* güvercin
down *adj* neşesiz
down *adv* aşağıda
down payment *n* peşinat
downcast *adj* morali bozuk
downfall *n* yıkılış
downhill *adv* yokuş aşağı
downpour *n* sağanak
downsize *v* işgücünü azaltmak
downstairs *adv* aşağıda
down-to-earth *adj* gerçekçi
downtown *n* çarşı

downtrodden *adj* mazlum
downturn *n* sıkıntılı dönem
dowry *n* çeyiz
doze *n* hafif uyku
doze *v* şekerleme yapmak
dozen *n* düzine
draft *n* taslak; askere alma
draft *v* taslak çizmek
draftsman *n* teknik ressam
drag *v* sürüklemek
dragon *n* dragon
drain *v* akıtmak
drainage *n* kanalizasyon
dramatic *adj* dramatik
dramatize *v* dramatize etmek
drape *n* kumaşla örtmek
drastic *adj* şiddetli
draw *n* kura; berabere biten oyun
draw *iv* çizmek; çekiliş yapmak
drawback *n* sakınca
drawer *n* çekmece
drawing *n* çizim
dread *v* çok korkmak
dreaded *adj* dehşet
dreadful *adj* ürkütücü
dream *n* hayal, rüya
dream *iv* hayal kurmak
dress *n* giysi
dress *v* giyinmek
dresser *n* şifoniyer
dressing *n* sargı
dried *adj* kuru

drift *v* sürüklemek
drift apart *v* kendini koyvermek
drifter *n* avare
drill *v* matkaplamak; sondaj yapmak
drill *n* matkap; talim
drink *iv* içmek
drink *n* içecek
drinkable *adj* içilir
drinker *n* içkici
drip *v* damlatmak
drip *n* damla
drive *n* araba gezintisi; top sürme
drive *iv* araç sürmek;
drive at *v* demek istemek
drive away *v* kovmak
driver *n* sürücü
driveway *n* özel araba yolu
drizzle *v* çiselemek
drizzle *n* çisenti
drop *v* damlamak; düşmek
drop *n* damla; düşüş
drop in *v* uğramak
drop off *v* uyuyakalmak
drop out *v* okulu terk etmek
drought *n* kuraklık
drown *v* boğulmak
drowsy *adj* uykulu
drug *n* ilaç
drug *v* ilaç vermek
drugstore *n* eczane
drum *n* davul; şarjör

drunk *adj* sarhoş
drunkenness *n* sarhoşluk
dry *v* kurutmak
dry *adj* kuru
dry-clean *v* kuru temizlemek
dryer *n* kurutucu
dual *adj* ikili
dubious *adj* kuşkulu
duchess *n* düşes
duck *n* ördek
duck *v* suya daldırmak
duct *n* oluk
due *adj* gereken; kalan
duel *n* düello
dues *n* aidat
duke *n* dük
dull *v* donuklaşmak
dull *adj* kalın kafalı
duly *adv* usulüne uygun
dumb *adj* dilsiz; budala
dummy *n* maket
dummy *adj* sözde
dump *v* terketmek
dump *n* dökmek
dung *n* gübre
dungeon *n* zindan
dupe *v* dolandırmak
duplicate *v* kopyalamak
duplication *n* kopyalama
durable *adj* dayanıklı
duration *n* müddet
during *pre* sırasında

D

dusk *n* alacakaranlık
dust *n* toz
dusty *adj* tozlu
Dutch *adj* Hollandalı
duty *n* görev
dwarf *n* cüce
dwell *iv* ikamet etmek
dwelling *n* ikametgah
dwindle *v* gittikçe küçülmek
dye *v* boyamak
dye *n* boya
dying *adj* ölmekte olan
dynamic *adj* dinamik
dynamite *n* dinamit
dynasty *n* hanedan

each *adj* her
each other *adj* her bir
eager *adj* hevesli
eagerness *n* heveslilik
eagle *n* kartal
ear *n* kulak; başak
earache *n* kulak ağrısı
eardrum *n* kulak zarı
early *adv* erken
earmark *v* tayin etmek

earn *v* kazanmak
earnestly *adv* ciddiyetle
earnings *n* kazanç
earphones *n* kulaklık
earring *n* küpe
earth *n* toprak; dünya
earthquake *n* deprem
earwax *n* kulak kiri
ease *v* kolaylaştırmak
ease *n* kolaylık, rahatlık
easily *adv* kolayca
east *n* doğu
eastbound *adj* doğuya giden
Easter *n* Paskalya
eastern *adj* doğusal
easterner *n* doğulu
eastward *adv* doğuya doğru
easy *adj* kolay; rahat
eat *iv* yemek
eat away *v* aşındırmak
eavesdrop *v* kulak misafiri olmak
ebb *v* cezir
eccentric *adj* acayip
echo *n* yankı
eclipse *n* gök tutulması
ecology *n* ekoloji
economical *adj* ekonomik
economize *v* tasarruf etmek
economy *n* ekonomi
ecstasy *n* mutluluk
ecstatic *adj* çok mutlu
edge *v* keskinleştirmek

edge *n* uç
edgy *adj* sinirli
edible *adj* yenilebilir
edifice *n* büyük yapı
edit *v* düzenlemek
edition *n* sürüm
educate *v* eğitmek
educational *adj* eğitimsel
eerie *adj* ürkütücü
effect *n* etki
effective *adj* etkili
effectiveness *n* tesirlilik
efficiency *n* etkenlik
efficient *adj* verimli
effigy *n* büst
effort *n* çaba
effusive *adj* coşkun
egg *n* yumurta
egg white *n* yumurta akı
egoism *n* bencillik
egoist *n* egoist
eight *adj* sekiz
eighteen *adj* on sekiz
eighth *adj* sekizinci
eighty *adj* seksen
either *adj* ikisinden biri
either *adv* ikisinden biri
eject *v* çıkarmak
elapse *v* akıp gitmek
elastic *adj* elastik
elated *adj* sevinçli
elbow *n* dirsek

elder *n* yaşlı
elderly *adj* yaşlıca
elect *v* seçmek
election *n* seçim
electric *adj* elektrik
electrician *n* elektrikçi
electricity *n* elektrik
electrify *v* elektrik vermek
electrocute *v* elektrikle idam etmek
electronic *adj* elektronik
elegance *n* zerafet
elegant *adj* zarif
element *n* eleman
elementary *adj* temel; kolay
elephant *n* fil
elevate *v* yükseltmek
elevation *n* yükselti
elevator *n* asansör
eleven *adj* on bir
eleventh *adj* on birinci
eligible *adj* seçilebilir
eliminate *v* elemek
elm *n* karaağaç
eloquence *n* belagat
else *adv* başka
elsewhere *adv* başka bir yere
elude *v* atlatmak
elusive *adj* ele geçmez
emaciated *adj* çok zayıf
emanate *v* yayılmak
emancipate *v* azat etmek

embalm *v* mumyalamak
embark *v* binmek
embarrass *v* utandırmak
embassy *n* elçilik
embellish *v* süslemek
embers *n* köz
embezzle *v* zimmetine geçirmek
embitter *v* gücendirmek
emblem *n* amblem
embody *v* kapsamak
emboss *v* kabartmak
embrace *v* kucaklaşmak
embrace *n* kucak
embroider *v* süslemek
embroidery *n* süs
embroil *v* karıştırmak
embryo *n* embriyon
emerald *n* zümrüt
emerge *v* meydana çıkmak
emergency *n* acil
emigrant *n* göçmen
emigrate *v* göçmek
emission *n* salım
emit *v* salmak
emotion *n* duygu
emotional *adj* duygusal
emperor *n* imparator
emphasis *n* vurgu
emphasize *v* vurgulamak
empire *n* imparator
employ *v* kullanmak; işe almak
employee *n* çalışan

employer *n* işveren
employment *n* istihdam
empress *n* imparatoriçe
emptiness *n* boşluk
empty *adj* boş
empty *v* boşaltmak
enable *v* etkinleştirmek
enchant *v* büyülemek
enchanting *adj* büyüleyici
encircle *v* kuşatmak
enclave *n* yerleşim bölgesi
enclose *v* kapsamak
enclosure *n* kapsam
encompass *v* ihtiva etmek
encounter *v* karşılamak
encounter *n* karşılaşma
encourage *v* cesaret vermek
encroach *v* saldırmak
encyclopedia *n* ansiklopedi
end *n* son
end *v* sonlandırmak
end up *v* olup çıkmak
endanger *v* tehlikeye sokmak
endeavor *v* gayret etmek
endeavor *n* gayret
ending *n* bitiş
endless *adj* sonsuz
endorse *v* telkin etmek
endorsement *n* ciro
endure *v* dayanmak
enemy *n* düşman
energetic *adj* enerji dolu

energy *n* enerji
enforce *v* uygulamak
engage *v* meşgul etmek
engaged *adj* meşgul
engagement *n* nişanlı
engine *n* makina
engineer *n* mühendis
England *n* İngiltere
English *adj* İngiliz
engrave *v* kazımak
engraving *n* kazı
engrossed *adj* meşgul
engulf *v* içine çekmek
enhance *v* geliştirmek
enjoy *v* keyfini çıkarmak
enjoyable *adj* keyifli
enjoyment *n* keyif
enlarge *v* büyütmek
enlargement *n* büyütme
enlighten *v* aydınlatmak
enlist *v* askere kaydolmak
enormous *adj* kocaman
enough *adv* yeteri kadar
enrage *v* öfkelendirmek
enrich *v* zenginleştirmek
enroll *v* kaydolmak
enrollment *n* sicile kaydetmek
ensure *v* garanti etmek
entail *v* icap ettirmek
entangle *v* başını derde sokmak
enter *v* girmek
enterprise *n* girişim; kuruluş

entertain *v* eğlendirmek
entertaining *adj* eğlenceli
entertainment *n* eğlence
enthrall *v* büyülemek
enthralling *adj* büyüleyici
enthuse *v* göklere çıkarmak
enthusiasm *n* şevk
entice *v* ayartmak
enticement *n* cazibe
enticing *adj* cezbedici
entire *adj* hepsi
entirely *adv* tamamıyla
entrance *n* giriş
entreat *v* yalvarmak
entree *n* esas yemek
entrenched *adj* sağlam
entrepreneur *n* girişimci
entrust *v* emanet etmek
entry *n* giriş
enumerate *v* saymak
envelop *v* kuşatmak
envelope *n* zarf
envious *adj* kıskanç
environment *n* çevre
envisage *v* tasavvur etmek
envoy *n* delege; son söz
envy *n* haset
envy *v* haset etmek
epidemic *n* salgın
epilepsy *n* sara
episode *n* bölüm; fasıl
epistle *n* risale; mektup

E

epitaph *n* mezar kitabesi
epitomize *v* özetlemek
epoch *n* devir
equal *adj* eşit
equality *n* eşitlik
equate *v* eşitlemek
equation *n* denklem
equator *n* ekvator
equilibrium *n* denge
equip *v* donatmak
equipment *n* donatım; gereç
equivalent *adj* eşdeğer
era *n* çağ
eradicate *v* yok etmek
erase *v* silmek
eraser *n* silgi
erect *v* kalkmak
erect *adj* kalkık
err *v* yanılmak
errand *n* ayak işi
erroneous *adj* hatalı
error *n* hata
erupt *v* püskürmek
eruption *n* patlak verme
escalate *v* yükseltmek
escalator *n* asansör
escapade *n* macera
escape *v* kaçmak
escort *n* refakatçi
esophagus *n* yemek borusu
especially *adv* özellikle
espionage *n* casusluk

essay *n* rapor; deneme
essence *n* öz varlık
essential *adj* temel
establish *v* kurmak
estate *n* arazi
esteem *v* itibar
estimate *v* kestirmek
estimation *n* tahmin
estranged *adj* ayrı yaşayan
estuary *n* haliç
eternity *n* ebediyet
ethical *adj* ahlaki
ethics *n* ahlak
etiquette *n* görgü kuralları
euphoria *n* coşku
Europe *n* Avrupa
European *adj* Avrupalı
evacuate *v* boşaltmak
evade *v* kurtulmak
evaluate *v* değerlendirmek
evaporate *v* buharlaştırmak
evasion *n* kaçamak
evasive *adj* baştansavma
eve *n* arife
even *adj* bile; çift
even if *c* olsa bile
even more *c* daha da
evening *n* akşam
event *n* olay
eventuality *n* ihtimal
eventually *adv* nihayet
ever *adv* hiç; hep

everlasting *adj* sonsuz
every *adj* her
everybody *pro* herkes
everyday *adj* her gün
everyone *pro* herkes
everything *pro* her şey
evict *v* tahliye ettirmek
evidence *n* delil
evil *n* kötülük
evil *adj* uğursuz
evoke *v* uyandırmak
evolution *n* evrim
evolve *v* evrim geçirmek
exact *adj* tamı tamına
exaggerate *v* abartmak
exalt *v* yüceltmek
examination *n* sınav
examine *v* sınamak
example *n* örnek
exasperate *v* çileden çıkarmak
excavate *v* kazı yapmak
exceed *v* aşmak
exceedingly *adv* aşırı
excel *v* üstün olmak
excellence *n* mükemmellik
excellent *adj* mükemmel
except *pre* haricinde
exception *n* istisna
exceptional *adj* istisnai
excerpt *n* alıntı
excess *n* fazlalık
excessive *adj* aşırı

exchange *v* takas etmek
excite *v* heyecanlandırmak
excitement *n* heyecan
exciting *adj* heyecan verici
exclaim *v* çığlık atmak
exclamation *n* ünlem
exclude *v* dışlamak
excruciating *adj* dayanılmaz
excursion *n* gezinti
excuse *v* mazur görmek
excuse *n* mazeret
execute *v* yürütmek
executive *n* yönetim
exemplary *adj* örnek olarak
exemplify *v* örnek vermek
exempt *adj* muaf
exemption *n* muafiyet
exercise *n* egzersiz
exercise *v* alıştırma yapmak
exert *v* güç kullanmak
exertion *n* gayret
exhaust *v* tüketmek
exhausting *adj* yorucu
exhaustion *n* yorgunluk
exhibit *v* sergilemek
exhibition *n* sergi
exhilarating *adj* neşelendirici
exhort *v* teşvik etmek
exile *v* sügüne göndermek
exile *n* sürgün
exist *v* var olmak
existence *n* varlık

exit *n* çıkış
exodus *n* akın
exonerate *v* aklamak
exorbitant *adj* aşırı yüksek
exorcist *n* üfürükçü
exotic *adj* egzotik
expand *v* genişletmek
expansion *n* genişleme
expect *v* tahmin etmek
expectancy *n* umut
expectation *n* beklenti
expediency *n* menfaat
expedient *adj* uygun
expedition *n* keşif gezisi
expel *v* kovmak
expenditure *n* masraf
expense *n* masraf
expensive *adj* pahalı
experience *n* deneyim
experiment *n* deney
expert *adj* uzman
expiate *v* cezasını çekmek
expiation *n* kefaret
expiration *n* sürenin dolması
expire *v* süresi bitmek
explain *v* açıklamak
explicit *adj* net
explode *v* patlamak
exploit *v* sömürmek
exploit *n* istismar
exploration *n* keşif
explore *v* keşfetmek

explorer *n* kaşif
explosion *n* patlama
explosive *adj* patlayıcı
export *v* ihracat
expose *v* maruz bırakmak
exposed *adj* maruz
express *adj* hızlı; kesin
express *v* beyan etmek
expression *n* anlatım
expressly *adv* hızlıca
expropriate *v* kamulaştırmak
expulsion *n* ihraç
exquisite *adj* üstün
extend *v* uzatmak
extension *n* uzatma
extent *n* kapsam
extenuating *adj* hafiflemiş
exterior *adj* harici
exterminate *v* yok etmek
external *adj* dış
extinct *adj* nesli tükenmiş
extinguish *v* söndürmek
extort *v* sızdırmak
extortion *n* haraç
extra *adv* ekstra
extract *v* çıkartmak
extradite *v* iade etmek
extradition *n* iade
extraneous *adj* yabancı
extravagance *n* israf
extravagant *adj* savurgan
extreme *adj* aşırı

extremist *adj* radikal
extremities *n* uç nokta
extricate *v* kurtarmak
extroverted *adj* dışadönük
exude *v* sızmak
exult *v* bayram etmek
eye *n* göz
eyebrow *n* kaş
eye-catching *adj* göz alan
eyeglasses *n* gözlük
eyelash *n* kirpik
eyelid *n* göz kapağı
eyesight *n* görüş yeteneği; alanı
eyewitness *n* görgü tanığı

fable *n* masal
fabric *n* kumaş
fabricate *v* uydurmak
fabulous *adj* harika
face *n* yüz
face up to *v* karşı koymak
facet *n* yüzey; façeta
facilitate *v* kolaylaştırmak
facing *pre* yüz yüze
fact *n* gerçek
factor *n* etken

factory *n* fabrika
factual *adj* gerçekçi
faculty *n* fakülte
fad *n* geçici heves
fade *v* sönmek
faded *adj* sönük
fail *v* başaramamak
failure *n* başarısızlık
faint *adj* zayıf; belli belirsiz
faint *v* bayılmak
faint *n* donuk
fair *adj* adil; hoş
fair *n* fuar
fairness *n* adaletlilik
fairy *n* peri
faith *n* inanç; güven
faithful *adj* inançlı; dürüst
fake *v* uydurmak
fake *adj* sahte
fall *n* düşüş; sonbahar
fall *iv* düşmek
fall back *v* geri çekilmek
fall behind *v* geride kalmak
fall down *v* düşmek
fall through *v* gerçekleşmemek
fallacy *n* yanıltmaca
fallout *n* radyoaktif serpinti
falsehood *n* yalan
falsify *v* çarpıtmak
falter *v* tereddüt etmek
fame *n* ün
familiar *adj* tanıdık

E
F

family *n* aile
famine *n* kıtlık
famous *adj* ünlü
fan *n* yelpaze; hayran
fanatic *adj* fanatik
fancy *adj* özel
fang *n* köpek dişi
fantastic *adj* enfes
fantasy *n* fantezi
far *adv* uzağa
faraway *adj* dalgın
farce *n* fars
fare *n* yol parası
farewell *n* elveda
farm *v* işlemek; ekip biçmek
farm *n* çiftlik
farmer *n* çiftçi
farming *n* tarım
farmyard *n* çiftlik
farther *adv* daha uzak
fascinate *v* etkilemek
fashion *n* moda
fashionable *adj* modaya uygun
fast *v* oruç tutmak
fast *adj* hızlı
fasten *v* bağlamak
fat *n* yağ
fat *adj* şişman
fatal *adj* ölümcül
fate *n* kader
fateful *adj* vahim
father *n* baba

fatherhood *n* babalık
father-in-law *n* kayınpeder
fatherly *adj* babacan
fathom out *v* çözmek
fatigue *n* yorgunluk
fatten *v* şişmanlamak
fatty *adj* yağlı
faucet *n* musluk
fault *n* hata
faulty *adj* hatalı
favor *n* iyilik
favorable *adj* hoşa giden
favorite *adj* favori
fear *n* korku
fearful *adj* korkunç
feasible *adj* mümkün
feast *n* ziyafet
feat *n* marifet
feather *n* tüy
feature *n* özellik
February *n* Şubat
fed up *adj* sıkkın
federal *adj* federal
fee *n* ücret
feeble *adj* kuvvetsiz
feed *iv* beslemek
feedback *n* geribildirim
feel *iv* hissetmek
feeling *n* duygu
feelings *n* his
feet *n* ayaklar
feign *v* numara yapmak

filthy

fellow *n* arkadaş
fellowship *n* grup
felon *n* suçlu
felony *n* ağır suç
felt *n* keçe
felt *v* keçelemek
female *n* kadın; dişi
feminine *adj* kadınsı
fence *v* çit ile çevirmek
fence *n* çit
fencing *n* eskrim
fend *v* savunmak
fend off *v* kovmak
fender *n* çamurluk
ferment *v* mayalamak
ferment *n* maya
ferocious *adj* vahşi
ferocity *n* vahişilik
ferry *n* feribot
fertile *adj* verimli
fertility *n* verimlilik
fertilize *v* gübrelemek
fervent *adj* hararetli
fester *v* iltihaplanmak
festive *adj* şen
festivity *n* şenlik
fetid *adj* kokuşmuş
fetus *n* cenin
feud *n* kan davası
fever *n* humma
feverish *adj* hummalı
few *adj* az

fewer *adj* daha az
fiancé *n* nişanlı
fiber *n* fiber
fickle *adj* vefasız
fiction *n* masal
fictitious *adj* hayali
fiddle *n* keman
fidelity *n* sadakat
field *n* alan; otlak
field *v* sahaya çıkarmak
fierce *adj* şiddetli
fiery *adj* kızgın
fifteen *adj* on beş
fifth *adj* beşinci
fifty *adj* elli
fifty-fifty *adv* yarı yarıya
fig *n* incir
fight *iv* kavga etmek
fight *n* kavga
fighter *n* kavgacı
figure *n* şekil; rakam
figure out *v* anlamak
file *v* dosyalamak
file *n* dosya; törpü
fill *v* doldurmak
filling *n* dolgu
film *v* film çekmek
film *n* film
filter *n* filtre
filter *v* filtrelemek
filth *n* pislik
filthy *adj* pis

F

fin *n* yüzgeç
final *adj* son
finalize *v* bitirmek
finance *v* finans
financial *adj* finansal
find *iv* bulmak
find out *v* keşfetmek
fine *n* iyi; para cezası
fine *v* para cezası vermek
fine *adv* iyi
fine *adj* iyi
fine print *n* dipnot
finger *n* parmak
fingernail *n* tırnak
fingerprint *n* parmak izi
fingertip *n* parmak ucu
finish *v* bitirmek
Finland *n* Finlandiya
Finnish *adj* Fince
fire *v* ateşlemek; kovmak
fire *n* ateş
firearm *n* ateşli silah
firecracker *n* kestane fişeği
firefighter *n* itfaiyeci
fireman *n* itfaiye eri
fireplace *n* şömine
firewood *n* yakacak
fireworks *n* havai fişek
firm *n* firma, şirket
firm *adj* sıkı
firmness *n* sıkılık
first *adj* birinci; ilk

fish *v* balık tutmak
fish *n* balık
fisherman *n* balıkçı
fishy *adj* şüphe uyandıran
fist *n* yumruk
fit *n* sağlıklı; nöbet
fit *v* uymak
fitness *n* sağlık; spor
fitting *adj* uygun
five *adj* beş
fix *v* onarmak
fjord *n* fiyort
flag *n* bayrak
flagpole *n* gönder
flamboyant *adj* frapan
flame *n* alev
flammable *adj* yanıcı
flank *n* böğür
flare *n* parıltı
flare-up *v* hiddetlenmek
flash *n* flaş
flashlight *n* el feneri
flashy *adj* parıltılı
flat *n* apartman dairesi
flat *adj* düz
flatten *v* düzleştirmek
flatter *v* yağ çekmek
flattery *n* kompliman
flaunt *v* sergilemek
flavor *n* çeşni
flaw *n* kusur
flawless *adj* kusursuz

flea *n* pire
flee *iv* firar etmek
fleece *n* yün
fleet *v* seyretmek
fleet *n* filo
fleeting *adj* donanma
flesh *n* et
flex *v* bükmek
flexible *adj* esnek
flicker *v* titreşmek
flier *n* pilot; uçak
flight *n* uçuş; firar
flimsy *adj* dayanıksız
flip *v* çevirmek
flirt *v* flört etmek
float *v* su üstünde durmak
flock *n* sürü
flog *v* dövmek
flood *n* su basmak
flood *v* sel
floodgate *n* bent kapağı
flooding *n* sel basma
floodlight *n* projektör
floor *n* zemin
flop *n* fiyasko
floss *n* diş ipliği
flour *n* un
flourish *v* serpilmek
flow *v* akmak
flow *n* akış
flower *n* çiçek
flowerpot *n* saksı

flu *n* grip
fluctuate *v* yükselip alçalmak
fluently *adv* akıcı bir şekilde
fluid *n* sıvı
flunk *v* sınavda çakmak
flush *v* birden akmak
flute *n* flüt
flutter *v* çırpınmak
fly *iv* uçmak
fly *n* uçuş
foam *n* köpük
focus *n* odak
focus on *v* odaklanmak
foe *n* düşman
fog *n* sis
foggy *adj* sisli
foil *v* set çekmek
fold *v* katlamak
folder *n* klasör
folks *n* ev halkı
folksy *adj* arkadaşça
follow *v* takip etmek
follower *n* yandaş
folly *n* delilik
fond *adj* sevgi dolu; meraklı
fondle *v* okşamak
fondness *n* düşkünlük
food *n* yemek
foodstuff *n* yiyecek
fool *v* kandırmak
fool *adj* budala
foolproof *adj* dört dörtlük

foot *n* ayak; piyade
football *n* futbol
footnote *n* dipnot
footprint *n* ayak izi
footstep *n* adım
footwear *n* ayakkabılar
for *pre* için
forbid *iv* yasaklamak
force *n* güç
force *v* zorlamak
forceful *adj* kuvvetli
forcibly *adv* zorla
forecast *iv* tahmin
forefront *n* ön sıra
foreground *n* ön plan
forehead *n* alın
foreign *adj* yabancı; harici
foreigner *n* yabancı
foreman *n* ustabaşı
foremost *adj* başta gelen
foresee *iv* ileriyi görmek
foreshadow *v* habercisi olmak
foresight *n* tedbir
forest *n* orman
foretaste *n* önceden tatma
foretell *v* kehanette bulunmak
forever *adv* ebediyen
forewarn *v* uyarmak
foreword *n* önsöz
forfeit *v* ceza olarak vermek
forge *v* sahtesini yapmak
forgery *n* sahte

forget *v* unutmak
forgivable *adj* affedilir
forgive *v* affetmek
forgiveness *n* bağışlama
fork *n* çatal
form *n* şekil
formal *adj* resmi
formality *n* resmiyet
formalize *v* resmileştirmek
formally *adv* resmi olarak
format *n* biçim
formation *n* düzen
former *adj* önceki
formerly *adv* eskiden
formidable *adj* korkunç
formula *n* formül
forsake *iv* vazgeçmek
fort *n* kale
forthcoming *adj* mevcut
forthright *adj* açıksözlü
fortify *v* kuvvetlendirmek
fortitude *n* metanetli
fortress *n* büyük kale
fortunate *adj* şanslı
fortune *n* kısmet
forty *adj* kırk
forward *adv* ileride
fossil *n* fosil
foster *v* beslemek
foul *adj* kirli
foundation *n* tesis; vakıf
founder *n* kurucu

foundry *n* dökümhane
fountain *n* çeşme
four *adj* dört
fourteen *adj* on dört
fourth *adj* dördüncü
fox *n* tilki
foxy *adj* kurnaz
fraction *n* kesir
fracture *n* kırık
fragile *adj* kırılgan
fragment *n* parça
fragrance *n* koku
fragrant *adj* kokulu
frail *adj* narin
frailty *n* zaaf
frame *n* çerçeve; iskelet
frame *v* ifade etmek
framework *n* taslak
France *n* Fransa
franchise *n* imtiyaz
frank *adj* dürüst
frankly *adv* dürüstçe
frankness *n* dürüstlük
frantic *adj* dellenmiş
fraternal *adj* kardeşçe
fraternity *n* kardeşlik
fraud *n* hile
fraudulent *adj* hileli
freckle *n* çil
freckled *adj* çilli
free *v* özgür bırakmak
free *adj* özgür; bedava

freedom *n* özgürlük
freeway *n* otoyol
freeze *iv* dondurmak
freezer *n* buzluk
freezing *adj* soğuk
freight *n* nakliye
French *adj* Fransız
frenetic *adj* telaşlı
frenzied *adj* çılgın
frenzy *n* çılgın
frequency *n* sıklık
frequent *adj* sık; yaygın
frequent *v* dadanmak
fresh *adj* taze
freshen *v* tazelemek
freshness *n* tazelik
friar *n* papaz
friction *n* sürtünme
Friday *n* Cuma
fried *adj* kızarmış
friend *n* arkadaş
friendship *n* arkadaşlık
fries *n* cips
frigate *n* fırkateyn
fright *n* korku
frighten *v* korkutmak
frightening *adj* korkunç
frigid *adj* duygusuz
fringe *n* kahkül; özenti
frivolous *adj* önemsiz
frog *n* kurbağa
from *pre* den

F

F

front *n* ön; cephe
front *adj* ön
frontage *n* bina cephesi
frontier *n* hudut
frost *n* ayaz
frostbite *n* soğuk ısırması
frostbitten *adj* donmuş
frosty *adj* kırağılı
frown *v* kaşlarını çatmak
frozen *adj* donmuş
frugal *adj* tutumlu
frugality *n* tutumluluk
fruit *n* meyve
fruitful *adj* verimli
fruity *adj* meyveli
frustrate *v* engellemek
frustration *n* hüsran
fry *v* kızartmak
frying pan *n* tava
fuel *n* yakıt
fuel *v* yakıt almak
fugitive *n* kaçak
fulfill *v* tamamlamak
fulfillment *n* tamamlama
full *adj* dolu
fully *adv* tamamen
fumes *n* duman
fumigate *v* dezenfekte etmek
fun *n* eğlenceli
function *n* işlev
fund *n* bütçe
fund *v* sermaye bulmak

fundamental *adj* temel
funds *n* sermaye
funeral *n* cenaze
fungus *n* küf mantar
funny *adj* komik
fur *n* kürk
furious *adj* sinirli
furiously *adv* sinirli bir şekilde
furnace *n* ocak
furnish *v* döşemek
furnishings *n* donatmak
furniture *n* mobilya
furor *n* kızgınlık
furrow *n* kırışık
furry *adj* tüyleri kabarık
further *adv* ötede
furthermore *adv* dahası
fury *n* gazap
fuse *n* elektrik sigortası
fusion *n* kaynaşma
fuss *n* yaygara
fussy *adj* yaygaracı
futile *adj* nafile
futility *n* faydasızlık
future *n* gelecek
fuzzy *adj* tüylü

G

gadget *n* alet
gag *n* şaka
gag *v* susturmak
gage *v* bahse girmek
gain *v* elde etmek
gain *n* kazanç
gal *n* kız
galaxy *n* galaksi
gale *n* sert rüzgar
gall bladder *n* safra kesesi
gallant *adj* efendi
gallery *n* galeri
gallon *n* galon
gallop *v* dörtnala gitmek
gallows *n* darağacı
galvanize *v* galvanizlemek
gamble *v* kumar oynamak
game *n* oyun
gang *n* çete
gangrene *n* kangren
gangster *n* gangster
gap *n* boşluk; fiyat aralığı
garage *n* garaj
garbage *n* çöplük
garden *n* bahçe
gardener *n* bahçıvan
gargle *v* gargara yapmak
garland *n* çelenk
garlic *n* sarımsak

garment *n* giysi
garnish *v* donatmak
garnish *n* garnitür
garrison *n* garnizon
garrulous *adj* geveze
garter *n* jartiyer
gas *n* gaz; benzin
gash *n* derin yara
gasoline *n* benzin
gasp *v* solumak
gastric *adj* midesel
gate *n* geçit
gather *v* toplamak
gathering *n* toplantı
gauge *v* kalibrasyon
gauze *n* gazlı bez
gaze *v* gözünü dikmek
gear *n* alet; vites
geese *n* kaz
gem *n* mücevher
gender *n* cinsiyet
gene *n* gen
general *n* genel; general
generalize *v* genellemek
generate *v* üretmek
generation *n* nesil
generator *n* jeneratör
generic *adj* soysal
generosity *n* cömertlik
genetic *adj* genetik
genial *adj* cana yakın
genius *n* deha**

genocide *n* soykırım
genteel *adj* efendi
gentle *adj* kibar
gentleman *n* beyefendi
gentleness *n* kibarlık
genuflect *v* diz çökmek
genuine *adj* hakiki
geography *n* coğrafya
geology *n* jeoloji
geometry *n* geometri
germ *n* mikrop
German *adj* Alman
Germany *n* Almanya
germinate *v* çimlenmek
gerund *n* ulaç
gestation *n* gebelik
gesticulate *v* jest yapmak
gesture *n* jest
get *iv* almak
get along *v* anlaşmak
get away *v* kaçmak
get back *v* öç almak
get by *v* geçmek
get down *v* indirmek
get down to *v* başlamak
get in *v* içeri girmek
get off *v* inmek
get out *v* çıkarmak
get over *v* unutmak
get together *v* buluşmak
get up *v* kalkmak
geyser *n* kaynaç

ghastly *adj* korkunç
ghost *n* hayalet
giant *n* dev
gift *n* hediye
gifted *adj* yetenekli
gigantic *adj* kocaman
giggle *v* kıkırdamak
gimmick *n* hile
ginger *n* zencefil; kızıl
gingerly *adv* ihtiyatla
giraffe *n* zürafa
girl *n* kız
girlfriend *n* kız arkadaş
give *iv* vermek
give away *v* hediye etmek
give back *v* iade etmek
give in *v* razı olmak
give out *v* duyurmak
give up *v* vazgeçmek
glacier *n* buzul
glad *adj* memnun
gladiator *n* gladyatör
glamorous *adj* çekici
glance *v* göz atmak
glance *n* bakış
gland *n* salgı bezi
glare *n* parıltı
glass *n* cam; bardak
glasses *n* gözlük
glassware *n* züccaciye
gleam *n* pırıltı
gleam *v* parıldamak

G

glide *v* süzülmek

glimmer *n* ışık

glimpse *n* gözüne ilişme

glimpse *v* gözüne ilişmek

glitter *v* pırıldamak

globe *n* küre

globule *n* kürecik

gloom *n* sıkıntı

gloomy *adj* kasvetli

glorify *v* yüceltmek

glorious *adj* şerefli

glory *n* şan

gloss *n* parlaklık

glossary *n* sözlük

glossy *adj* parlak

glove *n* eldiven

glow *v* parlamak

glucose *n* glikoz

glue *n* tutkal

glue *v* tutkallamak

glut *n* aşırı

glutton *n* obur

gnaw *v* kemirmek

go *iv* gitmek

go ahead *v* ilerlemek

go away *v* uzaklaşmak

go back *v* dönmek

go down *v* düşmek

go in *v* girmek

go on *v* devam etmek

go out *v* dışarı çıkmak

go over *v* incelemek

go through *v* gözden geçirmek

go under *v* batmak

go up *v* yükselmek

goad *v* dürtmek

goal *n* gol; amaç

goalkeeper *n* kaleci

goat *n* keçi

gobble *v* hızlı yemek

God *n* Tanrı

goddess *n* tanrıça

godless *adj* tanrıtanımaz

goggles *n* koruyucu gözlük

gold *n* altın

golden *adj* altından

good *adj* iyi

good-looking *adj* yakışıklı

goodness *n* iyilik

goods *n* mallar

goodwill *n* iyi niyet

goof *v* hata yapmak

goof *n* aptal

goose *n* kaz

gorge *n* geçit

gorgeous *adj* güzel

gorilla *n* goril

gory *adj* kanlı

gospel *n* incil

gossip *v* dedikodu yapmak

gossip *n* dedikodu

gout *n* gut

govern *v* yönetmek

government *n* hükümet

governor *n* vali
gown *n* gecelik
grab *v* kavramak
grace *n* zarafet
graceful *adj* zarif
gracious *adj* kibar
grade *v* derecelendirmek
grade *n* derece
gradual *adj* kademeli
graduate *v* mezun olmak
graduation *n* mezuniyet
graft *v* yamalamak
graft *n* yama
grain *n* tahıl
gram *n* gram
grammar *n* gramer, dilbilgisi
grand *adj* görkemli
grandchild *n* torun
granddad *n* dede
grandfather *n* büyükbaba
grandmother *n* büyükanne
grandparents *n* $
grandson *n* erkek torun
grandstand *n* tribün
granite *n* granit
granny *n* nine
grant *v* kabul etmek
grant *n* ödenek
grape *n* üzüm
grapefruit *n* greyfurt
grapevine *n* asma
graphic *adj* grafik

grasp *n* yakalama
grasp *v* kavramak; anlamak
grass *n* çimen
grassroots *adj* ortadirek
grateful *adj* minnettar
gratify *v* hoşnut etmek
gratifying *adj* tatminkar
gratitude *n* minnettarlık
gratuity *n* teberru
grave *adj* ciddi
grave *n* mezar
gravel *n* çakıl
gravely *adv* ciddi şekilde
gravestone *n* mezar taşı
graveyard *n* mezarlık
gravitate *v* yönelmek
gravity *n* yer çekimi
gravy *n* sos
gray *adj* gri
grayish *adj* grimsi
graze *v* otlamak
graze *n* otlama; sıyrık
grease *n* makine yağı
grease *v* yağlamak
greasy *adj* yağlı; kaygan
great *adj* büyük
greatness *n* fevkalade
Greece *n* Yunanistan
greed *n* açgözlülük
greedy *adj* açgözlü
Greek *adj* Yunan
green *adj* yeşil

green bean *n* taze fasulye
greenhouse *n* sera
Greenland *n* grönland
greet *v* selamlamak
greetings *n* selamlama
gregarious *adj* girişken
grenade *n* el bombası
greyhound *n* tazı
grief *n* keder
grievance *n* yakınma
grieve *v* kederlen
grill *v* ızgara yapmak
grill *n* ızgara
grim *adj* korkunç
grimace *n* yüz ekşitme
grime *n* kir
grin *n* sırıtma
grin *v* sırıtmak
grind *iv* öğütmek
grip *v* sımsıkı tutmak
grip *n* sap
gripe *n* sancı
grisly *adj* ürkütücü
groan *n* figan
groan *v* inlemek
groceries *n* bakkaliye
groin *n* kasık
groom *n* güvey
groove *n* oluk
gross *adj* iğrenç; brüt
grossly *adv* fena halde
grotesque *adj* gülünç

grotto *n* mağara
grouch *v* söylenmek
grouchy *adj* dırdırcı
ground *n* zemin
ground floor *n* zemin kat
groundless *adj* asılsız
groundwork *n* ön hazırlık
group *n* grup
grow *iv* yetiştirmek
grow up *v* büyümek
growl *v* hırlamak
grown-up *n* yetişkin
growth *n* büyüme
grudge *n* garez
grudgingly *adv* istemeyerek
grueling *adj* yorucu
gruesome *adj* iğrenç
grumble *v* homurdanma
grumpy *adj* huysuz
guarantee *v* garanti etmek
guarantee *n* garanti
guarantor *n* garantör
guard *n* nöbet
guardian *n* koruyucu
guerrilla *n* gerilla
guess *v* tahmin etmek
guess *n* tahmin
guest *n* misafir
guidance *n* kılavuzluk
guide *v* kılavuzluk etmek
guide *n* kılavuz
guidebook *n* rehber

G

guidelines *n* ana noktalar
guild *n* lonca
guile *n* kurnazlık
guillotine *n* giyotin
guilt *n* suç
guilty *adj* suçlu
guise *n* kılık
guitar *n* gitar
gulf *n* körfez
gull *n* martı
gullible *adj* saf
gulp *v* dedikodu
gulp *n* yudum
gulp down *v* yutmak
gum *n* sakız; damak
gun *n* silah
gun down *v* öldürmek
gunfire *n* ateş etme
gunman *n* tüfekçi
gunpowder *n* barut
gunshot *n* atış menzili
gust *n* bora
gusto *n* zevk
gusty *adj* fırtınalı
gut *n* mide
guts *n* yürek; metanet
gutter *n* oluk; sefalet
guy *n* adam
guzzle *v* hızlı içmek
gymnasium *n* spor salonu
gynecology *n* jinekoloji
gypsy *n* çingene

habit *n* alışkanlık
habitable *adj* oturulur
habitual *adj* alışılmış
hack *v* yarmak
haggle *v* pazarlık etmek
hail *n* selam; dolu fırtınası
hail *v* selamlamak; dolu yağmak
hair *n* saç
hairbrush *n* saç fırçası
haircut *n* saç kesimi
hairdo *n* saç şekli
hairdresser *n* kuaför
hairpiece *n* peruk
hairy *adj* kıllı
half *n* yarım
half *adj* yarı
hall *n* koridor
hallucinate *v* sanrılamak
hallway *n* hol
halt *v* durdurmak
halve *v* yarıya bölmek
ham *n* domuz eti
hamburger *n* hamburger
hamlet *n* mezra
hammer *v* çekiçle vurmak
hammer *n* çekiç
hammock *n* hamak
hand *n* el
hand down *v* devretmek

hand in *v* teslim etmek	**harbor** *n* liman; barınak
hand out *v* dağıtmak	**hard** *adj* zor
hand over *v* havale etmek	**harden** *v* sertleştirmek
handbag *n* el çantası	**hardly** *adv* zorla
handbook *n* el kitabı	**hardness** *n* sertlik
handcuff *v* kelepçelemek	**hardship** *n* sıkıntı
handcuffs *n* kelepçe	**hardware** *n* donanım
handful *n* avuç dolusu	**hardwood** *n* kereste
handgun *n* tabanca	**hardy** *adj* dayanıklı
handicap *n* engel	**hare** *n* tavşan
handkerchief *n* mendil	**harm** *v* zarar vermek
handle *v* işlemek	**harm** *n* zarar
handle *n* el sürmek	**harmful** *adj* zararlı
handmade *adj* el yapımı	**harmless** *adj* zararsız
handout *n* sadaka	**harmonize** *v* bağdaştırmak
handrail *n* tırabzan	**harmony** *n* uyum
handshake *n* el sıkışma	**harp** *n* harp
handsome *adj* yakışıklı	**harpoon** *n* zıpkın
handwriting *n* el yazısı	**harrowing** *adj* acıklı
handy *adj* kullanışlı	**harsh** *adj* hırçın
hang *iv* asmak	**harshly** *adv* insafsızca
hang around *v* etrafta takılmak	**harshness** *n* hırçınlık
hang on *v* sıkı tutunmak	**harvest** *n* hasat
hang up *v* çamaşır asmak	**harvest** *v* hasat etmek
hanger *n* askı	**hashish** *n* haşhaş
hang-up *n* güçlük	**hassle** *v* tartışmak
happen *v* olmak	**hassle** *n* zorluk
happening *n* vaka	**haste** *n* acele
happiness *n* mutluluk	**hasten** *v* hız vermek
happy *adj* mutlu	**hastily** *adv* acele şekilde
harass *v* rahatsız etmek	**hasty** *adj* düşüncesiz
harassment *n* usanç	**hat** *n* şapka

hatchet *n* balta
hate *v* nefret etmek
hateful *adj* nefret dolu
hatred *n* nefret
haughty *adj* kibirli
haul *v* çekmek
haunt *v* sık uğramak
have *iv* sahip olmak
have to *v* gerekmek
haven *n* sığınak
havoc *n* hasar
hawk *n* atmaca
hay *n* saman
haystack *n* saman sapı
hazard *n* tehlike
hazardous *adj* tehlikeli
haze *n* sis
hazelnut *n* fındık
hazy *adj* dumanlı
he *pro* o erkek
head *n* baş
head for *v* yol almak
headache *n* baş ağrısı
heading *n* reis
head-on *adv* gerçekten
headphones *n* kulaklık
headquarters *n* garnizon
headway *n* ilerleme
heal *v* iyileştirmek
healer *n* iyileştirici
health *n* sağlık
healthy *adj* sağlıklı

heap *n* yığın
heap *v* kümelemek
hear *iv* işitmek
hearing *n* duruşma
hearsay *n* söylenti
hearse *n* cenaze arabası
heart *n* kalp
heartbeat *n* kalp atışı
heartburn *n* mide ekşimesi
hearten *v* yüreklendirmek
heartfelt *adj* candan
hearth *n* şömine
heartless *adj* kalpsiz
hearty *adj* yürekten
heat *v* ısıtmak
heat *n* ısı
heat wave *n* sıcak dalgası
heater *n* ısıtıcı
heathen *n* kafir
heating *n* kalorifer
heatstroke *n* güneş çarpması
heaven *n* cennet
heavenly *adj* cennet gibi
heaviness *n* ağırlık
heavy *adj* ağır
heckle *v* sözünü kesmek
hectic *adj* heyecanlı
heed *v* önemsemek
heel *n* topuk
height *n* boy
heighten *v* yükseltmek
heinous *adj* tiksindirici

heir *n* mirasçı
heiress *n* kadın mirasçı
heist *n* soygun
helicopter *n* helikopter
hell *n* cehennem
hello *e* selam
helm *n* dümen
helmet *n* miğfer
help *v* yardım etmek
help *n* yardım
helper *n* yardımcı
helpful *adj* yardımsever
helpless *adj* savunmasız
hem *n* baskı
hemisphere *n* yarıküre
hemorrhage *n* kanama
hen *n* tavuk
hence *adv* dolayısıyla
henchman *n* dalkavuk
her *adj* o kıza; o kızın
herald *v* müjdecisi olmak
herald *n* müjdeci
herb *n* baharat
here *adv* burada
hereafter *adv* ileride
hereby *adv* bu vesileyle
hereditary *adj* ırsi
heresy *n* dalalet
heretic *adj* kafir
heritage *n* miras
hermetic *adj* hava yalıtımlı
hermit *n* keşiş

hernia *n* fıtık
hero *n* kahraman
heroic *adj* şanlı
heroin *n* eroin
heroism *n* kahramanlık
hers *pro* o kızın
herself *pro* kendisine
hesitant *adj* tereddütlü
hesitate *v* tereddüt etmek
hesitation *n* tereddüt
heyday *n* altın çağ
hiccup *n* hıçkırık
hidden *adj* gizli
hide *iv* gizlenmek
hideaway *n* gizlenme yeri
hideous *adj* korkunç
hierarchy *n* hiyerarşi
high *adj* yüksek
highlight *n* önemli olay
highly *adv* pek çok
Highness *n* Ekselanslar
highway *n* anayol
hijack *v* uçak kaçırmak
hijack *n* kaçırma
hijacker *n* korsan
hike *v* yürüyüş yapmak
hike *n* yürüyüş
hilarious *adj* komik
hill *n* tepe
hillside *n* yamaç
hilltop *n* tepe üstü
hilly *adj* tepelik

hilt *n* kabza
hinder *v* engellemek
hindrance *n* engel
hindsight *n* tüfeğin gezi
hinge *v* menteşe takmak
hinge *n* menteşe
hint *n* ipucu
hint *v* ipucu vermek
hip *n* kalça
hire *v* kiralamak
his *adj* o erkek
his *pro* o erkeğin
Hispanic *adj* İspanyol
hiss *v* tıslamak
historian *n* tarihçi
history *n* tarih
hit *n* isabet; başarı
hit *iv* vurmak
hit back *v* misilleme yapmak
hitch *n* engel
hitch up *v* koşmak
hitchhike *n* otostop yapmak
hitherto *adv* şimdiye kadar
hive *n* arı kovanı
hoard *v* biriktirmek
hoarse *adj* boğuk
hoax *n* şaka
hobby *n* hobi
hog *n* domuz
hoist *v* yukarı çekmek
hoist *n* vinç
hold *iv* tutmak

hold back *v* kendini tutmak
hold on to *v* tutunmak
hold out *v* sabırla beklemek
hold up *v* yukarı kaldırmak
holdup *n* durdurma
hole *n* delik
holiday *n* tatil
holiness *n* kutsallık
Holland *n* Hollanda
hollow *adj* boş
holocaust *n* facia
holy *adj* ilahi
homage *n* hürmet
home *n* ev
homeland *n* yurt
homeless *adj* evsiz
homely *adj* sade
homemade *adj* ev yapımı
homesick *adj* evini özlemiş
hometown *n* memleket
homework *n* ev ödevi
homicide *n* cinayet
homily *n* hitabe
honest *adj* dürüst
honesty *n* dürüstlük
honey *n* bal
honeymoon *n* balayı
honk *v* korna çalmak
honor *n* onur
hood *n* kukuleta
hoodlum *n* kabadayı
hoof *n* toynak

hook *n* kanca; orak
hooligan *n* holigan
hop *v* zıplamak
hope *v* umut etmek
hope *n* umut
hopeful *adj* umutlu
hopefully *adv* ümitle
hopeless *adj* ümitsiz
horizon *n* ufuk
horizontal *adj* yatay
hormone *n* hormon
horn *n* boynuz
horrendous *adj* tüyler ürpertici
horrible *adj* korkunç
horrify *v* korkutmak
horror *n* korku
horse *n* at
hose *n* su hortumu
hospital *n* hastane
hospitality *n* konukseverlik
hospitalize *v* hastaneye yatırmak
host *n* ev sahibi
hostage *n* rehine
hostess *n* sahibe
hostile *adj* düşmanca
hostility *n* düşmanlık
hot *adj* sıcak
hotel *n* otel
hound *n* tazı
hour *n* saat
hourly *adv* saatlik
house *n* ev

household *n* ev halkı
housekeeper *n* kahya
housewife *n* ev hanımı
housework *n* ev işi
hover *v* dolaşmak
how *adv* neden; nasıl
however *c* ancak
howl *v* ulumak
howl *n* uluma
hub *n* göbek
huddle *v* sıkışmak
hug *v* kucaklamak
hug *n* kucak
huge *adj* kocaman
hull *n* kavuz
hum *v* mırıldanmak
human *adj* insancıl
human being *n* insanoğlu
humanities *n* insanlık
humankind *n* insanoğlu
humble *adj* alçakgönüllü
humbly *adv* mütevazı şekilde
humid *adj* nemli
humidity *n* rutubet
humiliate *v* küçük düşürmek
humility *n* alçak gönüllülük
humor *n* mizah
humorous *adj* güldürücü
hump *n* kambur
hunch *n* önsezi
hunchback *n* kambur
hunched *adj* çömelmiş

hundred *adj* yüz
hundredth *adj* yüzüncü
hunger *n* açlık
hungry *adj* aç
hunt *v* avlanmak
hunter *n* avcı
hunting *n* elek
hurdle *n* engel
hurl *v* fırlatmak
hurricane *n* kasırga
hurriedly *adv* aceleyle
hurry *v* acele ettirmek
hurry up *v* acele etmek
hurt *iv* yaralamak
hurt *adj* yaralı
hurtful *adj* kırıcı
husband *n* koca
hush *n* huşu
hush up *v* örtbas etmek
husky *adj* kısık
hustle *n* koşuşturma
hut *n* baraka
hydraulic *adj* hidrolik
hydrogen *n* hidrojen
hyena *n* sırtlan
hygiene *n* hijyen
hymn *n* ilahi
hyphen *n* kısa çizgi
hypnosis *n* hipnoz
hypnotize *v* hipnotize etmek
hypocrisy *n* ikiyüzlülük
hypocrite *adj* ikiyüzlü

hypothesis *n* varsayım
hysteria *n* histeri
hysterical *adj* isteri

I *pro* ben
ice *n* buz
ice cream *n* dondurma
ice cube *n* buz kalıbı
ice skate *v* buz pateni
iceberg *n* buz dağı
icebox *n* buzluk
ice-cold *adj* buz gibi
icon *n* ikon
icy *adj* buzlu
idea *n* fikir
ideal *adj* ideal
identical *adj* tıpkısı; özdeş
identify *v* tespit etmek
identity *n* kimlik
ideology *n* ideoloji
idiom *n* deyim
idiot *n* gerizekalı
idiotic *adj* aptalca
idle *adj* aylak
idol *n* idol
idolatry *n* putperestlik

if _c_ eğer
ignite _v_ aydınlatmak
ignorance _n_ cehalet
ignorant _adj_ cahil
ignore _v_ gözardı etmek
ill _adj_ hasta
illegal _adj_ yasa dışı
illegible _adj_ okunaksız
illegitimate _adj_ gayri meşru
illicit _adj_ yasa dışı
illiterate _adj_ okumamış
illness _n_ hastalık
illogical _adj_ mantıksız
illuminate _v_ aydınlatmak
illusion _n_ sanrı
illustrate _v_ örneklemek
illustration _n_ resim; örnek
illustrious _adj_ ünlü
image _n_ görüntü
imagination _n_ hayal gücü
imagine _v_ hayal etmek
imbalance _n_ dengesizlik
imitate _v_ taklit etmek
imitation _n_ taklit
immaculate _adj_ tertemiz
immature _adj_ olgunlaşmamış
immaturity _n_ hamlık
immediately _adv_ hemen
immense _adj_ bucaksız
immensity _n_ enginlik
immerse _v_ batırmak
immersion _n_ batma

immigrant _n_ göçmen
immigrate _v_ göç etmek
immigration _n_ göç
imminent _adj_ yakın
immobile _adj_ hareketsiz
immobilize _v_ hareketsizleştirmek
immoral _adj_ ahlaksız
immorality _n_ ahlaksızlık
immortal _adj_ ölümsüz
immortality _n_ ölümsüzlük
immune _adj_ bağışık
immunity _n_ bağışıklık
immunize _v_ bağışıklık
kazandırmak
immutable _adj_ sabit
impact _v_ etkilemek
impact _n_ vuruş; etki
impair _v_ bozmak
impartial _adj_ tarafsız
impatience _n_ sabırsızlık
impatient _adj_ sabırsız
impeccable _adj_ hatasız
impediment _n_ engel
impending _adj_ yakın
imperfection _n_ kusur
imperial _adj_ şahane
imperialism _n_ imparatorluk
impersonal _adj_ gayri şahsi
impertinence _n_ küstahlık
impertinent _adj_ terbiyesiz
impetuous _adj_ aceleci
implacable _adj_ yatıştırılmaz

implant v aşılamak

implement v uygulamak

implicate v karıştırmak

implication n ima

implicit adj dahili

implore v dilemek

imply v ima etmek

impolite adj kaba

import v ithal etmek

importance n önem

importation n ithalat

impose v aldatmak

imposing adj heybetli

imposition n hile; ceza

impossibility n imkansızlık

impossible adj imkansız

impotent adj iktidarsız

impound v el koymak

impoverished adj yoksul

impractical adj pratik olmayan

imprecise adj dikkatsiz

impress v etkilemek

impressive adj çarpıcı

imprison v hapse atmak

improbable adj beklenmedik

impromptu adv doğaçlama

improper adj münasebetsiz

improve v geliştirmek

improvement n gelişme

improvise v doğaçlama yapmak

impulse n dürtü

impulsive adj atılgan

impunity n muaf olma

impure adj ahlaksız

in pre içinde

in depth adv derinlemesine

inability n acizlik

inaccessible adj erişilemez

inaccurate adj yanlış

inadequate adj yetersiz

inadmissible adj kabul edilemez

inappropriate adj uygunsuz

inasmuch as c madem ki

inaugurate v açılış yapmak

inauguration n açılış

incalculable adj değişken

incapable adj kabiliyetsiz

incapacitate v aciz bırakmak

incarcerate v hapsedilme

incense n tütsü; günlük

incentive n dürtü; neden

inception n başlangıç

incessant adj aralıksız

inch n inç

incident n hadise

incidentally adv tesadüfen

incision n açım; insizyon

incite v kışkırtmak

incitement n fitnecilik; tahrik

inclination n eğilim

incline v eğilmek

include v içermek

inclusive adv dahil

incoherent adj abuk sabuk

income *n* gelir
incoming *adj* gelen; yeni
incompatible *adj* uyuşmaz
incompetence *n* beceriksizlik
incompetent *adj* beceriksiz
incomplete *adj* bitmemiş
inconsistent *adj* tutarsız
incontinence *n* kendini
　tutamama
inconvenient *adj* zahmetli
incorporate *v* anonim
incorrect *adj* yanlış
incorrigible *adj* akıllanmaz
increase *v* artmak
increase *n* artış
increasing *adj* artan
incredible *adj* inanılmaz
increment *n* artış; kazanç
incriminate *v* suçlamak
incur *v* maruz kalmak
incurable *adj* devasız
indecency *n* ahlaksızlık
indecision *n* kararsızlık
indecisive *adj* kararsız
indeed *adv* gerçekten
indefinite *adj* belirsiz
indemnify *v* dokunulmazlık
　vermek
indemnity *n* tazminat
independence *n* bağımsızlık
independent *adj* bağımsız
index *n* içindekiler

indicate *v* göstermek
indication *n* belirti
indict *v* itham etmek
indifference *n* ilgisizlik
indifferent *adj* ilgisiz
indigent *adj* muhtaç
indigestion *n* hazımsızlık
indirect *adj* dolaylı
indiscreet *adj* patavatsız
indiscretion *n* boşboğazlık
indispensable *adj* zorunlu
indisposed *adj* isteksiz
indisputable *adj* su götürmez
indivisible *adj* bölünmez
indoctrinate *v* telkinde
　bulunmak
indoor *adv* yapı içi
induce *v* neden olmak
indulge *v* teslim olmak
indulgent *adj* yüz veren
industrious *adj* endüstriyel
industry *n* endüstri
ineffective *adj* etkisiz
inefficient *adj* etkisiz
inept *adj* uygunsuz
inequality *n* eşitsizlik
inevitable *adj* kaçınılmaz
inexcusable *adj* bağışlanamaz
inexpensive *adj* ucuz
inexperienced *adj* deneyimsiz
inexplicable *adj* açıklanamaz
infallible *adj* yanılmaz

infamous *adj* adı çıkmış
infancy *n* bebeklik
infant *n* bebek
infantry *n* piyadeler
infect *v* bulaştırmak
infection *n* enfeksiyon
infectious *adj* bulaşıcı
infer *v* çıkarmak
inferior *adj* aşağılık
infertile *adj* çorak
infested *adj* istila et
infidelity *n* sadakatsizlik
infiltrate *v* sızmak
infiltration *n* sızma
infinite *adj* sonsuz
infirmary *n* revir
inflammation *n* alevlendirici
inflate *v* şişirmek
inflation *n* enflasyon
inflexible *adj* eğilmez
inflict *v* acı çektirmek
influence *n* etki
influential *adj* nüfuzlu
influenza *n* nezle
influx *n* istila
inform *v* haber vermek
informal *adj* resmi olmayan
informality *n* teklifsiz
informant *n* haber kaynağı
information *n* bilgi
informer *n* ihbarcı; haberci
infraction *n* ihlal

infrequent *adj* seyrek
infuriate *v* çıldırtmak
infusion *n* içine dökme
ingenuity *n* ustalık
ingest *v* yemek
ingot *n* külçe
ingrained *adj* kökleşmiş
ingratiate *v* sevdirmek
ingratitude *n* nankörlük
ingredient *n* malzeme
inhabit *v* yerleşmek
inhabitable *adj* oturmaya elverişli
inhabitant *n* oturan kimse
inhale *v* içine çekmek
inherit *v* miras kalmak
inheritance *n* kalıt
inhibit *v* ket vurmak
inhuman *adj* acımasız
initial *n* baş harf
initial *v* parafe etmek
initial *adj* başlangıç
initially *adv* baştaki
initials *n* ismin ilk harfleri
initiate *v* başlatmak
initiative *n* inisiyatif
inject *v* enjekte etmek
injection *n* enjeksiyon
injure *v* zarar vermek
injurious *adj* zararlı
injury *n* hasar
injustice *n* haksızlık
ink *n* mürekkep

inkling *n* ipucu
inlaid *adj* işlemeli
inland *adv* içerilerde
inland *adj* ülkenin iç kısmı
in-laws *n* akraba
inmate *n* oturan kimse
inn *n* han
innate *adj* temelinde
inner *adj* iç
innocence *n* masumiyet
innocent *adj* masum
innovation *n* yenilik
innuendo *n* kinaye
innumerable *adj* hesapsız
input *n* girdi
inquest *n* soruşturma
inquire *v* araştırmak
inquiry *n* araştırma
inquisition *n* soruşturma
insane *adj* deli·
insanity *n* delilik
insatiable *adj* doymaz
inscription *n* kitabe
insect *n* böcek
insecurity *n* endişeli
insensitive *adj* düşüncesiz
inseparable *adj* ayrılmaz
insert *v* takmak
insertion *n* ekleme
inside *adj* içinde
inside *pre* içinde
inside out *adv* tersyüz

insignificant *adj* önemsiz
insincere *adj* samimiyetsiz
insincerity *n* ikiyüzlülük
insinuate *v* ima etmek
insinuation *n* üstü kapalı
insipid *adj* sönük
insist *v* ısrar etmek
insistence *n* ısrar
insolent *adj* küstah
insoluble *adj* çözülmez
insomnia *n* uykusuzluk
inspect *v* denetlemek
inspection *n* teftiş
inspector *n* müfettiş
inspiration *n* esin kaynağı
inspire *v* esinlemek
instability *n* istikrarsızlık
install *v* kurmak
installation *n* kuruluş
installment *n* taksit
instance *n* an; örnek
instant *n* ani
instantly *adv* anında
instead *adv* yerine
instigate *v* kışkırtmak
instill *v* işlemek
instinct *n* içgüdü
institute *v* tesis etmek
institution *n* müessese
instruct *v* okutmak
instructor *n* öğretmen
insufficient *adj* yetersiz

insulate *v* yalıtmak
insulation *n* yalıtım
insult *v* hakaret etmek
insult *n* hakaret
insurance *n* sigorta
insure *v* sigorta olmak
insurgency *n* isyan
insurrection *n* isyan
intact *adj* bozulmamış
intake *n* yeme
integrate *v* bütünleştirmek
integration *n* birleştirme
integrity *n* bütünlük
intelligent *adj* zeki
intend *v* kastetmek
intense *adj* şiddetli
intensify *v* yoğunlaşmak
intensity *n* yoğunluk
intensive *adj* yoğun
intention *n* amaç
intercede *v* aracılık etmek
intercept *v* kesişmek
intercession *n* araya girme
interchange *v* değiştirmek
interchange *n* değişim
interest *n* çıkar; ilgi
interested *adj* ilgili
interesting *adj* ilginç
interfere *v* karışmak
interference *n* engel
interior *adj* içinde
interlude *n* ara dönem

intermediary *n* arada bulunan
intern *v* staj yapmak
interpret *v* tercüme etmek
interpretation *n* tercüme
interpreter *n* tercüman
interrogate *v* sorgulamak
interrupt *v* yarıda kesmek
interruption *n* arasını kesme
intersect *v* kesişmek
intertwine *v* birbirine sarmak
interval *n* aralık
intervene *v* araya girmek
intervention *n* aracılık
interview *n* mülakat
intestine *n* bağırsak
intimacy *n* samimilik
intimate *adj* samimi
intimidate *v* korkutmak
intolerable *adj* çekilmez
intolerance *n* toleranssızlık
intoxicated *adj* alkollü
intravenous *adj* damar içi
intrepid *adj* yılmaz
intricate *adj* karışık
intrigue *n* entrika
intriguing *adj* ilgi çekici
intrinsic *adj* esas
introduce *v* tanıştırmak
introduction *n* giriş
introvert *adj* içe dönük
intrude *v* zorla girmek
intruder *n* davetsiz

intrusion *n* zorla girme	**iron** *n* demir
intuition *n* sezgi	**iron** *v* ütülemek
inundate *v* su basmak	**ironic** *adj* alaycı
invade *v* istila etmek	**irony** *n* ironi
invader *n* istilacı	**irrational** *adj* mantıksız
invalid *n* geçersiz	**irrefutable** *adj* çürütülemez
invalidate *v* geçersiz kılmak	**irregular** *adj* düzensiz
invaluable *adj* paha biçilemez	**irrelevant** *adj* alakasız
invasion *n* istila	**irreparable** *adj* onarılamaz
invent *v* icat etmek	**irresistible** *adj* dayanılmaz
invention *n* buluş	**irrespective** *adj* bakmaksızın
inventory *n* stok	**irreversible** *adj* değiştirilemez
invest *v* yatırım yapmak	**irrevocable** *adj* değişmez
investigate *v* soruşturmak	**irrigate** *v* sulamak
investigation *n* soruşturma	**irrigation** *n* sulama
investment *n* yatırım	**irritate** *v* can sıkmak
investor *n* yatırımcı	**irritating** *adj* can sıkıcı
invincible *adj* yenilmez	**Islamic** *adj* İslami
invisible *adj* görünmez	**island** *n* ada
invitation *n* davet	**isle** *n* adacık
invite *v* davet etmek	**isolate** *v* izole etmek
invoice *n* fatura	**isolation** *n* izolasyon
invoke *v* yardım istemek	**issue** *v* bildirmek
involve *v* içermek	**issue** *n* olay; sayı
involved *v* sarmak	**Italian** *adj* İtalyan
involvement *n* kuşatma	**italics** *adj* italik
inward *adj* dahili	**Italy** *n* İtalya
inwards *adv* ruhsal	**itch** *v* kaşınmak
iodine *n* iyot	**itchiness** *n* kaşıntı
irate *adj* öfkeli	**item** *n* öğe
Ireland *n* İrlanda	**itemize** *v* ayrıntılı yazmak
Irish *adj* İrlandalı	**itinerary** *n* yolcu rehberi

J

ivory *n* fildişi

jackal *n* çakal
jacket *n* ceket
jackpot *n* bingo
jaguar *n* jaguar
jail *n* hapis
jail *v* hapse atmak
jailer *n* gardiyan
jam *v* kıstırmak
jam *n* karışıklık; reçel
janitor *n* kapıcı
January *n* Ocak
Japan *n* Japonya
Japanese *adj* Japon
jar *v* sarsılmak
jar *n* kavanoz
jasmine *n* yasemin
jaw *n* çene
jealous *adj* kıskanç
jealousy *n* kıskançlık
jeans *n* kot
jeopardize *v* risk
jerk *v* ani çekiş
jerk *n* ahmak
jersey *n* kazak

Jew *n* Musevilik
jewel *n* cevher
jeweler *n* kuyumcu
jewelry store *n* kuyumcu
Jewish *adj* Musevi
jigsaw *n* yapboz
job *n* iş
jobless *adj* işsiz
join *v* katılmak
joint *n* eklem; esrar
jointly *adv* ortak olarak
joke *n* şaka; fıkra
joke *v* şaka yapmak
joker *n* joker
jokingly *adv* şakayla
jolly *adj* keyifli
jolt *v* dürtmek
jolt *n* darbe; etki
journal *n* gazete
journalist *n* gazeteci
journey *n* yolculuk
jovial *adj* keyifli
joy *n* neşe
joyful *adj* neşeli
joyfully *adv* neşeyle
jubilant *adj* çok sevinçli
Judaism *n* Musevi alemi
judge *v* yargılamak
judge *n* hakim
judgment *n* karar
judicious *adj* adaletli
jug *n* sürahi

juggler *n* hilebaz
juice *n* meyve suyu
juicy *adj* sulu
July *n* Temmuz
jump *v* zıplamak
jump *n* sıçrayış
jumpy *adj* gergin
junction *n* kavşak
June *n* Haziran
jungle *n* orman
junior *adj* ast
junk *v* çöpe atmak
junk *n* çöp
jury *n* jüri
just *adj* sadece
justice *n* adalet
justify *v* doğrulamak
justly *adv* adil bir şekilde
juvenile *adj* çocuksu
juvenile *n* çocuk

kangaroo *n* kanguru
karate *n* karate
keep *iv* saklamak
keep on *v* devam etmek
keep up *v* ayak uydurmak

keg *n* fıçı
kennel *n* köpek evi
kettle *n* çaydanlık
key *n* anahtar; tuş
key ring *n* anahtarlık
keyboard *n* klavye
kick *v* tekmelemek
kickback *n* rüşvet
kickoff *n* başlangıç
kid *v* şaka yapmak
kid *n* çocuk
kidnap *v* adam kaçırmak
kidnapper *n* adam kaçıran kişi
kidnapping *n* adam kaçırma
kidney *n* böbrek
kidney bean *n* barbunya
kill *v* öldürmek
killer *n* katil
killing *n* vurgun
kilogram *n* kilogram
kilometer *n* kilometre
kilowatt *n* kilovat
kind *adj* kibar
kindle *v* alevlendirmek
kindly *adv* kibarca
kindness *n* kibarlık
king *n* kral
kingdom *n* kraliyet
kinship *n* akrabalık
kiosk *n* büfe
kiss *v* öpmek
kiss *n* öpücük

J
K

kitchen *n* mutfak
kite *n* uçurtma
kitten *n* kedi
knee *n* diz
kneecap *n* diz kapağı
kneel *iv* dizlenmek
knife *n* bıçak
knight *n* şövalye
knit *v* örmek
knob *n* budak
knock *n* darbe
knock *v* kapı çalmak
knot *n* düğüm
know *iv* bilmek
know-how *n* beceri
knowingly *adv* bilerek
knowledge *n* bilgi

lab *n* laboratuar
label *n* etiket
labor *n* iş gücü
laborer *n* işçi
labyrinth *n* labirent
lace *n* dantel; şerit
lack *v* eksilmek
lack *n* eksik

lad *n* delikanlı
ladder *n* portatif merdiven
laden *adj* yüklü
lady *n* hanım
ladylike *adj* hanım gibi
lagoon *n* gölcük, lagün
lake *n* göl
lamb *n* kuzu
lame *adj* aksak; kusurlu
lament *v* ağıt yakmak
lament *n* ağıt
lamp *n* lamba
lamppost *n* elektrik direği
lampshade *n* abajur
land *n* arazi
land *v* uçağın konması
landfill *n* arazi doldurma
landing *n* karaya çıkarma
landlady *n* ev sahibesi
landlocked *adj* kara ile çevrili
landlord *n* ev sahibi
landscape *n* manzara
lane *n* yol şeridi
language *n* dil
languish *v* cansızlaşmak
lantern *n* fanus; fener
lap *n* kucak; etap
lapse *n* geçme
lapse *v* intikal etmek
larceny *n* hırsızlık
lard *n* domuz yağı
large *adj* geniş

K
L

larynx *n* boğaz
laser *n* lazer
lash *n* acı söz; kamçı
lash *v* ayıplamak
lash out *v* saldırmak
lasso *n* kement
lasso *v* kementle tutmak
last *v* sona ermek
last *adj* son
last name *n* soyadı
last night *adv* dün gece
lasting *adj* tükenmeyen
lastly *adv* nihayet
latch *n* mandal
late *adv* geç
lately *adv* son zamanlarda
later *adv* sonraları
later *adj* daha sonra
lateral *adj* büyüme
latest *adj* en sonuncu
lather *n* köpük; tornacı
latitude *n* enlem
latter *adj* sonraki
laugh *v* gülmek
laugh *n* kahkaha
laughable *adj* gülünç
laughing stock *n* maskara
laughter *n* kahkaha
launch *n* başlangıç
launch *v* fırlatmak
laundry *n* çamaşırhane
lavatory *n* lavabo

lavish *adj* bol
lavish *v* israf etmek
law *n* kanun
law-abiding *adj* yasaya uyan
lawful *adj* adil; meşru
lawmaker *n* kanuni
lawn *n* çimen
lawsuit *n* dava
lawyer *n* avukat
lax *adj* belirsiz
laxative *adj* yumuşatıcı
lay *n* örnek
lay *iv* sermek; yaymak
lay off *v* ara vermek
layer *n* katman
layman *n* mesleği olmayan
lay-out *n* düzenlemek
laziness *n* tembellik
lazy *adj* tembel
lead *iv* başı çekmek
lead *n* kurşun; ara kablosu
leaded *adj* kurşun kaplı
leader *n* lider
leadership *n* liderlik
leading *adj* ana
leaf *n* yaprak
leaflet *n* bildiri
league *n* lig
leak *v* sızmak
leak *n* akıntı
leakage *n* sızdırmazlık
lean *adj* cılız; eğik

L

lean *iv* dayanmak
lean back *v* geri yaslanmak
lean on *v* yaslanmak
leaning *n* meyil
leap *iv* zıplamak
leap *n* sıçrama
leap year *n* artık yıl
learn *iv* öğrenmek
learned *adj* okumuş
learner *n* öğrenci
learning *n* öğrenme
lease *v* kiralamak
lease *n* kira sözleşmesi
leash *n* tasma
least *adj* en ufak
leather *n* deri
leave *iv* geride bırakmak
leave out *v* ihmal etmek
leaves *n* yaprak
lectern *n* kürsü
lecture *n* ders
ledger *n* hesap defteri
leech *n* sülük
left *adv* sola
left *n* sol
left *adj* artık
leftovers *n* artıklar
leg *n* bacak
legacy *n* miras
legal *adj* yasal
legality *n* yasallık
legalize *v* yasallaştırmak

legend *n* efsane
legible *adj* okunur
legion *n* ordu; tümen
legislate *v* kanun yapmak
legislation *n* yasama
legislature *n* yasama meclisi
legitimate *adj* yasal
leisure *n* serbestlik
lemon *n* limon
lemonade *n* limonata
lend *iv* ödünç vermek
length *n* uzunluk
lengthen *v* uzatmak
lengthy *adj* fazlasıyla uzun
leniency *n* yumuşaklık
lenient *adj* hoşgörülü
lens *n* mercek
Lent *n* paskalya perhizi
lentil *n* mercimek
leopard *n* leopar
leper *n* cüzzamlı
leprosy *n* cüzam
less *adj* daha az
lessee *n* kiracı
lessen *v* azalmak
lesser *adj* daha az
lesson *n* ders
lessor *n* kiralayan
let *iv* bırakmak
let down *v* boşa çıkarmak
let go *v* vazgeçmek
let in *v* içeri almak

let out *v* azad etmek
lethal *adj* öldürücü
letter *n* yazı; mektup
lettuce *n* marul
leukemia *n* lösemi
level *v* eşitlemek
level *n* düzey; kademe
lever *n* manivela
leverage *n* piston
levy *v* el koymak
lewd *adj* müstehcen
liability *n* mesuliyet
liable *adj* sorumlu
liaison *n* irtibat
liar *adj* yalancı
libel *n* iftira
liberate *v* azat etmek
liberation *n* azat
liberty *n* özgürlük
librarian *n* kütüphaneci
library *n* kütüphane
lice *n* bitler
license *n* lisans
license *v* lisanslamak
lick *v* yalamak
lid *n* kapak
lie *iv* yalan söylemek
lie *v* uzanmak
lie *n* yalan
lieu *n* mahal
lieutenant *n* teğmen
life *n* yaşam

lifeguard *n* cankurtaran
lifeless *adj* cansız
lifestyle *n* yaşam stili
lifetime *adj* yaşam süreci
lift *v* kaldırmak
lift off *v* havalanmak
lift-off *n* kalkış
ligament *n* bağ; köprü
light *iv* aydınlatmak
light *adj* hafif; ışıklı
light *n* ışık
lighter *n* çakmak
lighthouse *n* deniz feneri
lighting *n* aydınlatma
lightly *adv* umursamazca
lightning *n* şimşek
lightweight *n* hafif sıklet
likable *adj* cana yakın
like *adj* eşit
like *pre* gibi; benzer
like *v* hoşlanmak
likelihood *n* ihtimal
likely *adv* muhtemelen
likeness *n* benzerlik
likewise *adv* benzer şekilde
liking *n* alaka
limb *n* bacak
lime *n* kireç
limestone *n* kireç taşı
limit *n* hudut; kenar
limit *v* sınırlandırmak
limitation *n* limit

L

limp *v* topallamak
limp *n* gevşek
linchpin *n* dingil çivisi
line *n* çizgi; sıra
line up *v* sıraya girmek
linen *n* keten
linger *v* ayrılamamak
lingerie *n* kadın iç çamaşırı
lingering *adj* çok yavaş
lining *n* dizgin
link *v* bağlamak
link *n* bağlantı; halka
lion *n* aslan
lioness *n* dişi aslan
lip *n* dudak
liqueur *n* likör
liquid *n* sıvı
liquidate *v* sıvılaştırmak
liquidation *n* sıvılaştırma
liquor *n* içki; et suyu
list *v* liste yapmak
list *n* liste
listen *v* dinlemek
listener *n* dinleyici
litany *n* ayin
liter *n* litre
literal *adj* değişmez
literally *adv* gerçekten
literate *adj* okuryazar
literature *n* edebiyat
litigate *v* dava açmak
litigation *n* dava

litter *n* çöp
little *adj* küçük
little bit *n* birazcık
little by little *adv* azar azar
liturgy *n* ayin
live *adj* canlı hayvan
live *v* yaşamak
live off *v* geçimini sağlamak
live up *v* hayatta kalmak
livelihood *n* geçim yolu
lively *adj* canlı
liver *n* ciğer
livestock *n* canlı hayvan
livid *adj* çok öfkeli
living room *n* oturma odası
lizard *n* kertenkele
load *v* yüklemek
load *n* yük
loaded *adj* doldurulmuş
loaf *v* aylaklık etmek
loaf *n* somun
loan *v* ödünç vermek
loan *n* ödünç
loathe *v* tiksinmek
loathing *n* nefret
lobby *n* lobi; geçiş
lobby *v* kulis yapmak
lobster *n* ıstakoz
local *adj* yerel
localize *v* lokalize etmek
locate *v* yerini belirlemek
located *adj* yerleştirilmiş

L

location n konum
lock v kilitlemek
lock n kilit
lock up v hapsetmek
locker room n soyunma odası
locksmith n çilingir
locust n ağustos böceği
lodge v konaklamak
lodging n ufak ev
lofty adj yüksek
log n kütük
log v ağaç kesmek
log in v oturum açmak
log off v oturum kapatmak
logic n mantık
logical adj mantıklı
loin n mantıksal
loiter v aylak aylak dolaşmak
loneliness n yalnızlık
lonely adv yalnız başına
loner n yalnız
lonesome adj yapayalnız
long adj uzun
long for v özlemek
longing n arzu
longitude n boylam
long-standing adj bitmez tükenmez
long-term adj uzun süreli
look n bakış; faal
look v bakmak
look after v gözetmek

look at v gözden geçirmek
look down v tepeden bakmak
look for v aramak; beklemek
look forward v beklemek
look into v incelemek
look out v dikkat etmek
look over v gözden geçirmek
look through v incelemek
looking glass n ayna
looks n görünüş
loom n dokuma tezgahı
loom v büyümek
loophole n gözetleme deliği
loose v ateşlemek
loose adj bol
loosen v gevşetmek
loot v ganimetlemek
loot n ganimet
lord n lord
lordship n lordluk
lose iv kaybetmek
loser n zavallı; mağlup
loss n kayıp
lot adv hepsi
lotion n losyon
lots adj birçok
lottery n piyango
loud adj gürültülü
loudly adv kaba
loudspeaker n hoparlör
lounge v uzanmak
lounge n lonca

L

louse *n* bit
lousy *adj* berbat; bitli
lovable *adj* sevimli
love *v* sevmek
love *n* sevgi
lovely *adj* güzel
lover *n* sevgili
loving *adj* sevecen
low *adj* alçak
lower *adj* daha alçak
low-key *adj* uyumlu
lowly *adj* alçakgönüllü
loyal *adj* sadık
loyalty *n* sadakat
lubricate *v* yağlamak
lubrication *n* gresleme
lucid *adj* açık seçik
luck *n* şans
lucky *adj* şanslı
lucrative *adj* kazançlı
ludicrous *adj* aptalca
luggage *n* bagaj
lukewarm *adj* ılık
lull *n* durgunluk
lumber *n* kereste
luminous *adj* aydınlık
lump *n* küme; şişkinlik
lump sum *n* götürü
lump together *v* aynı sınıfa girmek
lunacy *n* cinnet
lunatic *adj* ruh hastası

lunch *n* öğle yemeği
lung *n* akciğer
lure *v* ayartmak
lurid *adj* korkunç
lurk *v* pusuda beklemek
lush *adj* ayyaş
lust *v* arzulamak
lust *n* arzu
lustful *adj* azgın
luxurious *adj* konforlu
luxury *n* lüks
lynch *v* linç etmek
lynx *n* karakulak
lyrics *n* şarkı sözü

machine *n* makine
machine gun *n* makineli tüfek
mad *adj* sinirli
madam *n* hanımefendi
madden *v* delirtmek
madly *adv* delice
madman *n* deli
madness *n* delilik
magazine *n* magazin
magic *n* sihir
magical *adj* sihirli

L
M

magician *n* sihirbaz
magistrate *n* yargıç
magnet *n* mıknatıs
magnetic *adj* manyetik
magnetism *n* manyetizma
magnificent *adj* görkemli
magnify *v* büyütmek
magnitude *n* boyut
mahogany *n* maun
maid *n* bayan hizmetçi
maiden *n* bakire
mail *v* postalamak
mail *n* posta
mailbox *n* posta kutusu
mailman *n* postacı
maim *v* sakatlamak
main *adj* ana
mainland *n* ana kara
mainly *adv* başlıca
maintain *v* devam ettirmek
maintenance *n* bakım
majestic *adj* görkemli
majesty *n* majeste
major *n* binbaşı
major *adj* önemli; ana
major in *v* bir konuda
uzmanlaşmak
majority *n* çoğunluk
make *n* yapım
make *iv* yapmak
make up *v* barışmak
make up for *v* telafi etmek

maker *n* fail; imalatçı
makeup *n* makyaj
malaria *n* sıtma
male *n* erkek
malevolent *adj* art niyetli
malfunction *v* arızalı çalışmak
malfunction *n* arızalı çalışma
malice *n* fesat
malign *v* çamur atmak
malignancy *n* habislik
malignant *adj* kötü niyetli
mall *n* kapalı çarşı
malnutrition *n* yetersiz beslenme
malpractice *v* görevini kötüye
kullanmak
mammal *n* memeli
mammoth *n* mamut
man *n* adam
manage *v* yönetmek
manageable *adj* yönetilir
management *n* yönetim
manager *n* müdür
mandate *n* ferman
mandatory *adj* zorunlu
maneuver *n* manevra
manger *n* yemlik
mangle *v* parçalamak
manhandle *v* tartaklamak
manhunt *n* insan avı
maniac *adj* manyak
manifest *v* manifesto
manipulate *v* hile yapmak

M

mankind *n* insan soyu
manliness *n* erkeklik
manly *adj* erkeksi
manner *n* tavır
mannerism *n* kişisel özellik
manners *n* adap
manpower *n* insan gücü
mansion *n* konak
manslaughter *n* adam öldürme
manual *n* el kitabı
manual *adj* elle yapılan
manufacture *v* imal etmek
manure *n* gübre
manuscript *n* el yazısı
many *adj* birçok
map *v* eşlemek
map *n* harita
marble *n* bilye
march *v* uygun adım yürümek
march *n* askeri yürüyüş
March *n* Mart
mare *n* kısrak
margin *n* hudut; fazlalık
marginal *adj* marjinal
marinate *v* marine etmek
marine *adj* bahriyeli
marital *adj* evlilikle ilgili
mark *n* işaret
mark *v* işaretlemek
mark down *v* fiyat düşürmek
marker *n* belirteç
market *v* satmak

market *n* market
marksman *n* nişancı
marmalade *n* marmelat
marriage *n* evlilik
married *adj* evli
marrow *n* ilik
marry *v* evlenmek
Mars *n* Mars
marshal *n* mareşal; polis şefi
martyr *n* şehit
martyrdom *n* şehitlik
marvel *n* harika
marvelous *adj* fevkalade
Marxist *adj* Marksçı
masculine *adj* maskülen
mash *v* ezmek
mask *v* maskelemek
mask *n* maske
masochism *n* mazoşizm
mason *n* mason; duvarcı
masquerade *v* kılık değiştirmek
mass *n* kütle; kilise ayini
massacre *n* kırım
massage *n* masaj
massage *v* masaj yapmak
masseur *n* masör
masseuse *n* masöz
massive *adj* kocaman
mast *n* bayrak direği
master *v* uzmanlaşmak
master *n* usta
mastermind *n* beyin

meek

mastermind *v* yönetmek
masterpiece *n* başyapıt
mastery *n* egemenlik
mat *n* hasır
match *n* yarışma; akran
match *v* eşlemek
mate *n* arkadaş
material *n* madde; kumaş
materialism *n* maddecilik
maternal *adj* anaç
maternity *n* annelik
math *n* matematik
matriculate *v* kaydetmek
matrimony *n* evlenme
matter *v* önemli olmak
matter *n* cisim; konu
mattress *n* şilte
mature *adj* olgun
maturity *n* olgunluk
maul *v* berelemek
maxim *n* atasözü
maximum *adj* maksimum
May *n* Mayıs
may *iv* olabilir
may-be *adv* belki
mayhem *n* kargaşa
mayor *n* belediye başkanı
maze *n* hayret
meadow *n* çayır
meager *adj* bereketsiz
meal *n* yemek
mean *n* kaba

mean *iv* demek istemek
mean *adj* kötü kalpli
meaning *n* anlam
meaningful *adj* anlamlı
meaningless *adj* anlamsız
meanness *n* kötülük
means *n* araç
meantime *adv* bu arada
meanwhile *adv* bu sırada
measles *n* kızamık
measure *v* ölçmek
measurement *n* ölçüm
meat *n* et
meatball *n* köfte
mechanic *n* mekanik
mechanism *n* mekanizma
mechanize *v* mekanize etmek
medal *n* madalya
medallion *n* madalyon
meddle *v* burnunu sokmak
mediate *v* ara bulmak
mediator *n* ara bulucu
medication *n* ilaç tedavisi
medicinal *adj* gezgin
medicine *n* ilaç
medieval *adj* orta çağ
mediocre *adj* alelade
mediocrity *n* aleladelik
meditate *v* meditasyon yapmak
meditation *n* meditasyon
medium *adj* orta
meek *adj* alçakgönüllü

M

meekness *n* alçakgönüllülük
meet *iv* buluşmak
meeting *n* toplantı
melancholy *n* melankoli
mellow *adj* cana yakın
mellow *v* olgunlaştırmak
melodic *adj* melodik
melody *n* melodi
melon *n* kavun
melt *v* erimek
member *n* üye
membership *n* üyelik
membrane *n* membran
memento *n* hatıra
memo *n* kısa not
memoirs *n* anılar
memorable *adj* unutulmaz
memorize *v* ezberlemek
memory *n* hafıza
men *n* erkekler
menace *n* göz dağı
mend *v* onarmak
meningitis *n* menenjit
menopause *n* menapoz
menstruation *n* aybaşı
mental *adj* kaçık
mentality *n* zihniyet
mentally *adv* aklen
mention *v* bahsetmek
mention *n* ima
menu *n* menü
merchandise *n* alıp satmak

merchant *n* tüccar
merciful *adj* insaflı
merciless *adj* insafsız
mercury *n* cıva
mercy *n* insaf
merely *adv* adeta
merge *v* birleşmek
merger *n* birleşme
merit *n* değer
merit *v* layık olmak
mermaid *n* deniz kızı
merry *adj* mutlu
mesh *n* ağ; elek
mesmerize *v* büyülemek
mess *n* dağınıklık
mess around *v* oyalanmak
mess up *v* altüst etmek
message *n* mesaj
messenger *n* haberci
Messiah *n* Mesih
messy *adj* dağınık
metal *n* metal
metallic *adj* metalik
metaphor *n* istiare
meteor *n* meteor
meter *n* metre
method *n* metod
methodical *adj* düzenli
meticulous *adj* titiz
metric *adj* ölçülü
metropolis *n* büyükşehir
Mexican *adj* Meksikalı

M

mice *n* fareler
microbe *n* mikrop
microphone *n* mikrofon
microscope *n* mikroskop
microwave *n* mikrodalga
midair *n* gökyüzündeki nokta
midday *n* gün ortası
middle *n* orta
middleman *n* aracı
midget *n* cüce
midnight *n* geceyarısı
midsummer *n* yaz ortası
midwife *n* ebe
might *n* abilmek eki
mighty *adj* güçlü
migraine *n* migren
migrant *n* göçmen
migrate *v* göçmek
mild *adj* hafif
mildew *n* küf
mile *n* mil
mileage *n* dönem
milestone *n* dönüm noktası
militant *adj* azimli
milk *n* süt
milky *adj* sütlü
mill *n* değirmen
millennium *n* milenyum
milligram *n* miligram
millimeter *n* milimetre
million *n* milyon
millionaire *n* milyoner

mime *v* mimik yapmak
mince *v* doğramak
mincemeat *n* kıyma
mind *v* dikkat etmek
mind *n* zeka; hafıza
mind-boggling *adj* parmak ısırtan
mindful *adj* dikkatli
mindless *adj* akılsız
mine *n* kaynak; mayın
mine *v* mayın döşemek
mine *pro* benimki
minefield *n* mayın tarlası
miner *n* mayıncı
mineral *n* mineral
mingle *v* birbirine karıştırmak
miniature *n* minyatür
minimize *v* en aza indirgemek
minimum *n* minimum
miniskirt *n* mini etek
minister *n* bakan; papaz
minister *v* hizmet etmek
ministry *n* bakanlık
minor *n* küçük çocuk; minör
minor *v* yardımcı ders almak
minor *adj* önemsiz
minority *n* azınlık
mint *n* nane
mint *v* para basmak
minus *adj* eksi
minute *n* dakika
miracle *n* mucize
miraculous *adj* mucizevi

M

mirage n serap
mirror n ayna
misbehave v uygunsuz davranmak
miscalculate v yanlış hesaplamak
miscarriage n yanlışlık yapmak
miscarry v düşük yapmak
mischief n fenalık
mischievous adj afacan
misconduct n kabahat
misconstrue v tersten anlamak
misdemeanor n kabahat
miser n hasis
miserable adj zavallı
misery n acı
misfit adj uyumsuz
misfortune n aksilik
misgiving n endişe
misguided adj yanıltılmış
misinterpret v yanlış anlamak
misjudge v yanlış değerlendirmek
mislead v aldatmak
misleading adj aldatıcı
mismanage v kötü yönetmek
misplace v kaybetmek
misprint n baskı hatası
miss v özlemek; kaçırmak
miss n bayan
missile n misil
missing adj kayıp
mission n amaç; elçilik
missionary n misyoner

mist n buğu
mistake iv hata yapmak
mistake n hata
mistaken adj yanlış
mister n bay
mistreat v hor kullanmak
mistreatment n kıyım
mistress n bayan; dost
mistrust n kuşku
mistrust v güvenmemek
misty adj belirsiz
misunderstand v yanlış anlamak
misuse n hatalı kullanım
mitigate v azaltmak
mix v karıştırmak
mixed-up adj arapsaçı gibi
mixer n mikser
mixture n karışım
mix-up n anlaşmazlık
moan v inlemek
moan n inilti
mob v üşüşmek
mob n ayak takımı
mobile adj hareketli
mobilize v harekete geçirmek
mobster n gangster
mock v alay etmek
mockery n alay
mode n mod
model iv model olmak
model n örnek; model
moderate adj ılımlı

M

mosaic

moderation *n* azalma
modern *adj* modern
modernize *v* modernleştirmek
modest *adj* alçakgönüllü
modesty *n* alçakgönüllülük
modify *v* azaltmak
module *n* modül
moisten *v* nemlendirmek
moisture *n* nem
molar *n* kütlesel
mold *v* kalıp dökmek
mold *n* kalıp; küf
moldy *adj* küflü
mole *n* ben; köstebek
molecule *n* molekül
molest *v* uğraşmak
mom *n* anne
moment *n* an
momentarily *adv* bir an için
momentous *adj* ciddi
monarch *n* hükümdar
monarchy *n* monarşi
monastery *n* manastır
monastic *adj* keşiş
Monday *n* Pazartesi
money *n* para
money order *n* havale
monitor *v* izlemek
monk *n* papaz
monkey *n* maymun
monogamy *n* tek eşlilik
monologue *n* monolog

monopolize *v* tekelleştirmek
monopoly *n* monopol
monotonous *adj* monoton
monotony *n* monoton
monster *n* canavar
monstrous *adj* azman
month *n* ay
monthly *adv* aylık
monument *n* anıt
monumental *adj* devasa
mood *n* ruh hali
moody *adj* huysuz
moon *n* ay
moor *v* demir atmak
mop *v* paspas yapmak
moral *adj* ahlaki
moral *n* ahlak
morality *n* etik
more *adj* daha
moreover *adv* dahası
morning *n* sabah
moron *adj* gerizekalı
morphine *n* morfin
morsel *n* lokma
mortal *adj* ölümlü
mortality *n* fanilik
mortar *n* havan topu
mortgage *n* ipotek
mortification *n* aşağılama
mortify *v* çürütmek
mortuary *n* morg
mosaic *n* mozaik

M

mosque *n* cami
mosquito *n* sivrisinek
moss *n* yosun
most *adj* en çok
mostly *adv* başlıca
motel *n* motel
moth *n* güve; pervane
mother *n* anne
motherhood *n* annelik
mother-in-law *n* kaynana
motion *n* hareket; teklif
motion *v* işaret etmek
motionless *adj* hareketsiz
motivate *v* motive etmek
motive *n* dürtü; sebep
motor *n* motor
motorcycle *n* motosiklet
motto *n* ilke
mount *n* binek
mount *v* tırmanmak
mountain *n* dağ
mountainous *adj* dağlık
mourn *v* yas tutmak
mourning *n* yas
mouse *n* fare
mouth *n* ağız
move *n* hareket; adım
move *v* hareket etmek
move back *v* geri çekilmek
move forward *v* ilerlemek
move out *v* çıkmak
move up *v* yukarı taşımak

movement *n* hareket
movie *n* film
mow *v* biçmek
much *adv* çok
mucus *n* mukus
mud *n* çamur
muddle *n* dağınıklık
muddy *adj* çamurlu
muffle *v* susturmak
muffler *n* boyun atkısı
mug *n* bardak
mug *v* saldırıp soymak
mugging *n* saldırı
mule *n* katır
multiple *adj* çoklu
multiplication *n* çoğalma
multiply *v* çoğalmak
multitude *n* izdiham
mumble *v* mırıldanmak
mummy *n* anne
mumps *n* kabakulak
munch *v* kıtırdatarak yemek
munitions *n* cephane
murder *n* cinayet
murderer *n* katil
murky *adj* anlaşılması güç
murmur *v* homurdanma
murmur *n* hırıltı
muscle *n* kas
museum *n* müze
mushroom *n* mantar
music *n* müzik

musician *n* müzisyen
Muslim *adj* Müslüman
must *iv* gerekmek
mustache *n* bıyık
mustard *n* hardal
muster *v* içtima yapmak
mutate *v* değişmek
mute *adj* dilsiz; sessiz
mutilate *v* değiştirmek
mutiny *n* ayaklanma
mutually *adv* karşılıklı olarak
muzzle *v* susturmak
muzzle *n* namlu ağzı
my *adj* benim
myopic *adj* miyop
myself *pro* kendim
mysterious *adj* gizemli
mystery *n* gizem
mystic *adj* esrarengiz
mystify *v* aklını karıştırmak
myth *n* efsane

nag *v* dırdır etmek
nagging *adj* dırdır
nail *v* çivilemek
nail *n* tırnak; çivi
naive *adj* saf
naked *adj* çıplak
name *v* isimlendirmek
name *n* isim
namely *adv* yani
nanny *n* bakıcı
nap *v* şekerlemek
nap *n* kısa uyku
napkin *n* mendil
narcotic *n* narkotik
narrate *v* betimlemek
narrow *adj* dar
narrowly *adv* anca
nasty *adj* edepsiz
nation *n* ulus
national *adj* ulusal
nationality *n* vatandaşlık
nationalize *v* millileştirmek
native *adj* yerli
natural *adj* doğal
naturally *adv* doğal olarak
nature *n* doğa
naughty *adj* yaramaz
nausea *n* mide bulantısı
nave *n* dingil başlığı

M
N

navel *n* merkez
navigate *v* seyretmek
navigation *n* seyir
navy *n* bahriye
navy blue *adj* deniz mavisi
near *pre* yakın
nearby *adj* yakınlarda
nearly *adv* neredeyse
nearsighted *adj* miyop
neat *adj* düzenli
neatly *adv* düzenli bir şekilde
necessary *adj* gerekli
necessitate *v* gerekli kılmak
necessity *n* gereklilik
neck *n* boyun
necklace *n* kolye
necktie *n* kravat
need *v* gerekmek
need *n* yardım; gerek
needle *n* iğne
needless *adj* gereksiz
needy *adj* yardıma muhtaç
negative *n* olumsuz
negative *adj* negatif
neglect *v* ihmal etmek
neglect *n* ihmal
negligence *n* dikkatsizlik
negligent *adj* ihmalkar
negotiate *v* pazarlık etmek
negotiation *n* pazarlık
neighbor *n* komşu
neighborhood *n* komşuluk

neither *adj* hiçbiri
neither *adv* hiçbiri
nephew *n* yeğen
nerve *n* sinir
nervous *adj* sinirli; endişeli
nest *n* yuva
net *n* ağ
Netherlands *n* Hollanda
network *n* çevrim
neurotic *adj* evhamlı
neutral *adj* nötr
neutralize *v* etkisiz bırakmak
never *adv* asla
nevertheless *adv* yine de
new *adj* yeni
newborn *n* yeni doğmuş
newcomer *n* yeni gelen
newly *adv* yeni
newlywed *adj* yeni evli
news *n* haberler
newscast *n* haber bülteni
newsletter *n* bülten
newspaper *n* gazete
newsstand *n* gazete bayii
next *adj* sıradaki
next door *adj* yan kapı
nibble *v* kemirmek
nice *adj* güzel
nicely *adv* güzelce
nickel *n* nikel
nickname *n* lakap
nicotine *n* nikotin

N

niece *n* kuzen

night *n* gece

nightfall *n* alacakaranlık

nightgown *n* gecelik

nightingale *n* bülbül

nightmare *n* karabasan

nine *adj* dokuz

nineteen *adj* on dokuz

ninety *adj* doksan

ninth *adj* dokuzuncu

nip *n* ayaz; çimdik

nip *v* çimdik atmak

nipple *n* meme ucu

nitpicking *adj* eften püften

nitrogen *n* nitrojen

no one *pro* kimse

nobility *n* asalet

noble *adj* asil

nobleman *n* asilzade

nobody *pro* kimse

nocturnal *adj* geceleyin

nod *v* baş işareti

noise *n* gürültü

noisily *adv* gürültülü biçimde

noisy *adj* gürültücü

nominate *v* aday göstermek

none *pre* hiçbiri

nonetheless *c* yine de

nonsense *n* saçma

nonsmoker *n* sigara içmeyen

nonstop *adv* durmadan

noon *n* öğlen

noose *n* ilişki; tuzak

nor *c* ne de

norm *n* kural

normal *adj* normal

normalize *v* normalleştirmek

normally *adv* normalde

north *n* kuzey

northeast *n* kuzeydoğu

northern *adj* kuzeye ait

northerner *adj* kuzeyli

Norway *n* Norveç

Norwegian *adj* Norveçli

nose *n* burun

nosedive *v* pike yapmak

nostalgia *n* nostalji

nostril *n* burun deliği

nosy *adj* meraklı

not *adv* değil

notable *adj* önemli

notably *adv* kayda değer

notary *n* noter

notation *n* formül

note *n* not etmek; önem vermek

note *v* not

notebook *n* not defteri

noteworthy *adj* kayda değer

nothing *n* hiçbir şey

notice *v* farketmek

notice *n* bildiri; ihtar

noticeable *adj* önemli

notification *n* bildiri

notify *v* bildirmek

N

notion *n* düşünce
notorious *adj* adı çıkmış
noun *n* isim
nourish *v* beslemek
nourishment *n* beslenme
novel *n* hikaye
novelist *n* yazar
novelty *n* acayiplik
November *n* Kasım
novice *n* çaylak
now *adv* şimdi
nowadays *adv* bugünlerde
nowhere *adv* hiçbir yerde
noxious *adj* ahlakı bozan
nozzle *n* ağızlık
nuance *n* ayrıntı
nuclear *adj* nükleer
nude *adj* çıplak
nudism *n* çıplaklık
nudist *n* nüdist
nudity *n* çıplaklık
nuisance *n* baş ağrısı
null *adj* sıfır
nullify *v* sıfırlamak
numb *adj* uyuşuk
number *n* sayı
numbness *n* uyuşukluk
numerous *adj* sayısız
nun *n* rahibe
nurse *n* hemşire
nurse *v* bakıcılık yapmak
nursery *n* kreş; fidanlık

nurture *v* büyütmek
nut *n* fındık; çatlak
nutrition *n* beslenme
nutritious *adj* besleyici
nut-shell *n* fındık kabuğu
nutty *adj* çatlak; lezzetli

oak *n* meşe ağacı
oar *n* işçi
oasis *n* vaha
oath *n* yemin
oatmeal *n* yulaf ezmesi
obedience *n* itaat
obedient *adj* itaatkar
obese *adj* obez
obey *v* uymak
object *v* karşı çıkmak
object *n* obje
objection *n* itiraz
objective *n* amaç
obligate *v* mecbur etmek
obligation *n* mecburiyet
obligatory *adj* zorunlu
oblige *v* zorlamak
obliged *adj* borçlu olmak
oblique *adj* dolambaçlı**

N
O

obliterate *v* aşındırmak
oblivion *n* unutma
oblivious *adj* dikkatsiz
oblong *adj* uzunca
obnoxious *adj* çirkin
obscene *adj* açık saçık
obscenity *n* açık saçık laf
obscure *adj* anlaşılması güç
obscurity *n* anlaşılmazlık
observation *n* gözlem
observatory *n* gözlemevi
observe *v* gözlemlemek
obsess *v* aklına takılmak
obsession *n* saplantı
obsolete *adj* eski
obstacle *n* engel
obstinacy *n* inat
obstinate *adj* dik başlı
obstruct *v* engellemek
obstruction *n* arıza
obtain *v* elde etmek
obvious *adj* belli
obviously *adv* belli ki
occasion *n* fırsat
occasionally *adv* ara sıra
occult *adj* anlaşılmaz
occupant *n* oturan
occupation *n* uğraş
occupy *v* işgal etmek
occur *v* vuku bulmak
occurrence *n* oluş
ocean *n* okyanus

October *n* Ekim
octopus *n* ahtapot
odd *adj* garip
oddity *n* gariplik
odds *n* eşitsizlik
odious *adj* iğrenç
odometer *n* yol sayacı
odor *n* koku
odyssey *n* odise
of *pre* onun
off *adv* açıkta
offend *v* utandırmak
offense *n* gücenme
offensive *adj* hakaret edici
offer *v* teklif etmek
offer *n* teklif
offering *n* adak
office *n* ofis
officer *n* memur
official *adj* resmi
officiate *v* görev yapmak
offset *v* daldırma
offspring *n* ürün; evlat
off-the-record *adj* kayıt dışı
konuşma
often *adv* sıklıkla
oil *n* yağ
ointment *n* merhem
okay *adv* tamam
old *adj* yaşlı
old age *n* yaşlılık
old-fashioned *adj* eski moda

O

olive *n* zeytin
Olympics *n* olimpiyat
omelet *n* omlet
omen *n* alamet
ominous *adj* uğursuz
omission *n* ihmal
omit *v* dahil etmemek
on *pre* üstünde
once *adv* bir kerede
once *c* bir kere
one *adj* bir
oneself *pre* biri
ongoing *adj* süren
onion *n* soğan
onlooker *n* izleyici
only *adv* yalnız
onset *n* başlangıç
onslaught *n* hamle
onwards *adv* beri
opaque *adj* opak
open *v* açmak
open *adj* açık
open up *v* açılmak
opening *n* açılış
open-minded *adj* açık fikirli
openness *n* açıklık
opera *n* opera
operate *v* işletmek
operation *n* operasyon
opinion *n* fikir
opinionated *adj* dik kafalı
opium *n* afyon

opponent *n* muhalif
opportune *adj* elverişli
opportunity *n* fırsat
oppose *v* karşı koymak
opposite *adj* karşıt
opposite *adv* karşıda
opposite *n* karşı
opposition *n* direniş
oppress *v* baskı yapmak
oppression *n* baskı
opt for *v* tercih etmek
optical *adj* optik
optician *n* göz doktoru
optimism *n* iyimserlik
optimistic *adj* iyimser
option *n* seçenek
optional *adj* isteğe bağlı
opulence *n* bolluk
or *c* veya
oracle *n* ayrıcalık
orally *adv* ağızdan
orange *n* portakal
orangutan *n* orangutan
orbit *n* yörünge
orchard *n* bostan
orchestra *n* orkestra
ordain *v* atamak
ordeal *n* çile
order *v* emretmek; sipariş vermek
order *n* buyruk; sıra
ordinarily *adv* genelde
ordinary *adj* basit; sıradan

ordination *n* buyurma
ore *n* maden
organ *n* organ; org
organism *n* organizma
organist *n* orgcu
organization *n* kuruluş
organize *v* organize etmek
orient *n* doğu
oriental *adj* doğuya özgü
orientation *n* alışma
oriented *adj* yönlü
origin *n* köken
original *adj* orjinal
originally *adv* orjinal olarak
originate *v* başlamak
ornament *n* aksesuar
ornamental *adj* bezemeli
orphan *n* kimsesiz
orphanage *n* öksüzler yurdu
orthodox *adj* göreneksel
ostentatious *adj* azametli
ostrich *n* devekuşu
other *adj* başka
otherwise *adv* aksi takdirde
otter *n* su samuru
ought to *iv* malı eki
ounce *n* ons
our *adj* bizim
ours *pro* bizimki
ourselves *pro* bizler
oust *v* defetmek
out *adv* dışarıda

outbreak *n* baş gösterme
outburst *n* feveran
outcast *adj* kimsesiz
outcome *n* akıbet
outcry *n* bağırış
outdated *adj* çağ dışı
outdo *v* bastırmak
outdoor *adv* ev dışında
outdoors *adv* açık havada
outer *adj* dış
outfit *n* donatım
outgoing *adj* açık yürekli
outgrow *v* büyümek
outing *n* gezinti
outlast *v* daha fazla sürmek
outlaw *v* feshetmek
outlet *n* satış yeri
outline *v* taslak çizmek
outline *n* ana çizgiler
outlook *n* bakış açısı
outmoded *adj* demode
outnumber *v* sayıca çok olmak
outpatient *n* ayakta tedavi edilen hasta
outperform *v* aşmak
outpouring *n* taşma
output *n* çıktı
outrage *n* büyük ayıp
outrageous *adj* acımasız
outright *adj* açık sözlü
outrun *v* aşmak
outset *n* başlangıç

outshine *v* daha çok parlamak
outside *adv* dışarıda
outsider *n* dışlanmış
outskirts *n* civar
outspoken *adj* açık sözlü
outstanding *adj* göze çarpan
outstretched *adj* uzanmış
outward *adj* dışa doğru
outweigh *v* ağır basmak
oval *adj* oval
ovary *n* yumurtalık
ovation *n* tezahürat
oven *n* fırın
over *pre* üstünde
overall *adv* toplamda
overbearing *adj* ağır basan
overboard *adv* gemiden denize
overcast *adj* basık
overcharge *v* abartmak
overcoat *n* manto
overcome *v* alt etmek
overcrowded *adj* aşırı kalabalık
overdo *v* abartmak
overdone *adj* abartılı
overdose *n* dozaşımı
overdue *adj* gecikmiş
overestimate *v* fazla tahmin
etmek
overflow *v* akmak
overhaul *v* elden geçirmek
overlap *v* üstüste binmek
overlook *v* aldırmamak

overnight *adv* bir gecede
overpower *v* boyun eğdirmek
overrate *v* büyütmek
override *v* ağır basmak
overrule *v* geçersiz kılmak
overrun *v* aşmak
overseas *adv* deniz aşırı
oversee *v* denetlemek
overshadow *v* gölgede bırakmak
oversight *n* dikkatsizlik
overstate *v* abartmak
overstep *v* çok ileri gitmek
overtake *v* arkadan yetişmek
overthrow *v* çökertmek
overthrow *n* alaşağı edilme
overtime *adv* fazla mesai
overturn *v* alabora etmek
overview *n* genel bakış
overweight *adj* fazla kilolu
overwhelm *v* alt etmek
owe *v* borçlu olmak
owing to *adv* nedeniyle
owl *n* baykuş
own *v* sahibi olmak
own *adj* kendi
owner *n* mal sahibi
ownership *n* mülkiyet
ox *n* öküz
oxen *n* öküz
oxygen *n* oksijen
oyster *n* istiridye

P

pace *v* yürümek
pace *n* adım
pacify *v* yatıştırmak
pack *n* sigara paketi; bohça
pack *v* paketlemek
package *n* paket
pact *n* anlaşma
pad *v* doldurmak
padding *n* yastık
paddle *n* kürek
paddle *v* kürek çekmek
padlock *n* kilit
pagan *adj* putperest
page *n* sayfa; uşak
pail *n* kova
pain *n* eziyet
painful *adj* acı veren
painkiller *n* ağrı kesici
painless *adj* zahmetsiz
paint *v* boyamak
paint *n* boya
paintbrush *n* boya fırçası
painter *n* ressam
painting *n* tablo; levha
pair *n* çift
pajamas *n* pijama
pal *n* ahbap
palace *n* saray
palate *n* damak

pale *adj* soluk
paleness *n* solukluk
palm *n* avuç; palmiye
palm *v* kazıklamak
palpable *adj* hissedilebilir
paltry *adj* değersiz
pamper *v* şımartmak
pamphlet *n* broşür
pan *n* tava
pancreas *n* pankreas
pander *v* yaltaklanmak
pang *n* ıstırap
panic *n* panik
panorama *n* panorama
panther *n* panter
pantry *n* kiler
pants *n* pantolon; don
pantyhose *n* tayt
papacy *n* papalık
paper *n* kağıt
paperclip *n* ataş
paperwork *n* formalite
parable *n* kıssa
parachute *n* paraşüt
parade *n* gösteri
paradise *n* cennet
paradox *n* paradoks
paragraph *n* paragraf
parakeet *n* papağan
parallel *n* paralel
paralysis *n* felç
paralyze *v* felç olmak

P

parameters *n* parametre
paramount *adj* fevkalade
paranoid *adj* paranoyak
parasite *n* parazit
paratrooper *n* paraşütçü
parcel *n* paket
parcel post *n* paket postası
parch *v* kavurmak
parchment *n* parşömen
pardon *v* özür dilemek
pardon *n* özür
parenthesis *n* parantez
parents *n* ebeveyn
parish *n* mahalle
parishioner *n* kilise üyesi
parity *n* parite
park *v* park etmek
park *n* park
parking *n* park yeri
parliament *n* parlamento
parochial *adj* yerel
parrot *n* papağan
parsley *n* maydonoz
parsnip *n* behmen
part *v* parçalanmak
part *n* parça
partial *adj* kısmi
partially *adv* kısmen
participate *v* katılmak
participation *n* katılma
participle *n* sıfat
particle *n* tanecik

particular *adj* belirli
particularly *adv* özellikle
parting *n* bölünme çizgisi
partisan *n* partizan
partition *n* bölümlemek
partly *adv* kısmi
partner *n* ortak
partnership *n* ortaklık
partridge *n* keklik
party *v* parti yapmak
party *n* parti; toplantı
pass *n* geçiş
pass *v* geçmek
pass around *v* dilden dile
  dolaşmak
pass away *v* ölmek
pass out *v* bayılmak
passage *n* geçit
passenger *n* yolcu
passer-by *n* yoldan geçen
passion *n* tutku
passionate *adj* tutkulu
passive *adj* pasif
passport *n* pasaport
password *n* şifre
past *n* mazi
past *adj* geçmiş
paste *v* yapıştırmak
paste *n* zamk; çiriş
pasteurize *v* pastorize etmek
pastime *n* eğlence
pastor *n* rahip

pastoral *adj* kırsal	**pay slip** *n* maaş makbuzu
pastry *n* hamur işi	**payable** *adj* ödenecek
pasture *n* çayır	**paycheck** *n* maaş çeki
pat *n* okşamak	**payee** *n* ödenen kişi
patch *v* yamalamak	**payment** *n* ödeme
patch *n* yama	**payroll** *n* maaş bordrosu
patent *n* patent	**pea** *n* bezelye
patent *adj* patentli	**peace** *n* huzur; barış
paternity *n* babalık	**peaceful** *adj* huzurlu
path *n* yol	**peach** *n* şeftali
pathetic *adj* acınası	**peacock** *n* tavuskuşu
patience *n* sabır	**peak** *n* doruk
patient *adj* sabırlı	**peanut** *n* yerfıstığı
patio *n* avlu	**pear** *n* armut
patriarch *n* ata	**pearl** *n* inci
patrimony *n* baba mirası	**peasant** *n* köylü
patriot *n* vatansever	**pebble** *n* çakıl
patriotic *adj* yurtsever	**peck** *v* gagalamak
patrol *n* karakol	**peck** *n* sürü
patron *n* patron; efendi	**peculiar** *adj* özgün
patronage *n* hamilik	**pedagogy** *n* pedagoji
patronize *v* korumak	**pedal** *n* pedal
pattern *n* desen	**pedantic** *adj* mektepli
pavement *n* kaldırım	**pedestrian** *n* yaya
pavilion *n* pavyon	**peel** *v* soymak
paw *n* pençe	**peel** *n* kabuk
pawn *v* rehine koyma	**peep** *v* dikizlemek
pawnbroker *n* tefeci	**peer** *n* eş
pay *n* ödeme	**pelican** *n* pelikan
pay *iv* ödemek	**pellet** *n* tane
pay back *v* geri ödemek	**pen** *n* mürekkepli kalem
pay off *v* tazminat vermek	**penalize** *v* cezalandırmak

P

penalty *n* ceza
penance *n* kefaret
penchant *n* eğilim
pencil *n* kalem
pendant *n* asılı şey
pending *adj* beklemede
pendulum *n* sarkaç
penetrate *v* içine işlemek
penguin *n* penguen
penicillin *n* penisilin
peninsula *n* yarımada
penitent *n* tövbekar
penniless *adj* parasız
penny *n* peni
pension *n* emekli aylığı
pentagon *n* beşgen
pent-up *adj* hapsedilmiş
people *n* insanlar
pepper *n* biber

per *pre* kişi başına
perceive *v* anlamak
percent *adv* yüzde
percentage *n* yüzdelik
perception *n* algılama
perennial *adj* yıl boyu süren
perfect *adj* mükemmel
perfection *n* mükemmeliyet
perforate *v* içine işlemek
perforation *n* delik
perform *v* işlemek
performance *n* performans
perfume *n* parfüm

perhaps *adv* belki de
peril *n* tehlike
perilous *adj* tehlikeli
perimeter *n* çevre
period *n* çağ; süre
perish *v* ölmek
perishable *adj* dayanıksız
perjury *n* yalancı şahit
permanent *adj* kalıcı
permeate *v* içine işlemek
permission *n* izin
permit *v* izin vermek
pernicious *adj* zararlı
perpetrate *v* icra etmek
persecute *v* zulmetmek
persevere *v* ısrar etmek
persist *v* üstelemek
persistence *n* direnme
persistent *adj* inatçı
person *n* şahıs
personal *adj* şahsi
personality *n* kişilik
personify *v* kişiselleştirmek
personnel *n* personel
perspective *n* bakış açısı
perspiration *n* ter
perspire *v* terlemek
persuade *v* ikna etmek
persuasion *n* ikna
persuasive *adj* ikna edici
pertain *v* ait olmak
pertinent *adj* uygun

perturb v bozmak
perverse adj ters
pervert v saptırmak
pervert n sapık
pervert adj sapık
pessimism n karamsarlık
pessimistic adj karamsar
pest n böcek
pester v kafa ütülemek
pesticide n tarım ilacı
pet n evcil hayvan
pet v okşamak
petal n taç yaprağı
petite adj zarif
petition n dilekçe
petrified adj donakalmış
petroleum n petrol
pettiness n küçüklük
petty adj önemsiz; adi
pew n uzun bank
phantom n hayalet
pharmacist n eczacı
pharmacy n eczane
phase n evre
pheasant n sülün
phenomenon n görüngü, fenomen
philosopher n filozof
philosophy n felsefe
phobia n fobi
phone n telefon
phone v telefon etmek

phony adj sahte
phosphorus n fosfor
photo n fotoğraf
photocopy n fotokopi
photograph v fotoğraf çekmek
photographer n fotoğrafçı
photography n fotoğraf
phrase n deyim
physically adv fiziksel olarak
physician n hekim
physics n fizik
pianist n piyanist
piano n piyano
pick n kazma; seçme hakkı
pick v almak; koparmak
pick up v kaldırmak
pickpocket n yankesicilik
pickup n kamyonet
picture n resim
picture v resimlemek
picturesque adj güzel
pie n tart
piece n parça
piecemeal adv yavaş yavaş
pier n rıhtım
pierce v içine işlemek
piercing n delme
piety n dindarlık
pig n domuz
pigeon n güvercin
piggy bank n kumbara
pile v yığmak

P

pile *n* yığın
pile up *v* yığmak
pilfer *v* çalmak
pilgrim *n* hacı
pilgrimage *n* hac
pill *n* ilaç
pillage *v* soymak
pillar *n* direk
pillow *n* yastık
pillowcase *n* yastık kılıfı
pilot *n* pilot
pimple *n* sivilce
pin *v* iğneyle tutturmak
pin *n* iğne
pincers *n* kerpeten
pinch *v* çimdiklemek
pinch *n* çimdik; tutam
pine *n* çam ağacı
pineapple *n* ananas
pink *adj* pembe
pinpoint *v* nokta atışı yapmak
pint *n* pinta
pioneer *n* öncü
pious *adj* dindar
pipe *n* düdük; boru
pipeline *n* boru hattı
piracy *n* korsanlık
pirate *n* korsan
pistol *n* tabanca
pit *n* çukur; ocak
pitch *v* fırlatmak; çadır kurmak
pitch-black *adj* kapkara

pitcher *n* beyzbol atıcısı
pitchfork *n* saman tırmığı
pitfall *n* tuzak; tehlike
pitiful *adj* hazin
pity *n* şefkat
placard *n* pankart
placate *v* yatıştırmak
place *v* yerleştirmek
place *n* yer
placid *adj* sessiz
plague *n* uğraşmak
plain *n* sade
plain *adj* sade; düz
plainly *adv* anlaşılıyor ki
plaintiff *n* davacı
plan *v* planlamak
plan *n* plan
plane *n* uçak; düzlem
planet *n* gezegen
plant *v* ekmek
plant *n* bitki
plaster *n* sıva
plaster *v* sıva vurmak
plastic *n* plastik
plate *n* tabak
plateau *n* yayla, plato
platform *n* düzlem
platinum *n* platin
platoon *n* takım
plausible *adj* akla yatkın
play *v* eğlenmek
play *n* oyun; faaliyet

player *n* oyuncu
playful *adj* oyunbaz
playground *n* oyun alanı
plea *n* iddia
plead *v* yalvarmak
pleasant *adj* memnun
please *v* memnun etmek
pleasing *adj* hoş
pleasure *n* sevinç
pleat *n* kıvrım
pleated *adj* kırmalı
pledge *v* rehine koymak
pledge *n* rehin
plentiful *adj* çok
plenty *n* bolca
pliable *adj* katlanabilir
pliers *n* kerpeten
plot *v* yerini belirlemek
plot *n* arsa; suikast
plow *v* çift sürmek
ploy *n* manevra
pluck *v* koparmak
plug *v* çalışmak
plug *n* fiş; piston
plum *n* erik
plumber *n* tesisatçı
plumbing *n* boru tesisatı
plummet *v* dibe vurmak
plump *adj* tıknaz
plunder *v* talan etmek
plunge *v* saplamak
plunge *n* dalış; atılma

plural *n* çoğul
plus *adj* artı
plush *adj* pelüş; lüks
plutonium *n* plütonyum
pneumonia *n* zatürree
pocket *n* cep
poem *n* şiir
poet *n* şair
poetry *n* şiir
poignant *adj* keskin
point *n* nokta; maksat
point *v* yöneltmek
pointed *adj* sivri
pointless *adj* mantıksız
poise *n* dengelemek
poison *v* zehirlemek
poison *n* zehir
poisoning *n* zehirleyen
poisonous *adj* zehirli
Poland *n* Polonya
polar *adj* kutupsal
pole *n* kutup
police *n* polis
policeman *n* polis
policy *n* poliçe
Polish *adj* Polonyalı
polish *n* cila
polish *v* cilalamak
polite *adj* kibar
politeness *n* kibarlık
politician *n* siyasetçi
politics *n* politika

P

poll *n* oylama
pollen *n* polen
pollute *v* kirletmek
pollution *n* kirlilik
polygamist *adj* çokeşli
polygamy *n* çokeşlilik
pomegranate *n* nar
pomposity *n* tafra
pond *n* gölet
ponder *v* zihninde tartmak
pontiff *n* piskopos
pool *n* havuz; ekip
pool *v* birleştirmek
poor *n* fakir
poorly *adv* başarısızlıkla
pop *v* patlamak
popcorn *n* patlamış mısır
Pope *n* Papa
poppy *n* gelincik
popular *adj* popüler
popularize *v* popülerleştirmek
populate *v* nüfusu artırmak
population *n* nüfus
porcelain *n* porselen
porch *n* veranda
porcupine *n* oklu kirpi
pore *n* gözenek
pork *n* domuz eti
porous *adj* geçirgen
port *n* liman; kapı
portable *adj* taşınabilir
portent *n* belirtisi

porter *n* kapıcı
portion *n* porsiyon
portrait *n* portre
portray *v* betimlemek
Portugal *n* Portekiz
Portuguese *adj* Portekizli
pose *v* poz vermek
pose *n* poz
posh *adj* lüks
position *n* pozisyon
positive *adj* pozitif
possess *v* sahip olmak
possession *n* mülk
possibility *n* olanak
possible *adj* mümkün
post *v* postalamak
post *n* posta
post office *n* postahane
postage *n* posta ücreti
postcard *n* kart
poster *n* poster
posterity *n* zürriyet
postman *n* postacı
postmark *n* posta damgası
postpone *v* ertelemek
postponement *n* erteleme
pot *n* kap; ödül
potato *n* patates
potent *adj* güçlü
potential *adj* potansiyel
pothole *n* derin çukur
poultry *n* kümes hayvanı

pound *v* vurmak
pound *n* darbe; libre
pour *v* dökmek
poverty *n* yoksulluk
powder *n* pudra; toz
power *n* güç; iktidar
powerful *adj* güçlü
powerless *adj* güçsüz
practical *adj* pratik
practice *n* talim
practice *v* alıştırma yapmak
practicing *adj* avukatlık yapan
pragmatist *adj* çıkarcı
prairie *n* yayla
praise *v* övmek
praise *n* övgü
praiseworthy *adj* övgüye değer
prank *n* muziplik
prawn *n* karides
pray *v* dua etmek
prayer *n* dua
preach *v* vaaz vermek
preacher *n* vaiz
preaching *n* vaaz
preamble *n* giriş
precarious *adj* güvenilmez
precaution *n* önlem
precede *v* önde olmak
precedent *n* emsal
preceding *adj* sabık
precept *n* emir
precious *adj* değerli

precipice *n* uçurum
precipitate *v* neden olmak
precise *adj* tam; doğru
precision *n* isabet
precocious *adj* turfanda
precursor *n* öncü
predecessor *n* ata
predicament *n* hal
predict *v* öngörmek
prediction *n* öngörü
predilection *n* hoşlanma
predisposed *adj* eğilimli
predominate *v* üstün olmak
preempt *v* önlemek
prefabricate *v* kurmak
preface *n* önsöz
prefer *v* tercih etmek
preference *n* tercih
prefix *n* önek
pregnancy *n* hamilelik
pregnant *adj* hamile
prehistoric *adj* tarih öncesi
prejudice *n* önyargı
preliminary *adj* hazırlayıcı
prelude *n* giriş
premature *adj* erken
premeditate *v* tasarlamak
premeditation *n* kasıt
premier *adj* birinci
premise *n* arazi
premises *n* arazi
premonition *n* önsezi

P

preoccupation *n* tasa
preoccupy *v* işgal etmek
preparation *n* hazırlık
prepare *v* hazırlamak
preposition *n* ilgeç
prerequisite *n* önkoşul
prerogative *n* ayrıcalık
prescribe *v* emretmek
prescription *n* talimat
presence *n* varlık
present *n* hediye
present *adj* şimdiki
present *v* sunmak
presentation *n* sunum
preserve *v* saklamak
preside *v* nezaret etmek
presidency *n* başkanlık
president *n* başkan
press *n* basın; basımevi
press *v* baskı yapmak
pressing *adj* acil; sıkışık
pressure *v* sıkıştırmak
pressure *n* basınç
prestige *n* prestij
presume *v* zannetmek
presumption *n* zan
presuppose *v* varsaymak
presupposition *n* varsayılan
pretend *v* yapar görünmek
pretense *n* hile
pretension *n* iddia
pretty *adj* güzel

prevail *v* yenmek
prevalent *adj* yaygın
prevent *v* önlemek
prevention *n* önleme
preventive *adj* önleyici
preview *n* önizleme
previous *adj* önceki
previously *adv* önceden
prey *n* av
price *n* fiyat
pricey *adj* pahalı
prick *v* delmek
pride *n* gurur
priest *n* rahip
priestess *n* rahibe
priesthood *n* papazlık
primacy *n* üstünlük
primarily *adv* başlıca
prime *adj* asıl
primitive *adj* ilkel
prince *n* prens
princess *n* prenses
principal *adj* başlıca
principle *n* ilke
print *v* çıktı almak
print *n* çıktı
printer *n* yazıcı
printing *n* basma
prior *adj* evvel
priority *n* öncelik
prism *n* prizma
prison *n* hapis

prisoner *n* tutsak
privacy *n* gizlilik
private *adj* özel
privilege *n* imtiyaz
prize *n* ödül
probability *n* ihtimal
probable *adj* olası
probe *v* araştırmak
probing *n* sınama
problem *n* sorun
problematic *adj* sorunlu
procedure *n* prosedür
proceed *v* ileri gitmek
proceedings *n* takibat
proceeds *n* hasılat
process *v* işleme tabi tutmak
process *n* süreç
procession *n* kafile
proclaim *v* beyan etmek
proclamation *n* ilan
procrastinate *v* ertelemek
procreate *v* doğurmak
procure *v* edinmek
prod *v* dürtmek
prodigious *adj* olağanüstü
prodigy *n* harika
produce *v* üretmek
produce *n* ürün
product *n* ürün; çarpım
production *n* üretim
productive *adj* üretken
profane *adj* kafir

profess *v* itiraf etmek
profession *n* uğraş
professional *adj* profesyonel
professor *n* profesör
proficiency *n* ehliyet
proficient *adj* mahir
profile *n* belgi
profit *v* kar etmek
profit *n* kar
profitable *adj* kar getiren
profound *adj* önemli
program *v* programlamak
program *n* program
programmer *n* programcı
progress *v* ilerlemek
progress *n* ilerleme
progressive *adj* aşamalı
prohibit *v* menetmek
prohibition *n* yasak
project *v* proje yapmak
project *n* proje
projectile *n* itici
prologue *n* öndeyiş
prolong *v* uzatmak
promenade *n* gezinti
prominent *adj* ileri gelen
promiscuous *adj* karmakarışık
promise *n* vaat
promote *v* terfi ettirmek
promotion *n* terfi
prompt *adj* çabuk
prone *adj* eğilimli

P

pronoun *n* adıl, zamir
pronounce *v* telaffuz etmek
proof *n* kanıt
propaganda *n* propaganda
propagate *v* yaymak
propel *v* sürmek
propensity *n* eğilim
proper *adj* düzgün; uygun
properly *adv* uygun şekilde
property *n* mal
prophecy *n* kehanet
prophet *n* peygamber
proportion *n* oran
proposal *n* teklif
propose *v* teklif etmek
proposition *n* teşebbüs
prose *n* düzyazı
prosecute *v* dava açmak
prosecutor *n* savcı
prospect *n* umut
prosper *v* gelişmek
prosperity *n* refah
prosperous *adj* başarılı
prostate *n* prostat
prostrate *adj* bitkin
protect *v* korumak
protection *n* koruma
protein *n* protein
protest *v* protesto etmek
protest *n* protesto
protocol *n* protokol
prototype *n* ön ürün

protract *v* uzatmak
protracted *adj* uzatılmış
protrude *v* pırtlamak
proud *adj* gururlu
proudly *adv* gurulu biçimde
prove *v* kanıtlamak
proven *adj* kanıtlanmış
proverb *n* atasözü
provide *v* sağlamak
providence *n* basiret
providing that *c* şartıyla
province *n* vilayet
provision *n* karşılık
provisional *adj* geçici
provocation *n* korkutma
provoke *v* kışkırtmak
prow *n* pruva
prowler *n* serseri
proximity *n* yakınlık
proxy *n* vekaletname
prudence *n* sağgörü
prudent *adj* akıllı
prune *v* budamak
prune *n* kuru erik
prurient *adj* şehvet düşkünü
pseudonym *n* rumuz
psychiatrist *n* psikiyatrist
psychiatry *n* psikiyatri
psychic *adj* psişik
psychology *n* psikoloji
psychopath *n* psikopat
puberty *n* buluğ

public *adj* genel
publication *n* yayın
publicity *n* reklam
publicly *adv* alenen
publish *v* basmak
publisher *n* yayımcı
pudding *n* muhallebi
puerile *adj* çocukça
puff *n* üfürük
puffy *adj* kabarık
pull *v* çekmek
pull ahead *v* önüne geçmek
pull down *v* yıkmak
pull out *v* uzaklaşmak
pulley *n* makara
pulp *n* ezme
pulpit *n* kürsü
pulsate *v* sıçramak
pulse *n* nabız
pulverize *v* yenmek
pump *v* emmek
pump *n* pompa
pumpkin *n* bal kabağı
punch *v* yumruklamak
punch *n* zımba; kuvvet
punctual *adj* dakik
puncture *n* delik; patlama
punish *v* cezalandırmak
punishable *adj* cezalandırılabilir
punishment *n* ceza
pupil *n* öğrenci
puppet *n* kukla

puppy *n* köpek yavrusu
purchase *v* kazanmak
purchase *n* iştira; alınım
pure *adj* saf
puree *n* püre
purgatory *n* araf
purge *n* tasfiye
purge *v* temizlemek
purification *n* arındırma
purify *v* durulamak
purity *n* saflık
purple *adj* mor
purpose *n* amaç
purposely *adv* kasten
purse *n* cüzdan
pursue *v* kovalamak
pursuit *n* kovalama
pus *n* iltihap
push *v* itmek
pushy *adj* aceleci
put *iv* koymak
put aside *v* saklamak
put away *v* bir kenera bırakmak
put off *v* ertelemek
put out *v* söndürmek
put up *v* misafir etmek
put up with *v* dayanmak
putrid *adj* kokmuş
puzzle *n* bilmece
puzzling *adj* şaşırtıcı
pyramid *n* piramid
python *n* piton

P

quagmire *n* batak
quail *n* sinmek
quake *v* sallanmak
qualify *v* hak kazanmak
quality *n* nitelik
qualm *n* umutsuzluk
quandary *n* tereddüt
quantity *n* nicelik
quarrel *v* kavga etmek
quarrel *n* kavga
quarrelsome *adj* kavgacı
quarry *n* taş ocağı
quarter *n* çeyrek
quarterly *adj* üç ayda bir
quarters *n* kışla
quash *v* iptal etmek
queen *n* kraliçe
queer *adj* garip
quell *v* bastırmak
quench *v* tatmin etmek
quest *n* araştırma
question *v* sorgulamak
question *n* soru
questionable *adj* sorgulanabilir
questionnaire *n* anket
queue *n* sıra
quick *adj* çabuk
quicken *v* hızlandırmak
quickly *adv* acele

quicksand *n* bataklık
quiet *adj* sessiz
quietness *n* sessizlik
quilt *n* yorgan
quit *iv* çıkmak
quite *adv* oldukça
quiver *v* ürpermek
quiz *v* sınav
quotation *n* alıntı
quote *v* alıntı yapmak
quotient *n* bölüm

rabbi *n* haham
rabbit *n* tavşan
rabies *n* kuduz
raccoon *n* rakun
race *v* yarışmak
race *n* yarış; ırk
racism *n* ırkçılık
racist *adj* ırkçı
racket *n* raket; gürültü
racketeering *n* gangsterlik
radar *n* radar
radiation *n* radyasyon
radiator *n* radyatör
radical *adj* radikal

radio *n* radyo
radish *n* turp
radius *n* yarıçap
raffle *n* piyango
raft *n* sal
rag *n* bez
rage *n* öfke
ragged *adj* yırtık pırtık
raid *n* baskın; akın
raid *v* baskın yapmak
raider *n* baskıncı
rail *n* ray
railroad *n* demir yolu
rain *n* yağmur
rain *v* yağmur yağmak
rainbow *n* gökkuşağı
raincoat *n* yağmurluk
rainfall *n* sağanak
rainy *adj* yağmurlu
raise *n* artış
raise *v* arttırmak
raisin *n* kuru üzüm
rake *n* tarak; tırmık
rally *n* ralli; miting
ram *n* koç; çekiç
ram *v* dövmek
ramification *n* dallanma
ramp *n* rampa
rampage *v* öfkelenmek
rampant *adj* şahlanmış
ranch *n* hayvan çiftliği
rancor *n* garez

randomly *adv* rastgele
range *n* saha; dağ sırası
rank *n* rütbe
rank *v* düzenlemek
ransack *v* yoklamak
ransom *v* fidye ile kurtarmak
ransom *n* sarımsak
rape *v* tecavüz etmek
rape *n* şalgam
rapid *adj* hızlı
rapist *n* tecavüzcü
rapport *n* ahenk; yakınlık
rare *adj* nadir
rarely *adv* nadiren
rascal *n* yaramaz kimse
rash *v* çekip almak
rash *n* atak
raspberry *n* ahududu
rat *n* sıçan
rate *v* oranlamak
rate *n* hız; oran
rather *adv* oldukça
ratification *n* onaylama
ratify *v* onaylamak
ratio *n* oran
ration *v* karne ile vermek
ration *n* hisse
rational *adj* rasyonel
rationalize *v* bahane bulmak
rattle *v* tıkırdamak
ravage *v* harap etmek
ravage *n* yıkım

R

rave *v* çıldırmak
raven *n* kuzgun
ravine *n* geçit
raw *adj* çiğ
ray *n* ışın
raze *v* tahrip etmek
razor *n* jilet
reach *v* uzatmak
reach *n* görüş sahası
react *v* tepki vermek
reaction *n* tepki
read *iv* okumak
reader *n* okuyucu
readiness *n* gönüllülük
reading *n* okuma; anlam
ready *adj* hazır
real *adj* gerçek
realism *n* gerçekçilik
reality *n* hakikat
realize *v* farkına varmak
really *adv* gerçekten
realm *n* memleket
realty *n* emlak
reap *v* biçmek
reappear *v* tekrar belirmek
rear *v* yetiştirmek
rear *n* geri
rear *adj* art
reason *v* sonuç çıkarmak
reason *n* sebep
reasonable *adj* makul
reasoning *n* muhakeme

reassure *v* güven vermek
rebate *n* indirim
rebel *v* isyan etmek
rebel *n* isyancı
rebellion *n* isyan
rebirth *n* yeniden doğuş
rebound *v* yansımak
rebuff *v* reddetmek
rebuff *n* azarlama
rebuild *v* tekrar inşa etmek
rebuke *v* azarlamak
rebuke *n* azar
rebut *v* çürütmek
recall *v* anımsamak
recant *v* caymak
recap *v* özetlemek
recapture *v* yeniden ele geçirmek
recede *v* çekilmek
receipt *n* fatura
receive *v* almak
recent *adj* geçmiş
reception *n* resepsiyon
receptionist *n* resepsiyoncu
receptive *adj* kavrayışlı
recess *n* çekilmek
recession *n* geri çekilme
recharge *v* şarj etmek
recipe *n* yemek tarifi
reciprocal *adj* karşılıklı
recital *n* ifade
recite *v* nakletmek
reckless *adj* umursamaz

R

reckon *v* farz etmek
reckon on *v* bel bağlamak
reclaim *v* geri istemek
recline *v* dayanmak
recluse *n* münzevi
recognition *n* tanıma; kabul
recognize *v* tanımak
recollect *v* anımsamak
recollection *n* anılar
recommend *v* önermek
recompense *n* mükafat
reconcile *v* uzlaştırmak
reconsider *v* yeniden düşünmek
reconstruct *v* yeniden inşa etmek
record *v* kaydetmek
record *n* plak; belge
recorder *n* kaydedici
recording *n* kayıt
recount *n* nakletmek
recoup *v* telafi etmek
recourse *v* başvurmak
recourse *n* başvuru
recover *v* kurtarmak
recovery *n* iyileşme
recreate *v* ihya etmek
recreation *n* rekreasyon
recruit *v* işe almak
recruit *n* acemi asker
recruitment *n* personel alma
rectangle *n* dikdörtgen
rectangular *adj* dikdörtgen
rectify *v* ıslah etmek

rector *n* rektör
rectum *n* rektum
recuperate *v* iyileşmek
recur *v* nüksetmek
recurrence *n* tekerrür
recycle *v* geri kazanmak
red *adj* kırmızı
red tape *n* bürokrasi
redden *v* kırmızılaşmak
redeem *v* kefaret vermek
redemption *n* itfa
red-hot *adj* çok hevesli
redo *v* tekrar yapmak
redouble *v* yoğunlaştırmak
redress *v* doğrultmak
reduce *v* azaltmak
redundant *adj* ağdalı
reed *n* saz
reef *n* resif
reel *n* makara; tura
reelect *v* yeniden seçmek
reenactment *n* yeniden sahneleme
reentry *n* yeniden girme
refer to *v* tekabül etmek
referee *n* hakem
reference *n* referans
referendum *n* referandum
refill *v* tekrar doldurmak
refinance *v* yeniden finanse etmek
refine *v* rafine etmek

R

refinery *n* rafineri
reflect *v* yansıtmak
reflection *n* yansıtma
reflexive *adj* dönüşlü
reform *v* ıslahat; reform
reform *n* reform
refrain *v* kaçınmak
refresh *v* yenilemek
refreshing *adj* tazeleyici
refreshment *n* soğuk içecek
refrigerate *v* soğutmak
refuel *v* yakıt almak
refuge *n* sığınak
refugee *n* mülteci
refund *v* geri ödemek
refund *n* geri ödeme
refurbish *v* yeniden cilalamak
refusal *n* geri çevirme
refuse *v* reddetmek
refuse *n* ret
refute *v* yalanlamak
regal *adj* krala ait
regard *v* saymak
regarding *pre* hakkında
regardless *adv* bakmaksızın
regards *n* saygılar
regeneration *n* rejenerasyon
regent *n* kral vekili
regime *n* rejim
regiment *n* alay
region *n* bölge
regional *adj* bölgesel

register *v* kaydolmak
registration *n* kayıt
regret *v* pişman olmak
regret *n* pişmanlık
regrettable *adj* üzücü
regularity *n* düzen
regularly *adv* düzenli şekilde
regulate *v* düzenlemek
regulation *n* düzenleme
rehabilitate *v* tamir etmek
rehearsal *n* prova
rehearse *v* prova etmek
reign *n* saltanat
reimburse *v* iade etmek
reimbursement *n* iade
rein *v* dizginlemek
rein *n* dizgin
reindeer *n* Ren geyiği
reinforce *v* takviye etmek
reinforcements *n* takviye
reiterate *v* yinelemek
reject *v* reddetmek
rejection *n* ret
rejoice *v* çok sevinmek
rejoin *v* yeniden katılmak
rejuvenate *v* gençleştirmek
relapse *n* kötüye gitmek
related *adj* ilişkili
relationship *n* ilişki
relative *adj* göreli
relative *n* akraba
relax *v* rahatlamak

relaxation *n* rahatlama
relaxing *adj* rahatlatıcı
relay *v* anahtarlamak
release *v* yayımlamak
relegate *v* göndermek
relent *v* yumuşamak
relentless *adj* amansız
relevant *adj* yerinde
reliable *adj* güvenilir
reliance *n* itimat
relic *n* kalıntı
relief *n* ferahlama
relieve *v* ferahlamak
religion *n* din
religious *adj* dindar
relinquish *v* feragat etmek
relish *v* lezzet vermek
relive *v* tekrar yaşamak
relocate *v* yer değiştirmek
relocation *n* yerleşme
reluctant *adj* gönülsüz
reluctantly *adv* gönülsüzlükle
rely on *v* itimat etmek
remain *v* kalmak
remainder *n* kalıntı
remaining *adj* geri kalan
remains *n* ceset
remake *v* tekrar yapmak
remark *v* açıklamak
remark *n* açıklama
remarkable *adj* dikkate değer
remarry *v* tekrar evlenmek

remedy *v* deva olmak
remedy *n* deva
remember *v* hatırlamak
remembrance *n* anma
remind *v* hatırlatmak
reminder *n* hatırlatma
remission *n* hafifletme
remit *v* vazgeçmek
remittance *n* havale
remnant *n* kalıntı
remodel *v* tadilat yapmak
remorse *n* vicdan azabı
remorseful *adj* çok pişman
remote *adj* uzak
removal *n* kaldırma
remove *v* çıkarmak
remunerate *v* hakkını vermek
renew *v* yenileştirmek
renewal *n* yenileme
renounce *v* vazgeçmek
renovate *v* yenilemek
renovation *n* yenileme
renowned *adj* yenilenmiş
rent *v* kiralamak
rent *n* kira
reorganize *v* ıslah etmek
repair *v* onarmak
reparation *n* tamirat
repatriate *v* ülkesine iade etmek
repay *v* ödemek
repayment *n* iade
repeal *v* feshetmek

repeal *n* feshetme
repeat *v* tekrarlamak
repel *v* geri atmak
repent *v* pişman olmak
repentance *n* pişmanlık
repetition *n* tekrar
replace *v* yerine koymak
replacement *n* ikame
replay *n* tekrar
replenish *v* ikmal etmek
replete *adj* dolgun
replica *n* kopya
replicate *v* yinelemek
reply *v* cevaplamak
reply *n* cevap
report *v* anlatmak
report *n* rapor
reportedly *adv* söylendiğine göre
reporter *n* muhbir
repose *v* yatmak
repose *n* istirahat
represent *v* temsil etmek
repress *v* bastırmak
repression *n* baskı
reprieve *n* cezanın tecili
reprint *v* suret çıkarmak
reprint *n* yeni baskı
reprisal *n* misilleme
reproach *v* iftira etmek
reproach *n* ayıp
reproduce *v* tekrarlamak
reproduction *n* eserin kopyası

reptile *n* sürüngen
republic *n* cumhuriyet
repudiate *v* reddetmek
repugnant *adj* iğrenç
repulse *v* defetmek
repulse *n* kovma
repulsive *adj* tiksindirici
reputation *n* ün
reputedly *adv* sözde
request *v* talep etmek
request *n* istek
require *v* gerekmek
requirement *n* gereklilik
rescue *v* kurtarmak
rescue *n* kurtarma
research *v* araştırmak
research *n* araştırma
resemblance *n* benzerlik
resemble *v* benzemek
resent *v* içerlemek
resentment *n* gücenme
reservation *n* rezervasyon
reserve *v* ayırmak
reservoir *n* sarnıç; depo
reside *v* ikamet etmek
residence *n* ikametgah
residue *n* bakiye; kalıntı
resign *v* terk etmek
resignation *n* istifa
resilient *adj* esnek
resist *v* dayanmak
resistance *n* dayanıklılık

R

resolute *adj* kararlı
resolution *n* çözünürlük
resolve *v* çözmek
resort *v* müracaat etmek
resounding *adj* çınlayan
resource *n* kaynak
respect *v* saygı duymak
respect *n* saygı
respectful *adj* saygılı
respective *adj* ayrı ayrı
respiration *n* solunum
respite *n* ertelemek
respond *v* cevap vermek
response *n* cevap
responsibility *n* sorumluluk
responsible *adj* sorumlu
responsive *adj* hevesli
rest *v* dinlenmek
rest *n* istirahat
rest room *n* tuvalet
restaurant *n* restaurant
restful *adj* dinlendirici
restitution *n* onarma
restless *adj* huzursuz
restoration *n* onarma
restore *v* onarmak
restrain *v* geri tutmak
restraint *n* yasaklama
restrict *v* kısmak
result *n* sonuç
resume *v* devam etmek
resumption *n* geri alma

resurface *v* ortaya çıkmak
resurrection *n* diriliş
resuscitate *v* ölüyü diriltmek
retain *v* alıkoymak
retaliate *v* kısas etmek
retaliation *n* misilleme
retarded *adj* gecikmiş
retention *n* alıkoyma
retire *v* emekli olmak
retirement *n* emeklilik; inziva
retract *v* geri çekmek
retreat *v* geri adım atmak
retreat *n* sığınak; tenha yer
retrieval *n* bulup getirme
retrieve *v* erişmek
retroactive *adj* geçmişe dönük
return *v* geri dönmek
return *n* dönüş
reunion *n* kavuşma
reveal *v* açığa çıkarmak
revealing *adj* açıkta bırakan
revel *v* eğlenmek
revelation *n* ifşa
revenge *v* öç almak
revenge *n* öç
revenue *n* ciro
reverence *n* saygı göstermek
reversal *n* tersine çevirme
reverse *n* feshetmek
reversible *adj* dönüşür
revert *v* dönmek
review *v* gözden geçirmek

R

review *n* teftiş; eleştiri
revise *v* düzeltmek
revision *n* düzeltme
revive *v* canlandırmak
revoke *v* geçersiz kılmak
revolt *v* isyan etmek
revolt *n* isyan
revolting *adj* tiksindirici
revolve *v* döndürmek
revolver *v* tabanca
revue *n* revü
revulsion *n* tiksinti
reward *v* ödüllendirmek
reward *n* ödül
rewarding *adj* tatmin edici
rheumatism *n* romatizma
rhinoceros *n* gergedan
rhyme *n* kafiye
rhythm *n* ritm
rib *n* kaburga
ribbon *n* kurdela
rice *n* pirinç
rich *adj* zengin
rid of *iv* kurtulmak
riddle *n* bilmece
ride *iv* sürmek
ridge *n* bayır
ridicule *v* dalga geçmek
ridicule *n* alay
ridiculous *adj* saçma
rifle *n* tüfek
rift *n* yarık

right *adv* sağda
right *adj* sağ; doğru
right *n* doğru
rigid *adj* bükülmez, sert
rigor *n* sertlik
rim *n* kenar; tekerlek
ring *iv* çaldırmak
ring *n* yüzük; halka
ringleader *n* elebaşı
rinse *v* durulamak
riot *v* başkaldırmak
riot *n* başkaldırı, isyan
rip *v* parçalamak
rip apart *v* parçalara ayırmak
rip off *v* yürütmek
ripe *adj* olgun
ripen *v* olgunlaştırmak
ripple *n* çağıldamak
rise *iv* yükselmek
risk *v* riske atmak
risk *n* risk
risky *adj* riskli
rite *n* tören
rival *n* rakip
rivalry *n* rekabet
river *n* nehir
rivet *v* perçinlemek
riveting *adj* çok ilginç
road *n* yol
roam *v* dolaşmak
roar *v* kükremek
roar *n* gürleme

R

roast *v* kavurmak
roast *n* rosto
rob *v* soymak
robber *n* soyguncu
robbery *n* hırsızlık
robe *n* elbise
robust *adj* sağlam
rock *v* sallamak
rock *n* kaya
rocket *n* roket
rocky *adj* kayalık
rod *n* çubuk
rodent *n* kemirgen
roll *v* rulo yapmak
roll *n* rulo; top
romance *n* aşk hikayesi
roof *n* çatı
room *n* oda; yer
roomy *adj* ferah
rooster *n* horoz
root *n* kök
rope *n* ip
rosary *n* tesbih
rose *n* gül
rosy *adj* pembe
rot *v* çürümek
rot *n* çürümüş
rotate *v* döndürmek
rotation *n* rotasyon
rotten *adj* çürümüş
rough *adj* kaba
round *adj* yuvarlak

roundup *n* toparlama
rouse *v* kaldırmak
rousing *adj* hareketlendirici
route *n* rota
routine *n* rutin
row *v* kürek çekmek
row *n* kürek
rowdy *adj* gürültücü
royal *adj* krala ait
royalty *n* krallık
rub *v* ovalamak
rubber *n* kauçuk
rubbish *n* çöp
rubble *n* moloz
ruby *n* yakut
rudder *n* dümen
rude *adj* terbiyesiz
rudeness *n* terbiyesizlik
rudimentary *adj* temel
rug *n* halı
ruin *v* mahvetmek
ruin *n* harabe
rule *v* yönetmek
rule *n* yönetim
ruler *n* cetvel; hükümdar
rum *n* rom
rumble *v* gürüldemek
rumble *n* bagaj yeri
rumor *n* söylenti
run *iv* koşmak
run away *v* kaçmak
run into *v* karşılaşmak

run out *v* eksilmek
run over *v* adam çiğnemek
run up *v* birikmek
runner *n* koşucu
runway *n* pist
rupture *n* kopma
rupture *v* koparmak
rural *adj* kırsal
ruse *n* hile
rush *v* acele etmek
Russia *n* Rusya
Russian *adj* Rus
rust *v* paslanmak
rust *n* pas
rustic *adj* kırsal
rust-proof *adj* pas tutmaz
rusty *adj* paslı
ruthless *adj* insafsız
rye *n* çavdar

R
S

S

sabotage *v* sabote etmek
sabotage *n* sabotaj
sack *v* kovmak
sack *n* çuval; işten atma
sacrament *n* ayin
sacred *adj* kutsal

sacrifice *n* kurban
sacrilege *n* kutsal eşyaya
saygısızlık
sad *adj* üzgün
sadden *v* üzmek
saddle *n* semer
sadist *n* sadist
sadness *n* elem
safe *n* kasa
safe *adj* güvenli
safeguard *n* koruyucu
safety *n* güvenlik
sail *v* yelken açmak
sail *n* yelken
sailboat *n* yelkenli
sailor *n* gemici
saint *n* aziz
salad *n* salata
salary *n* maaş
sale *n* indirim
sale slip *n* satış fişi
salesman *n* satıcı
saliva *n* salya
salmon *n* som balığı
saloon *n* meyhane
salt *n* tuz
salty *adj* tuzlu
salvage *v* mal kurtarmak
salvation *n* kurtuluş
same *adj* aynı
sample *n* örnek
sanctify *v* kutsallaştırmak

sanction *v* tasdik etmek	**savior** *n* kurtarıcı
sanction *n* tasdik	**savor** *v* zevk almak
sanctity *n* kutsallık	**saw** *iv* doğramak
sanctuary *n* tapınak	**saw** *n* testere
sand *n* kum	**say** *iv* söylemek
sandal *n* sandal	**saying** *n* deyiş
sandpaper *n* zımpara kağıdı	**scaffolding** *n* inşaat iskelesi
sandwich *n* sandviç	**scald** *v* haşlamak
sane *adj* aklı başında	**scale** *v* ölçeklemek
sanity *n* aklı başındalık	**scale** *n* pul; terazi
sap *n* dirilik	**scalp** *n* kafa derisi
sap *v* tüketmek	**scam** *n* dolandırıcılık
sapphire *n* safir	**scan** *v* taramak
sarcasm *n* istihza	**scandal** *n* skandal
sarcastic *adj* iğneleyici	**scandalize** *v* skandal çıkarmak
sardine *n* sardalya	**scapegoat** *n* günah keçisi
satanic *adj* şeytanca	**scar** *n* yara izi
satellite *n* uydu	**scarce** *adj* seyrek
satire *n* hiciv	**scarcely** *adv* nadiren
satisfaction *n* memnuniyet	**scarcity** *n* kıtlık
satisfactory *adj* hoşnut edici	**scare** *v* korkutmak
satisfy *v* tatmin etmek	**scare** *n* korku
saturate *v* doymak	**scare away** *v* korkutup kaçırmak
Saturday *n* Cumartesi	**scarf** *n* şal; atkı
sauce *n* salça; sos	**scary** *adj* korkunç
saucepan *n* tava	**scatter** *v* dağıtmak
saucer *n* çay tabağı	**scenario** *n* senaryo
sausage *n* sosis	**scene** *n* sahne; manzara
savage *adj* vahşi	**scenery** *n* manzara
savagery *n* vahşilik	**scenic** *adj* manzaralı
save *v* kurtarmak	**scent** *n* koku
savings *n* birikim	**schedule** *v* planlamak

S

schedule *n* program
scheme *n* proje
schism *n* bölünme
scholar *n* bilgin
scholarship *n* irfan
school *n* okul
science *n* bilim
scientific *adj* bilimsel
scientist *n* bilim adamı
scissors *n* makas
scoff *v* hakaret
scold *v* azarlamak
scolding *n* azar
scooter *n* skuter
scope *n* kapsam
scorch *v* yakmak
score *v* gol atmak
score *n* puan
scorn *v* hor görmek
scornful *adj* küçümseyen
scorpion *n* akrep
scoundrel *n* hergele
scour *v* ovarak temizlemek
scourge *n* kırbaçlamak
scout *n* izci
scramble *v* tırmanmak
scrambled *adj* talan edilmiş
scrap *v* ıskartaya ayırmak
scrap *n* hurda
scrape *v* kazımak
scratch *v* kaşımak
scratch *n* karalama

scream *v* çığlık atmak
scream *n* çığlık
screech *v* acı acı bağırmak
screen *n* ekran; siper
screen *v* görüntülemek
screw *v* vidalamak
screw *n* vida
screwdriver *n* tornavida
scribble *v* karalamak
script *n* betik
scroll *n* tomar
scrub *v* ovalamak
scruples *n* tereddüt
scrupulous *adj* vicdanlı
scrutiny *n* dikkatle bakma
scuffle *n* didişme
sculptor *n* heykeltıraş
sculpture *n* heykel
sea *n* deniz
seafood *n* deniz ürünleri
seagull *n* martı
seal *v* mühürlemek
seal *n* fok; mühür
seal off *v* tıkamak
seam *n* dikiş yeri
seamless *adj* kusursuz
seamstress *n* kadın terzi
search *v* aramak
search *n* arayış
seashore *n* sahil
seasick *adj* deniz tutmuş
seaside *adj* deniz kenarı

S

season *v* baharat katmak
season *n* mevsim
seasonal *adj* mevsimlik
seasoning *n* çeşnilik
seat *n* oturacak yer
seated *adj* oturan
secede *v* çekilmek
secluded *adj* tenha
seclusion *n* çekilme
second *adj* ikinci
second *n* saniye
secondary *adj* ikincil
secrecy *n* gizlilik
secret *n* gizli
secretary *n* sekreter
secretly *adv* gizlice
sect *n* mezhep
section *n* bölüm
sector *n* kesim
secure *v* korumak
secure *adj* güvenli
security *n* güvenlik
sedate *v* yatıştırmak
sedation *n* yatıştırma
seduce *v* ayartmak
seduction *n* ayartma
see *iv* görmek
seed *n* tohum
seedless *adj* çekirdeksiz
seedy *adj* kılıksız
seek *iv* aramak
seem *v* görünmek

see-through *adj* saydam
segment *n* kesim
segregate *v* ayırmak
segregation *n* fark gözetme
seize *v* ele geçirmek
seizure *n* kriz
seldom *adv* nadiren
select *v* seçmek
selection *n* seçim
self-conscious *adj* utangaç
self-esteem *n* öz benlik
self-evident *adj* besbelli
self-interest *n* kişisel çıkar
selfish *adj* bencil
selfishness *n* bencillik
self-respect *n* öz saygı
sell *iv* satmak
seller *n* satıcı
sellout *n* elden çıkarma
semblance *n* biçim
semester *n* sömestre
seminary *n* ilahiyat fakültesi
senate *n* senato
senator *n* senatör
send *iv* göndermek
sender *n* gönderen
senile *adj* bunak
senior *adj* kıdemli
seniority *n* kıdem
sensation *n* sansasyon
sense *v* algılamak
sense *n* duyu; zeka

S

senseless *adj* saçma
sensible *adj* mantıklı
sensitive *adj* hassas
sensual *adj* tensel
sentence *v* mahkum etmek
sentence *n* cümle; hüküm
sentiment *n* duygu
sentimental *adj* duygusal
sentry *n* nöbetçi
separate *v* ayırmak
separate *adj* ayrı
separation *n* ayırma
September *n* Eylül
sequel *n* devam
sequence *n* ardışıklık
serenade *n* serenat
serene *adj* dingin
serenity *n* dinginlik
sergeant *n* çavuş
series *n* dizi
serious *adj* ciddi; tehlikeli
seriousness *n* ciddiyet
sermon *n* vaaz
serpent *n* yılan
serum *n* serum
servant *n* hizmetçi
serve *v* hizmet etmek
service *n* servis
service *v* hizmet vermek
session *n* sezon
set *n* küme
set *iv* kurmak

set about *v* girişmek
set off *v* yola çıkmak
set out *v* koyulmak
set up *v* kurmak
setback *n* aksama
setting *n* ayar
settle *v* yerleşmek
settle down *v* dibe oturmak
settle for *v* razı olmak
settlement *n* yerleşim
settler *n* göçmen
setup *n* düzenek
seven *adj* yedi
seventeen *adj* on yedi
seventh *adj* yedinci
seventy *adj* yetmiş
sever *v* kesmek
several *adj* birçok
severance *n* kesme
severe *adj* haşin
severity *n* zorluk
sew *v* dikmek
sewage *n* lağım suyu
sewer *n* kanalizasyon
sewing *n* dikim
sex *n* cinsel ilişki
sexuality *n* cinsellik
shabby *adj* pejmürde
shack *n* baraka
shackle *n* engel
shade *n* gölge; göz siperi
shadow *n* gölge

shady *adj* gölgeli
shake *iv* sarsmak
shaken *adj* sarsılmış
shaky *adj* titrek
shallow *adj* sığ
sham *n* yapmacık
shame *v* utanmak
shame *n* utanç
shameful *adj* utanç verici
shameless *adj* utanmaz
shape *v* şekillendirmek
shape *n* şekil
share *v* paylaşmak
share *n* paylaşım; hisse
shareholder *n* hissedar
shark *n* köpek balığı
sharp *adj* keskin; kurnaz
sharpen *v* bilemek
sharpener *n* kalemtıraş
shatter *v* mahvetmek
shattering *adj* yıkıcı
shave *v* traş olmak
she *pro* o kız
shear *iv* kaykılma
shed *n* akıtmak
shed *iv* dökmek
sheep *n* koyun
sheet *n* çarşaf; yaprak
sheets *n* yelken iskotası
shelf *n* sergen; raf
shell *v* soymak
shell *n* kabuk

shellfish *n* su kabuklusu
shelter *v* sığınmak
shelter *n* sığınak
shelves *n* kaya tabakası
shepherd *n* çoban
sherry *n* şeri
shield *v* kalkan
shield *n* siper etmek
shift *n* kayma; hile
shift *v* ötelemek
shine *n* parıltı
shine *iv* parlatmak
shiny *adj* parlak
ship *v* nakletmek
ship *n* gemi
shipment *n* nakliyat
shipwreck *n* gemi enkazı
shipyard *n* tersane
shirk *v* yan çizmek
shirt *n* gömlek
shiver *v* ürpermek
shiver *n* ürperti
shock *v* şoke olmak
shock *n* şok; darbe
shocking *adj* inanılmaz
shoddy *adj* kalitesiz
shoe *n* ayakkabı
shoe polish *n* ayakkabı cilası
shoe store *n* ayakkabıcı
shoelace *n* ayakkabı bağı
shoot *iv* kurşun atmak
shoot down *v* ateş edip
   düşürmek

S

shop v alışveriş yapmak
shop n dükkan
shoplifting n mal aşırma
shopping n alışveriş yapmak
shore n sahil
short adj kısa; parasız
shortage n eksiklik
shortcoming n noksan
shortcut n kestirme
shorten v kısaltmak
shorthand n steno
short-lived adj kısa ömürlü
shortly adv kısa sürede
shorts n şort
shortsighted adj miyop
shot n atış; iğne
shotgun n av tüfeği
shoulder n omuz
shout v bağırmak
shout n bağırış
shouting n feryat
shove v sokmak
shove n itiş
shovel v küreklemek
shovel n kürek
show iv göstermek
show off v gösteriş yapmak
show up v ortaya çıkmak
showdown n hesaplaşma
shower n duş
shrapnel n şarapnel
shred v kıymak

shred n ince şerit
shrewd adj kurnaz
shriek v çığlık atmak
shriek n feryat
shrimp n karides
shrine n tapınak
shrink iv küçültmek
shroud n kefen
shrouded adj örtülü
shrub n çalılık
shrug v omuz silkmek
shudder n ürperti
shudder v ürpermek
shuffle v karıştırmak
shun v uzak durmak
shut iv kapatmak
shut off v durdurmak
shut up v ağzını kapamak
shuttle v mekik dokumak
shy adj utangaç
shyness n çekingenlik
sick adj hasta
sicken v tiksindirmek
sickening adj tiksindirici
sickle n orak
sickness n kusma
side n yan; taraf
sideburns n favori
sidestep v yan çizmek
sidewalk n kaldırım
sideways adv yandan
siege n kuşatma

siege *v* kuşatmak
sift *v* elemek
sigh *n* iç çekme
sigh *v* iç çekmek
sight *n* görüş
sightseeing *v* gezi
sign *v* işaret etmek
sign *n* işaret; levha
signal *v* sinyal vermek
signal *n* sinyal
signature *n* imza
significance *n* önem
significant *adj* önemli
signify *v* anlamına gelmek
silence *n* sessizlik
silence *v* susmak
silent *adj* sessiz
silhouette *n* silüet
silk *n* ipek
silly *adj* aptal
silver *n* gümüş
silver-plated *adj* gümüş kaplama
silversmith *n* gümüşçü
silverware *n* gümüş eşya
similar *adj* benzer
similarity *n* benzerlik
simmer *v* kaynamak
simple *adj* kolay; sade
simplicity *n* sadelik
simplify *v* sadeleştirmek
simply *adv* basitçe
simulate *v* benzeştirmek

simultaneous *adj* simültane
sin *v* günaha girmek
sin *n* günah
since *c* olduğundan
since *pre* den beri
since then *adv* o gün bugündür
sincere *adj* samimi
sincerity *n* samimiyet
sinful *adj* günahkar
sing *iv* şarkı söylemek
singer *n* şarkıcı
single *n* tek
single *adj* bekar; tek
singlehanded *adj* tek elli
single-minded *adj* hilesiz
singular *adj* tekil
sinister *adj* netameli
sink *n* lavabo
sink *iv* batmak
sink in *v* nüfuz etmek
sinner *n* günahkar
sip *v* yudumlamak
sip *n* yudum
sir *n* beyefendi
siren *n* siren
sirloin *n* sığır filetosu
sissy *adj* hanım evladı
sister *n* abla
sister-in-law *n* görümce
sit *iv* oturmak
site *n* site
sitting *n* oturma

S

situated *adj* bulunan
situation *n* durum
six *adj* altı
sixteen *adj* on altı
sixth *adj* altıncı
sixty *adj* altmış
sizable *adj* oldukça büyük
size *n* ölçü
size up *v* ölçüp biçmek
skate *v* paten kaymak
skate *n* paten
skeleton *n* iskelet
skeptic *adj* kuşkucu, şüpheci
sketch *v* taslak çizmek
sketch *n* taslak
sketchy *adj* kabataslak
ski *v* kayak yapmak
skill *n* beceri
skillful *adj* becerikli
skim *v* sıyırmak
skin *v* soymak
skin *n* deri
skinny *adj* sıska
skip *v* sıçramak
skip *n* sıçrama
skirmish *n* çarpışma
skirt *n* etek
skull *n* kafatası
sky *n* gökyüzü
skylight *n* dam penceresi
skyscraper *n* gökdelen
slab *n* taraça

slack *adj* özensiz
slacken *v* yavaşlatmak
slacks *n* bol pantolon
slam *v* yenmek
slander *n* iftira
slanted *adj* eğik
slap *n* tokat
slap *v* tokatlamak
slash *n* eğik çizgi
slash *v* indirmek
slate *n* kayrak
slaughter *v* katletmek
slaughter *n* katliam
slave *n* köle
slavery *n* kölelik
slay *iv* öldürmek
sleazy *adj* çürük
sleep *iv* uyumak
sleep *n* uyku
sleeve *n* elbise kolu
sleeveless *adj* kolsuz
sleigh *n* kızak
slender *adj* narin
slice *v* dilimlemek
slice *n* dilim
slide *iv* kaymak
slightly *adv* birazcık
slim *adj* zayıf; ince uzun
slip *v* kaymak
slip *n* fiş; külot
slipper *n* terlik
slippery *adj* kaygan

S

slit *iv* yarmak
slob *adj* serseri
slogan *n* slogan
slope *n* yamaç
sloppy *adj* yarım yamalak
slot *n* dar uzun delik
slow *adj* yavaş
slow down *v* yavaşlamak
slow motion *n* ağır çekim
slowly *adv* yavaşça
sluggish *adj* durgun
slum *n* harabe
slump *v* çöküvermek
slump *n* düşüş
slur *v* aşağılamak
sly *adj* kurnaz
smack *n* tokat
smack *v* tokat atmak
small *adj* küçük
smallpox *n* çiçek hastalığı
smart *adj* akıllı
smash *v* sert vurmak
smear *n* leke
smear *v* sürmek
smell *n* koku
smell *iv* koklamak
smelly *adj* pis kokulu
smile *v* gülümsemek
smile *n* gülümseme
smith *n* nalbant
smoke *v* sigara içmek
smoked *adj* füme

smoker *n* sigara içen
smoking gun *n* açık delil
smooth *v* düzleştirmek
smooth *adj* pürüzsüz
smoothly *adv* pürüzsüzce
smoothness *n* pürüzsüzlük
smother *v* boğmak
smuggler *n* kaçakçı
snack *n* aperatif
snack *v* hafif şeyler yemek
snail *n* salyangoz
snake *n* yılan
snap *v* çıtırdatmak; şakırdatmak
snapshot *n* enstantane
snare *v* tuzağa düşürmek
snare *n* tuzak
snatch *v* kapmak
sneak *v* sinsice ilerlemek
sneeze *v* aksırmak
sneeze *n* aksırık
sniff *v* koklamak
sniper *n* keskin nişancı
snitch *v* çalmak
snooze *v* uyuklamak
snore *v* horlamak
snore *n* horultu
snow *v* kar yağmak
snow *n* kar
snowfall *n* kar yağışı
snowflake *n* kar tanesi
snub *v* hiçe saymak
snub *n* kötü muamele

S

soak *v* suya bastırmak
soak in *v* emmek
soak up *v* ıslanmak
soar *v* hızla yükselmek
sob *v* hıçkırarak ağlamak
sob *n* hıçkırık
sober *adj* ayık
so-called *adj* sözde
sociable *adj* sosyal
socialism *n* sosyalizm
socialist *adj* sosyalist
socialize *v* sosyalleşmek
society *n* topluluk
sock *n* çorap
sod *n* çim
soda *n* gazoz
sofa *n* kanepe
soft *adj* yumuşak
soften *v* yumuşatmak
softly *adv* yumuşakça
softness *n* yumuşaklık
soggy *adj* sırsıklam
soil *v* kirletmek
soil *n* toprak
soiled *adj* lekelenmiş
solace *n* teselli
solar *adj* güneşe ait
solder *v* lehimlemek
soldier *n* asker
sold-out *adj* satılıp biten
sole *n* taban
sole *adj* tek

solely *adv* yalnızca
solemn *adj* ağırbaşlı
solicit *v* rica etmek
solid *adj* sert; somut
solidarity *n* dayanışma
solitary *adj* yalnız
solitude *n* yalnızlık
soluble *adj* çözünür
solution *n* çözüm
solve *v* çözmek
solvent *adj* çözücü
somber *adj* kasvetli
some *adj* biraz
somebody *pro* birisi; birileri
someday *adv* bir gün
somehow *adv* bir şekilde
someone *pro* birine; birini
something *pro* bir şey
sometimes *adv* bazen
someway *adv* her nasılsa
somewhat *adv* bir nebze
son *n* oğul
song *n* şarkı
son-in-law *n* damat
soon *adv* yakında
soothe *v* sakinleştirmek
sorcerer *n* sihirbaz
sorcery *n* büyücülük
sore *n* ağrıyan
sore *adj* hassas
sorrow *n* keder
sorrowful *adj* kederli

S

sorry *adj* üzgün

sort *n* çeşit

sort out *v* seçip ayırmak

soul *n* ruh

sound *n* ses; ima

sound *v* dillendirmek

sound out *v* ağzını aramak

soup *n* çorba

sour *adj* ekşi

source *n* kaynak

south *n* güney

southbound *adv* güneye giden

southeast *n* güneydoğu

southern *adj* güneye ait

southerner *n* güneyli

southwest *n* güneybatı

souvenir *n* andaç

sovereign *adj* özerk

sovereignty *n* özerklik

soviet *adj* sovyet

sow *iv* tohum ekmek

spa *n* kaplıca

space *n* uzay; boşluk

space out *v* dalıp gitmek

spacious *adj* ferah

spade *n* kürek

Spain *n* İspanya

span *v* yayılmak

span *n* süre; genişlik

Spaniard *n* İspanyol

Spanish *adj* İspanyol

spank *v* şaplak atmak

spanking *n* şaplak atma

spare *v* ayırmak

spare *adj* yedek

spare part *n* yedek parça

sparingly *adv* tutumlu bir şekilde

spark *n* kıvılcım

spark off *v* neden olmak

spark plug *n* buji

sparkle *v* pırıldamak

sparrow *n* serçe

sparse *adj* seyrek

spasm *n* spazm

speak *iv* konuşmak

speaker *n* konuşmacı; hoparlör

spear *n* mızrak

spearhead *v* öncülük etmek

special *adj* özel

specialize *v* özelleşmek

specialty *n* uzmanlık alanı

species *n* madeni para

specific *adj* belirli

specimen *n* numune

speck *n* benek

spectacle *n* görünüş

spectator *n* seyirci

speculate *v* spekülasyon yapmak

speculation *n* spekülasyon

speech *n* konuşma

speechless *adj* dili tutulmuş

speed *iv* hız yapmak

speed *n* hız

speedily *adv* hızlıca

S

speedy *adj* hızlı
spell *iv* hecelemek
spell *n* büyü; nöbet vakti
spelling *n* belirtmek
spend *iv* harcamak
spending *n* harcama
sperm *n* sperm
sphere *n* küre
spice *n* baharat
spicy *adj* baharatlı
spider *n* örümcek
spider web *n* örümcek ağı
spill *iv* dökmek
spill *n* döküntü
spin *iv* döndürmek
spine *n* omurga
spineless *adj* cesaretsiz
spinster *n* kız kurusu
spirit *n* ruh
spiritual *adj* ruhani
spit *iv* tükürmek
spite *n* garez
spiteful *adj* garazlı
splash *v* sıçratmak
splendid *adj* şahane
splendor *n* ihtişam
splint *n* kırık çıkık
splinter *v* parçalamak
splinter *n* kıymık
split *n* yarık
split *iv* bölmek
split up *v* bölüştürmek

spoil *v* yıkmak
spoils *n* randıman
sponge *n* sünger
sponsor *n* sponsor
spontaneity *n* doğaçlama
spontaneous *adj* spontane
spooky *adj* ürkütücü
spool *n* makara
spoon *n* kaşık
spoonful *n* kaşık dolusu
sporadic *adj* tek tük
sport *n* spor
sportsman *n* sporcu
sporty *adj* sportmen
spot *v* tanımak
spot *n* leke; mevki
spotless *adj* lekesiz
spotlight *n* projektör ışığı
spouse *n* eş
sprain *v* burkmak
sprawl *v* yayılıp yatmak
spray *v* püskürtmek
spread *iv* yaymak
spring *iv* ileri atılmak
spring *n* yay; ilkbahar
springboard *n* tramplen
sprinkle *v* püskürtmek
sprout *v* filizlenmek
spruce up *v* düzenlemek
spur *v* dürtüklemek
spur *n* mahmuz
spy *v* casusluk etmek

S

spy *n* casus
squalid *adj* bakımsız
squander *v* boşa harcamak
square *adj* kare
square *n* gönye
squash *v* eşmek
squeak *v* gıcırdamak
squeaky *adj* gıcırtılı
squeamish *adj* çok titiz
squeeze *v* sıkıştırmak
squeeze in *v* sokuşturmak
squeeze up *v* sıkışmak
squid *n* mürekkep balığı
squirrel *n* sincap
stab *v* bıçaklamak
stab *n* saplama
stability *n* istikrar
stable *adj* durağan
stable *n* ahır
stack *v* istif etmek
stack *n* büyük yığın
staff *v* kadrolaşmak
staff *n* kurmay; çalışan
stage *n* sahne; posta arabası
stage *v* sahnelemek
stagger *v* tereddüt etmek
staggering *adj* çok şaşırtıcı
stagnant *adj* durgun
stagnate *v* durgunlaşmak
stagnation *n* durgunlaşma
stain *v* leke sürmek
stain *n* leke

stair *n* basamak
staircase *n* merdiven
stairs *n* merdiven
stake *v* kazığa bağlamak
stake *n* kazık; bahis
stale *adj* bayat
stalemate *n* çıkmaz
stalk *v* iz sürmek
stalk *n* azametle yürüme
stall *n* ahır; stand
stall *v* ertelemek
stammer *v* kekelemek
stamp *v* damgalamak
stamp *n* damga
stamp out *v* kökünü kazımak
stampede *n* ayaklanma
stand *iv* ayakta durmak
stand *n* duruş
stand for *v* desteklemek
stand out *v* göze çarpmak
stand up *v* ayağa kalkmak
standard *n* standart
standardize *v* standart duruma getirmek
standing *n* sabit olmak
standpoint *n* açı
standstill *adj* durgun
staple *v* zımbalamak
staple *n* zımba
stapler *n* zımba
star *n* yıldız
starch *n* nişasta

S

starchy *adj* nişastalı
stare *v* gözlerini dikmek
stark *adj* sert
start *v* başlamak
start *n* başlangıç
startle *v* korkutmak
startled *adj* korkmuş
starvation *n* açlıktan ölme
starve *v* acıkmak
state *n* durum; devlet
state *v* beyan etmek
statement *n* beyanname
station *n* istasyon
stationary *adj* durağan
stationery *n* kırtasiye
statistic *n* istatistik
statue *n* heykel
status *n* hal; medeni hal
statute *n* kanun
staunch *adj* sadık
stay *v* kalmak
stay *n* kalış
steady *adj* sabit; muntazam
steak *n* biftek
steal *iv* çalmak
stealthy *adj* gizli
steam *n* buhar
steel *n* çelik
steep *adj* sarp
stem *n* ağaç gövdesi
stem *v* başvermek
stench *n* taaffün

step *v* adım atmak
step *n* adım; basamak
step down *v* inmek
step out *v* dışarı çıkmak
step up *v* kuvvetlendirmek
stepbrother *n* üvey erkek kardeş
step-by-step *adv* adım adım
stepdaughter *n* üvey kız
stepfather *n* üvey baba
stepladder *n* ayaklı merdiven
stepmother *n* üvey anne
stepsister *n* üvey kız kardeş
stepson *n* üvey oğul
sterile *adj* steril
sterilize *v* sterilize etmek
stern *n* sandal kıçı
stern *adj* yavuz
sternly *adv* sert bir biçimde
stew *n* güveç
stewardess *n* hostes
stick *n* sopa
stick *iv* yapıştırmak
stick around *v* çakılı kalmak
stick out *v* çıkarmak
stick to *v* ayrılmamak
sticker *n* etiket
sticky *adj* yapışkan
stiff *adj* katı
stiffen *v* sertleşmek
stiffness *n* katılık
stifle *v* boğmak
stifling *adj* boğucu

still *adv* yine de
still *adj* durgun
stimulant *n* uyarıcı
stimulate *v* uyarmak
stimulus *n* uyarıcı unsur
sting *iv* sokmak
sting *n* iğne; dürtü
stinging *adj* batan
stingy *adj* cimri
stink *iv* kokmak
stink *n* pis koku
stinking *adj* pis kokan
stipulate *v* söz vermek
stir *v* karıştırmak
stir up *v* kışkırtmak
stitch *v* dikmek
stitch *n* dikiş
stock *v* depolamak
stock *n* hisse senedi
stocking *n* çorap; stoklama
stockpile *n* stok yığını
stockroom *n* mal deposu
stoic *adj* sabırlı
stomach *n* mide
stone *n* taş
stone *v* taşlamak
stool *n* iskemle
stop *v* durmak
stop *n* durak
stop by *v* uğramak
stop over *v* kısa ziyaret
storage *n* depo

store *v* depolamak
store *n* ambar
stork *n* leylek
storm *n* fırtına
stormy *adj* fırtınalı
story *n* öykü; kat
stove *n* soba
straight *adj* dümdüz
straighten out *v* düzeltmek
strain *v* germek
strain *n* germe
strained *adj* zoraki
strainer *n* süzgeç
strait *n* geçit
stranded *adj* yolda kalmış
strange *adj* garip
stranger *n* yabancı
strangle *v* boğmak
strap *n* kayış
strategy *n* strateji
straw *n* çöp
strawberry *n* çilek
stray *adj* aylak
stray *v* yoldan çıkmak
stream *n* dere; cereyan
street *n* sokak
streetcar *n* tramvay
streetlight *n* sokak lambası
strength *n* kuvvet
strengthen *v* güçlendirmek
strenuous *adj* yorucu
stress *n* gerilim; stres

S

stressful *adj* stres verici
stretch *n* hapis süresi
stretch *v* esnetmek
stretcher *n* sedye
strict *adj* sert
stride *iv* aşmak
strife *n* çekişme
strike *n* vuruş; grev
strike *iv* vurmak
strike back *v* karşılık vermek
strike out *v* çıkartmak
strike up *v* başlamak
striking *adj* göze çarpan
string *n* şerit; seri
stringent *adj* zorlu
strip *n* şerit
strip *v* soymak
stripe *n* çubuk
striped *adj* çizgili
strive *iv* gayret etmek
stroke *n* darbe; hat
stroll *v* gezinmek
strong *adj* güçlü
structure *n* yapı
struggle *v* mücadele etmek
struggle *n* mücadele
stub *n* izmarit
stubborn *adj* inatçı
student *n* öğrenci
study *v* ders çalışmak
stuff *n* madde; eşya
stuff *v* tıkıştırmak

stuffing *n* dolgu
stuffy *adj* havasız
stumble *v* tökezlemek
stun *v* şaşırtmak
stunning *adj* nefis
stupendous *adj* muazzam
stupid *adj* aptal
stupidity *n* aptallık
sturdy *adj* sağlam
stutter *v* kekelemek
style *n* biçem
subdue *v* bastırmak
subdued *adj* bastırılmış
subject *v* maruz kalmak
subject *n* özne; konu
sublime *adj* yüce
submerge *v* batırmak
submissive *adj* uysal
submit *v* arz etmek
subpoena *v* mahkemeye
çağırmak
subpoena *n* celpname
subscribe *v* imzalamak
subscription *n* abonelik
subsequent *adj* sonraki
subsidiary *adj* yardımcı
subsidize *v* destek sağlamak
subsidy *n* sübvansiyon
subsist *v* geçinmek
substance *n* madde
substandard *adj* acemi
substantial *adj* dayanıklı

S

substitute *v* yerine koymak
substitute *n* yedek
subtitle *n* altbaşlık
subtle *adj* kurnaz
subtract *v* çıkartmak
subtraction *n* çıkarma
suburb *n* şehir dışı
subway *n* tünel
succeed *v* başarılı olmak
success *n* başarı
successful *adj* başarılı
successor *n* varis
succulent *adj* sulu
succumb *v* boyun eğmek
such *adj* bunun gibi
suck *v* emmek
sucker *adj* enayi
sudden *adj* ani
suddenly *adv* aniden
sue *v* dava açmak
suffer *v* acı çekmek
suffer from *v* dan acı çekmek
suffering *n* ıstırap
sufficient *adj* yeterli
suffocate *v* boğulmak
sugar *n* şeker
suggest *v* önermek
suggestion *n* öneri
suggestive *adj* anlamlı
suicide *n* intihar
suit *n* hukuk davası
suitable *adj* uygun

suitcase *n* valiz
sulfur *n* kükürt
sullen *adj* somurtkan
sum *n* toplam
sum up *v* toplamak
summarize *v* özetlemek
summary *n* özet
summer *n* yaz
summit *n* zirve
summon *v* çağırmak
sumptuous *adj* görkemli
sun *n* güneş
sun block *n* güneş koruması
sunblock *n* güneş kremi
sunburn *n* güneş yanığı
Sunday *n* Pazar
sundown *n* gurup
sunglasses *n* güneş gözlüğü
sunken *adj* çökük
sunny *adj* güneşli
sunrise *n* gün doğumu
sunset *n* gün batımı
superb *adj* süper
superfluous *adj* fuzuli
superior *adj* üstün
superiority *n* üstünlük
supermarket *n* süpermarket
superpower *n* süper güç
supersede *v* yerini almak
superstition *n* batıl inanç
supervise *v* teftiş etmek
supervision *n* teftiş

S

supper *n* akşam yemeği
supple *adj* esnek
supplier *n* tedarikçi
supplies *n* erzak
supply *v* tedarik etmek
support *v* desteklemek
supporter *n* destekçi
suppose *v* farzetmek
supposing *c* faraza
supposition *n* zan
suppress *v* sindirmek
supremacy *n* üstünlük
supreme *adj* ulu
surcharge *n* sürşarj
sure *adj* güvenilir
surely *adv* elbette
surf *v* sörf yapmak
surface *n* yüzey
surge *n* büyük dalga
surgeon *n* cerrah
surgical *adv* cerrahi
surname *n* soyisim
surpass *v* baskın çıkmak
surplus *n* fazlalık
surprise *v* sürpriz yapmak
surprise *n* sürpriz
surrender *v* teslim olmak
surrender *n* teslimiyet
surround *v* çevrelemek
surroundings *n* çevre
surveillance *n* gözetme
survey *n* anket

survival *n* kurtuluş
survive *v* hayatta kalmak
survivor *n* sağ kalan, kurtulan
susceptible *adj* alıngan
suspect *v* kuşkulanmak
suspect *n* kuşku
suspend *v* askıya almak
suspenders *n* askı
suspense *n* askıda kalış
suspension *n* asılma
suspicion *n* kuşku
suspicious *adj* şüpheli
sustain *v* tedarik etmek
sustenance *n* gıda
swallow *v* yutmak
swamp *n* batak
swamped *adj* batmış
swan *n* kuğu
swap *v* değiş tokuş etmek
swap *n* değiş tokuş
swarm *v* dolup taşmak
swarm *n* küme
sway *v* sallamak
swear *iv* küfretmek
sweat *n* ter
sweat *v* terlemek
sweater *n* kazak
Sweden *n* İsveç
Swedish *adj* İsveçli
sweep *iv* süpürmek
sweet *adj* tatlı
sweeten *v* tatlılaştırmak

S

sweetheart *n* sevgili
sweetness *n* tatlılık
sweets *n* şeker
swell *iv* şişmek
swelling *n* büyümek
swift *adj* atik
swim *iv* yüzmek
swimmer *n* yüzücü
swimming *n* yüzme
swindle *v* dolandırmak
swindle *n* dolandırıcılık
swindler *n* dolandırıcı
swing *iv* sallanmak
swing *n* salıncak; devre
Swiss *adj* İsviçreli
switch *v* değiştirmek
switch *n* anahtar
switch off *v* kapatmak
switch on *v* açmak
Switzerland *n* İsviçre
swivel *v* mil etrafında dönmek
swollen *adj* şiş
sword *n* kılıç
swordfish *n* kılıçbalığı
syllable *n* hece
symbol *n* sembol
symbolic *adj* sembolik
symmetry *n* simetri
sympathize *v* başsağlığı dilemek
sympathy *n* sempati
symphony *n* senfoni
symptom *n* semptom

synagogue *n* sinagog
synchronize *v* senkronize etmek
synod *n* sinod
synonym *n* eş anlamlı, anlamdaş
synthesis *n* sentez
syphilis *n* frengi
syringe *n* şırınga
syrup *n* şurup
system *n* sistem
systematic *adj* sistemli

table *n* masa
tablecloth *n* sofra örtüsü
tablespoon *n* büyük kaşık
tablet *n* tablet
tack *n* ufak çivi
tackle *v* girişmek
tact *n* ince bir anlayış
tactful *adj* nazik
tactical *adj* taktiksel
tactics *n* taktik
tag *n* etiket
tail *n* kuyruk; tuğ
tail *v* peşine takılmak
tailor *n* terzi
tainted *adj* lekeli

S
T

take *iv* almak
take apart *v* ayırmak
take away *v* alıp götürmek
take back *v* geri almak
take in *v* daraltmak
take off *v* havalanmak
take out *v* çıkarmak
take over *v* devralmak
tale *n* masal
talent *n* yetenek
talk *v* konuşmak
talkative *adj* konuşkan
tall *adj* uzun boylu
tame *v* ehlileştirmek
tangent *n* teğet
tangerine *n* mandalina
tangible *adj* gerçek
tangle *n* kördüğüm
tank *n* tank
tanned *adj* serili
tantamount to *adj* farksız
tantrum *n* öfke nöbeti
tap *n* tapa
tap into *v* pençe vurmak
tape *n* kaset
tape recorder *n* teyp kaydedici
tapestry *n* resimli örtü
tar *n* katran
tarantula *n* tarantula
tardy *adv* geç
target *n* hedef; nişan
tariff *n* tarife

tarnish *v* karartmak
tart *n* turta
tartar *n* tartar
task *n* görev
taste *v* denemek
taste *n* tat
tasteful *adj* zevk sahibi
tasteless *adj* tatsız
tasty *adj* leziz
tavern *n* taverna
tax *n* vergi
tea *n* çay
teach *iv* öğretmek
teacher *n* öğretmen
team *n* takım
teapot *n* çay fincanı
tear *iv* yırtmak; kopmak
tear *n* gözyaşı
tearful *adj* ağlayan
tease *v* alay etmek
teaspoon *n* çay kaşığı
technical *adj* teknik
technicality *n* teknik detay
technician *n* teknisyen
technique *n* teknik
technology *n* teknoloji
tedious *adj* sıkıcı
tedium *n* can sıkıntısı
teenager *n* genç
teeth *n* dişler
telegram *n* telegram
telepathy *n* telepati**

T

telephone *n* telefon
telescope *n* teleskop
televise *v* yayınlamak
television *n* televizyon
tell *iv* anlatmak
teller *n* veznedar
telling *adj* tesirli
temper *n* tabiat; öfke
temperature *n* ısı derecesi
tempest *n* bora
temple *n* tapınak
temporary *adj* geçici
tempt *v* baştan çıkarmak
temptation *n* günaha teşvik
tempting *adj* cezbedici
ten *adj* on
tenacity *n* azim
tenant *n* kiracı
tendency *n* eğilim
tender *adj* gevrek; narin
tenderness *n* şefkat; taravet
tennis *n* tenis
tenor *n* tenör
tense *adj* gergin
tension *n* gerilim
tent *n* çadır
tentacle *n* dokunaç
tentative *adj* farazi
tenth *n* onuncu
tenuous *adj* belirsiz
tepid *adj* ılık
term *n* terim; müddet

terminate *v* sonlandırmak
terminology *n* terminoloji
termite *n* termit
terms *n* şartlar
terrace *n* teras
terrain *n* arazi
terrestrial *adj* karasal
terrible *adj* korkunç
terrific *adj* harika
terrify *v* dehşete düşürmek
terrifying *adj* korkunç
territory *n* arazi
terror *n* terör
terrorism *n* terörizm
terrorist *n* terörist
terrorize *v* yıldırmak
terse *adj* özlü
test *v* test etmek
test *n* test
testament *n* ahit
testify *v* tanıklık etmek
testimony *n* şahadet
text *n* metin
textbook *n* ders kitabı
texture *n* doku
thank *v* teşekkür etmek
thankful *adj* minnet dolu
thanks *n* teşekkürler
that *adj* o; onu
thaw *v* buzları çözülmek
thaw *n* erime
theater *n* tiyatro

T

theft *n* hırsızlık

theme *n* tema

themselves *pro* kendileri

then *adv* o zaman

theologian *n* ilahiyatçı

theology *n* ilahiyat

theory *n* teori

therapy *n* terapi

there *adv* orada; oradan

therefore *adv* o yüzden

thermometer *n* termometre

thermostat *n* termostat

these *adj* bunlar; bunları

thesis *n* tez

they *pro* onlar

thick *adj* kalın; koyu

thicken *v* kalınlaştırmak

thickness *n* kalınlık

thief *n* hırsız

thigh *n* uyluk

thin *adj* ince; seyrek

thing *n* şey

think *iv* düşünmek

thinly *adv* ince şekilde

third *adj* üçüncü

thirst *v* susamak

thirsty *adj* susamış

thirteen *adj* on üç

thirty *adj* otuz

this *adj* bu

thorn *n* diken

thorny *adj* dikenli

thorough *adj* esaslı

those *adj* onlar

though *c* rağmen

thought *n* düşünce

thoughtful *adj* düşünceli

thousand *adj* bin

thread *v* ipliğe dizmek

thread *n* iplik

threat *n* tehdit

threaten *v* tehdit etmek

three *adj* üç

thresh *v* konuşmak

threshold *n* eşik; basamak

thrifty *adj* tutumlu

thrill *v* heyecanlanmak

thrill *n* heyecan

thrive *v* uğraşıp başarmak

throat *n* boğaz

throb *n* vuruş; ağrı

throb *v* zonklamak

thrombosis *n* tromboz

throne *n* taht

throng *n* kalabalık

through *pre* boyunca

throw *iv* fırlatmak

throw away *v* çöpe atmak

throw up *v* kusmak

thug *n* cani

thumb *n* baş parmak

thumbtack *n* raptiye

thunder *n* gök gürültüsü

thunderbolt *n* yıldırım

thunderstorm *n* sağanak
Thursday *n* Perşembe
thus *adv* böylece
thwart *v* engellemek
thyroid *n* tiroit
tickle *v* gıdıklamak
tickle *n* gıdıklanma
ticklish *adj* gıdıklanan
tidal wave *n* med cezir dalgası
tide *n* med cezir
tidy *adj* muntazam
tie *v* bağlamak
tie *n* düğüm; kravat
tiger *n* kaplan
tight *adj* sıkı
tighten *v* sıkılaştırmak
tile *n* fayans; kiremit
till *adv* e kadar
till *v* çift sürmek
tilt *v* eğmek
timber *n* kereste
time *n* vakit
time *v* zamanlamak
timeless *adj* ebedi
timely *adj* zamanında
times *n* süre
timetable *n* çizelge
timid *adj* ürkek
timidity *n* ürkeklik
tin *n* teneke
tiny *adj* ufacık
tip *n* uç; bahşiş

tiptoe *n* parmak ucu
tire *n* araba lastiği
tire *v* yorulmak
tired *adj* yorgun
tiredness *n* yorgunluk
tireless *adj* yorulmak bilmez
tiresome *adj* yorucu
tissue *n* mendil; doku
title *n* başlık; unvan
to *pre* ona
toad *n* kara kurbağa
toast *v* ekmek kızartmak
toast *n* kutlama; tost
toaster *n* tost makinesi
tobacco *n* tütün
today *adv* bugün
toddler *n* küçük çocuk
toe *n* ayak parmağı
toenail *n* ayak tırnağı
together *adv* birlikte
toil *v* zahmet çekmek
toilet *n* tuvalet
token *n* simge
tolerable *adj* hoşgörülebilir
tolerance *n* tahammül
tolerate *v* göz yummak
toll *n* sabit ücret
toll *v* çan çalmak
tomato *n* domates
tomb *n* mezar
tombstone *n* mezar taşı
tomorrow *adv* yarın

T

ton _n_ ton
tone _n_ ses
tongs _n_ maşa
tongue _n_ dil
tonic _n_ tonik
tonight _adv_ bu gece
tonsil _n_ bademcik
too _adv_ o da
tool _n_ gereç
tooth _n_ diş
toothache _n_ diş ağrısı
toothpick _n_ kürdan
top _n_ üst giyecek
topic _n_ konu
topple _v_ devrilmek
torch _n_ meşale; el feneri
torment _v_ işkence etmek
torment _n_ işkence
torrent _n_ sel
torrid _adj_ çok sıcak
torso _n_ heykel gövdesi
tortoise _n_ tosbağa
torture _v_ işkence etmek
torture _n_ işkence
toss _v_ sallamak
total _adj_ tamamen
totalitarian _adj_ totaliter
totality _n_ toplam
touch _n_ dokunuş; tesir
touch _v_ dokunmak
touch on _v_ değinmek
touch up _v_ rötuş yapmak

touching _adj_ dokunaklı
tough _adj_ zor
toughen _v_ sertleştirmek
tour _n_ tur; nöbet
tourism _n_ turizm
tourist _n_ turist
tournament _n_ turnuva
tow _v_ çekmek
tow truck _n_ kurtarıcı
towards _pre_ a doğru
towel _n_ havlu
tower _n_ kule
towering _adj_ kule gibi
town _n_ kasaba
town hall _n_ belediye binası
toxic _adj_ toksinli
toxin _n_ toksin
toy _n_ oyuncak
trace _v_ iz sürmek
track _n_ iz; ray
track _v_ takip etmek
traction _n_ çekiş
tractor _n_ traktör
trade _n_ ticaret
trade _v_ ticaret yapmak
trademark _n_ ticari marka
trader _n_ tüccar
tradition _n_ gelenek
traffic _v_ ticareti yapmak
traffic _n_ trafik
tragedy _n_ trajedi
tragic _adj_ trajik

trail v izlemek

trail n iz

trailer n film parçası

train n tren

train v talim ettirmek

trainee n stajyer

trainer n terbiyeci

training n talim

trait n özellik

traitor n vatan haini

trajectory n mermi yolu

tram n tramvay

trample v ezmek

trance n hipnoz

tranquility n sükunet

transaction n işlem

transcend v sınırını aşmak

transcribe v kopyasını çıkarmak

transfer v taşımak

transfer n taşıma

transform v dönüşmek

transformation n dönüşüm

transfusion n kan nakil

transient adj geçici

transit n transit

transition n geçiş

translate v tercüme etmek

translator n tercüman

transmit v iletmek

transparent adj saydam

transplant v transplantasyon

transport v taşımak

trap v tuzak kurmak

trap n hendek; tuzak

trash n çerçöp

trash can n çöp sepeti

traumatic adj travmatik

traumatize v travma geçirmek

travel v seyahat etmek

traveler n yolcu

tray n tepsi

treacherous adj hain

treachery n ihanet

tread iv basmak

treason n vatana ihanet

treasure n hazine

treasurer n haznedar

treat v davranmak

treat n ikram

treatment n tedavi; muamele

treaty n antlaşma

tree n ağaç

tremble v titremek

tremendous adj muazzam

tremor n ürperme

trench n hendek

trend n eğilim

trendy adj modaya uygun

trespass v ihlal etmek

trial n duruşma

triangle n üçgen

tribe n kabile

tribulation n felaket

tribunal n mahkeme

tribute *n* hediye
trick *v* hile yapmak
trick *n* hile; şaka
trickle *v* akıtmak
tricky *adj* ustalık isteyen
trigger *v* tetiklemek
trigger *n* tetik
trim *v* kesip düzeltmek
trimester *n* üç aylık
trimmings *n* mağlubiyet
trip *n* gezi; çelme
trip *v* gezmeye çıkmak
triple *adj* üçlü
tripod *n* tripod, fotoğraf sehpası
triumph *n* zafer
triumphant *adj* galip
trivial *adj* önemsiz
trivialize *v* değersizleştirmek
trolley *n* el arabası
troop *n* tabur
trophy *n* ganimet; andaç
tropic *n* dönence; tropik
tropical *adj* tropik
trouble *n* zahmet; bela
trouble *v* canını sıkmak
troublesome *adj* baş belası
trousers *n* pantolon
trout *n* alabalık
truce *n* ateşkes
truck *n* kamyon
trucker *n* kamyoncu
trumped-up *adj* yalan

trumpet *n* borazan
trunk *n* bagaj; gövde
trust *v* itimat etmek
trust *n* itimat
truth *n* gerçek
truthful *adj* samimi
try *v* denemek
tub *n* banyo küveti
tuberculosis *n* tüberküloz
Tuesday *n* Salı
tuition *n* öğretim
tulip *n* lale
tumble *v* yuvarlanmak
tummy *n* karın
tumor *n* tümör
tumult *n* gürültü
tumultuous *adj* düzensiz
tuna *n* tonbalığı
tune *n* ayar
tune *v* ayarlamak
tune up *v* akort etmek
tunic *n* tünik
tunnel *n* tünel
turbine *n* türbin
turbulence *n* çalkantı
turf *n* çim; kesek
Turk *adj* Türk
Turkey *n* Türkiye
turmoil *n* karışıklık
turn *n* dönüş
turn *v* dönmek
turn back *v* geri dönmek

T

turn down *v* reddetmek
turn in *v* teslim etmek
turn off *v* kapatmak
turn on *v* açmak
turn out *v* kovmak
turn over *v* değiştirmek
turn up *v* gelmek
turret *n* zırhlı gemi
turtle *n* kaplumbağa
tusk *n* fildişi
tutor *n* özel öğretmen
tweezers *n* cımbız
twelfth *adj* onikinci
twelve *adj* on iki
twentieth *adj* yirminci
twenty *adj* yirmi
twice *adv* iki kere
twilight *n* alacakaranlık
twin *n* ikiz
twinkle *v* ışıldamak
twist *v* bükmek
twist *n* sicim; değişiklik
twisted *adj* çarpık
twister *n* hortum
two *adj* iki
tycoon *n* büyük işadamı
type *n* çeşit; sınıf
type *v* daktiloda yazmak
typical *adj* tipik
tyranny *n* zulüm
tyrant *n* zalim

ugliness *n* çirkinlik
ugly *adj* çirkin
ulcer *n* ülser
ultimate *adj* nihai
ultimatum *n* ültimatom
ultrasound *n* ültrason
umbrella *n* şemsiye
umpire *n* hakem
unable *adj* olanaksız
unanimity *n* oybirliği
unarmed *adj* silahsız
unassuming *adj* gösterişsiz
unattached *adj* bekar
unavoidable *adj* kaçınılmaz
unaware *adj* habersiz
unbearable *adj* çekilmez
unbeatable *adj* yenilmez
unbelievable *adj* inanılmaz
unbiased *adj* önyargısız
unbroken *adj* kırılmamış
unbutton *v* düğmeyi açmak
uncertain *adj* şüpheli
uncle *n* amca; dayı
uncomfortable *adj* rahatsız
uncommon *adj* nadir
unconscious *adj* habersiz
uncover *v* meydana çıkarmak
undecided *adj* kararsız
undeniable *adj* inkar edilemez

under *pre* altında
undercover *adj* gizli
underdog *n* güçsüz takım
undergo *v* geçirmek
underground *adj* yeraltı
underlie *v* altında yatmak
underline *v* altını çizmek
underlying *adj* altında yatan
undermine *v* altını kazmak
underneath *pre* altında
underpass *n* altgeçit
understand *v* anlamak
understandable *adj* anlaşılabilir
understanding *n* anlayış
undertake *v* yüklenmek
underwear *n* iç çamaşırı
underwrite *v* sigorta etmek
undeserved *adj* hak edilmemiş
undesirable *adj* istenilmeyen
undisputed *adj* tartışılmaz
undo *v* geri almak
undoubtedly *adv* şüphesiz
undress *v* soyunmak
undue *adj* aşırı
unearth *v* gün yüzüne çıkarmak
uneasiness *n* huzursuzluk
uneasy *adj* huzursuz
uneducated *adj* cahil
unemployed *adj* işsiz
unemployment *n* işsizlik
unending *adj* sonsuz
unequal *adj* eşit olmayan

unequivocal *adj* belirsiz
uneven *adj* düz olmayan
uneventful *adj* olaysız
unexpected *adj* beklenmedik
unfailing *adj* yanılmaz
unfair *adj* adaletsiz
unfairly *adv* adaletsizce
unfairness *n* adaletsizlik
unfaithful *adj* sadakatsiz
unfamiliar *adj* alışılmadık
unfasten *v* çözmek
unfavorable *adj* olumsuz
unfit *adj* uygun olmayan
unfold *v* açmak
unforeseen *adj* beklenmedik
unforgettable *adj* unutulmaz
unfounded *adj* temelsiz
unfriendly *adj* içtensiz
unfurnished *adj* mobilyasız
ungrateful *adj* nankör
unhappiness *n* mutsuzluk
unhappy *adj* mutsuz
unharmed *adj* sağ salim
unhealthy *adj* sağlıksız
unheard-of *adj* duyulmadık
unhurt *adj* incinmemiş
unification *n* birleşme
uniform *n* tekbiçimli
uniformity *n* tekbiçimlilik
unify *v* birleştirmek
unilateral *adj* tek yanlı
union *n* bileşim

unique *adj* tek
unit *n* birim
unite *v* birleşmek
unity *n* birlik
universal *adj* evrensel
universe *n* evren
university *n* üniversite
unjust *adj* adaletsiz
unjustified *adj* haksız
unknown *adj* bilinmeyen
unlawful *adj* kanunsuz
unleaded *adj* kurşunsuz
unleash *v* salıvermek
unless *c* meğer ki
unlike *adj* den farklı
unlikely *adj* alışılmadık
unlimited *adj* sınırsız
unload *v* yükü boşaltmak
unlock *v* kilidi açmak
unlucky *adj* şanssız
unmarried *adj* bekar
unmask *v* foyasını çıkarmak
unmistakable *adj* aşikar
unnecessary *adj* gereksiz
unnoticed *adj* fark edilmemiş
unoccupied *adj* boş
unofficially *adv* gayri resmi olarak
unpack *v* paketi açmak
unpleasant *adj* çirkin
unplug *v* prizden çekmek
unpopular *adj* sıradan
unpredictable *adj* öngörülemez

unprofitable *adj* karsız
unprotected *adj* korunmasız
unravel *v* ortaya çıkarmak
unreal *adj* gerçekdışı
unrealistic *adj* hayali
unreasonable *adj* mantıksız
unrelated *adj* ilgisiz
unreliable *adj* güvenilmez
unrest *n* tedirginlik
unsafe *adj* emniyetsiz
unselfish *adj* cömert
unspeakable *adj* tarifsiz
unstable *adj* dengesiz
unsteady *adj* istikrarsız
unsuccessful *adj* başarısız
unsuitable *adj* uygunsuz
unsuspecting *adj* masum
unthinkable *adj* olanaksız
untie *v* çözmek
until *pre* e kadar
untimely *adj* zamansız
untouchable *adj* dokunulmaz
untrue *adj* uydurma
unusual *adj* nadir
unveil *v* açığa çıkarmak
unwillingly *adv* isteksizce
unwind *v* sarılı birşeyi açmak
unwise *adj* akılsızca
unwrap *v* ambalajı açmak
upbringing *n* terbiye
upcoming *adj* gelecek
update *v* güncellemek

upgrade *v* yükseltmek
upheaval *n* karışıklık
uphill *adv* yokuş
uphold *v* yukarı kaldırmak
upholstery *n* döşemelik
upkeep *n* bakım
upon *pre* üzerine
upper *adj* üst
upright *adj* dikey
uprising *n* ayaklanma
uproar *n* arbede
uproot *v* kökünden sökmek
upset *v* keyfini bozmak
upside-down *adv* baş aşağı
upstairs *adv* yukarda
uptight *adj* sinirli
up-to-date *adj* güncel
upturn *n* yükseliş
upwards *adv* yukarıya doğru
urban *adj* kentsel
urge *n* dürtü
urge *v* zorlamak
urgency *n* aciliyet
urgent *adj* acil
urinate *v* işemek
urine *n* çiş
urn *n* semaver
us *pro* biz
usage *n* kullanım
use *v* kullanmak
use *n* kullanım
used to *adj* alışık

useful *adj* kullanışlı
usefulness *n* kullanışlılık
useless *adj* yararsız
user *n* kullanıcı
usher *n* yer gösterici
usual *adj* alışılmış
usurp *v* gaspetmek
utensil *n* alet
uterus *n* döl yatağı
utilize *v* faydalanmak
utmost *adj* en uzak
utter *v* dile getirmek

vacancy *n* boşluk
vacant *adj* boş
vacate *v* boşaltmak
vacation *n* tatil
vaccinate *v* aşı yapmak
vaccine *n* aşı
vacillate *v* bocalamak
vagrant *n* başıboş
vague *adj* belirsiz
vain *adj* boş; kibirli
vainly *adv* nafile
valiant *adj* yiğit
valid *adj* geçerli

validate *v* geçerli kılmak	**veil** *n* peçe
validity *n* geçerlilik	**vein** *n* damar
valley *n* vadi	**velocity** *n* sürat
valuable *adj* değerli	**velvet** *n* kadife
value *v* değer biçmek	**venerate** *v* saygı duymak
value *n* değer	**vengeance** *n* intikam
valve *n* vana	**venison** *n* karaca
vampire *n* vampir	**venom** *n* hayvan zehiri
van *n* van	**vent** *n* menfez
vandal *n* vandal	**ventilate** *v* havalandırmak
vandalism *n* vandalizm	**ventilation** *n* havalandırma
vandalize *v* yıkıp dökmek	**venture** *v* tehlikeye atmak
vanguard *n* elebaşı	**venture** *n* tehlikeli girişim
vanish *v* ortadan kaybolmak	**verb** *n* eylem, fiil
vanity *n* kibir	**verbally** *adv* sözle
vanquish *v* mağlup etmek	**verbatim** *adv* aynen
vaporize *v* buharlaştırmak	**verdict** *n* hüküm
variable *adj* değişken	**verge** *n* sınır
varied *adj* çeşitli; değişik	**verification** *n* doğrulama
variety *n* çeşit	**verify** *v* doğrulamak
various *adj* türlü	**versatile** *adj* çok yönlü
varnish *v* verniklemek	**verse** *n* mısra
varnish *n* vernik	**versed** *adj* beyit
vary *v* değişmek	**version** *n* sürüm
vase *n* vazo	**versus** *pre* e karşı
vast *adj* engin	**vertebra** *n* omur
veal *n* dana	**very** *adv* çok; tıpkısı
veer *v* sapmak	**vessel** *n* tekne; damar
vegetable *v* sebze	**vest** *n* yelek
vegetarian *v* vejetaryen	**vestige** *n* kalıntı
vegetation *n* bitki örtüsü	**veteran** *n* gazi
vehicle *n* araç	**veterinarian** *n* veteriner

veto *v* veto etmek
viaduct *n* viyadük
vibrant *adj* titreşimli
vibrate *v* titreşmek
vibration *n* titreşim
vice *n* muavin
vicinity *n* civar
vicious *adj* hırçın; berbat
victim *n* kurban
victimize *v* mağdur etmek
victor *n* galip
victorious *adj* muzaffer
victory *n* zafer
view *n* bakış
view *v* görüntüleme
viewpoint *n* bakış açısı
vigil *n* nöbet tutma
village *n* köy
villager *n* köylü
villain *n* hain
vindicate *v* haklı çıkarmak
vindictive *adj* kinci
vine *n* asma
vinegar *n* sirke
vineyard *n* bağ
violate *v* ihlal etmek
violence *n* şiddet
violent *adj* zorlu
violet *n* menekşe
violin *n* keman
violinist *n* kemancı
viper *n* engerek

virgin *n* bakire
virginity *n* bakirelik
virile *adj* erkekçe
virility *n* kuvvetlilik
virtually *adv* neredeyse
virtue *n* erdem
virtuous *adj* erdemli
virulent *adj* öldürücü
virus *n* virüs
visibility *n* görünürlük
visible *adj* görülebilir
vision *n* görüş
visit *n* ziyaret
visit *v* ziyaret etmek
visitor *n* ziyaretçi
visual *adj* görsel
visualize *v* canlandırmak
vital *adj* hayati
vitality *n* canlılık
vitamin *n* vitamin
vivacious *adj* hayat dolu
vivid *adj* parlak
vocabulary *n* kelime hazinesi
vocation *n* kabiliyet
vogue *n* rağbet
voice *n* ses
void *adj* geçersiz
volatile *adj* uçucu
volcano *n* yanardağ
volleyball *n* voleybol
voltage *n* voltaj
volume *n* hacim

volunteer *n* gönüllü
vomit *v* kusmak
vomit *n* kusmuk
vote *v* oy vermek
vote *n* oy
voting *n* oylama
vouch for *v* doğrulamak
voucher *n* makbuz
vow *v* yemin etmek
vowel *n* sesli harf
voyage *v* deniz yolculuğu yapmak
voyager *n* gezgin
vulgar *adj* müstehcen
vulgarity *n* müstehcenlik
vulnerable *adj* savunmasız
vulture *n* akbaba

wafer *n* yonga plakası
wag *v* sallamak
wage *v* sürdürmek
wage *n* ücret; maaş
wagon *n* vagon
wail *v* feryat etmek
wail *n* feryat
waist *n* bel
wait *v* beklemek

waiter *n* garson
waiting *n* bekleme
waitress *n* bayan garson
waive *v* feragat etmek
wake up *iv* uyanmak
walk *v* yürümek
walk *n* yürüyüş
walkout *n* grev
wall *n* duvar
wallet *n* cüzdan
walnut *n* ceviz
walrus *n* deniz aygırı
waltz *n* vals
wander *v* dolaşmak
wanderer *n* avare
wane *v* azalmak
want *v* istemek
war *n* savaş
ward *n* semt
warden *n* muhafız
wardrobe *n* gardırop
warehouse *n* ambar
warfare *n* savaşım
warm *adj* ılık
warm up *v* ısınmak
warmth *n* ısı
warn *v* uyarmak
warning *n* uyarı
warp *v* eğrilmek
warped *adj* eğri
warrant *v* izin vermek
warrant *n* gerekçe

warranty *n* garanti
warrior *n* savaşçı
warship *n* savaş gemisi
wart *n* siğil
wary *adj* temkinli
wash *v* yıkamak
washable *adj* yıkanabilir
wasp *n* eşekarısı
waste *v* kaybetmek
waste *n* harap
waste basket *n* çöp kutusu
wasteful *adj* müsrif
watch *n* saat
watch *v* izlemek
watch out *v* sakınmak
watchful *adj* uyanık
watchmaker *n* saat üreticisi
water *n* su
water *v* sulamak
water down *v* sulandırmak
water heater *n* termosifon
waterfall *n* şelale
watermelon *n* karpuz
waterproof *adj* su geçirmez
watershed *n* dönüm noktası
watertight *adj* su geçirmez
watery *adj* sulu
watt *n* vat

wave *v* dalgalanmak
wave *n* dalga; hare
waver *v* sallanmak
wavy *adj* dalgalı

wax *n* mum; ağda
way *n* yol; durum
way in *n* giriş
way out *n* çıkış
we *pro* biz
weak *adj* zayıf
weaken *v* zayıflatmak
weakness *n* zayıflık
wealth *n* zenginlik
wealthy *adj* zengin
weapon *n* silah
wear *n* giyim eşyası
wear *iv* giyinmek
wear down *v* eskitmek
wear out *v* yormak
weary *adj* yorgun
weather *n* hava
weave *iv* dokumak
web *n* ağ; top
web site *n* web sitesi
wed *iv* evlenmek
wedding *n* düğün
wedge *n* takoz
Wednesday *n* Çarşamba
weed *n* ot
weed *v* ot yolmak
week *n* hafta
weekday *adj* hafta içi
weekend *n* hafta sonu
weekly *adv* haftalık
weep *iv* ağlamak
weigh *v* tartmak

weight *n* ağırlık
weird *adj* garip
welcome *v* karşılamak
welcome *n* sevindirici
weld *v* birleştirmek
welder *n* kaynakçı
welfare *n* refah
well *n* kuyu
well *adj* iyi
well-known *adj* iyi bilinen
well-to-do *adj* varlıklı
west *n* batı
westbound *adv* batıya giden
western *adj* batılı
westerner *adj* batılı
wet *adj* ıslak
whale *n* balina
wharf *n* iskele
what *adj* ne
whatever *adj* hepsi
wheat *n* buğday
wheel *n* tekerlek
wheelbarrow *n* çekçek
wheelchair *n* tekerlekli sandalye
wheeze *v* hırıldamak
when *adv* ne zaman
whenever *adv* herhangi bir zamanda
where *adv* nerede
whereabouts *n* nerelerde
whereas *c* iken
whereupon *c* bundan dolayı

wherever *c* her nerede
whether *c* olup olmadığını
which *adj* hangi
while *c* iken; sırasında
whim *n* kapris
whine *v* anırmak
whip *v* fırlatmak
whip *n* kırbaç
whirl *v* fırıldanmak
whirlpool *n* girdap
whiskers *n* favori
whisper *v* fısıldamak
whisper *n* fısıltı
whistle *v* ıslık çalmak
whistle *n* ıslık
white *adj* beyaz
whiten *v* beyazlatmak
whittle *v* yontmak
who *pro* kim
whoever *pro* kim olursa
whole *adj* bütün
wholehearted *adj* samimi
wholesale *n* toptan satış
wholesome *adj* erdemli
whom *pro* kimi; kime
why *adv* neden
wicked *adj* fena
wickedness *n* fenalık
wide *adj* geniş
widely *adv* genişçe
widen *v* genişletmek
widespread *adj* yaygın

widow *n* dul
widower *n* dul erkek
width *n* genişlik
wield *v* kullanmak
wife *n* eş; karı
wig *n* peruk
wiggle *v* oynamak
wild *adj* vahşi
wild boar *n* yaban domuzu
wilderness *n* vahşi doğa
wildlife *n* vahşi hayat
will *n* maksat; irade
willfully *adv* taammüden
willing *adj* istekli
willingly *adv* istekle
willingness *n* isteklilik
willow *n* söğüt
wily *adj* düzenbaz
wimp *adj* pısırık
win *iv* kazanmak
win back *v* geri kazanmak
wind *n* rüzgar
wind *iv* rüzgar esmek
wind up *v* kurmak
winding *adj* dolambaçlı
windmill *n* yel değirmeni
window *n* pencere
windpipe *n* nefes borusu

windshield *n* rüzgar siperi
windy *adj* rüzgarlı
wine *n* şarap
winery *n* şaraphane

wing *n* kanat
wink *n* pırıldamak
wink *v* göz kırpmak
winner *n* kazanan
winter *n* kış
wipe *v* silmek
wipe out *v* temizlemek
wire *n* tel; telgraf
wireless *adj* kablosuz
wisdom *n* bilgelik
wise *adj* bilge
wish *v* dilemek
wish *n* dilek
wit *n* nükte
witch *n* cadı
witchcraft *n* büyücülük
with *pre* ile birlikte
withdraw *v* fesh etmek
withdrawal *n* iptal
withdrawn *adj* iptal edilmiş
wither *v* solmak
withhold *iv* kısıtlamak
within *pre* içerden
without *pre* siz suz eki
withstand *v* dayanmak
witness *n* şahit
witty *adj* esprili
wives *n* eşler; karılar
wizard *n* büyücü
wobble *v* sallanmak
woes *n* acılar
wolf *n* kurt

woman *n* kadın
womb *n* dölyatağı
women *n* kadınlar
wonder *v* merak etmek
wonder *n* merak
wonderful *adj* harika
wood *n* tahta
wooden *adj* tahtadan
wool *n* yün
woolen *adj* yünden
word *n* kelime; sözcük
wording *n* üslup
work *n* iş
work *v* işlemek
work out *v* halletmek
workable *adj* işletilebilir
workbook *n* çalışma kitabı
worker *n* işçi
workshop *n* seminer
world *n* dünya
worldly *adj* dünyevi
worldwide *adj* dünya çapında
worm *n* solucan
worn-out *adj* bitkin
worrisome *adj* üzücü
worry *v* üzülmek
worry *n* üzüntü
worse *adj* daha kötü
worsen *v* kötüleşmek
worship *n* tapmak
worst *adj* en kötü
worth *adj* kıymetli

worthless *adj* değersiz
worthwhile *adj* değerli
worthy *adj* layık
would-be *adj* sözde
wound *n* yara
wound *v* yaralanmak
woven *adj* örülü
wrap *v* sarmak
wrap up *v* sarmalamak
wrapping *n* özel ambalaj
wrath *n* öfke
wreath *n* çember
wreck *v* harap etmek
wreckage *n* enkaz
wrench *n* İngiliz anahtarı
wrestle *v* güreşmek
wrestler *n* güreşçi
wrestling *n* güreş
wretched *adj* perişan
wring *iv* burmak
wrinkle *v* kırıştırmak
wrinkle *n* kırışık
wrist *n* bilek
write *iv* yazmak
write down *v* not etmek
writer *n* yazar
writhe *v* kıvranmak
writing *n* yazı
written *adj* yazılı
wrong *adj* yanlış

X-mas *n* Noel
X-ray *n* röntgen ışını

yacht *n* yat
yam *n* yün ipliği
yard *n* yarda
yarn *n* yün ipliği
yawn *n* esneme
yawn *v* esnemek
year *n* yıl
yearly *adv* yıllık
yearn *v* can atmak
yeast *n* maya
yell *v* bağırmak
yellow *adj* sarı
yes *adv* evet
yesterday *adv* dün
yet *c* henüz
yield *v* teslim olmak
yield *n* hasılat

yoke *n* boyunduruk
yolk *n* yumurta sarısı
you *pro* sen
young *adj* genç
youngster *n* delikanlı
your *adj* senin; sizin
yours *pro* seninki
yourself *pro* kendin
youth *n* gençlik
youthful *adj* genç

zap *v* vurmak
zeal *n* gayret
zealous *adj* gayretli
zebra *n* zebra
zero *n* sıfır
zest *n* zevk
zinc *n* çinko
zip code *n* posta kodu
zipper *n* fermuar
zone *n* bölge
zoo *n* hayvanat bahçesi
zoology *n* zooloji

X
Y
Z

Turkish-English

Bilingual Dictionaries, Inc.

Abbreviations

a - article
n - noun
e - exclamation
pro - pronoun
adj - adjective
adv - adverb
v - verb
pre - preposition
c - conjunction

a doğru *pre* towards
abajur *n* lampshade
abartılı *adj* overdone
abartmak *v* exaggerate, overcharge, overstate
abilmek eki *n* might
abla *n* sister
abluka *n* blockade
abluka etmek *v* blockade
abonelik *n* subscription
abuk sabuk *adj* incoherent
acayip *adj* bizarre, eccentric
acayiplik *n* novelty
acele *n* haste
acele *adv* quickly
acele etmek *v* hurry up, rush
acele ettirmek *v* hurry
acele şekilde *adv* hastily
aceleci *adj* impetuous, pushy
aceleyle *adv* hurriedly
aceleyle girmek *v* burst into
acemi *n* cub; beginner
acemi *adj* substandard
acemi asker *n* recruit
acenta *n* agent
acı *adj* bitter
acı *n* misery
acı *adv* bitterly
acı acı bağırmak *v* screech

acı çekmek *v* suffer
acı çektirmek *v* inflict
acı duymak *v* deplore
acı söz *n* lash
acı veren *adj* painful
acı vermek *v* afflict
acıklı *adj* harrowing
acıkmak *v* starve
acılar *n* woes
acılık *n* bitterness
acımasız *adj* cruel, inhuman, outrageous
acımasızlık *n* cruelty
acınası *adj* pathetic
acil *n* emergency
acil *adj* urgent, pressing
aciliyet *n* urgency
aciz bırakmak *v* incapacitate
acizlik *n* inability
aç *adj* hungry
açgözlü *adj* greedy
açgözlülük *n* greed
açı *n* angle, standpoint
açı vermek *v* angle
açığa çıkarmak *v* reveal, unveil
açığa vurmak *v* disclose
açık *adj* bare, open
açık delil *n* smoking gun
açık fikirli *adj* open-minded
açık havada *adv* outdoors
açık saçık *adj* obscene
açık saçık laf *n* obscenity

açık seçik *adj* lucid
açık sözlü *adj* outright, outspoken
açık yürekli *adj* outgoing
açıkça *adv* clearly
açıklama *n* clarification, remark
açıklama getirmek *v* clarify
açıklamak *v* explain, remark
açıklanamaz *adj* inexplicable
açıklayıcı not *n* annotation
açıklık *n* openness, clearness
açıksözlü *adj* forthright
açıkta *adv* off
açıkta bırakan *adj* revealing
açılış *n* inauguration, opening
açılış yapmak *v* inaugurate
açılmak *v* open up
açım *n* incision
açlık *n* hunger
açlıktan ölme *n* starvation
açmak *v* open, switch on, turn on, unfold
ada *n* island
adacık *n* isle
adak *n* dedication, offering
adalet *n* justice
adaletli *adj* judicious
adaletlilik *n* fairness
adaletsiz *adj* unfair, unjust
adaletsizce *adv* unfairly
adaletsizlik *n* unfairness
adam *n* guy, man
adam çiğnemek *v* run over

adam kaçıran kişi *n* kidnapper
adam kaçırma *n* kidnapping
adam kaçırmak *v* kidnap
adam öldürme *n* manslaughter
adamak *v* dedicate, devote, commit
adap *n* manners
adaptasyon *n* adaptation
adaptör *n* adapter
aday *n* applicant, candidate
aday göstermek *v* nominate
adaylık *n* candidacy
adeta *adv* merely
adı çıkmış *adj* infamous, notorious
adıl *n* pronoun
adım *n* move, footstep, pace, step
adım adım *adv* step-by-step
adım atmak *v* step
adi *adj* petty, despicable
adil *adj* fair, lawful
adil bir şekilde *adv* justly
adisyon *n* check
adliye sarayı *n* courthouse
adres *n* address
Advent *n* Advent
af *n* absolution
afacan *n* brat
afacan *adj* mischievous
afet *n* catastrophe
affedilir *adj* forgivable
affetmek *v* forgive

afrodizyak *adj* aphrodisiac
afyon *n* opium
agnostik *n* agnostic
ağ *n* net, mesh, web
ağabey *n* brother
ağaç *n* tree
ağaç gövdesi *n* stem
ağaç kesmek *v* log
ağartmak *v* bleach
ağda *n* wax
ağdalı *adj* redundant
ağır *adj* heavy
ağır basan *adj* overbearing
ağır basmak *v* outweigh, override
ağır çekim *n* slow motion
ağır silah *n* artillery
ağır suç *n* felony
ağırbaşlı *adj* solemn
ağırlık *n* heaviness, weight
ağıt *n* lament
ağıt yakmak *v* lament
ağız *n* mouth
ağızdan *adv* orally
ağızlık *n* nozzle
ağlamak *v* cry, weep
ağlayan *adj* tearful
ağrı *n* throb, ache
ağrı kesici *n* painkiller
ağrıyan *n* sore
Ağustos *n* August
ağustos böceği *n* locust

ağzını aramak *v* sound out
ağzını kapamak *v* shut up
ahbap *n* buddy, pal
ahenk *n* rapport
ahenksiz *adj* dissonant
ahır *n* barn, stable, stall
ahit *n* testament
ahlak *n* ethics, moral
ahlak bozukluğu *n* depravity
ahlak dışı *adj* amoral
ahlakı bozan *adj* noxious
ahlaki *adj* ethical, moral
ahlaksız *adj* immoral, impure
ahlaksızlık *n* immorality, indecency
ahmak *n* jerk
ahtapot *n* octopus
ahududu *n* raspberry
aidat *n* dues
aile *n* family
aile içi *adj* domestic
ait olmak *v* belong, pertain
ajan *n* agent
ajanda *n* agenda
ajans *n* agency
akademi *n* academy
akademik *adj* academic
akbaba *n* vulture, buzzard
akciğer *n* lung
akıbet *n* outcome
akıcı bir şekilde *adv* fluently
akıl hastanesi *n* asylum

akıllanmaz *adj* incorrigible
akıllı *adj* prudent, smart, clever
akılsız *adj* mindless
akılsızca *adj* unwise
akım *n* current
akın *n* raid, exodus
akıntı *n* current, leak
akıp gitmek *v* elapse
akış *n* flow
akıtmak *v* drain, trickle
akıtmak *n* shed
akla getirmek *v* connote
akla yatkın *adj* plausible
aklamak *v* acquit, exonerate
aklen *adv* mentally
aklı başında *adj* sane
aklı başındalık *n* sanity
aklına takılmak *v* obsess
aklını çelmek *v* beguile
aklını karıştırmak *v* mystify
akmak *v* flow, overflow
akordeon *n* accordion
akort etmek *v* tune up
akraba *n* in-laws, relative
akrabalık *n* kinship
akran *n* match
akrep *n* scorpion
akrobat *n* acrobat
aksak *adj* lame
aksama *n* setback
aksan *n* accent
aksesuar *n* ornament

aksırık *n* sneeze
aksırmak *v* sneeze
aksi takdirde *adv* otherwise
aksilik *n* misfortune
aksini kanıtlamak *v* disprove
aksiyom *n* axiom
akşam *n* evening
akşam yemeği *n* dinner, supper
akşam yemeği yemek *v* dine
aktör *n* actor
aktris *n* actress
akustik *adj* acoustic
akut *adj* acute
akvaryum *n* aquarium
alabalık *n* trout
alabora etmek *v* overturn
alabora olmak *v* capsize
alacakaranlık *n* dusk, nightfall, twilight
alacaklı *n* creditor
alaka *pre* concerning
alaka *n* liking
alakasız *adj* irrelevant
alamet *n* omen
alan *n* area, field
alanı *n* eyesight
alarm *n* alarm
alaşağı edilme *n* overthrow
alaşım *n* alloy
alay *n* mockery, regiment, ridicule
alay etmek *v* deride, mock, tease
alaycı *adj* ironic

albay *n* colonel
alçak *adj* dishonorable, low
alçak gönüllülük *n* humility
alçakgönüllü *adj* humble, lowly, meek
alçakgönüllülük *n* meekness, modesty
alçaklık *n* dishonor
alçaltıcı *adj* degrading
alçaltılmış *adj* demeaning
alçaltmak *v* demean
aldatıcı *adj* misleading
aldatma *n* deception
aldatmak *v* cheat, betray, delude, mislead, impose
aldırmamak *v* overlook
alelade *adj* mediocre
aleladelik *n* mediocrity
alenen *adv* publicly
alerji *n* allergy
alerjik *adj* allergic
alet *n* gadget, utensil, gear
alev *n* flame
alevlendirici *n* inflammation
alevlendirmek *v* kindle
alfabe *n* alphabet
algılama *n* perception
algılamak *v* sense
alıkoyma *n* detention, retention
alıkoymak *v* detain, retain
alın *n* forehead
alıngan *adj* susceptible

alınım *n* purchase
alıntı *n* excerpt, quotation
alıntı yapmak *v* quote
alıp götürmek *v* take away
alıp satmak *n* merchandise
alışık *adj* used to
alışılmadık *adj* unfamiliar, unlikely
alışılmış *adj* habitual, usual
alışkanlık *n* habit
alışma *n* orientation
alıştırma yapmak *v* exercise, practice
alıştırmak *v* acclimatize, accustom
alışveriş yapmak *v* shop, shopping
alkış *n* applause
alkışlamak *v* applaud
alkolik *adj* alcoholic
alkolizm *n* alcoholism
alkollü *adj* intoxicated
almak *v* get, receive, take, pick
Alman *adj* German
almanak *n* almanac
Almanya *n* Germany
alt *n* bottom
alt etmek *v* overcome, overwhelm
altbaşlık *n* subtitle
alternatif *n* alternative
altgeçit *n* underpass
altı *adj* six

altın *n* gold
altın çağ *n* heyday
altıncı *adj* sixth
altında *adv* below
altında *pre* under, underneath, beneath
altında yatan *adj* underlying
altında yatmak *v* underlie
altından *adj* golden
altını çizmek *v* underline
altını kazmak *v* undermine
altmış *adj* sixty
altüst etmek *v* mess up
alüminyum *n* aluminum
ama *c* but
âmâ *adj* blind
amaç *n* goal, intention, objective, purpose, mission
amaçlamak *v* aim
amaçsız *adj* aimless
âmâlık *n* blindness
amansız *adj* relentless
amatör *adj* amateur
ambalajı açmak *v* unwrap
ambar *n* store, warehouse
amblem *n* emblem
ambulans *n* ambulance
amca *n* uncle
Amerikalı *adj* American
Amerikan *adj* American
amfibi *adj* amphibious
amfiteatr *n* amphitheater

amiral *n* admiral
amirane *adj* bossy
amonyak *n* ammonia
amorti etmek *v* amortize
ampul *n* bulb
ampute etmek *v* amputate
ampütasyon *n* amputation
an *n* moment, instance
ana *adj* major
ana çizgiler *n* outline
ana kara *n* mainland
ana noktalar *n* guidelines
anaç *adj* maternal
anahtar *n* switch, key
anahtarlamak *v* relay
anahtarlık *n* key ring
analiz *n* analysis
analiz etmek *v* analyze
analoji *n* analogy
ananas *n* pineapple
anarşi *n* anarchy
anarşist *n* anarchist
anat *n* corpuscle
anatomi *n* anatomy
anayasa *n* constitution
anayol *n* highway
anca *adv* narrowly
ancak *c* however
ancüez *n* anchovy
andaç *n* trophy, souvenir
anekdot *n* anecdote
anemi *n* anemia

anemik *adj* anemic
anestezi *n* anesthesia
Anglikan *adj* Anglican
anılar *n* memoirs, recollection
anımsamak *v* recall, recollect
anımsatmak *v* conjure up
anında *adv* instantly
anırmak *v* whine
anıt *n* monument
ani *n* instant
ani *adj* sudden
ani çekiş *v* jerk
aniden *adv* suddenly
animasyon *n* animation
anjin *n* angina
anket *n* questionnaire, survey
anlam *n* reading, meaning
anlamak *v* grasp, perceive, understand, figure out
anlamdaş *n* synonym
anlamına gelmek *v* boil down to, signify
anlamlı *adj* meaningful, suggestive
anlamsız *adj* meaningless
anlaşılabilir *adj* understandable
anlaşılıyor ki *adv* plainly
anlaşılması güç *adj* murky, obscure
anlaşılmaz *adj* occult
anlaşılmazlık *n* obscurity
anlaşma *n* agreement, deal, pact

anlaşmak *v* agree, deal, get along
anlaşmamak *v* disagree
anlaşmazlık *n* disagreement, dispute, mix-up
anlatım *n* expression
anlatmak *v* report, tell
anlayış *n* understanding
anma *n* remembrance
anmak *v* commemorate
anne *n* mom, mother, mummy
annelik *n* maternity, motherhood
anonim *adj* anonymous
anonim *v* incorporate
anonim şirket *n* corporation
anonimlik *n* anonymity
anormal *adj* abnormal
anormallik *n* abnormality
ansiklopedi *n* encyclopedia
anten *n* antenna
antibiyotik *n* antibiotic
antidot *n* antidote
antik *adj* ancient
antikite *n* antiquity
antilop *n* antelope, buck
antipati *n* antipathy
antlaşma *n* treaty
antrenör *n* coach
antrenörlük etmek *n* coaching
apandis *n* appendix
apandisit *n* appendicitis
apartman *n* apartment
apartman dairesi *n* flat

aperatif *n* snack
aperitif *n* aperitif
aptal *n* goof
aptal *adj* silly, stupid
aptalca *adj* idiotic, ludicrous
aptallık *n* stupidity
ara bulmak *v* mediate
ara bulucu *n* mediator
ara dönem *n* interlude
ara kablosu *n* lead
ara sıra *adv* occasionally
ara vermek *v* lay off
araba *n* car, auto
araba gezintisi *n* drive
araba lastiği *n* tire
arabulucu *n* arbiter
aracı *n* middleman
aracılık *n* intervention
aracılık etmek *v* intercede
aracılık yapmak *v* arbitrate
araç *n* means, vehicle
araç sürmek *v* drive
arada bulunan *n* intermediary
araf *n* purgatory
aralık *adj* ajar
Aralık *n* December
aralık *n* interval, break
aralıksız *adj* incessant
aramak *v* search, seek, look for, call
Arap *adj* Arabic
arapsaçı gibi *adj* mixed-up

arasında *pre* among, between
arasını kesme *n* interruption
araştırma *n* inquiry, quest, research
araştırmak *v* inquire, probe, research
araya girme *n* intercession
araya girmek *v* intervene
arayış *n* search
arazi *n* estate, land, premises, terrain, territory
arazi doldurma *n* landfill
arbede *n* brawl, uproar
ardıl *adj* consecutive
ardında *adv* beyond
ardışıklık *n* sequence
arena *n* arena
arı *n* bee
arı kovanı *n* beehive, hive
arındırma *n* purification
arıza *n* obstruction
arızalı çalışma *n* malfunction
arızalı çalışmak *v* malfunction
arife *n* eve
aristokrasi *n* aristocracy
aristokrat *n* aristocrat
aritmetik *n* arithmetic
arka *n* back
arka kapı *n* backdoor
arkadan yetişmek *v* overtake
arkadaş *n* fellow, friend, mate
arkadaş olmak *v* befriend

arkadaşça *adj* folksy
arkadaşlık *n* company, friendship
arkaik *adj* archaic
arkaplan *n* background
arkasında *adv* back
arkasında *pre* behind
arkaya doğru *adv* backwards
arkeoloji *n* archaeology
arktik *adj* arctic
armağan etmek *v* bestow
armut *n* pear
aromatik *adj* aromatic
arpa *n* barley
arsa *n* plot
arsenik *n* arsenic
arşiv *n* archive
art *adj* rear
art niyetli *adj* malevolent
artan *adj* increasing
artı *adj* plus
artık *adj* left
artık yıl *n* leap year
artıklar *n* leftovers
artırıcı *n* conditioner
artış *n* increase, raise, increment
artikülasyon *n* articulation
artistik *adj* artistic
artizan *n* artisan
artmak *v* increase
artrit *n* arthritis
arttırmak *v* raise
arz etmek *v* submit

arzu *n* desire, longing, lust
arzulamak *v* crave, desire, lust
as *n* ace
asalet *n* dignity, nobility
asansör *n* elevator, escalator
asfalt *n* asphalt
asıl *adj* actual, prime
asılı şey *n* pendant
asılma *n* suspension
asılsız *adj* groundless, baseless
asil *adj* noble
asilzade *n* nobleman
asimilasyon *n* assimilation
asimile etmek *v* assimilate
asit *n* acid
asitlik *n* acidity
asker *n* soldier
askere alınmış *n* conscript
askere alma *n* draft
askere kaydolmak *v* enlist
askeri yürüyüş *n* march
askı *n* hanger, suspenders
askıda kalış *n* suspense
askıya almak *v* suspend
asla *adv* never
aslan *n* lion
aslında *adv* actually
asma *n* grapevine, vine
asmak *v* hang
aspirin *n* aspirin
ast *adj* junior
asteroit *n* asteroid

astım *n* asthma
astımlı *adj* asthmatic
astrolog *n* astrologer
astroloji *n* astrology
astronom *n* astronomer
astronomi *n* astronomy
astronomik *adj* astronomic
astronot *n* astronaut
aşağı indirmek *v* bring down
aşağı inmek *v* come down
aşağıda *adv* down; downstairs
aşağılama *n* mortification
aşağılamak *v* slur
aşağılık *adj* inferior
aşağısında *pre* below
aşağıya eğilmek *v* bend down
aşamalı *adj* progressive
aşçı *n* cook
aşerme *n* craving
aşı *n* vaccine
aşı yapmak *v* vaccinate
aşılamak *v* implant
aşındırmak *v* corrode, eat away, obliterate
aşırı *adv* exceedingly
aşırı *adj* excessive, extreme, undue
aşırı *n* glut
aşırı kalabalık *adj* overcrowded
aşırı yüksek *adj* exorbitant
aşikar *adj* unmistakable
aşk hikayesi *n* romance
aşk ilişkisi *n* affair
aşmak *v* exceed, outperform, outrun, overrun, stride
at *n* horse
at arabası *n* carriage
at başlığı *n* bridle
ata *n* ancestor, patriarch, predecessor
atak *n* rash
atalar *n* antecedents
atama *n* appointment
atamak *v* ordain
atardamar *n* artery
atasözü *n* maxim, proverb
ataş *n* paperclip
ateist *n* atheist
ateizm *n* atheism
ateş *n* fire
ateş edip düşürmek *v* shoot down
ateş etme *n* gunfire
ateşkes *n* armistice, cease-fire, truce
ateşlemek *v* loose, fire
ateşli silah *n* firearm
atılgan *adj* dashing, impulsive
atılım *n* breakthrough
atılma *n* plunge
atılmak *v* dart
atış *n* shot
atış menzili *n* gunshot
atik *adj* swift

atkı *n* scarf
atlamak *v* bypass
atlatmak *v* elude
atlet *n* athlete
atletik *adj* athletic
atmaca *n* hawk
atmak *v* discard
atmosfer *n* atmosphere
atmosferik *adj* atmospheric
atom *n* atom
atomik *adj* atomic
av *n* chase, prey
av tüfeği *n* shotgun
avantaj *n* advantage
avare *n* drifter, wanderer
avcı *n* hunter
avize *n* chandelier
avlanmak *v* hunt
avlu *n* backyard, patio, court
Avrupa *n* Europe
Avrupalı *adj* European
avuç *n* palm
avuç dolusu *n* handful
avukat *n* counselor, counsel, attorney, lawyer
avukatlık yapan *adj* practicing
ay *n* month; moon
ayağa kalkmak *v* stand up
ayak *n* foot
ayak bileği *n* ankle
ayak işi *n* errand
ayak izi *n* footprint

ayak parmağı *n* toe
ayak takımı *n* mob
ayak tırnağı *n* toenail
ayak uydurmak *v* keep up
ayakkabı *n* shoe
ayakkabı bağı *n* shoelace
ayakkabı cilası *n* shoe polish
ayakkabıcı *n* shoe store
ayakkabılar *n* footwear
ayaklanma *n* mutiny, stampede, uprising
ayaklar *n* feet
ayaklı merdiven *n* stepladder
ayakta durmak *v* stand
ayakta tedavi edilen hasta *n* outpatient
ayar *n* setting, tune
ayarlamak *v* calibrate, tune
ayartıcı *adj* deprave
ayartma *n* seduction
ayartmak *v* entice, lure, seduce
ayaz *n* frost, nip
aybaşı *n* menstruation
aydınlatma *n* lighting
aydınlatmak *v* enlighten, ignite, illuminate, light
aydınlık *adj* luminous
aygıt *n* device
ayı *n* bear
ayık *adj* sober
ayıp *n* reproach
ayıplamak *v* lash

ayırma *n* separation
ayırmak *v* allocate, reserve, spare; detach, segregate, separate, take apart
ayırt etmek *v* discern, distinguish
ayin *n* litany, liturgy, sacrament
aylak *adj* idle, stray
aylak aylak dolaşmak *v* loiter
aylaklık etmek *v* loaf
aylık *adv* monthly
ayna *n* looking glass, mirror
aynen *adv* verbatim
aynı *adj* same
aynı sınıfa girmek *v* lump together
ayraç *n* bracket
ayrı *adv* apart
ayrı *adj* separate
ayrı ayrı *adj* respective
ayrı yaşayan *adj* estranged
ayrıca *adv* also
ayrıcalık *n* oracle, prerogative
ayrılabilir *adj* detachable
ayrılamamak *v* linger
ayrılış *n* departure
ayrılmak *v* break away, break up
ayrılmamak *v* stick to
ayrılmaz *adj* inseparable
ayrım *n* discrimination
ayrıntı *n* nuance
ayrıntılı yazmak *v* itemize
ayrıntıya inmek *v* detail

ayrıştırmak *v* decompose
ayyaş *adj* lush
az *adj* few
azad etmek *v* let out
azalma *n* moderation
azalmak *v* decrease, lessen, wane
azaltmak *v* alleviate, cut down, dim, mitigate, reduce
azametle yürüme *n* stalk
azametli *adj* ostentatious
azar *n* rebuke, scolding
azar azar *adv* little by little
azarlama *n* rebuff
azarlamak *v* rebuke, scold
azat *n* liberation
azat etmek *v* emancipate, liberate
azgın *adj* lustful
azınlık *n* minority
azim *n* tenacity
azimli *adj* militant
aziz *adj* beloved
aziz *n* saint
aziz saymak *v* canonize
azman *adj* monstrous

B

baba *n* dad, father
baba mirası *n* patrimony
babacan *adj* fatherly
babalık *n* fatherhood, paternity
baca *n* chimney
bacak *n* leg, limb
badem *n* almond
bademcik *n* tonsil
bagaj *n* baggage, luggage, trunk
bagaj yeri *n* rumble
baget *n* baguette
bağ *n* connection, bond; vineyard; ligament
bağdaştırmak *v* correlate, harmonize
bağımlı *adj* addicted
bağımlılık *n* addiction
bağımlılık yapan *adj* addictive
bağımsız *adj* independent
bağımsızlık *n* independence
bağır *n* bosom
bağırış *n* outcry, shout
bağırmak *v* shout, yell
bağırsak *n* intestine
bağırsaklar *n* bowels
bağış *n* donation
bağış yapmak *v* donate
bağışçı *n* benefactor, donor
bağışık *adj* immune

bağışıklık *n* immunity
bağışıklık kazandırmak *v* immunize
bağışlama *n* forgiveness
bağışlamak *v* absolve
bağışlanamaz *adj* inexcusable
bağlaç *n* conjunction
bağlam *n* context
bağlamak *v* bind, connect, fasten, buckle up, link, tie
bağlantı *n* link
bağlantıyı kesmek *v* disconnect
bağlı olmak *v* depend
bağlılık *n* attachment, dependence
bağnaz *adj* bigot
bahane bulmak *v* rationalize
baharat *n* condiment, herb, spice
baharat katmak *v* season
baharatlı *adj* spicy
bahçe *n* garden
bahçıvan *n* gardener
bahis *n* stake, bet
bahriye *n* navy
bahriyeli *adj* marine
bahse girmek *v* bet, gage
bahsetmek *v* mention
bahşiş *n* tip
bakan *n* minister
bakanlık *n* ministry
bakıcı *n* caretaker, nanny
bakıcılık yapmak *v* nurse

B

bakım *n* maintenance, upkeep
bakımsız *adj* squalid
bakımsızlık *n* disrepair
bakır *n* copper
bakış *n* glance, view, look, outlook
bakış açısı *n* outlook, perspective, viewpoint
bakire *n* maiden, virgin
bakirelik *n* virginity
bakiye *n* balance, residue
bakkaliye *n* groceries
bakmak *v* look
bakmaksızın *adj* irrespective
bakmaksızın *adv* regardless
bakteri *n* bacteria
bal *n* honey
bal kabağı *n* pumpkin
balayı *n* honeymoon
baldır *n* calf
balık *n* fish
balık tutmak *v* fish
balıkçı *n* fisherman
balina *n* whale
balkon *n* balcony
balo *n* ball
balo salonu *n* ballroom
balon *n* balloon
balta *n* ax, hatchet
balya *n* bale
bambu *n* bamboo
band *n* band

bandaj *n* bandage
bandajlamak *v* bandage
bank *n* bank, bench
banka *n* bank
banyo *n* bath, bathroom
banyo küveti *n* bathtub, tub
banyo yapmak *v* bathe
bar *n* bar
baraj *n* barrage, dam
baraka *n* barracks, hut, shack
barbar *n* barbarian
barbarca *adj* barbaric
barbarlık *n* barbarism
barbunya *n* kidney bean
bardak *n* glass, mug
bardak ağzı *n* brim
barınak *n* harbor
barış *n* peace
barışmak *v* make up
barikat *n* barricade
bariyer *n* barrier
barmen *n* barman, bartender
barometre *n* barometer
barut *n* gunpowder
bas *n* bass
basamak *n* step, stair, threshold; digit
basamaklamak *n* cascade
basık *adj* overcast
basımevi *n* press
basın *n* press
basınç *n* pressure

basiret *n* providence
basit *adj* ordinary
basitçe *adv* simply
basketbol *n* basketball
baskı *n* constraint, oppression, repression; compulsion, coercion
baskı hatası *n* misprint
baskı yapmak *v* oppress, press
baskın *n* raid
baskın çıkmak *v* surpass
baskın yapmak *v* raid
baskıncı *n* raider
basma *n* printing
basmak *v* publish; tread
bastırılmış *adj* subdued
bastırmak *v* outdo, quell, repress, subdue
baston *n* cane
baş *n* head
baş ağrısı *n* headache, nuisance
baş aşağı *adv* upside-down
baş belası *adj* troublesome
baş gösterme *n* outbreak
baş harf *n* initial
baş işareti *v* nod
baş parmak *n* thumb
başak *n* ear
başaramamak *v* fail
başarı *n* hit, accomplishment, achievement, success
başarılı *adj* prosperous, successful

başarılı olmak *v* succeed
başarısız *adj* unsuccessful
başarısızlık *n* failure
başarısızlıkla *adv* poorly
başarmak *v* accomplish, achieve
başı çekmek *v* lead
başı dönen *n* dizziness
başıboş *n* vagrant
başından savmak *v* bow out
başını derde sokmak *v* entangle
başını kesmek *v* decapitate, behead
başka *adj* another, other
başka *adv* else
başka bir yere *adv* elsewhere
başka olmak *v* differ
başkaldırı *n* riot
başkaldırmak *v* riot
başkan *n* president
başkanlık *n* presidency
başkanlık etmek *v* chair
başkent *n* capital
başlamak *v* begin, commence, originate, start,
başlangıç *n* beginning, debut, kickoff, launch, onset, outset, start
başlangıç *adj* initial
başlatmak *v* initiate
başlıca *adv* chiefly, mainly, primarily, mostly
başlıca *adj* principal

B

başlık *n* title
başpiskopos *n* archbishop
başrahip *n* abbot
başsağlığı *n* condolences
başsağlığı dilemek *v* sympathize
başta gelen *adj* foremost
baştaki *adv* initially
baştan çıkarmak *v* tempt
baştansavma *adj* evasive
başvermek *v* stem
başvuru *n* recourse; application
başyapıt *n* masterpiece
batak *n* quagmire; swamp
bataklık *n* bog; quicksand
batan *adj* stinging
batı *n* west
batıl inanç *n* superstition
batılı *adj* western, westerner
batırmak *v* immerse, submerge
batıya giden *adv* westbound
batma *n* immersion
batmak *v* go under, sink
batmış *adj* swamped
baton *n* baton
battaniye *n* blanket
bay *n* mister
bayağı *n* banality
bayan *n* miss, mistress
bayan barmen *n* barmaid
bayan garson *n* waitress
bayan hizmetçi *n* maid
bayat *adj* stale

bayılmak *v* faint, pass out
bayır *n* ridge
baykuş *n* owl
bayrak *n* banner, flag
bayrak direği *n* mast
bayram etmek *v* exult
bazen *adv* sometimes
bebek *n* baby, infant
bebeklik *n* infancy
beceri *n* know-how, skill
becerikli *adj* deft, skillful
beceriksiz *adj* clumsy, incompetent
beceriksizlik *n* clumsiness, incompetence
bedava *adj* free
beden *n* body
bedeni *adj* corporal
beğenmek *v* admire
beğenmeme *n* distaste
behmen *n* parsnip
bekar *adj* celibate, unattached, unmarried, single
bekar *n* bachelor
bekarlık *n* celibacy
bekleme *n* waiting
beklemede *adj* pending
beklemek *v* look for, look forward, wait
beklenmedik *adj* improbable, unexpected, unforeseen
beklenti *n* anticipation, expectation

bel *n* waist
bel bağlamak *v* reckon on
bel vermek *n* bulge
bela *n* trouble
belagat *n* eloquence
Belçika *n* Belgium
Belçikalı *adj* Belgian
belediye *n* city hall
belediye başkanı *n* mayor
belediye binası *n* town hall
belge *n* record
belgeleme *n* documentation
belgelemek *v* authenticate
belgesel *n* documentary
belgi *n* profile
belirli *adj* particular, specific
belirsiz *adj* ambiguous, indefinite,
   lax, misty, tenuous, vague
belirteç *n* adverb; marker
belirti *n* indication
belirtisi *n* portent
belirtmek *v* denote
belirtmek *n* spelling
belit *n* axiom
belki *adv* may-be
belki de *adv* perhaps
belli *adj* apparent, obvious
belli belirsiz *adj* faint
belli ki *adv* apparently, obviously
ben *pro* I
ben *n* mole
bencil *adj* selfish

bencillik *n* egoism, selfishness
benç *n* bench
benek *n* speck
benim *adj* my
benimki *pro* mine
bent kapağı *n* floodgate
benzemek *v* resemble
benzer *pre* like
benzer *adj* akin, alike, similar
benzer şekilde *adv* likewise
benzerlik *n* affinity, likeness,
   resemblance, similarity
benzeştirmek *v* simulate
benzin *n* gas, gasoline
beraat *n* acquittal
berabere biten oyun *n* draw
berbat *adj* vicious, abysmal,
   awful, lousy
berbat etmek *v* botch
berber *n* barber
bere *n* beret, bruise
bereketsiz *adj* meager
berelemek *v* maul, bruise
beri *adv* onwards
besbelli *adj* self-evident
beslemek *v* feed, foster, nourish
beslenme *n* nourishment,
   nutrition
besleyici *adj* nutritious
besteci *n* composer
bestelemek *v* compose
beş *adj* five

B

beş parasız *adj* broke
beşgen *n* pentagon
beşik *n* cradle
beşinci *adj* fifth
betik *n* script
betimlemek *v* depict, narrate, portray
beton *n* concrete
beyan etmek *v* proclaim, express, state
beyanname *n* statement
beyaz *adj* white
beyazlatıcı *n* bleach
beyazlatmak *v* whiten
beyefendi *n* gentleman, sir
beyin *n* brain, mastermind
beyin yıkamak *v* brainwash
beyinsel *adj* cerebral
beyit *adj* versed
beyzbol *n* baseball
beyzbol atıcısı *n* pitcher
bez *n* cloth, diaper, rag
bezelye *n* pea
bezemek *v* deck
bezemeli *adj* ornamental
bıçak *n* knife
bıçaklamak *v* stab
bıkkın *adj* bored
bıkkınlık *n* boredom
bırakmak *v* let
bıyık *n* mustache
biber *n* pepper

biçem *n* style
biçim *n* format, semblance
biçimini bozmak *v* distort
biçimsizleştirmek *v* deform, disfigure
biçimsizlik *n* deformity
biçmek *v* cut out, mow, reap
biftek *n* steak
bilardo *n* billiards
bildiri *n* bulletin, declaration, leaflet, notification
bildirmek *v* declare, issue, notify
bile *adj* even
bilek *n* wrist
bilemek *v* sharpen
bilerek *adv* knowingly
bileşen *n* component
bileşik *n* compound
bileşim *n* union
bilezik *n* bracelet
bilge *adj* wise
bilgelik *n* wisdom
bilgi *n* information, knowledge
bilgin *n* scholar
bilgisayar *n* computer
bilim *n* science
bilim adamı *n* scientist
bilimsel *adj* scientific
bilinçlilik *n* consciousness
bilinemezci *n* agnostic
bilinmeyen *adj* unknown
bilmece *n* puzzle, riddle

bilmek *v* know
bilye *n* marble
bin *adj* thousand
bina cephesi *n* frontage
binbaşı *n* major
binek *n* mount
bingo *n* jackpot
binmek *v* board, embark
bir *a* a, an
bir *adj* one
bir an için *adv* momentarily
bir gecede *adv* overnight
bir gün *adv* someday
bir kenera bırakmak *v* put away
bir kere *c* once
bir kerede *adv* once
bir konuda uzmanlaşmak *v* major in
bir kullanımlık *adj* disposable
bir nebze *adv* somewhat
bir şekilde *pro* anyhow
bir şekilde *adv* somehow
bir şey *pro* something
bir yerden gelmek *v* come from
bira *n* beer
birahane *n* brewery
biraz *adj* some
birazcık *n* little bit
birazcık *adv* slightly
birbirine karıştırmak *v* mingle
birbirine sarmak *v* intertwine
birçok *adj* lots, many, several

birden akmak *v* flush
birdenbire *adv* abruptly
biri *pre* oneself
birikim *n* backlog, savings
birikmek *v* run up
biriktirmek *v* accumulate, hoard
birileri *pro* somebody
birim *n* unit
birinci *adj* premier, first
birine *pro* someone
birini *pro* someone
birinin namına *adv* behalf (on)
birisi *pro* somebody
birleşim *n* combination
birleşme *n* conjunction, unification, merger
birleşmek *v* conjugate, merge, unite
birleştirme *n* integration
birleştirmek *v* affiliate, combine, pool, unify, weld
birlik *n* unity
birlikte *adv* together
birlikte varolmak *v* coexist
bisiklet *n* bicycle, bike
bisikletçi *n* cyclist
bisiklete binmek *v* cycle
bisküvi *n* biscuit
bit *n* louse
bitirmek *v* finalize, finish
bitiş *n* ending
bitişik *adj* adjacent

B

bitiştirmek *v* adjoin
bitki *n* plant
bitki örtüsü *n* vegetation
bitkin *adj* prostrate, worn-out
bitler *n* lice
bitli *adj* lousy
bitmemiş *adj* incomplete
bitmez tükenmez *adj* long-
  standing
biyografi *n* biography
biyoloji *n* biology
biyolojik *adj* biological
biz *pro* us, we
bizim *adj* our
bizimki *pro* ours
bizler *pro* ourselves
bizon *n* bison
blok *n* block
bloke etmek *v* block
blöf *n* bluff
blöf yapmak *v* bluff
bluz *n* blouse
bocalamak *v* vacillate
bodrum *n* cellar, basement
boğa *n* bull
boğa güreşçisi *n* bull fighter
boğa güreşi *n* bull fight
boğaz *n* larynx, throat
boğmak *v* asphyxiate, choke,
  smother, strangle, stifle
boğucu *adj* stifling
boğuk *adj* hoarse

boğulma *n* asphyxiation
boğulmak *v* drown, suffocate
bohça *n* pack, bundle
bohçalamak *v* bundle
bok *n* crap
boks *n* boxing
boks yapmak *v* box
boksör *n* boxer
boktan *adj* crappy
bol *adj* abundant, ample, lavish,
  loose, baggy
bol olmak *v* abound
bol pantolon *n* slacks
bolca *n* plenty
bolluk *n* abundance, opulence
bomba *n* bomb
bomba mermisi *n* bombshell
bombalama *n* bombing
bombalamak *v* bomb
bono *n* bond
bonus *n* bonus
bora *n* gust, tempest
borazan *n* trumpet
borç *n* debit, debt
borçlu *n* debtor
borçlu olmak *adj* obliged
borçlu olmak *v* owe
bornoz *n* bathrobe
boru *n* pipe
boru hattı *n* pipeline
boru tesisatı *n* plumbing
bostan *n* orchard

B

boş *adj* blank, empty, hollow, unoccupied, vacant; vain
boşa çıkarmak *v* let down
boşa harcamak *v* squander
boşaltma *n* discharge
boşaltmak *v* discharge, empty, evacuate, vacate
boşanan *n* divorcee
boşanma *n* divorce
boşanmak *v* divorce
boşboğazlık *n* indiscretion
boşluk *n* space, emptiness, vacancy, gap
bot *n* boat
botanik *n* botany
boy *n* height
boya *n* dye, paint
boya fırçası *n* paintbrush
boyamak *v* dye, paint
boykot etmek *v* boycott
boylam *n* longitude
boynuz *n* horn
boyun *n* neck
boyun atkısı *n* muffler
boyun eğdirmek *v* overpower
boyun eğmek *v* back down, succumb
boyunca *pre* along, through
boyunduruk *n* yoke
boyut *n* dimension, magnitude
bozma *n* disruption
bozmak *v* defile, disrupt, impair, perturb; break off

bozulmak *v* break down
bozulmamış *adj* intact
böbrek *n* kidney
böbürlenmek *v* boast, crow
böcek *n* beetle, bug, insect, pest
böğür *n* flank
böğürtlen *n* blackberry
bölge *n* region, zone
bölgesel *adj* regional
bölme *n* division, compartment
bölmek *v* divide, split
bölüm *n* chapter, section, episode; quotient
bölümlemek *n* partition
bölünebilir *adj* divisible
bölünen *n* dividend
bölünme *n* disintegration, schism
bölünme çizgisi *n* parting
bölünmez *adj* indivisible
bölüştürmek *v* split up
böylece *adv* thus
branç *n* brunch
brandayla örtmek *v* canvas
brifing *n* briefing
Britanya *n* Britain
Britanyalı *adj* British
bronşit *n* bronchitis
bronz *n* bronze
broşür *n* brochure, pamphlet
brüt *adj* gross
bu *adj* this
bu arada *adv* meantime

B

bu gece *adv* tonight
bu sırada *adv* meanwhile
bu vesileyle *adv* hereby
bucaksız *adj* immense
budak *n* knob
budala *adj* dumb, fool
budamak *v* prune
bufalo *n* buffalo
bugün *adv* today
bugünlerde *adv* nowadays
buğday *n* wheat
buğu *n* condensation, mist
buhar *n* steam
buharlaştırmak *v* evaporate,
  vaporize
buji *n* spark plug
bukle *adj* curly
bulanık *adj* blurred
bulanıklaştırmak *v* blur
bulaşıcı *adj* contagious, infectious
bulaşık makinası *n* dishwasher
bulaştırmak *v* contaminate,
  infect
bulldozerle düzenlemek *v*
  bulldoze
bulmak *v* find
buluğ *n* puberty
bulunan *adj* situated
bulup getirme *n* retrieval
buluş *n* invention
buluşma *n* date
buluşmak *v* get together, meet

bulut *n* cloud
bulutlu *adj* cloudy
bulutsuz *adj* cloudless
bulvar *n* boulevard
bunak *adj* senile
bundan dolayı *c* whereupon
bunlar *adj* these
bunları *adj* these
bunun gibi *adj* such
bunun yanında *pre* besides
burada *adv* here
burjuva *adj* bourgeois
burkmak *v* sprain
burmak *v* wring
burnunu sokmak *v* meddle
burun *n* cape, nose
burun deliği *n* nostril
buruşturmak *v* crease
buruşuk *n* crease
buyruk *n* commandment, order
buyurma *n* ordination
buyurmak *v* decree
buz *n* ice
buz dağı *n* iceberg
buz gibi *adj* ice-cold
buz kalıbı *n* ice cube
buz pateni *v* ice skate
buzları çözülmek *v* thaw
buzlarını çözmek *v* defrost
buzlu *adj* icy
buzluk *n* freezer, icebox
buzul *n* glacier

büfe *n* kiosk
büklüm *n* curl
bükmek *v* flex, twist
bükülmez *adj* rigid
bülbül *n* nightingale
bülten *n* newsletter
büro *n* bureau
bürokrasi *n* bureaucracy, red tape
bürokrat *n* bureaucrat
büst *n* bust, effigy
bütçe *n* budget, fund
bütün *adj* whole
bütünleştirmek *v* integrate
bütünlük *n* integrity
büyü *n* spell
büyü yapmak *v* bewitch
büyücü *n* wizard
büyücülük *n* sorcery, witchcraft
büyük *adj* big, great
büyük ayıp *n* outrage
büyük buluş *n* breakthrough
büyük dalga *n* surge
büyük harf *n* capital letter
büyük işadamı *n* tycoon
büyük kale *n* fortress
büyük kaşık *n* tablespoon
büyük parça *n* block
büyük yapı *n* edifice
büyük yığın *n* stack
büyükanne *n* grandmother
büyükbaba *n* grandfather

büyükelçi *n* ambassador
büyükşehir *n* metropolis
büyülemek *v* charm, enchant, enthrall, mesmerize
büyüleyici *adj* enchanting, enthralling
büyüme *n* buildup, growth
büyüme *adj* lateral
büyümek *v* grow up, loom, outgrow,
büyütme *n* enlargement
büyütmek *v* enlarge, magnify, nurture, overrate

C

cadde *n* avenue
cadı *n* witch
cahil *adj* ignorant, uneducated
cam *n* glass
cami *n* mosque
can alıcı *adj* crucial
can atmak *v* yearn
can sıkıcı *adj* depressing, irritating
can sıkıntısı *n* tedium
can sıkmak *v* bug, irritate
cana yakın *adj* affable, genial, likable, mellow

canavar *n* beast, monster
canavarlık *n* bestiality
candan *adj* heartfelt
canını sıkmak *v* depress, trouble
cani *n* thug
cankurtaran *n* lifeguard
canlandırmak *v* animate, arouse, revive, visualize
canlı *adj* alive, lively
canlı hayvan *adj* live
canlı hayvan *n* livestock
canlılık *n* vitality
cansız *adj* lifeless
cansızlaşmak *v* languish
casus *n* spy
casusluk *n* espionage
casusluk etmek *v* spy
caydırma *n* deterrence
caydırmak *v* deter, dissuade
caymak *v* recant
cazibe *n* appeal, allure, attraction, charm, enticement
cazibeli *adj* alluring, charming
cazip *adj* appealing
cebir *n* algebra
cehalet *n* ignorance
cehennem *n* hell
ceket *n* jacket
celpname *n* subpoena
cenaze *n* funeral
cenaze arabası *n* hearse
cenaze töreni *n* burial

cenin *n* fetus
cennet *n* heaven, paradise
cennet gibi *adj* heavenly
cep *n* pocket
cep telefonu *n* cell phone
cephane *n* ammunition, munitions
cephanelik *n* arsenal
cephe *n* front
cereyan *n* stream
cerrah *n* surgeon
cerrahi *adv* surgical
cesaret *n* audacity, courage
cesaret etmek *v* dare
cesaret vermek *v* encourage
cesaretini kırmak *v* discourage
cesaretli *adj* courageous
cesaretsiz *adj* spineless
cesaretsizlik *n* discouragement
ceset *n* carcass, corpse, remains
cesur *adj* bold, brave
cesurca *adv* bravely
cetvel *n* ruler
cevap *n* reply, response, answer
cevap vermek *v* respond
cevaplamak *v* answer, reply
cevher *n* jewel
ceviz *n* walnut
ceza *n* imposition, chastisement, penalty, punishment
ceza olarak vermek *v* forfeit
cezalandırılabilir *adj* punishable

cezalandırmak *v* chastise, penalize, punish
cezanın tecili *n* reprieve
cezasını çekmek *v* expiate
cezbedici *adj* enticing, tempting
cezbetmek *v* attract
cezir *v* ebb
cılız *adj* lean
cımbız *n* tweezers
cıva *n* mercury
cıvata *n* bolt
ciddi *adj* grave, momentous, serious
ciddi şekilde *adv* gravely
ciddiyet *n* seriousness
ciddiyetle *adv* earnestly
ciğer *n* liver
cihaz *n* appliance
cila *n* polish
cilalamak *v* polish
cimri *adj* stingy
cinayet *n* homicide, murder
cinnet *n* lunacy
cins *n* breed
cinsel *adj* carnal
cinsel ilişki *n* sex
cinsellik *n* sexuality
cinsiyet *n* gender
cips *n* fries
ciro *n* endorsement, revenue
cisim *n* matter
civar *n* outskirts, vicinity

civarında *pre* about
civciv *n* chick
coğrafya *n* geography
coplamak *v* bludgeon
coşku *n* euphoria
coşkun *adj* avid, effusive
cömert *adj* unselfish
cömertlik *n* bounty, generosity
Cuma *n* Friday
Cumartesi *n* Saturday
cumhuriyet *n* republic
cübbe *n* cassock
cüce *n* dwarf, midget
cümle *n* sentence
cümlecik *n* clause
cüret *n* boldness, dare
cüzam *n* leprosy
cüzdan *n* purse, wallet
cüzzamlı *n* leper

Ç

çaba *n* effort
çabuk *adj* prompt, quick
çadır *n* tent, booth
çadır bezi *n* canvas
çadır kurmak *v* pitch
çağ *n* era, period

çağ dışı *adj* outdated
çağdışı *adj* antiquated
çağıldamak *n* ripple
çağırmak *v* summon
çağrı *n* call
çakal *n* jackal
çakıl *n* gravel, pebble
çakılı kalmak *v* stick around
çakmak *n* lighter
çalar saat *n* alarm clock
çaldırmak *v* ring
çalı *n* bush
çalılık *n* shrub
çalışan *n* staff, employee
çalışma kitabı *n* workbook
çalışmak *v* plug
çalıştırmak *v* coach
çalkantı *n* turbulence
çalmak *v* pilfer, snitch, steal
çam ağacı *n* pine
çamaşır asmak *v* hang up
çamaşırhane *n* laundry
çamur *n* mud
çamur atmak *v* malign
çamurlu *adj* muddy
çamurluk *n* fender
çan *n* bell
çan çalmak *v* toll
çan kulesi *n* belfry
çanak çömlek *n* crockery
çanta *n* bag, case
çantaya koymak *v* bag

çap *n* diameter
çapa *n* anchor
çapkın *adj* dissolute
çapraz ateş *n* crossfire
çapraz bulmaca *n* crossword
çaprazlama *v* crisscross
çar *n* czar
çare *n* cure
çarmıh *n* crucifix
çarmıha germe *n* crucifixion
çarmıha germek *v* crucify
çarpı *n* cross
çarpıcı *adj* impressive
çarpık *adj* twisted
çarpılı *adj* cross
çarpım *n* product
çarpış *n* clash
çarpışma *n* collision, skirmish
çarpıtma *n* distortion
çarpıtmak *v* falsify
çarpmak *v* clash, collide
çarşaf *n* sheet
Çarşamba *n* Wednesday
çarşı *n* downtown
çatal *n* fork
çatal-bıçak takımı *n* cutlery
çatı *n* roof
çatlak *n* crack; nut
çatlak *adj* nutty
çatlamak *v* crack
çavdar *n* rye
çavuş *n* sergeant

çay *n* tea
çay fincanı *n* teapot
çay kaşığı *n* teaspoon
çay tabağı *n* saucer
çaydanlık *n* kettle
çayır *n* meadow, pasture
çaylak *n* novice
çehre *n* countenance
çek defteri *n* checkbook
çekçek *n* wheelbarrow
çekici *adj* attractive, desirable, glamorous
çekiç *n* hammer
çekiçle vurmak *v* hammer
çekiliş yapmak *v* draw
çekilme *n* abdication, seclusion
çekilmek *v* abdicate, recede, secede
çekilmek *n* recess
çekilmez *adj* intolerable, unbearable
çekingen *adj* backward
çekingenlik *n* shyness
çekip almak *v* rash
çekirdeksiz *adj* seedless
çekiş *n* traction
çekişme *n* altercation, strife
çekişmek *v* contend
çekmece *n* drawer
çekmek *v* haul, pull, tow
çelenk *n* garland
çelik *n* steel

çelişki *n* contradiction
çelişkili *adj* conflicting
çelişmek *v* contradict
çelme *n* trip
çember *n* wreath
çene *n* chin, jaw
çerçeve *n* frame
çerçöp *n* trash
çeşit *adj* diverse
çeşit *n* sort, variety, type
çeşitlendirmek *v* diversify
çeşitli *adj* assorted, varied
çeşitlilik *n* diversity
çeşme *n* fountain
çeşni *n* flavor
çeşnilik *n* seasoning
çete *n* gang
çevik *adj* agile
çevir sesi *n* dial tone
çevirmek *v* dial, flip
çevre *n* environment, perimeter, surroundings
çevrelemek *v* surround
çevrim *n* network
çeyiz *n* dowry
çeyrek *n* quarter
çığırtkanlık *n* bark
çığlık *n* crying, scream
çığlık atmak *v* exclaim, scream, shriek
çıkar *n* interest
çıkar sağlamak *v* capitalize

çıkarcı *adj* pragmatist
çıkarma *n* subtraction
çıkarmak *v* eject, get out, remove, take out; infer
çıkartmak *v* extract, strike out, subtract
çıkış *n* boom; exit, way out
çıkmak *v* move out, quit
çıkmaz *adj* deadlock
çıkmaz *n* stalemate
çıkmaz sokak *n* dead end
çıkmaza girmek *v* bog down
çıktı *n* output, print
çıktı almak *v* print
çıldırmak *v* rave
çıldırtmak *v* infuriate
çılgın *adj* crazy, frenzied
çılgın *n* frenzy
çılgına dönmüş *adv* berserk
çılgına dönmüş *adj* distraught
çılgınlık *n* craziness
çınlayan *adj* resounding
çıplak *adj* naked, nude, bare
çıplak ayak *adj* barefoot
çıplaklık *n* nudism, nudity
çırak *n* apprentice
çırpınmak *v* flutter
çıtır *adj* crispy, crunchy
çıtırdatmak *v* snap
çiçek *n* flower
çiçek açmak *v* bloom
çiçek hastalığı *n* smallpox

çiçek soğanı *n* bulb
çiçeklenmek *v* blossom
çift *adj* even, double
çift *n* pair, couple
çift sürmek *v* plow, till
çiftçi *n* farmer
çiftlik *n* farm, farmyard
çiğ *adj* raw
çiğnemek *v* chew
çikolata *n* chocolate
çil *n* freckle
çile *n* ordeal
çileden çıkarmak *v* exasperate
çilek *n* strawberry
çilingir *n* locksmith
çilli *adj* freckled
çim *n* sod, turf
çimdik *n* nip, pinch
çimdik atmak *v* nip
çimdiklemek *v* pinch
çimen *n* grass, lawn
çimento *n* cement
çimlenmek *v* germinate
çingene *n* gypsy
çinko *n* zinc
çip *n* chip
çiriş *n* paste
çirkin *adj* obnoxious, ugly, unpleasant
çirkinleştirmek *v* deface
çirkinlik *n* ugliness
çiselemek *v* drizzle

çisenti *n* drizzle
çiş *n* urine
çit *n* fence
çit ile çevirmek *v* fence
çivi *n* nail
çivilemek *v* nail
çiy *n* dew
çizelge *n* chart, timetable
çizgi *n* line
çizgi film *n* cartoon
çizgili *adj* striped
çizim *n* drawing
çizme *n* boot
çizmek *v* draw
çoban *n* shepherd
çocuk *n* child, juvenile, kid
çocuk bakıcısı *n* babysitter
çocukça *adj* childish, puerile
çocuklar *n* children
çocukluk *n* childhood
çocuksu *adj* juvenile
çocuksuz *adj* childless
çoğalma *n* multiplication
çoğalmak *v* multiply
çoğul *n* plural
çoğunluk *n* majority
çok *adv* much, very
çok *adj* plentiful
çok hevesli *adj* red-hot
çok ileri gitmek *v* overstep
çok ilginç *adj* riveting
çok korkmak *v* dread

çok mutlu *adj* ecstatic
çok öfkeli *adj* livid
çok pişman *adj* remorseful
çok sevinçli *adj* jubilant
çok sevinmek *v* rejoice
çok sıcak *adj* torrid
çok şaşırtıcı *adj* staggering
çok titiz *adj* squeamish
çok yavaş *adj* lingering
çok yönlü *adj* versatile
çok zayıf *adj* emaciated
çokeşli *adj* polygamist
çokeşlilik *n* polygamy
çoklu *adj* multiple
çorak *adj* barren, infertile
çorap *n* sock, stocking
çorba *n* soup
çökertmek *v* overthrow
çökmek *v* cave in
çökük *adj* sunken
çöküş *n* collapse
çöküvermek *v* slump
çöl *n* desert
çömelmek *v* crouch
çömelmiş *adj* hunched
çömez *n* disciple
çöp *n* bin, junk, litter, rubbish;
straw
çöp kutusu *n* waste basket
çöp sepeti *n* trash can
çöpe atmak *v* junk, throw away
çöplük *n* garbage

Ç
D

çörek *n* bun
çözmek *v* disentangle, unfasten, unite; fathom out, resolve, solve
çözücü *adj* solvent
çözülmez *adj* insoluble
çözüm *n* solution
çözünür *adj* soluble
çözünürlük *n* resolution
çubuk *n* bar, rod, stripe
çukur *n* ditch, pit
çuval *n* sack
çünkü *c* because
çürük *n* cavity, decay
çürük *adj* sleazy
çürümek *v* decay, rot
çürümüş *n* rot
çürümüş *adj* rotten
çürütmek *v* debunk, mortify, rebut
çürütülemez *adj* irrefutable

D

dadanmak *v* frequent
dağ *n* mountain
dağ sırası *n* range
dağılım *n* dispersal
dağılmak *v* disband

dağınık *adj* messy
dağınıklık *n* mess, muddle
dağıtım *n* distribution
dağıtımcı *n* dealer
dağıtma *n* dispensation
dağıtmak *v* diffuse, dispatch, dispense, disperse, dissipate, distribute, handout, scatter
dağlık *adj* mountainous
daha *adj* more
daha alçak *adj* lower
daha az *adj* fewer, less, lesser
daha çok parlamak *v* outshine
daha da *c* even more
daha fazla sürmek *v* outlast
daha iyi *adj* better
daha kötü *adj* worse
daha sonra *adv* afterwards
daha sonra *adj* later
daha uzak *adv* farther
dahası *adv* furthermore, moreover
dahil *adv* inclusive
dahil etmemek *v* omit
dahili *adj* implicit, inward
daire *n* apartment
dakik *adj* punctual
dakika *n* minute
daktiloda yazmak *v* type
dal *n* bough, branch
dal salmak *v* branch out
dalalet *n* heresy

daldırma *v* offset

dalga *n* wave

dalga geçmek *v* ridicule

dalgalanmak *v* wave

dalgalı *adj* wavy

dalgıç *n* diver

dalgın *adj* faraway

dalıp gitmek *v* space out

dalış *n* diving, plunge

dalkavuk *n* henchman

dalkavukluk *n* adulation

dallanma *n* ramification

dalmak *v* dive

dam penceresi *n* skylight

damak *n* gum, palate

damar *n* vessel, vein

damar içi *adj* intravenous

damat *n* bridegroom; son-in-law

damga *n* stamp

damgalamak *v* stamp

damıtmak *v* distill

damızlık *n* breed

damla *n* drip, drop

damlamak *v* drop

damlatmak *v* drip

dan acı çekmek *v* suffer from

dana *n* veal, calf

danışma *n* consultation

danışmak *v* consult

danışman *n* adviser, counselor

Danimarka *n* Denmark

dans *n* dance, dancing

dans etmek *v* dance

dantel *n* lace

dar *adj* narrow

dar geçit *n* bottleneck

dar uzun delik *n* slot

darağacı *n* gallows

daraltmak *v* take in

darbe *n* bump, shock, coup, knock, jolt, stroke, pound

dart *n* dart

dava *n* case, lawsuit, litigation

dava açmak *v* litigate, prosecute, sue

davacı *n* plaintiff

davalı *n* defendant

davet *n* calling, invitation

davet etmek *v* invite

davetsiz *n* intruder

davranış *n* behavior

davranmak *v* act, behave, treat

davul *n* drum

dayanıklı *adj* durable, hardy, substantial

dayanıklılık *n* resistance

dayanıksız *adj* flimsy, perishable

dayanılır *adj* bearable

dayanılmaz *adj* excruciating, irresistible

dayanışma *n* solidarity

dayanmak *v* base, lean, recline; endure, put up with, resist, withstand, bear

D

dayı *n* uncle
de *pre* at
debriyaj *n* clutch
dede *n* granddad
dedikodu *n* gossip, gulp
dedikodu yapmak *v* gossip
defetmek *v* dispel, oust, repulse
değer *n* merit, value
değer biçmek *v* appraise, value
değerini düşürmek *v* debase
değerlendirme *n* assessment
değerlendirmek *v* evaluate
değerli *adj* precious, valuable, worthwhile
değersiz *adj* paltry, worthless
değersiz eşya *n* crap
değersizleştirmek *v* trivialize
değil *adv* not
değinmek *v* touch on
değirmen *n* mill
değiş tokuş *n* swap
değiş tokuş etmek *v* swap
değişik *adj* varied
değişiklik *n* twist
değişim *n* alteration, change, interchange
değişken *adj* incalculable, variable
değişmek *v* mutate, vary
değişmez *adj* irrevocable, literal
değiştirilemez *adj* irreversible
değiştirmek *v* alter, change, interchange, mutilate, switch, turn over

değnek *n* baton
deha *n* genius
dehşet *n* consternation, dreaded
dehşet verici *adj* appalling
dehşete düşmek *v* appall
dehşete düşürmek *v* dismay, terrify
dejenerasyon *n* degeneration
dejenere *adj* degenerate
dekan *n* dean
dekor *n* décor
dekoratif *adj* decorative
dekore etmek *v* decorate
delegasyon *n* delegation
delege *n* delegate, envoy
deli *adj* deranged, insane
deli *n* madman
delice *adv* madly
delik *n* hole, perforation, puncture
delikanlı *n* lad, youngster
delil *n* evidence
delilik *n* folly, insanity, madness
delirtmek *v* madden
dellenmiş *adj* frantic
delme *n* piercing
delmek *v* prick
demek istemek *v* drive at, mean
demir *n* iron
demir atmak *v* moor
demir yolu *n* railroad
demirci *n* blacksmith

demlemek *v* brew
demode *adj* outmoded
demokrasi *n* democracy
demokratik *adj* democratic
den *pre* from
den beri *pre* since
den farklı *adj* unlike
denek *n* bale
deneme *n* essay
denemek *v* taste, try
denetim *n* check
denetlemek *v* audit, inspect, oversee
deney *n* experiment
deneyim *n* experience
deneyimsiz *adj* inexperienced
denge *n* equilibrium, balance
dengelemek *v* balance, poise
dengesiz *adj* unstable
dengesizlik *n* imbalance
deniz *n* sea
deniz aşırı *adv* overseas
deniz aygırı *n* walrus
deniz feneri *n* lighthouse
deniz kenarı *adj* seaside
deniz kızı *n* mermaid
deniz mavisi *adj* navy blue
deniz tutmuş *adj* seasick
deniz ürünleri *n* seafood
deniz yolculuğu yapmak *v* voyage
deniztarağı *n* clam

denklem *n* equation
deodorant *n* deodorant
departman *n* department
depo *n* reservoir, storage, depot
depolamak *v* stock, store
depozit *n* deposit
deprem *n* earthquake
depresyon *n* depression
dere *n* creek, stream
derece *n* grade, degree
derecelendirmek *v* grade
deri *n* leather; skin
derin *adj* deep
derin çukur *n* pothole
derin yara *n* gash
derinlemesine *adv* in depth
derinleştirmek *v* deepen
derinlik *n* depth
derlemek *v* compile
dernek *n* association
ders *n* lecture, lesson, course
ders çalışmak *v* study
ders kitabı *n* textbook
dert *n* affliction, care
desen *n* pattern
despot *n* despot
despotça *adj* despotic
deste *n* deck
destek *n* backing, crutch
destek sağlamak *v* subsidize
destekçi *n* supporter
desteklemek *v* back, back up, stand for, support

D

detay *n* detail
detektif *n* detective
detektör *n* detector
deterjan *n* detergent
dev *n* giant
deva *n* remedy
deva olmak *v* remedy
devaluasyon *n* devaluation
devalüe etmek *v* devalue
devam *n* sequel
devam etme *n* continuation
devam etmek *v* carry on, continue, go on, keep on, resume
devam ettirmek *v* maintain
devasa *adj* monumental
devasız *adj* incurable
deve *n* camel
devekuşu *n* ostrich
devir *n* cycle, epoch
devlet *n* state
devralmak *v* take over
devre *n* swing, circuit
devretmek *v* hand down
devreye sokmak *v* call out
devrilmek *v* topple
deyim *n* idiom, phrase
deyiş *n* saying
dezavantaj *n* disadvantage
dezenfektan *n* disinfectant
dezenfekte etmek *v* disinfect, fumigate

dırdır *adj* nagging
dırdır etmek *v* nag
dırdırcı *adj* grouchy
dış *adj* external, outer
dış hatlar *n* contour
dışa doğru *adj* outward
dışadönük *adj* extroverted
dışarı çıkmak *v* come out, go out, step out
dışarıda *adv* out, outside
dışında *adv* aside from
dışlamak *v* exclude
dışlanmış *n* outsider
dibe oturmak *v* settle down
dibe vurmak *v* plummet
didişme *n* scuffle
diftong *n* diphthong
dijestif *adj* digestive
dik başlı *adj* obstinate
dik kafalı *adj* opinionated
dikdörtgen *n* rectangle
dikdörtgen *adj* rectangular
diken *n* thorn
dikenli *adj* thorny
dikey *adj* upright
dikim *n* sewing
dikiş *n* stitch
dikiş yeri *n* seam
dikizlemek *v* peep
dikkat dağınıklığı *n* distraction
dikkat etmek *v* look out, mind
dikkate almak *v* consider

dikkate değer *adj* remarkable
dikkatini dağıtmak *v* distract
dikkatle bakma *n* scrutiny
dikkatle bakmak *v* behold
dikkatli *adj* attentive, careful, mindful
dikkatsiz *adj* careless, imprecise, oblivious
dikkatsizlik *n* carelessness, negligence, oversight
dikmek *v* sew, stitch
diktatör *n* dictator
diktatörce *adj* dictatorial
diktatörlük *n* dictatorship
dil *n* language, tongue
dil dökmek *v* coax
dilbilgisi *n* grammar
dilbudak ağacı *n* ash
dilden dile dolaşmak *v* pass around
dile getirmek *v* utter
dilek *n* wish
dilekçe *n* petition
dilemek *v* implore, wish
dilenci *n* beggar
dili tutulmuş *adj* speechless
dilim *n* slice
dilimlemek *v* slice
dillendirmek *v* sound
dilsiz *adj* dumb, mute
din *n* religion
din kardeşi *n* brethren

dinamik *adj* dynamic
dinamit *n* dynamite
dinazor *n* dinosaur
dindar *adj* devout, pious, religious
dindarlık *n* piety
dingil *n* axle
dingil başlığı *n* nave
dingil çivisi *n* linchpin
dingin *adj* serene
dinginlik *n* serenity
dinlemek *v* listen
dinlendirici *adj* restful
dinlenmek *v* rest
dinleyici *n* listener
diploma *n* diploma
diplomasi *n* diplomacy
diplomat *n* diplomat
diplomatik *adj* diplomatic
dipnot *n* fine print, footnote
dipsiz *adj* bottomless
direk *n* pillar
direniş *n* opposition
direnme *n* persistence
dirilik *n* sap
diriliş *n* resurrection
dirsek *n* elbow
disiplin *n* discipline
disk *n* disk
diskalifiye etmek *v* disqualify
disko *n* club
diş *n* tooth
diş ağrısı *n* toothache

diş doktoru *n* dentist
diş ipliği *n* floss
dişi *n* female
dişi aslan *n* lioness
dişler *n* teeth
dişsel *adj* dental
diyabet *n* diabetes
diyabetik *adj* diabetic
diyagram *n* diagram
diyakoz *n* deacon
diyalog *n* dialogue
diyet *n* diet
diyet yapmak *v* diet
diz *n* knee
diz çökmek *v* genuflect
diz kapağı *n* kneecap
dizgin *n* lining, rein
dizginlemek *v* rein
dizi *n* series
dizin *n* directory
dizlenmek *v* kneel
dobra *adj* blunt
dogmatik *adj* dogmatic
doğa *n* nature
doğaçlama *adv* impromptu
doğaçlama *n* spontaneity
doğaçlama yapmak *v* improvise
doğal *adj* natural
doğal olarak *adv* naturally
doğal sonuç *n* corollary
doğmak *v* be born, come about
doğmuş *adj* born

doğramak *v* chop, mince, saw
doğru *adj* right, precise, accurate, correct
doğru *n* right
doğru yoldan sapmış *v* astray
doğrudan *adj* direct
doğrulama *n* correction, verification
doğrulamak *v* affirm, attest, correct, justify, verify, vouch for
doğrultmak *v* redress
doğruluk *n* accuracy
doğu *n* east, orient
doğulu *n* easterner
doğum *n* delivery, birth
doğum günü *n* birthday
doğurmak *v* procreate
doğusal *adj* eastern
doğuya doğru *adv* eastward
doğuya giden *adj* eastbound
doğuya özgü *adj* oriental
doksan *adj* ninety
doktor *n* doctor
doku *n* tissue, texture
dokuma tezgahı *n* loom
dokumak *v* weave
dokunaç *n* tentacle
dokunaklı *adj* touching
dokunmak *v* touch
dokunulmaz *adj* untouchable
dokunulmazlık vermek *v* indemnify

dokunuş *n* touch
dokuz *adj* nine
dokuzuncu *adj* ninth
doküman *n* document
dolamak *v* curl
dolambaçlı *adj* oblique, winding
dolambaçlı yol *n* detour
dolandırıcı *n* swindler
dolandırıcılık *n* scam, swindle
dolandırmak *v* defraud, dupe, swindle, cheat
dolap *n* cupboard, cabinet
dolar *n* dollar
dolaşmak *v* hover, roam, wander
dolayısıyla *adv* hence
dolaylı *adj* indirect
doldurmak *v* fill, pad
doldurulmuş *adj* loaded
dolgu *n* filling, stuffing
dolgun *adj* replete
dolmalık biber *n* bell pepper
dolmuş uçak *n* charter
dolu *adj* full
dolu fırtınası *n* hail
dolu yağmak *v* hail
dolup taşmak *v* swarm
doluşmak *v* crowd
domates *n* tomato
domuz *n* hog, pig
domuz eti *n* pork, ham
domuz pastırması *n* bacon
domuz yağı *n* lard

don *n* pants
donakalmış *adj* aghast, petrified
donanım *n* hardware
donanma *adj* fleeting
donatım *n* outfit, equipment
donatmak *v* equip, garnish
donatmak *n* furnishings
dondurma *n* ice cream
dondurmak *v* freeze
donmuş *adj* frostbitten, frozen
donuk *n* faint
donuklaşmak *v* dull
doruk *n* cap, peak
dost *n* mistress
dostane *adj* amicable
dosya *n* dossier, file
dosyalamak *v* file
doymak *v* saturate
doymaz *adj* insatiable
dozaj *n* dosage
dozaşımı *n* overdose
dökmek *n* dump
dökmek *v* pour, shed, spill
dökümhane *n* foundry
döküntü *n* debris, spill
döl yatağı *n* uterus
dölyatağı *n* womb
döndürmek *v* revolve, rotate, spin
dönem *n* mileage
dönemeç *n* crook
dönence *n* tropic

D

dönme *n* convert
dönmek *v* go back, revert, turn
dönüm *n* acre
dönüm noktası *n* milestone, watershed
dönüş *n* comeback, return, turn, cycle
dönüşlü *adj* reflexive
dönüşmek *v* transform
dönüştürmek *v* convert
dönüşüm *n* transformation, conversion
dönüşür *adj* reversible
dördüncü *adj* fourth
dört *adj* four
dört dörtlük *adj* foolproof
dörtnala gitmek *v* gallop
dörtyol *n* crossroads
döşemek *v* furnish
döşemelik *n* upholstery
döviz *n* currency
dövmek *v* batter, flog, ram, club, beat
dövüşçü *n* combatant
dragon *n* dragon
dramatik *adj* dramatic
dramatize etmek *v* dramatize
dua *n* prayer
dua etmek *v* pray
dudak *n* lip
dul *n* widow
dul erkek *n* widower

duman *n* fumes
dumanlı *adj* hazy
durağan *adj* stable, stationary
durak *n* stop
durdurma *n* holdup
durdurmak *v* abort, cease, discontinue, halt, shut off
durgun *adj* sluggish, stagnant, standstill, still
durgunlaşma *n* stagnation
durgunlaşmak *v* stagnate
durgunluk *n* lull
durmadan *adv* ceaselessly, nonstop
durmak *v* stop
durulamak *v* purify, rinse
durum *n* way, circumstance, situation, state
durumsallık *n* contingency
duruş *n* stand
duruşma *n* hearing, trial
duş *n* shower
duvar *n* wall
duvarcı *n* mason, bricklayer
duygu *n* emotion, feeling, sentiment
duygusal *adj* emotional, sentimental
duygusuz *adj* frigid
duyu *n* sense
duyulmadık *adj* unheard-of
duyulur *adj* audible

duyurmak *v* announce, give out
duyuru *n* announcement
düdük *n* pipe
düello *n* duel
düğme *n* button
düğme iliği *n* buttonhole
düğmeyi açmak *v* unbutton
düğüm *n* knot, tie
düğün *n* wedding
düğüne ait *adj* bridal
dük *n* duke
dükkan *n* shop
dümdüz *adj* straight
dümen *n* helm, rudder
dün *adv* yesterday
dün gece *adv* last night
dünya *n* earth, world
dünya çapında *adj* worldwide
dünyevi *adj* worldly
dürbün *n* binoculars
dürtmek *v* goad, prod, jolt
dürtü *n* sting; impulse, urge, incentive, motive
dürtüklemek *v* spur
dürüst *adj* faithful, candid, frank, honest
dürüstçe *adv* frankly
dürüstlük *n* frankness, honesty
düşes *n* duchess
düşkün *adj* affectionate
düşkünlük *n* affection, fondness
düşman *n* adversary, enemy, foe

düşman etmek *v* antagonize
düşmanca *adj* hostile
düşmanlık *n* hostility
düşmek *v* drop, fall, fall down, go down
düşük yapmak *v* miscarry
düşünce *n* consideration, notion, thought
düşünceli *adj* considerate, thoughtful
düşüncesiz *adj* brusque, hasty, insensitive
düşünmek *v* contemplate, think
düşüş *n* drop, decline, decrease, slump, fall
düz *adj* plain, flat
düz olmayan *adj* uneven
düzeltici *n* conditioner
düzeltme *n* amendment, revision
düzeltmek *v* amend, revise, straighten out
düzen *n* array, formation, regularity
düzenbaz *adj* wily
düzenek *n* setup
düzenleme *n* adjustment, regulation, arrangement
düzenlemek *v* adjust, edit, lay-out, rank, regulate, spruce up
düzenlenebilir *adj* adjustable
düzenli *adj* methodical, neat
düzenli bir şekilde *adv* neatly

düzenli şekilde *adv* regularly
düzensiz *adj* disorganized, irregular, tumultuous
düzey *n* level
düzgün *adj* proper
düzine *n* dozen
düzlem *n* plane, platform
düzleştirmek *v* flatten, smooth
düzyazı *n* prose

E

e göre *pre* according to
e kadar *adv* till
e kadar *pre* until
e karşı *pre* versus
e yapışmak *v* adhere
ebe *n* midwife
ebedi *adj* timeless
ebediyen *adv* forever
ebediyet *n* eternity
ebeveyn *n* parents
eczacı *n* pharmacist
eczane *n* drugstore, pharmacy
edebiyat *n* literature
edep *n* decency
edepli *adj* decent
edepsiz *adj* nasty

edinmek *v* procure
efendi *n* patron
efendi *adj* gallant, genteel
efsane *n* legend, myth
eften püften *adj* nitpicking
egemen olmak *v* dominate
egemenlik *n* dominion, mastery
egoist *n* egoist
egzersiz *n* exercise
egzotik *adj* exotic
eğer *c* if
eğik *adj* lean, slanted
eğik çizgi *n* slash
eğilim *n* inclination, penchant, propensity, tendency, trend
eğilimli *adj* predisposed, prone
eğilmek *v* incline
eğilmez *adj* inflexible
eğitimsel *adj* educational
eğitmek *v* educate
eğlence *n* amusement, diversion, entertainment, pastime
eğlenceli *adj* amusing, entertaining
eğlenceli *n* fun
eğlendirmek *v* amuse, entertain
eğlenmek *v* revel, play
eğmek *v* tilt, bend
eğri *adj* warped
eğrilmek *v* warp
ehil *adj* competent
ehlileştirmek *v* tame

ehliyet *n* proficiency
ek *adj* additional
ek *n* appendix, attachment
Ekim *n* October
ekin *n* crop
ekip *n* pool, crew
ekip biçme *n* cultivation
ekip biçmek *v* farm
eklem *n* joint
ekleme *n* addition, insertion
eklemek *v* add
ekmek *n* bread
ekmek *v* plant
ekmek kızartmak *v* toast
ekoloji *n* ecology
ekonomi *n* economy
ekonomik *adj* economical
ekonomik kriz *n* depression
ekran *n* screen
Ekselanslar *n* Highness
eksen *n* axis
eksi *adj* minus
eksik *adj* absent, deficient
eksik *n* lack
eksiklik *n* absence, deficiency, shortage
eksilmek *v* lack, run out
ekstra *adv* extra
ekşi *adj* sour
ekvator *n* equator
el *n* hand
el altından *adj* clandestine

el arabası *n* cart, trolley
el bombası *n* grenade
el çantası *n* handbag
el çırpmak *v* clap
el feneri *n* torch, flashlight
el kitabı *n* handbook, manual
el koymak *v* confiscate, impound, levy
el sıkışma *n* handshake
el sürmek *n* handle
el yapımı *adj* handmade
el yazısı *n* handwriting, manuscript
elastik *adj* elastic
elbette *adv* surely
elbise *n* robe
elbise kolu *n* sleeve
elçilik *n* mission, embassy
elde etmek *v* acquire, gain, obtain
elden çıkarma *n* disposal, sellout
elden çıkarmak *v* dispose
elden geçirmek *v* overhaul
eldiven *n* glove
ele geçirmek *v* capture, corner, seize
ele geçmez *adj* elusive
elebaşı *n* ringleader, vanguard
elek *n* mesh, hunting
elektrik *adj* electric, electricity
elektrik direği *n* lamppost
elektrik kesintisi *n* blackout

E

elektrik sigortası *n* fuse
elektrik vermek *v* electrify
elektrikçi *n* electrician
elektrikle idam etmek *v* electrocute
elektronik *adj* electronic
elem *n* sadness
eleman *n* element
elemek *v* eliminate, sift
eleştirel *adj* critical
eleştiri *n* review, critique, criticism
eleştirmek *v* criticize
elle yapılan *adj* manual
elli *adj* fifty
elma *n* apple
elma şarabı *n* cider
elmacık kemiği *n* cheekbone
elmas *n* diamond
elveda *n* farewell
elverişli *adj* convenient, opportune
elverişlilik *n* convenience
elverişsiz *adj* cumbersome
emanet *n* deposit
emanet etmek *v* entrust
embriyon *n* embryo
emeklemek *v* creep
emekli aylığı *n* pension
emekli olmak *v* retire
emeklilik *n* retirement
emici *adj* absorbent

emir *v* command
emir *n* precept, commandment
emlak *n* realty
emmek *v* absorb, pump, soak in, suck
emniyetsiz *adj* unsafe
emretmek *v* bid, direct, prescribe, order
emsal *n* precedent
en aza indirgemek *v* minimize
en çok *adj* most
en iyi *adj* best
en kötü *adj* worst
en sonuncu *adj* latest
en ufak *adj* least
en uzak *adj* utmost
enayi *adj* sucker
endişe *n* anxiety, misgiving
endişe *v* concern
endişe verici *adj* alarming, distressing
endişelenmek *v* distress
endişeli *adj* nervous, anxious
endişeli *n* insecurity
endüstri *n* industry
endüstriyel *adj* industrious
enerji *n* energy
enerji dolu *adj* energetic
enfeksiyon *n* infection
enfes *adj* fantastic
enflasyon *n* inflation
engel *n* handicap, hindrance, hitch, hurdle, impediment, interference, obstacle

engellemek *v* curb, frustrate, hinder, obstruct, thwart

engerek *n* viper

engin *adj* broad, vast

enginar *n* artichoke

enginlik *n* immensity

enişte *n* brother-in-law

enjeksiyon *n* injection

enjekte etmek *v* inject

enkaz *n* wreckage

enlem *n* latitude

enstantane *n* snapshot

entrika *n* intrigue

erdem *n* virtue

erdemli *adj* virtuous, wholesome

ergen *n* adolescent

ergenlik *n* adolescence

erik *n* plum

erime *n* dissolution, thaw

erimek *v* melt

erişilebilir *adj* accessible

erişilemez *adj* inaccessible

erişim *n* access

erişmek *v* retrieve

eritmek *v* dissolve

erkek *n* male

erkek arkadaş *n* boyfriend

erkek torun *n* grandson

erkekçe *adj* virile

erkekler *n* men

erkeklik *n* manliness

erkeksi *adj* manly

erken *adv* early

erken *adj* premature

eroin *n* heroin

erteleme *n* postponement

ertelemek *v* defer, delay, postpone, procrastinate, respite, stall

erzak *n* supplies

esas *adj* intrinsic

esas yemek *n* entree

esaslı *adj* thorough

eserin kopyası *n* reproduction

esin kaynağı *n* inspiration

esinlemek *v* inspire

esinti *n* blow

eski *adj* obsolete

eski moda *adj* old-fashioned

eskiden *adv* formerly

eskitmek *v* wear down

eskrim *n* fencing

esmek *v* blow

esnek *adj* flexible, resilient, supple

esneme *n* yawn

esnemek *v* yawn

esnetmek *v* stretch

esprili *adj* witty

esrar *n* joint

esrarengiz *adj* mystic

estetik *adj* aesthetic

eş *n* spouse, wife; peer

eş anlamlı *n* synonym

eş zamanlı *adj* concurrent

eşdeğer *adj* equivalent
eşek *n* donkey
eşekarısı *n* wasp
eşgüdümlemek *v* coordinate
eşik *n* brink, threshold
eşit *adj* equal, like
eşit olmayan *adj* unequal
eşitlemek *v* equate, level
eşitlik *n* equality
eşitsizlik *n* inequality, odds
eşlemek *v* map; match
eşler *n* wives
eşlik etmek *v* accompany
eşmek *v* squash
eşya *n* stuff
et *n* flesh, meat
et suyu *n* liquor
etap *n* lap
etek *n* skirt
etik *n* morality
etiket *n* label, sticker, tag
etken *n* factor
etkenlik *n* efficiency
etki *n* jolt, impact, effect, influence
etkilemek *v* affect, fascinate, impact, impress
etkili *adj* effective
etkinleştirme *n* activation
etkinleştirmek *v* enable
etkisiz *adj* ineffective, inefficient
etkisiz bırakmak *v* neutralize

etmek *v* do
etrafında *pre* around
etrafını sarmak *v* beset
etrafta takılmak *v* hang around
etsuyu *n* broth
ev *n* home, house
ev dışında *adv* outdoor
ev halkı *n* folks, household
ev hanımı *n* housewife
ev işi *n* housework
ev ödevi *n* homework
ev sahibesi *n* landlady
ev sahibi *n* host, landlord
ev yapımı *adj* homemade
evcil hayvan *n* pet
evcilleştirmek *v* domesticate
evet *adv* yes
evhamlı *adj* apprehensive, neurotic
evini özlemiş *adj* homesick
evlat *n* offspring
evlat edinme *n* adoption
evlat edinmek *v* adopt
evlatlıktan reddetmek *v* disinherit
evlenme *n* matrimony
evlenmek *v* marry, wed
evli *adj* married
evlilik *n* marriage
evlilikle ilgili *adj* conjugal, marital
evrak çantası *n* briefcase
evre *n* phase

evren *n* universe
evrensel *adj* universal
evrim *n* evolution
evrim geçirmek *v* evolve
evsiz *adj* homeless
evvel *adj* prior
eylem *n* deed, verb, action
Eylül *n* September
eyvallah *e* bye
ezberlemek *v* memorize
ezik *n* bruise
eziyet *n* pain
ezme *n* pulp
ezmek *v* crush, mash, trample

F

faal *n* look
faal *adj* active
faal olarak *adv* busily
faaliyet *n* play; activity
fabrika *n* factory
facia *n* holocaust
façeta *n* facet
fail *n* maker
fakir *n* poor
fakülte *n* faculty
falez *n* cliff

fanatik *adj* fanatic
fanilik *n* mortality
fantezi *n* fantasy
fanus *n* lantern
faraza *c* supposing
farazi *adj* tentative
fare *n* mouse
fareler *n* mice
fark *n* difference
fark edilmemiş *adj* unnoticed
fark gözetme *n* segregation
fark gözetmek *v* discriminate
farketmek *v* notice
farkına varmak *v* realize
farkında *adj* aware
farkındalık *n* awareness
farklı *adj* different, distinct
farklı *n* disparity
farksız *adj* tantamount to
fars *n* farce
farz etmek *v* reckon
farzetmek *v* deem, suppose
fasıl *n* episode
fasulye *n* bean
fatih *n* conqueror
fatura *n* invoice, receipt, bill
favori *adj* favorite
favori *n* sideburns; whiskers
fayans *n* tile
fayda *v* avail, benefit
fayda sağlamak *v* court
faydalanan kişi *n* beneficiary

faydalanmak *v* utilize
faydası olmak *v* benefit
faydasızlık *n* futility
fazla kilolu *adj* overweight
fazla mesai *adv* overtime
fazla tahmin etmek *v* overestimate
fazlalık *n* margin, excess, surplus
fazlasıyla uzun *adj* lengthy
feci *adj* disastrous
federal *adj* federal
felaket *n* calamity, disaster, tribulation
felç *n* paralysis
felç olmak *v* paralyze
felsefe *n* philosophy
fena *adj* wicked
fena halde *adv* grossly
fenalık *n* mischief, wickedness
fener *n* lantern, beacon
fenomen *n* phenomenon
feragat etmek *v* relinquish, waive
ferah *adj* roomy, spacious
ferahlama *n* relief
ferahlamak *v* relieve
feribot *n* ferry
ferman *n* mandate
fermuar *n* zipper
feryat *n* cry, shouting, shriek, wail
feryat etmek *v* wail
fesat *n* malice

fesh etmek *v* withdraw
feshetme *n* repeal
feshetmek *v* abolish, abrogate, annul, outlaw, repeal
feshetmek *n* reverse
fesih *n* annulment
fethetmek *v* conquer
fetih *n* conquest
feveran *n* outburst
fevkalade *n* greatness
fevkalade *adj* marvelous, paramount
fıçı *n* barrel, keg
fıkra *n* joke
fındık *n* hazelnut, nut
fındık kabuğu *n* nut-shell
fırça *n* brush
fırçalamak *v* brush
fırıldanmak *v* whirl
fırın *n* bakery; oven
fırıncı *n* baker
fırında pişirmek *v* bake
fırkateyn *n* frigate
fırlamak *v* dodge, dart
fırlatmak *v* hurl, launch, throw, whip, pitch
fırsat *n* occasion, opportunity
fırtına *n* storm
fırtınalı *adj* gusty, stormy
fısıldamak *v* whisper
fısıltı *n* whisper
fıtık *n* hernia**

fiber *n* fiber
fidanlık *n* nursery
fidye ile kurtarmak *v* ransom
figan *n* groan
fiil *n* verb
fikir *n* idea, opinion
fikir birliği *n* consensus
fil *n* elephant
fildişi *n* ivory, tusk
filika *n* cutter
filizlenmek *v* sprout
film *n* film, movie
film çekmek *v* film
film parçası *n* trailer
filo *n* fleet
filozof *n* philosopher
filtre *n* filter
filtrelemek *v* filter
finans *v* finance
finansal *adj* financial
fincan *n* cup
Fince *adj* Finnish
Finlandiya *n* Finland
firar *n* flight
firar etmek *v* flee
firma *n* firm
fiş *n* plug
fitnecilik *n* incitement
fiyasko *n* flop
fiyat *n* price
fiyat aralığı *n* gap
fiyat düşürmek *v* mark down

fiyat teklifi *n* bid
fiyort *n* fjord
fizik *n* physics
fiziksel olarak *adv* physically
flaş *n* flash
flört etmek *v* flirt
flüt *n* flute
fobi *n* phobia
fok *n* seal
formalite *n* paperwork
formül *n* formula, notation
fosfor *n* phosphorus
fosil *n* fossil
fotoğraf *n* photo, photography
fotoğraf çekmek *v* photograph
fotoğraf makinesi *n* camera
fotoğraf sehpası *n* tripod
fotoğrafçı *n* photographer
fotokopi *n* photocopy
fotokopi makınası *n* copier
foyasını çıkarmak *v* unmask
Fransa *n* France
Fransız *adj* French
frapan *adj* flamboyant
fren *n* brake
frengi *n* syphilis
frenlemek *v* brake
fuar *n* fair
futbol *n* football
fuzuli *adj* superfluous
füme *adj* smoked

G

gaf *n* blunder

gaga *n* bill, beak

gagalamak *v* peck

galaksi *n* galaxy

galeri *n* gallery

galip *adj* triumphant

galip *n* victor

galon *n* gallon

galvanizlemek *v* galvanize

gangster *n* gangster, mobster

gangsterlik *n* racketeering

ganimet *n* booty, loot, trophy

ganimetlemek *v* loot

garaj *n* garage

garanti *n* guarantee, warranty

garanti etmek *v* ensure, guarantee

garantör *n* guarantor

garaz *n* bile

garazlı *adj* spiteful

gardırop *n* wardrobe

gardiyan *n* jailer

garez *n* grudge, rancor, spite

gargara yapmak *v* gargle

garip *adj* odd, queer, strange, weird

gariplik *n* oddity

garnitür *n* garnish

garnizon *n* garrison, headquarters

garson *n* waiter

gaspetmek *v* usurp

gayret *n* ardor, endeavor, exertion, zeal

gayret etmek *v* endeavor, strive

gayretli *adj* ardent, diligent, zealous

gayri meşru *adj* illegitimate

gayri resmi olarak *adv* unofficially

gayri şahsi *adj* impersonal

gaz *n* gas

gazap *n* fury

gazete *n* newspaper, journal

gazete bayii *n* newsstand

gazeteci *n* journalist

gazi *n* veteran

gazino *n* casino

gazlı bez *n* gauze

gazoz *n* soda

gebe kalma *n* conception

gebe kalmak *v* conceive

gebelik *n* gestation

gece *n* night

geceleyin *adj* nocturnal

gecelik *n* gown, nightgown

geceyarısı *n* midnight

gecikme *n* delay

gecikmiş *adj* overdue, retarded

geç *adv* late, tardy

geç kahvaltı *n* brunch

geç kalmış *adj* belated

geçerli *adj* binding, valid

geçerli kılmak *v* validate

geçerlilik *n* validity
geçersiz *n* invalid
geçersiz *adj* void
geçersiz kılmak *v* invalidate, overrule, revoke
geçici *adj* contemporary, provisional, temporary, transient
geçici heves *n* fad
geçim yolu *n* livelihood
geçimini sağlamak *v* live off
geçinmek *v* subsist
geçirgen *adj* porous
geçirmek *v* undergo
geçiş *n* lobby, pass, transition
geçme *n* lapse
geçmek *v* get by, pass
geçmiş *adj* past, recent
geçmişe dönük *adj* retroactive
geğirmek *v* belch, burp
geğirti *n* belch, burp
gelecek *n* future
gelecek *adj* upcoming
gelen *adj* coming, incoming
gelenek *n* custom, tradition
geleneksel *adj* conventional, customary
gelin *n* bride, daughter-in-law
gelincik *n* poppy
gelir *n* income
gelişme *n* improvement
gelişmek *v* prosper
geliştirmek *v* develop, entrance, improve

gelmek *v* come, turn up
gemi *n* ship, boat
gemi enkazı *n* shipwreck
gemi yolculuğu *v* cruise
gemici *n* sailor
gemiden denize *adv* overboard
gen *n* gene
genç *n* teenager
genç *adj* young, youthful
genç kız *n* chick
gençleştirmek *v* rejuvenate
gençlik *n* youth
genel *adj* common, public
genel *n* general
genel af *n* amnesty
genel bakış *n* overview
genelde *adv* ordinarily
genelev *n* brothel
genellemek *v* generalize
general *n* general
genetik *adj* genetic
geniş *adj* large, wide
geniş görüşlü *adj* broadminded
genişçe *adv* broadly, widely
genişleme *n* expansion
genişletmek *v* broaden, expand, widen
genişlik *n* span, breadth, width
geometri *n* geometry
gerçek *n* fact, truth
gerçek *adj* real, tangible
gerçekçi *adj* down-to-earth, factual

G

gerçekçilik *n* realism
gerçekdışı *adj* unreal
gerçekleşmemek *v* fall through
gerçekten *adv* head-on, indeed, literally, really
gereç *n* equipment, tool
gerek *n* need
gerekçe *n* warrant
gereken *adj* due
gerekli *adj* necessary
gerekli kılmak *v* necessitate
gereklilik *n* necessity, requirement
gerekmek *v* have to, must, need, require
gereksiz *adj* needless, unnecessary
gergedan *n* rhinoceros
gergin *adj* jumpy, tense
geri *n* rear
geri adım atmak *v* retreat
geri alma *n* resumption
geri almak *v* take back, undo
geri atmak *v* repel
geri çekilme *n* recession
geri çekilmek *v* fall back, move back
geri çekmek *v* retract
geri çevirme *n* refusal
geri dönmek *v* return, turn back
geri gelmek *v* come back
geri getirmek *v* bring back

geri istemek *v* reclaim
geri kalan *adj* remaining
geri kazanmak *v* recycle, win back
geri ödeme *n* refund
geri ödemek *v* pay back, refund
geri tepme *n* backlash
geri tepmek *v* backfire
geri tutmak *v* restrain
geri yaslanmak *v* lean back
geribildirim *n* feedback
geride bırakmak *v* leave
geride kalmak *v* fall behind
gerileme *n* declension
gerilim *n* tension, stress
gerilla *n* guerrilla
geriye sayım *n* countdown
gerizekalı *n* idiot
gerizekalı *adj* moron
germe *n* strain
germek *v* strain
getirmek *v* bring
geveze *adj* garrulous
gevezelik etmek *v* babble
gevrek *n* cereal
gevrek *adj* crisp, tender
gevşek *n* limp
gevşetmek *v* loosen
geyik *n* deer
gezegen *n* planet
gezgin *adj* medicinal
gezgin *n* voyager

gezi *v* sightseeing, trip
gezinmek *v* stroll
gezinti *n* excursion, outing, promenade
gezmeye çıkmak *v* trip
gıcırdamak *v* creak, squeak
gıcırtı *n* creak
gıcırtılı *adj* squeaky
gıda *n* sustenance
gıdıklamak *v* tickle
gıdıklanan *adj* ticklish
gıdıklanma *n* tickle
gibi *adv* as
gibi *pre* like
gidici *adj* bound
girdap *n* whirlpool
girdi *n* input
girinti *n* dent
giriş *n* entrance, entry, way in; introduction, preamble, prelude
girişim *n* enterprise
girişimci *n* entrepreneur
girişken *adj* gregarious
girişmek *v* set about, tackle
girmek *v* enter, go in
gişe *n* box office
gitar *n* guitar
gitmek *v* go
gitmek üzere *adj* bound for
gittikçe küçülmek *v* dwindle
giydirmek *v* clothe
giyim eşyası *n* wear

giyim kuşam *n* apparel
giyinmek *v* dress, wear
giyotin *n* guillotine
giysi *n* dress, garment, clothes
giysiler *n* clothes
gizem *n* mystery
gizemli *adj* mysterious
gizleme *n* cover-up
gizlemek *v* conceal
gizlenme yeri *n* hideaway
gizlenmek *v* hide
gizli *adj* confidential, covert, hidden, stealthy, undercover
gizli *n* secret
gizlice *adv* secretly
gizlice işbirliği yapmak *v* connive
gizlilik *n* privacy, secrecy
gladyatör *n* gladiator
glikoz *n* glucose
gol *n* goal
gol atmak *v* score
goril *n* gorilla
göbek *n* belly, hub
göbek deliği *n* belly button
göç *n* immigration
göç etmek *v* immigrate
göçmek *v* emigrate, migrate
göçmen *n* emigrant, immigrant, migrant, settler
göğüs *n* breast, chest
gök gürültüsü *n* thunder

G

G

gök tutulması *n* eclipse
gökdelen *n* skyscraper
gökkuşağı *n* rainbow
göklere çıkarmak *v* enthuse
gökyüzü *n* sky
gökyüzündeki nokta *n* midair
göl *n* lake
gölcük *n* lagoon
gölet *n* pond
gölge *n* shadow, shade
gölgede bırakmak *v* overshadow
gölgeli *adj* shady
gömlek *n* shirt
gömmek *v* bury
gönder *n* flagpole
gönderen *n* sender
göndermek *v* relegate, send
gönlünü almak *v* conciliate
gönüllü *n* volunteer
gönüllülük *n* readiness
gönülsüz *adj* reluctant
gönülsüzlükle *adv* reluctantly
gönye *n* square
göreli *adj* relative
göreneksel *adj* orthodox
görev *n* charge, task duty
görev yapmak *v* officiate
görevden almak *v* depose
görevini kötüye kullanmak *v* malpractice
görevlendirmek *v* charge
görevli *n* attendant

görgü kuralları *n* etiquette
görgü tanığı *n* eyewitness
görgüsüz *adj* coarse
görkemli *adj* grand, magnificent, majestic, sumptuous
görmek *v* see
görsel *adj* visual
görülebilir *adj* visible
görümce *n* sister-in-law
görüngü *n* phenomenon
görünmek *v* seem, appear
görünmez *adj* invisible
görüntü *n* image, display
görüntüleme *v* view
görüntülemek *v* display, screen
görünüm *n* appearance
görünürlük *n* visibility
görünüş *n* aspect, looks, spectacle
görüş *n* sight, vision
görüş sahası *n* reach
görüş yeteneği *n* eyesight
gösteri *n* parade
gösteriş yapmak *v* show off
gösterişsiz *adj* unassuming
göstermek *v* indicate, show
göstermelik *adj* conspicuous
götürü *n* lump sum
gövde *n* trunk
göz *n* eye
göz alan *adj* eye-catching
göz atmak *v* glance, browse

göz dağı *n* menace
göz doktoru *n* optician
göz kamaştıran *adj* dazzling
göz kamaştırmak *v* blind, dazzle
göz kapağı *n* eyelid
göz kırpmak *v* blink, wink
göz siperi *n* shade
göz yummak *v* condone, tolerate
gözardı etmek *v* ignore
gözden düşmek *v* disgrace
gözden düşürmek *v* discredit
gözden geçirmek *v* go through, look at, look over, review
göze çarpan *adj* outstanding, striking
göze çarpmak *v* stand out
gözenek *n* pore
gözetleme deliği *n* loophole
gözetme *n* surveillance
gözetmek *v* look after
gözlem *n* observation
gözlemek *v* await
gözlemevi *n* observatory
gözlemlemek *v* observe
gözleri bağlı *n* blindfold
gözlerini bağlamak *v* blindfold
gözlerini dikmek *v* stare
gözlük *n* eyeglasses, glasses
gözüne ilişme *n* glimpse
gözüne ilişmek *v* glimpse
gözünü dikmek *v* gaze
gözüpek *adj* daunting

gözyaşı *n* tear
grafik *adj* graphic
grafik *n* chart
gram *n* gram
gramer *n* grammar
granit *n* granite
gresleme *n* lubrication
grev *n* strike, walkout
greyfurt *n* grapefruit
gri *adj* gray
grimsi *adj* grayish
grip *n* flu
grönland *n* Greenland
grup *n* fellowship, group
gurulu biçimde *adv* proudly
gurup *n* sundown
gurur *n* pride
gururlu *adj* proud
gut *n* gout
gübre *n* dung, manure
gübrelemek *v* fertilize
gücendirmek *v* embitter
gücenme *n* offense, resentment
güç *adj* arduous
güç *n* force, power
güç bela *adv* barely
güç kullanmak *v* exert
güçlendirmek *v* boost, strengthen
güçlü *adj* mighty, potent, powerful, strong
güçlük *n* hang-up

G

G

güçsüz *adj* powerless
güçsüz takım *n* underdog
gül *n* rose
güldürücü *adj* humorous
güle güle *n* bypass
gülmek *v* laugh
gülümseme *n* smile
gülümsemek *v* smile
gülünç *adj* grotesque, laughable
gümbürdemek *v* boom
gümbürtü *n* boom
gümrük *n* customs
gümüş *n* silver
gümüş eşya *n* silverware
gümüş kaplama *adj* silver-plated
gümüşçü *n* silversmith
gün *n* day
gün batımı *n* sunset
gün doğumu *n* sunrise
gün ortası *n* midday
gün yüzüne çıkarmak *v* unearth
günah *n* sin
günah çıkarma odası *n*
  confessional
günah çıkartan papaz *n*
  confessor
günah keçisi *n* scapegoat
günaha girmek *v* sin
günaha teşvik *n* temptation
günahkar *adj* sinful
günahkar *n* sinner
günce *n* diary

güncel *adj* up-to-date
güncellemek *v* update
güneş *n* sun
güneş çarpması *n* heatstroke
güneş gözlüğü *n* sunglasses
güneş kremi *n* sunblock
güneş yanığı *n* sunburn
güneşe ait *adj* solar
güneşlenmek *v* bask
güneşli *adj* sunny
güney *n* south
güneybatı *n* southwest
güneydoğu *n* southeast
güneye ait *adj* southern
güneye giden *adv* southbound
güneyli *n* southerner
günlük *n* incense
günlük *adv* daily
güreş *n* wrestling
güreşçi *n* wrestler
güreşmek *v* wrestle
gürleme *n* roar
gürüldemek *v* rumble
gürültü *n* racket, noise, tumult
gürültücü *adj* noisy, rowdy,
  boisterous, loud
gürültülü biçimde *adv* noisily
güve *n* moth
güveç *n* casserole, stew
güven *n* faith, confidence
güven vermek *v* reassure
güvence *n* assurance

güvenilir *adj* credible,
  dependable, reliable, sure
güvenilirlik *n* credibility
güvenilmez *adj* precarious,
  unreliable
güvenli *adj* safe, secure
güvenlik *n* safety, security
güvenmek *v* depend
güvenmemek *v* mistrust
güvercin *n* dove, pigeon
güvey *n* groom
güzel *adj* beautiful, gorgeous,
  lovely, nice, picturesque, pretty
güzelce *adv* nicely
güzelleştirmek *v* beautify
güzellik *n* beauty

haber bülteni *n* newscast
haber kaynağı *n* informant
haber vermek *v* inform
haberci *n* informer, messenger
habercisi olmak *v* foreshadow
haberdar olmak *v* acquaint
haberler *n* news
habersiz *adj* unaware,
  unconscious

habislik *n* malignancy
hac *n* pilgrimage
hacı *n* pilgrim
hacim *n* bulk, volume
hacimli *adj* bulky
haczetmek *n* confiscation
Haçlı *n* crusader
haçlı seferi *n* crusade
hadise *n* incident
hafıza *n* mind, memory
hafıza kaybı *n* amnesia
hafif *adj* mild, light
hafif sıklet *n* lightweight
hafif şeyler yemek *v* snack
hafif uyku *n* doze
hafiflemiş *adj* extenuating
hafifletici *adj* attenuating
hafifletme *n* remission
hafifletmek *v* attenuate, cushion,
  deaden
hafta *n* week
hafta içi *adj* weekday
hafta sonu *n* weekend
haftalık *adv* weekly
haham *n* rabbi
hain *adj* treacherous
hain *n* villain
hak edilmemiş *adj* undeserved
hak etmek *v* deserve
hak kazanmak *v* qualify
hakaret *n* affront, insult
hakaret *v* scoff

G
H

hakaret edici *adj* offensive
hakaret etmek *v* affront, insult
hakem *n* referee, umpire
hakemlik *n* arbitration
hakikat *n* reality
hakiki *adj* genuine
hakim *n* judge
hakimiyet *n* domination
hakkında *adv* about
hakkında *pre* regarding
hakkını vermek *v* remunerate
haklı çıkarmak *v* vindicate
haksız *adj* unjustified
haksızlık *n* injustice
hal *n* predicament, status
hala *n* aunt
halı *n* carpet, rug
haliç *n* estuary
halka *n* link, ring
halletmek *v* work out, compound
ham *adj* crude
hamak *n* hammock
hamamböceği *n* cockroach
hamburger *n* burger, hamburger
hamile *adj* pregnant
hamilelik *n* pregnancy
hamilik *n* patronage
hamle *n* onslaught
hamlık *n* immaturity
hamur *n* dough
hamur işi *n* pastry
han *n* inn

hançer *n* dagger
hanedan *n* dynasty
hangi *adj* which
hanım *n* lady
hanım evladı *adj* sissy
hanım gibi *adj* ladylike
hanımefendi *n* madam
hapis *n* confinement, jail, prison
hapis süresi *n* stretch
hapse atmak *v* imprison, jail
hapsedilme *v* incarcerate
hapsedilmiş *adj* pent-up
hapsetmek *v* confine, lock up
harabe *n* ruin, slum
haraç *n* extortion
harap *adj* dilapidated
harap *n* waste
harap edici *adj* devastating
harap etmek *v* destroy, devastate, ravage, wreck
haraplık *n* desolation
hararetli *adj* fervent
harcama *n* spending
harcamak *v* spend
harçlık *n* allowance
hardal *n* mustard
hare *n* wave
hareket *n* movement, move, motion
hareket etmek *v* move
harekete geçirmek *v* mobilize
hareketlendirici *adj* rousing

hareketli *adj* brisk, mobile
hareketsiz *adj* immobile, motionless
hareketsizleştirmek *v* immobilize
harici *adj* foreign, exterior
haricinde *pre* barring, except
harika *adj* fabulous, terrific, wonderful
harika *n* marvel, prodigy
harita *n* map
harman *n* blend
harmanlamak *v* blend
harp *n* harp
hasar *n* havoc, injury
hasat *n* harvest
hasat etmek *v* harvest
haset *n* envy
haset etmek *v* envy
hasılat *n* proceeds, yield
hasır *n* mat
hasis *n* miser
hassas *adj* sensitive, sore
hasta *adj* ill, sick
hastalık *n* ailment, disease, illness
hastane *n* hospital
hastaneye yatırmak *v* hospitalize
haşhaş *n* hashish
haşin *adj* severe
haşlamak *v* scald
hat *n* stroke
hata *n* error, fault, mistake
hata yapmak *v* goof, mistake

hatalı *adj* erroneous, faulty
hatalı kullanım *n* misuse
hatasız *adj* impeccable
hatıra *n* memento
hatırlamak *v* remember
hatırlatma *n* reminder
hatırlatmak *v* remind
hav hav *n* bark
hava *n* air, weather
hava akımı *n* circulation
hava boşluğu *n* airspace
hava geçirmez *adj* airtight
hava yalıtımlı *adj* hermetic
havaalanı *n* airport, airfield
havacı *n* aviator
havacılık *n* aviation
havai fişek *n* fireworks
havalandırma *n* ventilation
havalandırmak *v* ventilate, air
havalanmak *v* lift off, take off
havale *n* money order, remittance
havale etmek *v* hand over
havalimanı *n* airport
havan topu *n* mortar
havanın akması *v* circulate
havari *n* apostle, disciple
havasız *adj* stuffy
havayolu *n* airline
havlamak *v* bark
havlu *n* towel
havuç *n* carrot
havuz *n* pool

hayal *n* dream, delusion
hayal etmek *v* imagine
hayal gücü *n* imagination
hayal kırıklığı *n* disappointment, disillusion
hayal kırıklığına uğratmak *v* disappoint
hayal kurmak *v* daydream, dream
hayalet *n* apparition, ghost, phantom
hayali *adj* fictitious, unrealistic
hayat dolu *adj* vivacious
hayati *adj* vital
hayatta kalmak *v* live up, survive
haydut *n* bandit
hayırlı *adj* auspicious
hayırsever *adj* charitable
hayırseverlik *n* charity
haykırmak *v* cry out
hayran *n* fan, admirer, amazement, maze
hayret verici *adj* astounding
hayvan *n* animal
hayvan *adj* brute
hayvan çiftliği *n* ranch
hayvan zehiri *n* venom
hayvanat bahçesi *n* zoo
hayvani *adj* bestial
hazımsızlık *n* indigestion
hazır *adj* ready
hazırlamak *v* prepare

hazırlayıcı *adj* preliminary
hazırlık *n* preparation
hazin *adj* pitiful
hazine *n* treasure
Haziran *n* June
haznedar *n* treasurer
hece *n* syllable
hecelemek *v* spell
hedef *n* destination, target
hediye *n* gift, present, tribute
hediye etmek *v* give away
hekim *n* physician
helikopter *n* chopper, helicopter
hemen *adv* immediately
hemşire *n* nurse
hendek *n* trench, ditch, trap
henüz *c* yet
hep *adv* ever
hep beraber *adj* altogether
hepsi *adj* all, entire, whatever
hepsi *adv* lot
her *adj* each, every
her bir *adj* each other
her gün *adj* everyday
her ikisi de *adj* both
her nasılsa *adv* someway
her nerede *c* wherever
her şey *pro* everything
her zaman *adv* always
hergele *n* scoundrel
herhangi bir *adj* any
herhangi bir şey *pro* anything

herhangi bir zamanda *adv* whenever

herkes *pro* everybody, everyone

hesap *n* account

hesap defteri *n* ledger

hesap makinesi *n* calculator

hesap vermek *v* account for

hesaplama *n* calculation

hesaplamak *v* calculate, compute

hesaplaşma *n* showdown

hesapsız *adj* innumerable

hesaptan düşmek *v* deduct

hevesli *adj* eager, responsive

heveslilik *n* eagerness

heybetli *adj* imposing

heyecan *n* excitement, thrill

heyecan verici *adj* exciting

heyecanlandırmak *v* excite

heyecanlanmak *v* thrill

heyecanlı *adj* hectic

heyelan *n* avalanche

heykel *n* sculpture, statue

heykel gövdesi *n* torso

heykeltıraş *n* sculptor

hıçkırarak ağlamak *v* sob

hıçkırık *n* hiccup, sob

hırçın *adj* harsh, vicious

hırçınlık *n* harshness

hırıldamak *v* wheeze

hırıltı *n* murmur

hırlamak *v* growl

hırs *n* ambition

hırsız *n* burglar, thief

hırsızlık *n* burglary, larceny, robbery, theft

hırsızlık yapmak *v* break in, burglarize

hırslı *adj* ambitious

hıyar *n* cucumber

hız *n* speed, rate

hız vermek *v* hasten

hız yapmak *v* speed

hızla yükselmek *v* soar

hızlandırıcı *n* accelerator

hızlandırmak *v* accelerate, quicken

hızlı *adj* fast, rapid, speedy, express

hızlı içmek *v* guzzle

hızlı koşmak *v* dash

hızlı yemek *v* gobble

hızlıca *adv* expressly, speedily

hiciv *n* satire

hiç *adv* ever

hiç biri *pro* anyone

hiçbir şey *n* nothing

hiçbir yerde *adv* nowhere

hiçbiri *adj* neither

hiçbiri *adv* neither

hiçbiri *pre* none

hiçe saymak *v* snub

hiddetlenmek *v* flare-up

hidrojen *n* hydrogen

hidrolik *adj* hydraulic
hijyen *n* hygiene
hikaye *n* novel
hile *n* delusion, deceit, pretense, ruse, imposition, trick
hile yapmak *v* manipulate, trick
hilebaz *n* juggler
hilekar *n* cheater, con man
hilekar *adj* deceitful
hileli *adj* fraudulent
hilesiz *adj* single-minded
hindistan cevizi *n* coconut
hipnotize etmek *v* hypnotize
hipnoz *n* hypnosis, trance
his *n* feelings
hisse *n* share, allotment, ration
hisse senedi *n* stock
hissedar *n* shareholder
hissedilebilir *adj* palpable
hissetmek *v* feel
hissiz *adj* callous
histeri *n* hysteria
hitabe *n* homily
hitap etmek *v* address
hiyerarşi *n* hierarchy
hiza *n* alignment
hizaya getirmek *v* align
hizmet etmek *v* minister, serve
hizmet vermek *v* service
hizmetçi *n* servant
hobi *n* hobby
hol *n* hallway

holigan *n* hooligan
Hollanda *n* Holland, Netherlands
Hollandalı *adj* Dutch
homurdanma *v* grumble, murmur
hoparlör *n* speaker, loudspeaker
hor görme *n* contempt
hor görmek *v* despise, scorn
hor kullanmak *v* mistreat
horlamak *v* snore
hormon *n* hormone
horoz *n* cock, rooster
hortum *n* twister
horultu *n* snore
hostes *n* stewardess
hoş *adj* fair, delightful, pleasing
hoşa giden *adj* favorable
hoşgörülebilir *adj* tolerable
hoşgörülü *adj* lenient
hoşlanma *n* predilection
hoşlanmak *v* care for, like
hoşlanmama *n* dislike
hoşlanmamak *v* dislike
hoşnut edici *adj* satisfactory
hoşnut etmek *v* gratify
hoşnutsuzluk *adj* discontent
hoşnutsuzluk *n* displeasure
Hristiyan *adj* Christian
Hristiyanlık *n* Christianity
hudut *n* frontier, margin, border, limit
hukuk davası *n* suit

humma *n* fever
hummalı *adj* feverish
hurda *n* scrap
husumet *n* animosity
huşu *n* awe, hush
huysuz *adj* grumpy, moody
huzur *n* peace
huzurlu *adj* peaceful
huzursuz *adj* uneasy
huzursuzluk *n* uneasiness
hüküm *n* sentence, ascendancy, verdict
hükümdar *n* ruler, monarch
hükümdarlık *n* crown
hükümet *n* government
hülasa *n* compendium
hürmet *n* homage
hüsran *n* frustration
hüzünlü *adj* blue

I

ılık *adj* lukewarm, tepid, warm
ılımlı *adj* moderate
ırk *n* race
ırk ayrımına son vermek *v* desegregate

ırkçı *adj* racist
ırkçılık *n* racism
ırsi *adj* hereditary
ısı *n* heat, warmth
ısı derecesi *n* temperature
ısınmak *v* warm up
ısırık *n* bite
ısırmak *v* bite
ısıtıcı *n* heater
ısıtmak *v* heat
ıskartaya ayırmak *v* scrap
ıslah etmek *v* rectify, reorganize
ıslahat *v* reform
ıslak *adj* wet
ıslanmak *v* soak up
ıslık *n* whistle
ıslık çalmak *v* whistle
ısmarlama *adj* custom-made
ısrar *n* insistence
ısrar etmek *v* insist, preserve
ısrarcı *adj* demanding
ıssız *adj* deserted
ıstakoz *n* lobster
ıstırap *n* anguish, suffering, pang
ışık *n* glimmer, light
ışıklı *adj* light
ışıldamak *v* twinkle
ışıltılı *adj* ablaze
ışın *n* beam, ray
ızdırap *n* agony
ızdırap çekmek *v* agonize
ızdırap verici *adj* agonizing

H
I

ızgara *n* broiler, grill
ızgara yapmak *v* broil, charbroil, grill
ızgaralanmış *adj* charbroiled

i

iade *n* extradition, reimbursement, repayment
iade etmek *v* extradite, give back, reimburse
icap ettirmek *v* entail
icat etmek *v* invent
icra etmek *v* perpetrate
iç *adj* inner
iç bahçe *n* courtyard
iç çamaşırı *n* underwear
iç çekme *n* sigh
iç çekmek *v* sigh
içe dönük *adj* introvert
içecek *n* beverage, drink
içerden *pre* within
içeri almak *v* let in
içeri girmek *v* come in, get in
içerik *adj* content
içerilerde *adv* inland
içerlemek *v* resent
içermek *v* contain, include, involve

içgüdü *n* instinct
içilir *adj* drinkable
için *pre* for
içinde *adv* aboard
içinde *pre* in, inside
içinde *adj* inside, interior
içindekiler *n* index
içine çekmek *v* engulf, inhale
içine dökme *n* infusion
içine işlemek *v* penetrate, perforate, permeate, pierce
içki *n* booze, liquor
içkici *n* drinker
içler acısı *adj* deplorable
içmek *v* drink
içtensiz *adj* unfriendly
içtima yapmak *v* muster
idare *n* conduct
idare etmek *v* conduct
iddia *n* claim, allegation, assertion, plea, pretension
iddia etmek *v* allege
ideal *adj* ideal
ideoloji *n* ideology
idol *n* idol
idrak etmek *v* apprehend
ifade *n* recital
ifade etmek *v* articulate, frame
iffet *n* chastity
iflas *n* bankruptcy
iflas etmek *v* bankrupt
iflas etmiş *adj* bankrupt

ifşa *n* revelation
ifşa etmek *v* divulge
iftira *n* calumny, libel, slander
iftira etmek *v* denigrate, reproach
iğne *n* shot, needle, pin, sting
iğneleyici *adj* sarcastic
iğneyle tutturmak *v* pin
iğrenç *adj* disgusting, gruesome, odious, repugnant, gross
iğrenmek *v* abhor, disgust
ihanet *n* betrayal, treachery
ihbar etmek *v* denounce
ihbarcı *n* informer
ihlal *n* infraction, breach
ihlal etmek *v* trespass, violate
ihmal *n* neglect, omission
ihmal etmek *v* leave out, neglect
ihmalkar *adj* negligent
ihracat *v* export
ihraç *n* expulsion
ihtar *n* notice
ihtimal *n* eventuality, likelihood, probability
ihtişam *n* splendor
ihtiva etmek *v* comprise, encompass
ihtiyacı karşılamak *v* cater to
ihtiyatla *adv* gingerly
ihtiyatlı *adj* cautious
ihya etmek *v* recreate
ikame *n* replacement

ikamet etmek *v* dwell, reside
ikametgah *n* dwelling, residence
iken *c* whereas, while
iki *adj* two
iki ayda bir *adj* bimonthly
iki dilli *adj* bilingual
iki katına çıkarmak *v* double
iki kere *adv* twice
iki tane *n* couple
ikieşlilik *n* bigamy
ikilem *n* dilemma
ikili *adj* dual
ikinci *adj* second
ikincil *adj* secondary
ikisinden biri *adj* either
ikiyüzlü *adj* hypocrite
ikiyüzlülük *n* hypocrisy, insincerity
ikiz *n* twin
iklim *n* climate
iklimsel *adj* climatic
ikmal etmek *v* replenish
ikna *n* persuasion
ikna edici *adj* convincing, persuasive
ikna etmek *v* convince, persuade
ikon *n* icon
ikram *n* treat
iktidar *n* power
iktidarsız *adj* impotent
il *n* city
ilaç *n* drug, medicine, pill

i

ilaç tedavisi *n* medication
ilaç vermek *v* drug
ilah *n* deity
ilahi *n* chant, hymn
ilahi *adj* divine, holy
ilahilik *n* divinity
ilahiyat *n* theology
ilahiyat fakültesi *n* seminary
ilahiyatçı *n* theologian
ilan *n* proclamation, banner
ilave *v* augment
ilçe *n* county
ile birlikte *pre* with
ileri atılmak *v* spring
ileri gelen *adj* prominent
ileri gitmek *v* proceed
ileride *pre* ahead
ileride *adv* forward, hereafter
ileriyi görmek *v* foresee
ilerleme *n* advance, headway, progress
ilerlemek *v* advance, go ahead, move forward, progress
iletişim *n* communication
iletişim kurmak *v* communicate
iletken *n* conductor
iletmek *v* transmit
ilgeç *n* preposition
ilgi *n* interest
ilgi çekici *adj* intriguing
ilgilendiren şey *n* concern
ilgili *adj* interested

ilginç *adj* interesting
ilgisiz *adj* indifferent, unrelated, aloof
ilgisizlik *n* apathy, indifference
ilhak *n* annex
ilik *n* marrow
ilişik *adj* attached
ilişki *n* relationship, association; noose
ilişkilendirmek *v* associate
ilişkili *adj* related
iliştirmek *v* attach
ilk *adj* first
ilkbahar *n* spring
ilke *n* motto, principle
ilkel *adj* primitive
ilmihal *n* catechism
iltica *n* defection
iltica etmek *v* defect
iltifat *n* compliment, courtship
iltihap *n* pus
iltihaplanmak *v* fester
ima *n* sound, allusion, implication, mention
ima etmek *v* imply, insinuate
imal etmek *v* manufacture
imalatçı *n* maker
iman *n* creed
imha *n* annihilation
imha etmek *v* annihilate
imkansız *adj* impossible
imkansızlık *n* impossibility

imparator *n* emperor
imparatoriçe *n* empress
imparatorluk *n* imperialism, empire
imrenmek *v* covet
imtiyaz *n* franchise, privilege
imza *n* autograph, signature
imzalamak *v* subscribe
inanan *n* believer
inancını yitirmiş *adj* disenchanted
inanç *n* conviction, belief, faith
inançlı *adj* faithful
inanılır *adj* believable
inanılmaz *adj* incredible, shocking, unbelievable
inanmak *v* believe
inanmama *n* disbelief
inat *n* obstinacy
inatçı *adj* persistent, stubborn
ince *adj* thin
ince bir anlayış *n* tact
ince şekilde *adv* thinly
ince şerit *n* shred
ince uzun *adj* slim
incelemek *v* go over, look into, look through
inci *n* pearl
incil *n* bible, gospel
incilden *adj* biblical
incinmemiş *adj* unhurt
incir *n* fig

inç *n* inch
indirgemek *v* demote
indirim *n* deduction, discount, rebate, sale
indirim yapmak *v* discount
indirimli *adj* deductible
indirmek *v* dismount, get down; slash
inek *n* cow
infilak *n* blast
İngiliz *adj* English
İngiliz anahtarı *n* wrench
İngiltere *n* England
inilti *n* moan
inisiyatif *n* initiative
iniş *n* descent
inkar *n* denial
inkar edilemez *adj* undeniable
inkar etmek *v* deny
inlemek *v* groan, moan
inmek *v* descend, get off, step down
insaf *n* mercy
insaflı *adj* merciful
insafsız *adj* merciless, ruthless
insafsızca *adv* harshly
insan avı *n* manhunt
insan gücü *n* manpower
insan soyu *n* mankind
insancıl *adj* human
insanlar *n* people
insanlık *n* humanities

insanoğlu *n* human being, humankind

insizyon *n* incision

inşa etmek *v* construct

inşaa etmek *v* build

inşaat *n* building, construction

inşaat iskelesi *n* scaffolding

inşaat işçisi *n* builder

internet sitesi *n* web site

intihar *n* suicide

intikal etmek *v* lapse

intikam *n* vengeance

intikam almak *v* avenge

inziva *n* retirement

ip *n* rope

ipek *n* silk

ipliğe dizmek *v* thread

iplik *n* thread

ipotek *n* mortgage

iptal *n* cancellation, withdrawal

iptal edilmiş *adj* withdrawn

iptal etmek *v* call off, cancel, quash

ipucu *n* clue, hint, inkling

ipucu vermek *v* hint

irade *n* will

irfan *n* scholarship

iriyarı *adj* burly

İrlanda *n* Ireland

İrlandalı *adj* Irish

ironi *n* irony

irtibat *n* liaison

isabet *n* precision, hit

ishal *n* diarrhea

isim *n* name; noun

isimlendirmek *v* name

iskele *n* wharf

iskelet *n* frame, skeleton

iskemle *n* stool

İslami *adj* Islamic

ismin ilk harfleri *n* initials

İspanya *n* Spain

İspanyol *n* Spaniard

ispat etmek *v* demonstrate

israf *n* extravagance

israf etmek *v* lavish

istasyon *n* station

istatistik *n* statistic

isteğe bağlı *adj* optional

istek *n* request

istekle *adv* willingly

istekli *adj* willing

isteklilik *n* willingness

isteksiz *adj* averse, indisposed

isteksizce *adv* unwillingly

isteksizlik *n* aversion

istemek *v* call, ask, want

istemeyerek *adv* grudgingly

istenilmeyen *adj* undesirable

isteri *adj* hysterical

istiare *n* metaphor

istif etmek *v* stack

istifa *n* resignation

istihdam *n* employment

istihza *n* sarcasm
istikrar *n* stability
istikrarlı *adj* consistent
istikrarsız *adj* unsteady
istikrarsızlık *n* instability
istila *n* annexation, influx, invasion
istila et *adj* infested
istila etmek *v* invade
istilacı *n* invader
istirahat *n* repose, rest
istiridye *n* oyster
istismar *n* exploit
istisna *n* exception
istisnai *adj* exceptional
İsveç *n* Sweden
İsveçli *adj* Swedish
İsviçre *n* Switzerland
İsviçreli *adj* Swiss
isyan *n* riot, rebellion revolt, insurgency, insurrection
isyan etmek *v* rebel, revolt
isyancı *n* rebel
iş *n* business, job, work; affair, deed
iş adamı *n* businessman
iş arkadaşı *n* colleague
iş gücü *n* labor
işaret *n* mark, sign
işaret etmek *v* designate, motion, sign
işaretle çağırmak *v* beckon

işaretlemek *v* mark
işbirliği *n* collaboration, cooperation
işbirliği yapmak *v* collaborate, cooperate
işbirlikçi *n* collaborator
işçi *n* laborer, oar, worker
işe almak *v* employ, recruit
işemek *v* urinate
işgal etmek *v* occupy, preoccupy
işgücünü azaltmak *v* downsize
işitmek *v* hear
işkence *n* torment, torture
işkence etmek *v* torment, torture
işlem *n* transaction
işleme tabi tutmak *v* process
işlemek *v* handle, instill, perform, work, farm
işlemeli *adj* inlaid
işletilebilir *adj* workable
işletmek *v* operate
işlev *n* function
işsiz *adj* jobless, unemployed
işsizlik *n* unemployment
iştah *n* appetite
işten atma *n* sack
işten çıkarma *n* dismissal
iştira *n* purchase
işveren *n* employer
itaat *v* abide by
itaat *n* compliance, compliance, obedience

j

itaat etmek *v* conform
itaat etmemek *v* disobey
itaatkar *adj* obedient
itaatsiz *adj* disobedient
itaatsizlik *n* disobedience, distrust
italik *adj* italics
İtalya *n* Italy
İtalyan *adj* Italian
itfa *n* redemption
itfaiye eri *n* fireman
itfaiyeci *n* firefighter
ithaf *v* deduce
ithal etmek *v* import
ithalat *n* importation
itham etmek *v* indict
itibar *v* esteem
itibar etmek *v* credit
itibarsızlık *n* degradation
itici *n* projectile
itilaf *n* conflict
itimat *n* reliance, trust, confidence
itimat etmek *v* rely on, trust
itimat etmemek *v* distrust
itimatsız *adj* distrustful
itiraf *n* admission, confession
itiraf etmek *v* confess, profess
itirafçı *n* confessor
itiraz *n* contest, objection
itiş *n* shove
itmek *v* push

ittifak *n* alliance
ittifak etmek *v* ally
iyi *adv* well
iyi *adj* fine, good
iyi bilinen *adj* well-known
iyi kalpli *adj* benign
iyi niyet *n* benevolence, goodwill
iyi niyetli *adj* benevolent
iyileşen *adj* convalescent
iyileşme *n* recovery
iyileşmek *v* recuperate
iyileştirici *adj* balmy
iyileştirici *n* healer
iyileştirmek *v* heal
iyilik *n* favor, goodness
iyimser *adj* optimistic
iyimserlik *n* optimism
iyot *n* iodine
iz *n* trail, track
iz sürmek *v* stalk, trace
izci *n* scout
izdiham *n* congestion; multitude
izdiham *adj* crushing
izin *n* authorization, permission
izin vermek *v* allow, permit, warrant
izlemek *v* monitor, watch, trail
izleyici *n* onlooker
izmarit *n* stub
izolasyon *n* isolation
izole etmek *v* isolate

J

jaguar *n* jaguar
Japon *adj* Japanese
Japonya *n* Japan
jartiyer *n* garter
jeneratör *n* generator
jeoloji *n* geology
jest *n* gesture
jest yapmak *v* gesticulate
jilet *n* razor
jinekoloji *n* gynecology
joker *n* joker
jüri *n* jury

K

kaba *adj* crude, crass, impolite; rough, coarse
kaba *n* mean
kaba *adv* loudly
kabadayı *n* hoodlum
kabahat *n* misconduct, misdemeanor
kabahatli *n* culpability
kabakulak *n* mumps
kabarcık *n* blister; bubble

kabarık *adj* puffy
kabartmak *v* emboss
kabataslak *adj* sketchy
kabız *adj* constipated
kabızlık *n* constipation
kabızlık vermek *v* constipate
kabile *n* clan, tribe
kabiliyet *n* aptitude, competence, vocation
kabiliyetsiz *adj* incapable
kabin *n* booth, cabin
kabine *n* cabinet
kablo *n* cable, cord
kablosuz *adj* cordless, wireless
kabuk *n* crust, peel, shell
kabuklu *adj* crusty
kabul *n* recognition, acceptance, admittance, admission, concession
kabul edilebilir *adj* acceptable
kabul edilemez *adj* inadmissible
kabul etmek *v* accept, acknowledge, grant, admit
kabul etmemek *v* dissent
kaburga *n* rib
kabza *n* hilt
kaçak *n* contraband; deserter, fugitive
kaçakçı *n* smuggler
kaçamak *n* evasion
kaçık *adj* demented, mental
kaçınılabilir *adj* avoidable

J
K

kaçınılmaz *adj* inevitable, unavoidable
kaçınma *n* avoidance
kaçınmak *v* abstain, abstinence, avoid, refrain
kaçırma *n* abduction, hijack
kaçırmak *v* miss, abduct
kaçmak *v* break free, escape, get away, run away
kadar etmek *v* amount to
kadeh *n* chalice
kademe *n* level
kademeli *adj* gradual
kader *n* destiny, fate
kadın *n* woman, female
kadın iç çamaşırı *n* lingerie
kadın mirasçı *n* heiress
kadın terzi *n* seamstress
kadınlar *n* women
kadınsı *adj* feminine
kadife *n* velvet
kadran *n* dial
kadrolaşmak *v* staff
kafa derisi *n* scalp
kafa karıştıran *adj* confusing
kafa tutmak *v* defy
kafa ütülemek *v* pester
kafadar *n* crony
kafası karışmış *adj* disoriented
kafasını karıştırmak *v* confuse
kafatası *n* skull
kafein *n* caffeine

kafeinsiz *adj* decaf
kafes *n* cage
kafeterya *n* cafeteria
kafile *n* procession
kafir *n* heathen
kafir *adj* heretic, profane
kafiye *n* rhyme
kağıt *n* paper
kahkaha *n* laugh, laughter
kahkül *n* fringe
kahraman *n* hero
kahramanlık *n* heroism
kahretmek *v* damn
kahvaltı *n* breakfast
kahve *n* coffee
kahverengi *adj* brown
kahya *n* housekeeper
kakao *n* cocoa
kâkül *n* bangs
kalabalık *adj* crowded
kalabalık *n* throng
kalan *adj* due
kalbe ait *adj* cardiac
kalça *n* hip
kaldıraç *n* crowbar
kaldırım *n* pavement, sidewalk
kaldırma *n* removal
kaldırmak *v* lift, pick up; rouse; dismount
kale *n* castle, fort
kaleci *n* goalkeeper
kalem *n* pencil

kalemtıraş *n* sharpener
kalıcı *adj* permanent
kalın *adj* thick
kalın kafalı *adj* dull
kalınlaştırmak *v* thicken
kalınlık *n* thickness
kalıntı *n* residue, relic, remainder, remnant, vestige
kalıp *n* mold
kalıp dökmek *v* mold
kalış *n* stay
kalıt *n* inheritance
kalibrasyon *v* gauge
kalibre *n* caliber
kalitesiz *adj* shoddy
kalkan *v* shield
kalkık *adj* erect
kalkınma *n* development
kalkış *n* lift-off
kalkmak *v* erect, get up
kalmak *v* remain, stay
kalori *n* calorie
kalorifer *n* heating
kalp *n* heart
kalp atışı *n* heartbeat
kalp krizi *n* cardiac arrest
kalple ilgili *adj* coronary
kalpsiz *adj* heartless
kambur *n* hump, hunchback
kamçı *n* lash
kamp *n* camp
kamp ateşi *n* campfire

kamp yapmak *v* camp
kampanya *n* campaign
kampanya yapmak *v* campaign
kamuflaj *n* camouflage
kamufle etmek *v* camouflage
kamulaştırmak *v* expropriate
kamyon *n* truck
kamyoncu *n* trucker
kamyonet *n* pickup
kan *n* blood
kan davası *n* feud
kan nakil *n* transfusion
kana susamış *adj* bloodthirsty
kanal *n* canal, channel
kanalizasyon *n* drainage, sewer
kanama *n* hemorrhage
kanamak *v* bleed
kanarya *n* canary
kanat *n* wing
kanayan *n* bleeding
kanca *n* hook
kandırmak *v* deceive, fool
kanepe *n* couch, sofa
kangren *n* gangrene
kanguru *n* kangaroo
kanıt *n* proof
kanıtlamak *v* prove
kanıtlanmış *adj* proven
kanıtlayan *adj* demonstrative
kanlı *adj* bloody, gory
kano *n* canoe
kanser *n* cancer

K

kanserli *adj* cancerous

kantin *n* canteen

kanun *n* code, law, statute, act

kanun yapmak *v* legislate

kanuni *n* lawmaker

kanunsuz *adj* unlawful

kanyon *n* canyon, chasm

kaos *n* chaos

kap *n* pot

kapak *n* lid, cap

kapalı *adj* close, closed

kapalı çarşı *n* mall

kapanış *n* closure

kapasite *n* capacity

kapatmak *v* close, shut, switch off, turn off

kapı *n* port, door

kapı aralığı *n* doorway

kapı çalmak *v* knock

kapı girişi *n* doorstep

kapı zili *n* doorbell

kapıcı *n* janitor, porter

kapitalizm *n* capitalism

kapkara *adj* pitch-black

kaplan *n* tiger

kaplıca *n* spa

kaplumbağa *n* turtle

kapmak *v* snatch

kapris *n* whim

kapsam *n* coverage, enclosure, cover; extent, scope

kapsamak *v* enclose, cover, embody

kapsamlı *adj* comprehensive

kapsül *n* capsule

kaptan *n* captain

kar *n* profit; snow

kar etmek *v* profit

kar getiren *adj* profitable

kar tanesi *n* snowflake

kar yağışı *n* snowfall

kar yağmak *v* snow

kara çalmak *v* defame

kara ile çevrili *adj* landlocked

kara kurbağa *n* toad

karaağaç *n* elm

karabasan *n* nightmare

karaca *n* venison

karakol *n* patrol

karakter *n* character

karakteristik *adj* characteristic

karakulak *n* lynx

karalama *n* scratch

karalamak *v* scribble

karalık *n* blackness

karamsar *adj* pessimistic

karamsarlık *n* pessimism

karanfil *n* carnation

karanlık *n* darkness

karar *n* decision, judgment

karar vermek *v* decide, determine

kararlı *adj* adamant, decisive, resolute

kararlılık *n* determination

kararname *n* decree
kararsız *adj* ambivalent, indecisive, undecided
kararsızlık *n* indecision
karartmak *v* darken, tarnish
karasal *adj* terrestrial
karat *n* carat
karatahta *n* blackboard, chalkboard
karate *n* karate
karavan *n* caravan
karaya çıkarma *n* landing
karaya çıkarmak *v* disembark
karbüratör *n* carburetor
kardeş *n* brother
kardeşçe *adj* brotherly, fraternal
kardeşlik *n* brotherhood, fraternity
kardiyoloji *n* cardiology
kare *adj* square
karga *n* crow
kargaşa *n* disorder, mayhem
kargo *n* cargo
karı *n* wife
karılar *n* wives
karın *n* abdomen, tummy
karınca *n* ant
karışık *adj* intricate
karışıklık *n* confusion, turmoil, upheaval, jam
karışım *n* assortment, mixture, concoction

karışmak *v* interfere
karıştırmak *v* adulterate, embroil, implicate, mix, shuffle, stir
karides *n* prawn, shrimp
karikatür *n* caricature
kariyer *n* career
karizma *n* charisma
karizmatik *adj* charismatic
karmakarışık *adj* chaotic; promiscuous
karmaşık *adj* complex
karmaşıklık *n* complexity
karnabahar *n* cauliflower
karne ile vermek *v* ration
karpuz *n* watermelon
karsız *adj* unprofitable
karşı *pre* against
karşı *n* opposite
karşı çıkmak *v* object
karşı koymak *v* counteract, face up to, oppose
karşıda *adv* opposite
karşılamak *v* afford, encounter, welcome
karşılanabilir *adj* affordable, comparable
karşılaşma *n* encounter
karşılaşmak *v* bump into, come across, run into
karşılaştırma *n* comparison, contrast

K

karşılaştırmak *v* compare
karşılaştırmalı *adj* comparative
karşılık *n* provision
karşılık vermek *v* strike back
karşılıklı *adj* alternate; reciprocal
karşılıklı olarak *adv* mutually
karşıt *adj* adverse, contrary, opposite
karşıtlık *n* contrast
karşıya geçmek *v* cross
kart *n* postcard, card
kartal *n* eagle
kartvizit *n* card
kas *n* muscle
kasa *n* safe
kasaba *n* borough, town
kasap *n* butcher
kase *n* bowl
kaset *n* tape
kasık *n* groin
kasılma *n* contraction
Kasım *n* November
kasırga *n* cyclone, hurricane
kasıt *n* premeditation
kasiyer *n* cashier
kast *n* caste
kasten *adv* purposely
kastetmek *v* intend
kasvetli *adj* bleak, gloomy, somber
kaş *n* brow, eyebrow
kaşık *n* spoon

kaşık dolusu *n* spoonful
kaşımak *v* scratch
kaşınmak *v* itch
kaşıntı *n* itchiness
kaşif *n* explorer
kaşlarını çatmak *v* frown
kat *n* story
katakomb *n* catacomb
katalog *n* catalog
katalog yapmak *v* catalog
katarakt *n* cataract
katedral *n* cathedral
kategori *n* category
katı *adj* stiff
katılık *n* stiffness
katılım *n* attendance
katılma *n* participation
katılmak *v* join, participate, attend
katır *n* mule
kati *adj* definitive
katil *n* killer, murderer
katip *n* clerk
katkı *n* contribution
katkıda bulunmak *v* contribute
katlamak *v* fold
katlanabilir *adj* pliable
katletmek *v* slaughter
katliam *n* carnage, slaughter
katman *n* layer
katolik *adj* catholic
Katolik *n* Catholicism

K

katran *n* tar
katsayı *n* coefficient
kauçuk *n* rubber
kavanoz *n* jar
kavga *n* fight, quarrel
kavga etmek *v* fight, quarrel
kavgacı *adj* aggressive, belligerent, contentious, quarrelsome
kavgacı *n* fighter
kavramak *v* comprehend, grab, grasp
kavrayışlı *adj* receptive
kavşak *n* crossroads, junction
kavun *n* cantaloupe, melon
kavurmak *v* roast, parch
kavuşma *n* reunion
kavuz *n* hull
kaya *n* boulder, rock
kaya tabakası *n* shelves
kayak yapmak *v* ski
kayalık *adj* rocky
kaybetmek *v* lose, misplace, waste
kaybolma *n* disappearance
kaybolmak *v* disappear
kayda değer *adv* notably
kayda değer *adj* noteworthy
kaydedici *n* recorder
kaydetmek *v* matriculate, record
kaydını yaptırmak *v* check in
kaydolmak *v* enroll, register

kaygan *adj* greasy, slippery
kayınbirader *n* brother-in-law
kayınpeder *n* father-in-law
kayıp *n* loss
kayıp *adj* missing
kayısı *n* apricot
kayış *n* strap
kayıt *n* recording, registration
kayıt dışı konuşma *adj* off-the-record
kaykılma *v* shear
kayma *n* shift
kaymak *v* slide, slip
kaynaç *n* geyser
kaynak *n* basis, source; resource; mine
kaynakça *n* bibliography
kaynakçı *n* welder
kaynamak *v* boil, simmer
kaynana *n* mother-in-law
kaynaşma *n* fusion
kayrak *n* slate
kaz *n* geese, goose
kaza *n* accident
kaza yapmak *v* crash
kazak *n* jersey, sweater
kazan *n* boiler
kazanan *n* winner
kazanç *n* increment, gains, earnings
kazançlı *adj* lucrative
kazanım *n* acquisition

kazanmak *v* earn, win, purchase
kazazede *n* castaway, casualty
kazı *n* engraving
kazı yapmak *v* excavate
kazığa bağlamak *v* stake
kazık *n* stake
kazık atmak *v* double-cross
kazıklamak *v* palm
kazımak *v* engrave, scrape
kazma *n* pick
kazmak *v* dig
keçe *n* felt
keçelemek *v* felt
keçi *n* goat

keder *n* grief, sorrow
kederlen *v* grieve
kederli *adj* dejected, sorrowful
kedi *n* cat, kitten
kefalet *n* bail
kefaletle kurtarmak *v* bail out
kefaret *n* atonement, expiation, penance
kefaret etmek *v* atone
kefaret vermek *v* redeem
kefen *n* shroud
keferli *adj* dismal
kehanet *n* prophecy
kehanette bulunmak *v* foretell
kek *n* cake
kekelemek *v* stammer, stutter
keklik *n* partridge
kel *adj* bald

kelebek *n* butterfly
kelepçe *n* handcuffs
kelepçelemek *v* handcuff
kelime *n* word
kelime hazinesi *n* vocabulary
keman *n* fiddle, violin
kemancı *n* violinist
kement *n* lasso
kementle tutmak *v* lasso
kemer *n* arch, belt
kemik *n* bone
kemik iliği *n* bone marrow
kemirgen *n* rodent
kemirmek *v* gnaw, nibble
kenar *n* border, limit, rim
kenara *adv* aside
kendi *adj* own
kendileri *pro* themselves
kendim *pro* myself
kendin *pro* yourself
kendinden emin *adj* confident
kendine hakimiyet *n* composure
kendine özgü *adj* distinctive
kendini koyvermek *v* drift apart
kendini tutamama *n* incontinence
kendini tutmak *v* hold back
kendisine *pro* herself
kentsel *adj* urban
kereste *n* hardwood, lumber, timber
kereviz *n* celery
kerpeten *n* pincers, pliers
kertenkele *n* lizard

kesek *n* turf
kesici *n* cutter
kesik *n* cut
kesim *n* sector, segment
kesin *adj* express, certain, clear-cut, conclusive, deciding, definite
kesinlik *n* certainty
kesip düzeltmek *v* trim
kesir *n* fraction
kesişmek *v* intercept, intersect
keski *n* chisel
keskin *adv* bitterly
keskin *adj* poignant, acute, sharp
keskin nişancı *n* sniper
keskinleştirmek *v* edge
kesme *n* clipping, severance
kesme işareti *n* apostrophe
kesmek *v* break off, cut, sever, cut off, cut out
kestane *n* chestnut
kestane fişeği *n* firecracker
kestirme *n* shortcut
kestirmek *v* estimate
keşfetmek *v* ascertain, discover, explore, find out
keşif *n* discovery, exploration
keşif gezisi *n* expedition
keşiş *n* hermit
keşiş *adj* monastic
ket vurmak *v* inhibit
keten *n* linen

keyfi *adj* arbitrary
keyfini bozmak *v* upset
keyfini çıkarmak *v* enjoy
keyif *n* enjoyment
keyifli *adj* enjoyable, jolly, jovial
kıç *n* bum
kıdem *n* seniority
kıdemli *adj* senior
kıkırdamak *v* chuckle, giggle
kılavuz *n* guide
kılavuzluk *n* guidance
kılavuzluk etmek *v* guide
kılıç *n* blade, sword
kılıçbalığı *n* swordfish
kılık *n* guise
kılık değiştirmek *v* disguise, masquerade
kılık değiştirmiş *n* disguise
kılıksız *adj* seedy
kıllı *adj* hairy
kımıldamak *v* budge
kınama *n* blame, condemnation
kınamak *v* censure, condemn
kırağılı *adj* frosty
kırbaç *n* whip
kırbaçlamak *n* scourge
kırıcı *adj* hurtful
kırık *adj* broken
kırık *n* fracture
kırık çıkık *n* splint
kırılgan *adj* brittle, fragile
kırılır *adj* breakable

kırılma *n* crash
kırılmamış *adj* unbroken
kırım *n* massacre
kırıntı *n* crumb
kırıp açmak *v* break open
kırıp geçirmek *v* decimate
kırışık *n* furrow, wrinkle
kırıştırmak *v* wrinkle
kırk *adj* forty
kırma *n* crease
kırmak *v* break
kırmalı *adj* pleated
kırmızı *adj* red
kırmızılaşmak *v* redden
kırpma *n* clipping
kırpmak *v* clip
kırsal *adj* country, pastoral, rural, rustic
kırsal bölge *n* countryside
kırtasiye *n* stationery
kısa *adj* short
kısa çizgi *n* hyphen
kısa kesmek *v* curtail
kısa not *n* memo
kısa ömürlü *adj* short-lived
kısa sürede *adv* shortly
kısa uyku *n* nap
kısa ziyaret *v* stop over
kısaca *adv* briefly
kısalık *n* brevity
kısaltma *n* abbreviation
kısaltmak *v* abbreviate, cut back, shorten

kısas etmek *v* retaliate
kısık *adj* husky
kısım *n* division
kısıtlama *n* constraint
kısıtlamak *v* withhold
kıskaç *n* clamp
kıskanç *adj* envious, jealous
kıskançlık *n* jealousy
kısmak *v* restrict
kısmen *adv* partially
kısmet *n* fortune
kısmi *adv* partly
kısmi *adj* partial
kısrak *n* mare
kıssa *n* parable
kıstırmak *v* jam
kış *n* winter
kışkırtıcı *n* agitator
kışkırtmak *v* incite, instigate, provoke, stir up
kışla *n* quarters, barracks
kıta *n* continent
kıtasal *adj* continental
kıtırdatarak yemek *v* munch
kıtlık *n* famine, scarcity
kıvılcım *n* spark
kıvırmak *v* curve
kıvranmak *v* writhe
kıvrım *n* curve, pleat
kıyafet *n* clothing
kıyamet *n* apocalypse
kıyı *n* coastline

kıyı boyunca *adj* coastal
kıyıda *adv* ashore
kıyım *n* mistreatment
kıyma *n* mincemeat
kıymak *v* shred
kıymet tahmini *n* appraisal
kıymetli *adj* worth
kıymık *n* splinter
kız *n* gal, girl
kız arkadaş *n* girlfriend
kız çocuk *n* daughter
kız kurusu *n* spinster
kızak *n* sleigh
kızamık *n* measles
kızarmış *adj* fried
kızartmak *v* fry
kızdırmak *v* annoy
kızgın *adj* fiery
kızgınlık *n* furor
kızıl *n* ginger
kibar *adj* gentle, gracious, kind, polite
kibarca *adv* kindly
kibarlık *n* courtesy, gentleness, kindness, politeness, delicacy
kibir *n* arrogance, vanity
kibir *adj* conceited
kibirli *adj* vain, arrogant, cocky, haughty
kil *n* clay
kiler *n* pantry
kilerci *n* butler

kilidi açmak *v* unlock
kilise *n* church
kilise ayini *n* mass
kilise üyesi *n* parishioner
kilit *n* lock, padlock
kilitlemek *v* lock
kilogram *n* kilogram
kilometre *n* kilometer
kilovat *n* kilowatt
kim *pro* who
kim olursa *pro* whoever
kime *pro* whom
kimi *pro* whom
kimlik *n* identity
kimse *pro* no one, nobody, anybody
kimsesiz *adj* desolate, outcast
kimsesiz *n* orphan
kimya *n* chemistry
kimyager *n* chemist
kimyasal *adj* chemical
kinaye *n* allegory, innuendo
kinci *adj* vindictive
kinik *adj* cynic
kinizm *n* cynicism
kir *n* dirt, grime
kira *n* rent
kira sözleşmesi *n* lease
kiracı *n* lessee, tenant
kiralamak *v* lease, rent, charter, hire
kiralayan *n* lessor

kiraz *n* cherry
kireç *n* lime
kireç taşı *n* limestone
kiremit *n* tile
kirletmek *v* pollute, soil
kirli *adj* dirty, foul
kirlilik *n* pollution
kirpik *n* eyelash
kist *n* cyst
kişi başına *pre* per
kişilik *n* character, personality
kişisel çıkar *n* self-interest
kişisel eşyalar *n* belongings
kişisel özellik *n* mannerism
kişiselleştirmek *v* personify
kitabe *n* inscription
kitap *n* book
kitap evi *n* bookstore
kitapçı *n* bookseller
kitapçık *n* booklet
kitaplık *n* bookcase
klarnet *n* clarinet
klas *adj* classy
klasik *adj* classic
klasör *n* folder
klavye *n* keyboard
klinik *n* clinic
klonlama *n* cloning
klonlamak *v* clone
klozet *n* closet
koalisyon *n* coalition
koca *n* husband

kocaman *adj* enormous, gigantic, huge, massive
koç *n* ram
kod *n* code
kodlamak *v* codify
kokain *n* cocaine
koklamak *v* smell, sniff
kokmak *v* stink
kokmuş *adj* putrid
kokpit *n* cockpit
kokteyl *n* cocktail
koku *n* fragrance, odor, scent, smell
kokulu *adj* fragrant
kokuşmuş *adj* fetid
kol *n* arm
kolay *adj* elementary, easy, simple
kolayca *adv* easily
kolaylaştırmak *v* facilitate, ease
kolaylık *n* ease
kolaylıklar *n* amenities
kolej *n* college
koleksiyon *n* collection
koleksiyoncu *n* collector
kolera *n* cholera
kolestorol *n* cholesterol
kolik *n* colic
kollateral *adj* collateral
kolluk *n* cuff
kolon *n* colon
kolonya *n* cologne
kolsuz *adj* sleeveless

K

koltuk *n* armchair
koltukaltı *n* armpit
kolye *n* necklace
koma *n* coma
komedi *n* comedy
komedyen *n* comedian
komik *adj* comical, funny, hilarious
komisyon *n* commission
komite *n* committee
kompakt *adj* compact
kompartıman *n* compartment
komplikasyon *n* complication
kompliman *n* flattery
komplo *n* conspiracy
komplo kurmak *v* conspire
komplocu *n* conspirator
komposto *n* compost
kompozisyon *n* composition
kompresyon *n* compression
kompülsif *adj* compulsive
komrad *n* comrade
komşu *n* neighbor
komşuluk *n* neighborhood
komünist *adj* communist
komünizm *n* communism
konak *n* mansion
konaklamak *v* lodge
konferans *n* conference
konfor *n* comfort
konforlu *adj* comfortable, luxurious

konformist *adj* conformist
kongre *n* congress
koni *n* cone
konsantrasyon *n* concentration
konsantre olmak *v* concentrate
konsept *n* concept
konser *n* concert
konserve *n* conserve
konserve *adj* canned
konserve açacağı *n* can opener
konsey *n* council
konsolos *n* consul
konsolosluk *n* consulate
kontes *n* countess
konteyner *n* container
kontrol *n* control
kontrol etmek *v* check, control, double-check
kontur *n* contour
konu *n* matter, subject, topic
konudan ayrılmak *v* digress
konukseverlik *n* hospitality
konum *n* location
konuşkan *adj* talkative
konuşlandırma *n* deployment
konuşlanmak *v* deploy
konuşma *n* conservation, speech
konuşmacı *n* speaker
konuşmak *v* converse, speak, talk, thresh
konvoy *n* convoy
konyak *n* brandy

K

koordinasyon *n* coordination
koordinatör *n* coordinator
koparmak *v* pick, pluck, rupture
kopma *n* rupture
kopmak *v* tear
kopukluk *n* disunity
kopuvermek *v* come apart
kopya *n* copy, replica
kopyalama *n* duplication
kopyalamak *v* copy, duplicate
kopyasını çıkarmak *v* transcribe
kordon *n* cord, braid, cordon
koridor *n* aisle, corridor, hall
korkak *n* coward
korkakça *adv* cowardly
korkaklık *n* cowardice
korkmuş *adj* afraid, startled
korku *n* fear, fright, horror, scare
korkunç *adj* awesome, formidable; terrible, horrible, creepy, hideous, dire, grim
korkunç son *n* doom
korkutma *n* provocation
korkutmak *v* frighten, horrify, intimidate, scare, startle
korkutup kaçırmak *v* scare away
korna çalmak *v* honk
korner *n* corner
kornet *n* cornet
koro *n* choir, chorus
korsan *n* hijacker, pirate
korsanlık *n* piracy

koruma *n* protection
korumak *v* patronize, protect, secure
korunmasız *adj* unprotected
koruyucu *n* guardian; safeguard
koruyucu gözlük *n* goggles
kostüm *n* costume
koşmak *v* hitch up, run
koşucu *n* runner
koşul *n* condition
koşullu *adj* conditional
koşuşturma *n* hustle
kot *n* jeans
kova *n* bucket, pail
kovalama *n* pursuit
kovalamak *v* chase, pursue
kovboy *n* cowboy
kovma *n* repulse
kovmak *v* fire, expel, dismiss; drive away, fend off, sack, turn out
koymak *v* put
koyu *adj* thick, dark, bold
koyulmak *v* set out
koyuluk *n* boldness
koyun *n* sheep
kozmetik *n* cosmetic
kozmik *adj* cosmic
kozmonot *n* cosmonaut
köfte *n* meatball
kök *n* root
köken *n* origin

kökleşmiş *adj* ingrained
kökünden sökmek *v* uproot
kökünü kazımak *v* stamp out
köle *n* slave
kölelik *n* bondage, slavery
kömür *n* coal
köpek *n* dog
köpek balığı *n* shark
köpek dişi *n* fang
köpek evi *n* kennel
köpek yavrusu *n* puppy
köprü *n* bridge
köprücük kemiği *n* collarbone
köpük *n* foam, lather
kör *adj* blind
kör gibi *adv* blindly
kördüğüm *n* tangle
körelmek *v* atrophy
körelmiş *adj* blunt
körfez *n* bay, cove, gulf
körlük *n* blindness, bluntness
köstebek *n* mole
köşe *n* corner
köşe taşı *n* cornerstone
köşegen *adj* diagonal
kötü *adj* bad
kötü bir şekilde *adv* badly
kötü kalpli *adj* mean
kötü muamele *n* snub
kötü niyetli *adj* malignant
kötü yönetmek *v* mismanage
kötüleşme *n* deterioration

kötüleşmek *v* worsen
kötüleştirme *n* aggravation
kötüleştirmek *v* aggravate, deteriorate
kötüleyici *adj* abusive
kötülük *n* evil, meanness
kötüye gitmek *n* relapse
kötüye kullanmak *v* abuse
köy *n* village
köylü *n* peasant, villager
köz *n* embers
kral *n* king
kral vekili *n* regent
krala ait *adj* regal, royal
kraliçe *n* queen
kraliyet *n* kingdom
krallık *n* royalty
kramp *n* cramp
kramp girmiş *adj* cramped
krank *n* crank
krater *n* crater
kravat *n* tie, necktie
kreasyon *n* creation
kredi *n* credit
krem *n* cream
kremalı *adj* creamy
kremasyon *v* cremate
krematoryum *n* crematorium
kreş *n* nursery
kriket *n* cricket
kristal *n* crystal
kriter *n* criterion

K

kritik *adj* critical
kriz *n* crisis, seizure
kronik *n* chronicle
kronoloji *n* chronology
kuaför *n* hairdresser
kubbe *n* dome
kucak *n* embrace, hug, lap
kucaklamak *v* cuddle, hug
kucaklaşmak *v* embrace
kuduz *n* rabies
kuğu *n* swan
kukla *n* puppet
kukuleta *n* hood
kulak *n* ear
kulak ağrısı *n* earache
kulak kiri *n* earwax
kulak misafiri olmak *v*
  eavesdrop
kulak zarı *n* eardrum
kulaklık *n* earphones,
  headphones
kule *n* tower
kule gibi *adj* towering
kulis yapmak *v* lobby
kullanıcı *n* user
kullanılmazlık *n* disuse
kullanım *n* usage, use
kullanışlı *adj* handy, useful
kullanışlılık *n* usefulness
kullanmak *v* use, wield, employ
kulübe *n* cottage
kulüp *n* club

kum *n* sand
kumandan *n* commander
kumar oynamak *v* gamble
kumaş *n* material, fabric
kumaş parçası *n* cloth
kumaşla örtmek *n* drape
kumbara *n* piggy bank
kumral *adj* brunette
kundakçı *n* arsonist
kundakçılık *n* arson
kunduz *n* beaver
kupon *n* coupon
kura *n* draw
kurabiye *n* cookie
kuraklık *n* drought
kural *n* norm
kurbağa *n* frog
kurban *n* butt, sacrifice, victim
kurdela *n* ribbon
kurmak *v* establish, install,
  prefabricate, set, set up, wind up
kurmay *n* staff
kurnaz *adj* sharp, astute, cunning,
  foxy, shrewd, sly, subtle
kurnazlık *n* guile
kurşun *n* bullet, lead
kurşun atmak *v* shoot
kurşun kaplı *adj* leaded
kurşunsuz *adj* unleaded
kurt *n* wolf
kurtarıcı *n* savior, tow truck
kurtarma *n* rescue

kurtarmak *v* extricate, recover, rescue, save
kurtulan *n* survivor
kurtulmak *v* evade, rid of
kurtuluş *n* salvation, survival
kuru *adj* arid, dried, dry
kuru erik *n* prune
kuru temizlemek *v* dry-clean
kuru üzüm *n* raisin
kurucu *n* founder
kurul başkanı *n* chairman
kuruluş *n* enterprise, organization; installation
kurutmak *v* dry
kurutucu *n* dryer
kurye *n* courier
kusma *n* sickness
kusmak *v* throw up, vomit
kusmuk *n* vomit
kusur *n* blemish, blot, defect, flaw, imperfection
kusur bulmak *v* chide
kusurlu *adj* lame, defective
kusursuz *adj* flawless, seamless
kuş *n* bird
kuşatma *n* siege
kuşatmak *v* besiege, cordon off, encircle, envelop, siege, circle
kuşkonmaz *n* asparagus
kuşku *n* mistrust, suspect, suspicion
kuşkucu *adj* skeptic

kuşkulanmak *v* suspect
kuşkulu *adj* dubious
kutlama *n* celebration
kutlamak *v* celebrate
kutsal *adj* celestial, sacred
kutsal eşyaya saygısızlık *n* sacrilege
kutsallaştırmak *v* sanctify
kutsallık *n* holiness, sanctity
kutsama *n* benediction, blessing, consecration
kutsamak *v* bless, consecrate
kutsanmış *adj* blessed
kutu *n* box
kutucuk *n* cartridge
kutulamak *v* box
kutup *n* pole
kutupsal *adj* polar
kuvvet *n* punch, boost, strength
kuvvetlendirmek *v* fortify, step up
kuvvetli *adj* forceful
kuvvetlilik *n* virility
kuvvetsiz *adj* feeble
kuyruk *n* tail
kuyruklu yıldız *n* comet
kuyu *n* well
kuyumcu *n* jeweler; jewelry store
kuzen *n* cousin
kuzey *n* north
kuzeydoğu *n* northeast
kuzeye ait *adj* northern
kuzeyli *adj* northerner

kuzgun *n* raven
kuzu *n* lamb
kübik *adj* cubic
küçük *adj* little, small
küçük bölme *n* cubicle
küçük çocuk *n* toddler, minor
küçük düşürmek *v* humiliate
küçük iş *n* chore
küçük kısım *n* bit
küçük köşk *n* chalet
küçük kutu *n* casket
küçüklük *n* pettiness
küçültmek *v* shrink
küçümsemek *v* belittle
küçümseyen *adj* scornful
küf *n* mold, mildew
küf mantar *n* fungus
küflü *adj* moldy
küfretmek *v* blaspheme, swear
küfür *v* cuss
kükremek *v* roar
kükürt *n* sulfur
kül *n* cinder, ash
külçe *n* chunk, ingot
küllük *n* ashtray
külot *n* slip
kült *n* cult
kültür *n* culture
kültürel *adj* cultural
küme *n* cluster, set, swarm, lump
kümelemek *v* heap
kümelenmek *v* cluster

kümes hayvanı *n* poultry
küp *n* cube
küp küp kesmek *v* dice
küpe *n* earring
küratör *n* curator
kürdan *n* toothpick
küre *n* globe, sphere
kürecik *n* globule
kürek *n* paddle; shovel, spade
kürek çekmek *v* paddle, row
küreklemek *v* shovel
kürk *n* fur
kürsü *n* lectern, pulpit
kürtaj *n* abortion
küskün *adj* disgruntled
küstah *adj* insolent
küstahlık *n* impertinence
kütle *n* body, mass
kütlesel *n* molar
kütük *n* log
kütüphane *n* library
kütüphaneci *n* librarian

L

labirent *n* labyrinth
laboratuar *n* lab
lagün *n* lagoon
lağım suyu *n* sewage
lahana *n* cabbage
lakap *n* nickname
lale *n* tulip
lamba *n* lamp
lanet *n* damnation
lanetlemek *v* curse
lastik patlaması *n* blowout
lavabo *n* lavatory, sink
layık *adj* deserving, worthy
layık olmak *v* merit
lazer *n* laser
leğen *n* basin
lehçe *n* dialect
lehimlemek *v* solder
leke *n* smear, stain, spot
leke sürmek *v* stain
lekelemek *v* blemish, blot
lekelenmiş *adj* soiled
lekeli *adj* tainted
lekesiz *adj* spotless
leopar *n* leopard
levha *n* sign, painting
levrek *n* bass
leylek *n* stork
leziz *adj* tasty

lezzet vermek *v* relish
lezzetli *adj* nutty, delicious
libre *n* pound
lider *n* conductor, leader
liderlik *n* leadership
lig *n* league
likör *n* liqueur
liman *n* harbor, port
limit *n* limitation
limon *n* lemon
limonata *n* lemonade
linç etmek *v* lynch
lisans *n* license
lisanslamak *v* license
liste *n* list
liste yapmak *v* list
listeleyici *n* browser
litre *n* liter
lobi *n* lobby
lokalize etmek *v* localize
lokma *n* bite, morsel
lonca *n* guild, lounge
lord *n* lord
lordluk *n* lordship
losyon *n* lotion
loş *adj* dim
lösemi *n* leukemia
lüks *adj* plush, deluxe, posh
lüks *n* luxury
lüle *n* curl
lüzum *n* calling

M

maaş *n* wage, salary
maaş bordrosu *n* payroll
maaş çeki *n* paycheck
maaş makbuzu *n* pay slip
macera *n* adventure, escapade
madalya *n* medal
madalyon *n* medallion
madde *n* substance, stuff, material; count
maddecilik *n* materialism
maddi *adj* bodily
madem ki *c* inasmuch as
maden *n* ore
madeni para *n* coin
magazin *n* magazine
mağara *n* cave, cavern, den, grotto
mağdur etmek *v* victimize
mağlubiyet *n* beating, trimmings
mağlup *n* loser
mağlup *adj* beaten
mağlup etmek *v* vanquish
mahal *n* lieu
mahalle *n* district, parish
mahcup *adj* ashamed
mahir *adj* proficient
mahkeme *n* tribunal
mahkemeye çağırmak *v* subpoena

mahkum etmek *v* convict, sentence
mahkumiyet *adj* doomed
mahkumiyet *n* conviction
mahmuz *n* spur
mahrum *adj* devoid
mahrumiyet *n* deprivation
mahvetmek *v* ruin, shatter
majeste *n* majesty
makale *n* contribution, article
makara *n* pulley, spool, reel
makas *n* scissors
makbul *adj* admissible
makbuz *n* voucher
maket *n* dummy
makina *n* engine
makine *n* machine
makine yağı *n* grease
makineli tüfek *n* machine gun
maksat *n* point; will
maksimum *adj* maximum
makul *adj* advisable, reasonable
makyaj *n* makeup
mal *n* asset, property
mal aşırma *n* shoplifting
mal deposu *n* stockroom
mal kurtarmak *v* salvage
mal olmak *v* cost
mal sahibi *n* owner
mal varlıkları *n* assets
malı eki *v* ought to
mallar *n* goods

malumat *n* dope
malzeme *n* ingredient
mamut *n* mammoth
manastır *n* abbey, cloister, monastery
mandal *n* latch
mandalina *n* tangerine
mandıra *n* dairy farm
manevra *n* maneuver, ploy
mangal *n* barbecue
mangal kömürü *n* charcoal
manifesto *v* manifest
manivela *n* lever, crank
manşet *n* cuff
mantar *n* mushroom
mantık *n* logic
mantıklı *adj* coherent, sensible, logical
mantıksal *n* loin
mantıksız *adj* illogical, irrational, pointless, unreasonable
manto *n* overcoat
manyak *adj* maniac
manyetik *adj* magnetic
manyetizma *n* magnetism
manzara *n* scene, landscape, scenery
manzaralı *adj* scenic
marangoz *n* carpenter
marangozluk *n* carpentry
mareşal *n* marshal
marifet *n* feat

marine etmek *v* marinate
marjinal *adj* marginal
marka *n* brand
markalamak *v* brand
market *n* market
Marksçı *adj* Marxist
marmelat *n* marmalade
Mars *n* Mars
marş *n* anthem
Mart *n* March
martı *n* gull, seagull
marul *n* lettuce
maruz *adj* exposed
maruz bırakmak *v* expose
maruz kalmak *v* subject, incur
masa *n* table, desk
masaj *n* massage
masaj yapmak *v* massage
masal *n* fable, fiction, tale
maskara *n* laughing stock
maskaralık *n* charade
maske *n* mask
maskelemek *v* mask
maskülen *adj* masculine
mason *n* mason
masör *n* masseur
masöz *n* masseuse
masraf *n* cost, expenditure, expense
masum *adj* innocent, unsuspecting
masumiyet *n* innocence

M

maşa *n* tongs
matador *n* bull fighter
matem *n* bereavement
matematik *n* math
matemli *adj* bereaved
matkap *n* drill
matkaplamak *v* drill
maun *n* mahogany
mavi *adj* blue
mavi kopya *n* blueprint
mavna *n* barge
maya *n* ferment, yeast
mayalamak *v* ferment
maydonoz *n* parsley
mayın *n* mine
mayın döşemek *v* mine
mayın tarlası *n* minefield
mayıncı *n* miner
Mayıs *n* May
maymun *n* ape, monkey
mazeret *n* excuse
mazi *n* past
mazlum *adj* downtrodden
mazoşizm *n* masochism
mazur görmek *v* excuse
mecbur etmek *v* obligate
mecburi *adj* compulsory
mecburiyet *n* obligation
meclis *n* council, chamber
med cezir *n* tide
med cezir dalgası *n* tidal wave
medeni *adj* civil

medeni hal *n* status
medenileştirmek *v* civilize
medeniyet *n* civilization
meditasyon *n* meditation
meditasyon yapmak *v* meditate
meğer ki *c* unless
mekanik *n* mechanic
mekanize etmek *v* mechanize
mekanizma *n* mechanism
mekik dokumak *v* shuttle
Meksikalı *adj* Mexican
mektepli *adj* pedantic
mektup *n* epistle, letter
mektuplaşmak *v* correspond
melankoli *n* melancholy
melek *n* angel
meleksi *adj* angelic
melodi *n* melody
melodik *adj* melodic
meltem *n* breeze
membran *n* membrane
meme ucu *n* nipple
memeli *n* mammal
memleket *n* hometown, realm
memnun *adj* glad, pleasant
memnun etmek *v* content, please
memnuniyet *n* satisfaction, contents
memur *n* officer
menapoz *n* menopause
mendil *n* handkerchief, napkin, tissue

M

menekşe *n* violet
menenjit *n* meningitis
menetmek *v* prohibit
menfaat *n* expediency
menfez *n* vent
menteşe *n* hinge
menteşe takmak *v* hinge
menü *n* menu
merak *n* curiosity, wonder
merak etmek *v* care about, wonder
meraklı *adj* fond, curious, nosy
mercek *n* lens
mercimek *n* lentil
merdiven *n* staircase, stairs
merhamet *n* clemency
merhem *n* balm, ointment
merhum *adj* deceased
merkez *n* center; navel
merkezi *adj* central
merkezleştirmek *v* centralize
mermi yolu *n* trajectory
mesaj *n* message
mesane *n* bladder
Mesih *n* Messiah
mesleği olmayan *n* layman
meslek *n* call
mesuliyet *n* liability
meşale *n* torch
meşe ağacı *n* oak
meşe palamudu *n* acorn
meşgul *adj* busy, engrossed, engaged

meşgul etmek *v* engage
meşru *adj* lawful
metal *n* metal
metalik *adj* metallic
metanet *n* guts
metanetli *n* fortitude
meteor *n* meteor
metin *n* text
metod *n* method
metre *n* meter
mevcut *adj* forthcoming, available
mevki *n* spot
mevsim *n* season
mevsimlik *adj* seasonal
meydan okuma *n* challenge
meydan okumak *v* challenge
meydana çıkarmak *v* detect, uncover
meydana çıkmak *v* emerge
meydana gelmek *v* consist
meyhane *n* saloon
meyil *n* leaning, decline
meyus *adj* despondent
meyve *n* fruit
meyve suyu *n* juice
meyveli *adj* fruity
meyvesiz *adj* barren
mezar *n* grave, tomb
mezar kitabesi *n* epitaph
mezar taşı *n* gravestone, tombstone
mezarlık *n* cemetery, graveyard

M

mezatçi *n* auctioneer
mezbaha *n* butchery
meze *n* appetizer
mezhep *n* cult, sect
mezra *n* hamlet
mezun olmak *v* graduate
mezuniyet *n* graduation
mıknatıs *n* magnet
mırıldanmak *v* hum; mumble
mısır *n* corn
mısır koçanı *n* cob
mısra *n* verse
mızrak *n* spear
mide *n* gut, stomach
mide bulantısı *n* nausea
mide ekşimesi *n* heartburn
midesel *adj* gastric
migren *n* migraine
miğfer *n* helmet
mikrodalga *n* microwave
mikrofon *n* microphone
mikrop *n* germ, microbe
mikroskop *n* microscope
mikser *n* blender, mixer
miktar *n* amount
mil *n* mile
mil etrafında dönmek *v* swivel
milenyum *n* millennium
miligram *n* milligram
milimetre *n* millimeter
millileştirmek *v* nationalize
milyar *n* billion

milyarder *n* billionaire
milyon *n* million
milyoner *n* millionaire
mimar *n* architect
mimari *n* architecture
mimik yapmak *v* mime
minder *v* bolster
minder *n* cushion
mineral *n* mineral
mini etek *n* miniskirt
minimum *n* minimum
minnet dolu *adj* thankful
minnettar *adj* grateful
minnettarlık *n* gratitude
minör *n* minor
minyatür *n* miniature
miras *n* heritage, legacy
miras kalmak *v* inherit
mirasçı *n* heir
misafir *n* guest
misafir etmek *v* put up
misil *n* missile
misilleme *n* reprisal, retaliation
misilleme yapmak *v* hit back
misyoner *n* missionary
miting *n* rally
miyop *adj* myopic, nearsighted, shortsighted
mizah *n* humor
mobilya *n* furniture
mobilyasız *adj* unfurnished
mod *n* mode**

M

moda *n* fashion
modaya uygun *adj* fashionable, trendy
model *n* model
model olmak *v* model
modern *adj* modern
modernleştirmek *v* modernize
modül *n* module
molekül *n* molecule
moloz *n* rubble
monarşi *n* monarchy
monolog *n* monologue
monopol *n* monopoly
monoton *adj* monotonous
monoton *n* monotony
montaj *n* assembly
mor *adj* purple
morali bozuk *adj* downcast
moralini bozmak *v* demoralize
morfin *n* morphine
morg *n* mortuary
morina *n* cod
motel *n* motel
motive etmek *v* motivate
motor *n* motor
motosiklet *n* motorcycle
mozaik *n* mosaic
muaf *adj* exempt
muaf olma *n* impunity
muafiyet *n* exemption
muamele *n* treatment, dealings
muavin *n* vice

muayene *n* check up
muazzam *adj* colossal, stupendous, tremendous
mucize *n* miracle
mucizevi *adj* miraculous
muhabbet *n* conversation
muhabir *n* correspondent
muhafaza *n* custody, conserve
muhafaza etmek *v* conserve
muhafız *n* custodian, warden
muhakeme *n* reasoning
muhalefet *n* defiance
muhalif *adj* defiant, dissident
muhalif *n* opponent
muhallebi *n* custard, pudding
muhasebe *n* bookkeeping
muhasebeci *n* accountant, bookkeeper
muhatap *n* addressee
muhbir *n* reporter
muhtaç *adj* dependent, indigent
muhtemelen *adv* likely
mukabil *n* counterpart
mukavele *n* covenant
mukavva *n* cardboard
muktedir *adj* able
mukus *n* mucus
mum *n* candle, candlestick, wax
mumyalamak *v* embalm
muntazam *adj* steady, tidy
Musevi *adj* Jewish
Musevi alemi *n* Judaism

Musevilik *n* Jew
musluk *n* faucet
mutabık *adj* corresponding
mutfak *n* cuisine; kitchen
mutlu *adj* happy, merry
mutluluk *n* ecstasy, happiness
mutsuz *adj* unhappy
mutsuzluk *n* unhappiness
muvafakat *n* accord
muz *n* banana
muzaffer *adj* victorious
muziplik *n* prank
mübaşir *n* bailiff
mücadele *n* combat, struggle,
   contest
mücadele etmek *v* combat,
   struggle
mücadeleci *adj* challenging
mücevher *n* gem
müddet *n* term, duration
müdür *n* manager
müessese *n* institution
müfettiş *n* inspector
mühendis *n* engineer
mühür *n* seal
mühürlemek *v* seal
müjdeci *n* herald
müjdecisi olmak *v* herald
mükafat *n* recompense
mükemmel *adj* brilliant,
   excellent, perfect
mükemmeliyet *n* perfection

mükemmellik *n* excellence
mülakat *n* interview
mülayim *adj* bland
mülk *n* condo; possession
mülkiyet *n* ownership
mülteci *n* refugee
mümin *n* believer
mümkün *adj* feasible, possible
münakaşa *n* dispute
münasebetsiz *adj* improper
münzevi *n* recluse
müracaat etmek *v* apply for,
   resort
mürekkep *n* ink
mürekkep balığı *n* squid
mürekkepli kalem *n* pen
müsait olma *n* availability
Müslüman *adj* Muslim
müsrif *adj* wasteful
müstehcen *adj* lewd, vulgar
müstehcenlik *n* vulgarity
müşkülpesent *adj* choosy
müşteri *n* buyer, client, customer
mütehakkim *adj* domineering
mütevazı şekilde *adv* humbly
müttefik *adj* allied
müttefik *n* ally
müvekkiller *n* clientele
müzakere etmek *v* confer,
   deliberate
müzayede *n* auction
müzayedeyle satmak *v* auction

müze *n* museum
müzik *n* music
müzik grubu *n* band
müzisyen *n* musician
müzmin *adj* chronic

N

nabız *n* pulse
nadir *adj* rare, uncommon, unusual
nadiren *adv* rarely, scarcely, seldom
nafile *adj* futile, vainly
nahoş *adj* disagreeable, displeasing
nakit para *n* cash
nakletmek *v* convey, recite, ship
nakletmek *n* recount
nakliyat *n* shipment
nakliye *n* freight
nalbant *n* smith
namlu ağzı *n* muzzle
namuslu *adj* chaste
namussuz *adj* corrupt
nane *n* mint
nankör *adj* ungrateful
nankörlük *n* ingratitude

nar *n* pomegranate
narin *adj* tender, delicate, frail, slender
narkotik *n* narcotic
nasıl *adv* how
nasır *n* corn
nasihat *n* advice
nazik *adj* courteous, tactful
ne *adj* what
ne de *c* nor
ne zaman *adv* when
neden *n* incentive, cause
neden *adv* why, how
neden olmak *v* induce, precipitate, spark off
nedeniyle *adv* owing to
nedeniyle *pre* because of
nedime *n* bridesmaid
nefes *n* breath
nefes alma *n* breathing
nefes almak *n* aspiration
nefes almak *v* breathe
nefes borusu *n* windpipe
nefes kesici *adj* breathtaking
nefesini tutmak *adj* catching
nefis *adj* stunning
nefret *n* hatred, loathing
nefret dolu *adj* hateful
nefret etmek *v* detest, hate
negatif *adj* negative
nehir *n* river
nehir yatağı *n* bed

nem *adj* damp
nem *n* moisture
nemlendirmek *v* moisten, dampen
nemli *adj* humid
nerede *adv* where
neredeyse *adv* almost, nearly, virtually
nerelerde *n* whereabouts
nesil *n* generation
nesli tükenmek *v* die out
nesli tükenmiş *adj* extinct
nesne *n* article
neşe *n* bliss, joy
neşelendirici *adj* exhilarating
neşelendirmek *v* cheer up
neşeli *adj* blissful, cheerful, joyful
neşesiz *adj* down
neşeyle *adv* joyfully
net *adv* clearly
net *adj* explicit
netameli *adj* sinister
netice *adj* consequent
netlik *n* clearness, clarity
nezaketsizlik *n* discourtesy
nezaret etmek *v* preside
nezle *n* influenza
nicelik *n* quantity
nihai *adj* ultimate
nihayet *adv* eventually, lastly
nikahsız yaşamak *v* cohabit
nikel *n* nickel

nikotin *n* nicotine
nine *n* granny
Nisan *n* April
nişan *n* target
nişancı *n* marksman
nişanlı *n* fiancé, engagement
nişasta *n* starch
nişastalı *adj* starchy
nitelik *n* quality
nitrojen *n* nitrogen
Noel *n* Christmas, X-mas
Noel ilahisi *n* carol
noksan *n* shortcoming
nokta *n* dot, point
nokta atışı yapmak *v* pinpoint
normal *adj* normal
normalde *adv* normally
normalleştirmek *v* normalize
Norveç *n* Norway
Norveçli *adj* Norwegian
nostalji *n* nostalgia
not *v* note
not defteri *n* notebook
not eklemek *v* annotate
not etmek *v* write down
not etmek *n* note
noter *n* notary
nöbet *n* tour, guard
nöbet tutma *n* vigil
nöbet vakti *n* spell
nöbetçi *n* sentry
nötr *adj* neutral

numara yapmak *v* feign
numune *n* specimen
nüdist *n* nudist
nüfus *n* population
nüfus sayımı *n* census
nüfusu artırmak *v* populate
nüfuz etmek *v* sink in
nüfuzlu *adj* influential
nükleer *adj* nuclear
nüksetmek *v* recur
nükte *n* wit

o *adj* that
o da *adv* too
o erkeğin *pro* his
o erkek *pro* he
o erkek *adj* his
o gün bugündür *adv* since then
o kız *pro* she
o kıza *adj* her
o kızın *adj* her
o kızın *pro* hers
o yüzden *adv* therefore
o zaman *adv* then
obez *adj* obese
obje *n* object

obur *n* glutton
ocak *n* furnace, stove; pit
Ocak *n* January
oda *n* room
odak *n* focus
odaklanmak *v* focus on
odise *n* odyssey
ofis *n* office
oğlan *n* boy
oğul *n* son
ok *n* arrow
oklu kirpi *n* porcupine
oksijen *n* oxygen
okşama *n* caress
okşamak *v* caress, fondle, pat,
   pet
okul *n* school
okulu terk etmek *v* drop out
okuma *n* reading
okumak *v* read
okumamış *adj* illiterate
okumuş *adj* learned
okunaksız *adj* illegible
okunur *adj* legible
okuryazar *adj* literate
okutmak *v* instruct
okuyucu *n* reader
okyanus *n* ocean
olabilir *v* may
olağanüstü *adj* prodigious
olanak *n* possibility
olanaksız *adj* unable, unthinkable

olarak *c* as
olası *adj* contingent, probable
olasılık *n* chance
olay *n* event, apparition, issue
olaysız *adj* uneventful
olduğundan *c* since
oldukça *adv* quite, rather
oldukça büyük *adj* sizable
olgun *adj* mature, ripe
olgunlaşmamış *adj* immature
olgunlaştırmak *v* mellow, ripen
olgunluk *n* maturity
olimpiyat *n* Olympics
olmak *v* be, become, happen
olsa bile *c* even if
oluk *n* duct, groove, gutter
olumlu *adj* affirmative
olumsuz *n* negative
olumsuz *adj* unfavorable
olup çıkmak *v* end up
olup olmadığını *c* whether
oluş *n* occurrence
oluşmuş *adj* composed
omlet *n* omelet
omur *n* vertebra
omurga *n* backbone, spine
omuz *n* shoulder
omuz silkmek *v* shrug
on *adj* ten
on altı *adj* sixteen
on beş *adj* fifteen
on bir *adj* eleven

on birinci *adj* eleventh
on dokuz *adj* nineteen
on dört *adj* fourteen
on iki *adj* twelve
on sekiz *adj* eighteen
on sent *n* dime
on üç *adj* thirteen
on yedi *adj* seventeen
on yıl *n* decade
ona *pre* to
onarılamaz *adj* irreparable
onarma *n* restitution, restoration
onarmak *v* fix, mend, repair, restore
onay *n* approval, confirmation
onaylama *n* ratification
onaylamak *v* approve, confirm, ratify
onaylamama *n* disapproval
onaylamamak *v* disapprove
onbaşı *n* corporal
ondalık sayı *adj* decimal
ondurlandırmak *v* dignify
onikinci *adj* twelfth
onlar *pro* they
onlar *adj* those
ons *n* ounce
onu *adj* that
onun *pre* of
onuncu *n* tenth
onur *n* honor
onur kırıcı *adj* derogatory

opak *adj* opaque
opera *n* opera
operasyon *n* operation
optik *adj* optical
orada *adv* there
oradan *adv* there
orak *n* hook, sickle
oran *n* rate, proportion, ratio
orangutan *n* orangutan
oranlamak *v* rate
ordu *n* army, legion
org *n* organ
organ *n* organ
organize etmek *v* organize
organizma *n* organism
orgcu *n* organist
orjinal *adj* original
orjinal olarak *adv* originally
orkestra *n* orchestra
orman *n* forest, jungle
orta *adj* medium
orta *n* middle
orta çağ *adj* medieval
ortadan kaybolmak *v* vanish
ortadirek *adj* grassroots
ortak *n* partner
ortak *adj* common
ortak merkezli *adj* concentric
ortak olarak *adv* jointly
ortaklık *n* partnership
ortalama *n* average
ortalamak *v* center

ortasına *pre* amid
ortaya çıkarmak *v* unravel
ortaya çıkmak *v* arise, resurface, show up, come up
oruç tutmak *v* fast
ot *n* weed
ot yolmak *v* weed
otantik *adj* authentic
otantiklik *n* authenticity
otel *n* hotel
otlak *n* field
otlama *n* graze
otlamak *v* crop, gaze
oto- *n* auto
otobüs *n* bus
otobüsle götürmek *v* bus
otomatik *adj* automatic
otomobil *n* automobile
otonom *adj* autonomous
otonomi *n* autonomy
otopsi *n* autopsy
otorite *n* authority
otoriter *adj* authoritarian
otostop yapmak *n* hitchhike
otoyol *n* freeway
oturacak yer *n* seat
oturan *n* occupant
oturan *adj* seated
oturan kimse *n* inhabitant, inmate
oturma *n* sitting
oturma odası *n* living room

oturmak *v* sit
oturmaya elverişli *adj* inhabitable
oturulur *adj* habitable
oturum açmak *v* log in
oturum kapatmak *v* log off
otuz *adj* thirty
oval *adj* oval
ovalamak *v* rub, scrub
ovarak temizlemek *v* scour
oy *n* vote
oy pusulası *n* ballot
oy vermek *v* vote
oyalanmak *v* mess around
oybirliği *n* unanimity
oylama *n* poll, voting
oymak *v* carve
oynamak *v* wiggle
oynayanlar *n* cast
oyuk *n* burrow
oyun *n* act, game, play
oyun alanı *n* playground
oyun zarları *n* dice
oyunbaz *adj* playful
oyuncak *n* toy
oyuncak bebek *n* doll
oyuncu *n* player

öbür tarafına *pre* across
öç *n* revenge
öç almak *v* revenge, get back
ödeme *n* pay, payment, discharge
ödemek *v* defray, pay, repay, discharge
ödenecek *adj* payable
ödenek *n* grant
ödenen kişi *n* payee
ödül *n* pot, award, prize, reward
ödüllendirmek *v* award, reward
ödünç *n* loan
ödünç almak *v* borrow
ödünç vermek *v* lend, loan
öfke *n* temper, rage, wrath
öfke nöbeti *n* tantrum
öfkelendirmek *v* enrage
öfkelenmek *v* rampage
öfkeli *adj* irate
öğe *n* item
öğle yemeği *n* lunch
öğleden sonra *n* afternoon
öğlen *n* noon
öğrenci *n* learner, pupil, student
öğrenme *n* learning
öğrenmek *v* learn
öğreti *n* doctrine
öğretim *n* tuition
öğretmek *v* teach

öğretmen *n* instructor, teacher
öğüt vermek *v* counsel
öğütmek *v* grind
öksürmek *v* cough
öksürük *n* cough
öksüzler yurdu *n* orphanage
öküz *n* ox, oxen
ölçeklemek *v* scale
ölçmek *v* measure
ölçü *n* size
ölçülü *adj* metric
ölçüm *n* measurement
ölçüp biçmek *v* size up
öldürmek *v* assassinate, gun down, kill, slay
öldürücü *adj* lethal, virulent
ölmek *v* die, pass away, perish
ölmekte olan *adj* dying
ölü *adj* dead
ölü sayısı *n* death toll
ölüm *n* death
ölüm tuzağı *n* death trap
ölüm yatağı *n* deathbed
ölümcül *adj* deadly, fatal
ölümlü *adj* mortal
ölümsüz *adj* immortal
ölümsüzlük *n* immortality
ölüyü diriltmek *v* resuscitate
ön *adj* front
ön *n* front
ön hazırlık *n* groundwork
ön plan *n* foreground

ön sıra *n* forefront
ön ürün *n* prototype
önce *pre* before
önce gelen *n* antecedent
önceden *adv* beforehand, previously
önceden tatma *n* foretaste
önceki *adv* before
önceki *adj* former, previous
öncelik *n* priority
öncü *n* pioneer, precursor
öncülük etmek *v* spearhead
önde olmak *v* precede
öndeyiş *n* prologue
öne sürmek *v* assert
önek *v* affix
önek *n* prefix
önem *n* importance, significance
önem vermek *n* note
önemli *adj* notable, noticeable, profound, significant, major
önemli olay *n* highlight
önemli olmak *v* matter
önemli oranda *adj* considerable
önemsemek *v* heed
önemsememek *v* brush aside, disregard
önemsiz *adj* frivolous, insignificant, minor, trivial, petty
öneri *n* suggestion
önermek *v* recommend, suggest
öngörmek *v* predict

öngörü *n* prediction
öngörülemez *adj* unpredictable
önizleme *n* preview
önkoşul *n* prerequisite
önlem *n* precaution
önleme *n* prevention
önlemek *v* preempt, prevent
önleyici *adj* preventive
önlük *n* apron
önsezi *n* hunch, premonition
önsöz *n* foreword, preface
önüne geçmek *v* pull ahead
önyargı *n* bias, prejudice
önyargısız *adj* unbiased
öpmek *v* kiss
öpücük *n* kiss
ördek *n* duck
örmek *v* knit
örnek *n* instance, illustration, example, lay, sample, model
örnek olarak *adj* exemplary
örnek vermek *v* exemplify
örneklemek *v* illustrate
örs *n* anvil
örtbas etmek *v* hush up
örtmek *v* cap
örtü *n* cover
örtülü *adj* shrouded
örülü *adj* woven
örümcek *n* spider
örümcek ağı *n* cobweb, spider web

ötede *adv* further
ötelemek *v* shift
övgü *n* commendation, praise
övgü dolu *adj* complimentary
övgüye değer *adj* praiseworthy
övmek *v* acclaim, praise
öykü *n* story
öz *n* core
öz benlik *n* self-esteem
öz saygı *n* self-respect
öz varlık *n* essence
özdeş *adj* identical
özel *adj* fancy, private, special
özel ambalaj *n* wrapping
özel araba yolu *n* driveway
özel öğretmen *n* tutor
özel şoför *n* chauffeur
özelleşmek *v* specialize
özellik *n* feature, trait
özellikle *adv* especially, particularly
özen *n* diligence
özensiz *adj* slack
özenti *n* fringe
özerk *adj* sovereign
özerklik *n* sovereignty
özet *n* compendium, briefs, summary
özetlemek *v* abridge, brief, epitomize, recap, summarize
özgün *adj* peculiar
özgür *adj* free

özgür bırakmak *v* free
özgürlük *n* freedom, liberty
özlemek *v* long for, miss
özlü *adj* brief, concise, terse
özlük *n* brevity
özne *n* subject
özür *n* apology, disability, pardon
özür dilemek *v* apologize, pardon

paha biçilemez *adj* invaluable
pahalı *adj* costly, expensive, pricey
pahalıya *adv* dearly
paket *n* package, parcel
paket postası *n* parcel post
paketi açmak *v* unpack
paketlemek *v* pack
palmiye *n* palm
palto *n* coat
palyaço *n* clown
pamuk *n* cotton
pancar *n* beet
panik *n* panic
pankart *n* placard
pankreas *n* pancreas
panorama *n* panorama

panter *n* panther
pantolon *n* trousers, pants
panzehir *n* antidote
Papa *n* Pope
papağan *n* parakeet, parrot
papalık *n* papacy
papatya *n* daisy
papaya ait *adj* apostolic
papaz *n* minister, clergyman, friar, monk
papazlık *n* priesthood
para *n* money
para basmak *v* mint
para cezası *n* fine
para cezası vermek *v* fine
para etmek *v* cost
para harcamak *v* disburse
para hırsı *n* avarice
para yedirmek *v* buy off
paradoks *n* paradox
parafe etmek *v* initial
paragraf *n* paragraph
paralel *n* parallel
parametre *n* parameters
paranoyak *adj* paranoid
parantez *n* parenthesis
parasız *adj* short, penniless
paraşüt *n* chute, parachute
paraşütçü *n* paratrooper
parazit *n* parasite
parça *n* fragment, part, piece, bit
parça başına *adv* apiece

parçalamak *v* disintegrate, mangle, rip, splinter
parçalanmak *v* part
parçalar halinde *adv* asunder
parçalara ayırmak *v* dismantle, rip apart
parfüm *n* perfume
parıldamak *v* gleam
parıltı *n* flare, glare, shine
parıltılı *adj* flashy
parite *n* parity
park *n* park
park etmek *v* park
park yeri *n* parking
parke taşı *n* cobblestone
parlak *adj* glossy, shiny, vivid, bright
parlaklık *n* brightness, gloss
parlamak *v* blaze, glow
parlamento *n* parliament
parlatmak *v* brighten, shine
parmak *n* finger
parmak ısırtan *adj* mind-boggling
parmak izi *n* fingerprint
parmak ucu *n* fingertip
parşömen *n* parchment
parti *n* party
parti yapmak *v* party
partizan *n* partisan
pas *n* rust
pas tutmaz *adj* rust-proof
pasaport *n* passport

pasif *adj* passive
Paskalya *n* Easter
paskalya perhizi *n* Lent
paslanmak *v* rust
paslı *adj* rusty
paspas yapmak *v* mop
pasta *n* cake
pastel *n* crayon
pastorize etmek *v* pasteurize
patates *n* potato
patavatsız *adj* indiscreet
paten *n* skate
paten kaymak *v* skate
patent *n* patent
patentli *adj* patent
patika *n* alley
patlak verme *n* eruption
patlak vermek *v* break out
patlama *n* puncture, detonation, explosion
patlamak *v* burst, pop, explode
patlamış mısır *n* popcorn
patlatıcı *n* detonator
patlatmak *v* blow up, detonate
patlayıcı *adj* explosive
patron *n* boss, patron
patronluk taslamak *v* boss around
pavyon *n* pavilion
pay *n* dividend
pay etmek *v* allot
payda *n* denominator

P

paylaşım *n* share
paylaşma *n* communion
paylaşmak *v* share
pazar *n* bazaar
Pazar *n* Sunday
pazarlık *n* bargain, negotiation
pazarlık etme *n* bargaining
pazarlık etmek *v* bargain, haggle, negotiate
Pazartesi *n* Monday
peçe *n* veil
pedagoji *n* pedagogy
pedal *n* pedal
pejmürde *adj* shabby
pek çok *adv* highly
peki *adv* alright
pekiştirmek *v* consolidate, corroborate
pelerin *n* cloak, cape
pelikan *n* pelican
pelüş *adj* plush
pembe *adj* pink, rosy
pembeleşmiş *n* blush
pencere *n* window
pençe *n* claw, paw
pençe vurmak *v* tap into
penguen *n* penguin
peni *n* penny
penisilin *n* penicillin
perçem *n* bangs
perçinlemek *v* clinch, rivet
perde *n* curtain

performans *n* performance
peri *n* fairy
perişan *adj* wretched
personel *n* personnel
personel alma *n* recruitment
Perşembe *n* Thursday
peruk *n* hairpiece, wig
pervane *n* moth
pervasız *n* bluntness
peşinat *n* down payment
peşine düşmek *v* chase away
peşine takılmak *v* tail
petrol *n* petroleum
peygamber *n* prophet
peynir *n* cheese
pıhtı *n* clot
pıhtılaşma *n* coagulation
pıhtılaşmak *v* coagulate, curdle
pırıldamak *v* glitter, sparkle, wink
pırıltı *n* gleam
pırtlamak *v* protrude
pısırık *adj* wimp
piç *n* bastard
pijama *n* pajamas
pike yapmak *v* nosedive
pil *n* battery
pilot *n* pilot, flier
pinta *n* pint
piramid *n* pyramid
pire *n* flea
pirinç *n* rice
pirzola *n* chop

pis *adj* filthy
pis kokan *adj* stinking
pis koku *n* stink
pis kokulu *adj* smelly
piskopos *n* bishop, pontiff
piskoposluk bölgesi *n* diocese
pislik *n* contamination, filth
pist *n* runway
piston *n* plug, leverage
pişirmek *v* cook
pişman olmak *v* regret, repent
pişmanlık *n* contrition, regret,
  repentance
piton *n* python
piyade *n* foot
piyadeler *n* infantry
piyango *n* lottery, raffle
piyanist *n* pianist
piyano *n* piano
plaj *n* beach
plak *n* record
plan *n* plan
planlamak *v* plan, schedule
plastik *n* plastic
platin *n* platinum
plato *n* plateau
plütonyum *n* plutonium
polen *n* pollen
poliçe *n* policy
polis *n* cop, police, policeman
polis şefi *n* marshal
politika *n* politics

Polonya *n* Poland
Polonyalı *adj* Polish
pompa *n* pump
popo *n* butt
popüler *adj* popular
popülerleştirmek *v* popularize
porselen *n* porcelain
porsiyon *n* portion
portakal *n* orange
portatif merdiven *n* ladder
Portekiz *n* Portugal
Portekizli *adj* Portuguese
portre *n* portrait
posta *n* mail, post
posta arabası *n* stage
posta damgası *n* postmark
posta kodu *n* zip code
posta kutusu *n* mailbox
posta ücreti *n* postage
postacı *n* mailman, postman
postahane *n* post office
postalamak *v* mail, post
poster *n* poster
potansiyel *adj* potential
poz *n* pose
poz vermek *v* pose
pozisyon *n* position
pozitif *adj* positive
pratik *adj* practical
pratik olmayan *adj* impractical
prens *n* prince
prenses *n* princess

prestij *n* prestige
prizden çekmek *v* unplug
prizma *n* prism
profesör *n* professor
profesyonel *adj* professional
program *n* program, schedule
programcı *n* programmer
programlamak *v* program
proje *n* project, scheme
proje yapmak *v* project
projektör *n* floodlight
projektör ışığı *n* spotlight
propaganda *n* propaganda
prosedür *n* procedure
prostat *n* prostate
protein *n* protein
protesto *n* protest
protesto etmek *v* protest
protokol *n* protocol
prova *n* rehearsal
prova etmek *v* rehearse
pruva *n* prow
psikiyatri *n* psychiatry
psikiyatrist *n* psychiatrist
psikoloji *n* psychology
psikopat *n* psychopath
psişik *adj* psychic
puan *n* score
pudra *n* powder
pul *n* scale
puro *n* cigar
pusuda beklemek *v* lurk

pusula *n* compass
pusuya düşürmek *v* ambush
putperest *adj* pagan
putperestlik *n* idolatry
püre *n* puree
pürüzsüz *adj* smooth
pürüzsüzce *adv* smoothly
pürüzsüzlük *n* smoothness
püskürmek *v* erupt
püskürtmek *v* spray, sprinkle

radar *n* radar
radikal *adj* extremist, radical
radyasyon *n* radiation
radyatör *n* radiator
radyo *n* radio
radyoaktif serpinti *n* fallout
raf *n* shelf
rafine etmek *v* refine
rafineri *n* refinery
rağbet *n* vogue
rağmen *c* although, despite, though
rahat *adj* easy, cozy
rahatlama *n* relaxation
rahatlamak *v* chill out, relax
rahatlatıcı *adj* relaxing

rahatlık *n* ease
rahatlıklar *n* amenities
rahatsız *adj* ailing, uncomfortable
rahatsız edici *adj* disturbing
rahatsız etmek *v* disturb, harass
rahatsızlık *n* discomfort, disturbance
rahibe *n* nun, priestess
rahibe manastırı *n* convent
rahip *n* pastor, priest
rakam *n* figure
raket *n* racket
rakip *adj* competitive
rakip *n* rival, competitor
rakun *n* raccoon
ralli *n* rally
rampa *n* ramp
randevu *n* appointment
randıman *n* spoils
ranza *n* berth, bunk bed
rapor *n* report, essay
raptiye *n* clip, thumbtack
rastgele *adv* randomly
rasyonel *adj* rational
ray *n* track, rail
raydan çıkma *n* derailment
raydan çıkmak *v* derail
razı olmak *v* assent, give in, settle for, comply
reçel *n* jam
reddetmek *v* decline, refuse, reject, repudiate, turn down, rebuff

refah *n* affluence, prosperity, welfare
refakatçi *n* escort
referandum *n* referendum
referans *n* reference
reform *v* reform
reform *n* reform
rehber *n* guidebook
rehin *n* pledge
rehine *n* hostage
rehine koyma *v* pawn
rehine koymak *v* pledge
reis *n* heading
rejenerasyon *n* regeneration
rejim *n* regime
rekabet *n* rivalry
rekabet etmek *v* compete
reklam *n* publicity
reklam yapmak *v* advertise
rekreasyon *n* recreation
rektör *n* chancellor, rector
rektum *n* rectum
Ren geyiği *n* reindeer
renk *n* color
renklendirmek *v* color
renkli *adj* colorful
resepsiyon *n* desk, reception
resepsiyoncu *n* receptionist
resif *n* reef
resim *n* picture, illustration
resimlemek *v* picture
resimli örtü *n* tapestry

R

resmi *adj* formal, official
resmi olarak *adv* formally
resmi olmayan *adj* informal
resmileştirmek *v* formalize
resmiyet *n* formality
ressam *n* painter
restaurant *n* restaurant
restoran *n* diner
ret *n* refuse, rejection
reverans *n* bow
reverans yapmak *v* bow
revir *n* infirmary
revü *n* revue
rezervasyon *n* reservation
rezil *adj* dissolute
rıhtım *n* dock, pier
rıza *n* consent
rızasını almak *v* consent
rica etmek *v* solicit
risale *n* epistle
risk *v* jeopardize
risk *n* risk
riske atmak *v* risk
riskli *adj* risky
ritm *n* beat, rhythm
roket *n* rocket
rol alanlar *n* cast
rom *n* rum
romatizma *n* rheumatism
rosto *n* roast
rota *n* route
rotasyon *n* rotation

rozet *n* badge
röntgen ışını *n* X-ray
rötuş yapmak *v* touch up
ruh *n* soul, spirit
ruh hali *n* mood
ruh hastası *adj* lunatic
ruhani *adj* spiritual
ruhban *n* clergy
ruhsal *adv* inwards
rulo *n* roll
rulo yapmak *v* roll
rumuz *n* pseudonym
Rus *adj* Russian
Rusya *n* Russia
rutin *n* routine
rutubet *n* humidity
rüşvet *n* bribe, kickback
rüşvet vermek *v* bribe
rüşvetçilik *n* bribery
rütbe *n* degree, dignitary, rank
rütbesini indirmek *v* degrade
rüya *n* dream
rüzgar *n* wind
rüzgar esmek *v* wind
rüzgar siperi *n* windshield
rüzgarlı *adj* windy

S

saat *n* clock, hour, watch
saat üreticisi *n* watchmaker
saatlik *adv* hourly
sabah *n* morning
sabık *adj* preceding
sabır *n* patience
sabırla beklemek *v* hold out
sabırlı *adj* patient, stoic
sabırsız *adj* impatient
sabırsızlık *n* impatience
sabit *adj* constant, immutable, steady
sabit olmak *n* standing
sabit ücret *n* toll
sabotaj *n* sabotage
sabote etmek *v* sabotage
saç *n* hair
saç fırçası *n* hairbrush
saç kepeği *n* dandruff
saç kesimi *n* haircut
saç şekli *n* hairdo
saçma *adj* absurd, ridiculous, senseless
saçma *n* nonsense
saçmak *v* disseminate
sadaka *n* handout
sadaka vermek *v* dole out
sadakat *n* allegiance, devotion, fidelity, loyalty

sadakatsız *adj* unfaithful
sadakatsizlik *n* infidelity
sade *adj* simple, austere, homely, plain
sade *n* plain
sadece *adj* just
sadeleştirmek *v* simplify
sadelik *n* austerity, simplicity
sadık *adj* loyal, staunch
sadist *n* sadist
saf *adj* gullible, naïve, pure
safir *n* sapphire
saflık *n* purity
safra kesesi *n* gall bladder
sağ *adj* right
sağ kalan *n* survivor
sağ salim *adj* unharmed
sağanak *n* downpour, rainfall, thunderstorm
sağda *adv* right
sağdıç *n* best man
sağduyu *n* discretion
sağgörü *n* prudence
sağır *adj* deaf
sağır edici *adj* deafening
sağır etmek *v* deafen
sağırlık *n* deafness
sağlam *adj* entrenched, robust, sturdy
sağlamak *v* provide
sağlamlaştırmak *v* brace for
sağlık *n* health, fitness

sağlıklı *adj* healthy, fit
sağlıksız *adj* unhealthy
saha *n* arena, range
sahaya çıkarmak *v* field
sahibe *n* hostess
sahibi olmak *v* own
sahil *n* coast, seashore, shore
sahip olmak *v* possess, have
sahipsiz *adj* derelict
sahne *n* scene, stage
sahnelemek *v* stage
sahra *v* desert
sahte *adj* counterfeit, fake, phony
sahte *n* forgery
sahtekar *adj* dishonest
sahtekarlık *n* dishonesty
sahtesini yapmak *v* forge
sakal *n* beard
sakallı *adj* bearded
sakat *adj* cripple
sakat etmek *v* cripple
sakatlamak *v* maim
sakatlık *adj* disabled
sakınca *n* drawback
sakınmak *v* watch out, beware
sakız *n* bubble gum, gum
sakin *adj* calm
sakin *n* calm
sakinleşmek *v* cool down, calm down
sakinleştirmek *v* soothe
saklamak *v* preserve, keep, put aside

saksı *n* flowerpot
sal *n* raft
salata *n* salad
salatalık *n* cucumber
salça *n* sauce
saldırgan *n* aggressor, assailant, attacker
saldırgan *adj* aggressive
saldırı *n* aggression, assault, attack, mugging
saldırıp soymak *v* mug
saldırmak *v* assail, assault, attack, encroach, lash out
salgı bezi *n* gland
salgın *n* epidemic
Salı *n* Tuesday
salım *n* emission
salıncak *n* swing
salıvermek *v* unleash
salkım *n* bunch
sallamak *v* rock, sway, wag
sallanmak *v* quake, swing, wobble
salmak *v* emit
saltanat *n* reign
salya *n* saliva
salyangoz *n* snail
saman *n* hay
saman sapı *n* haystack
saman tırmığı *n* pitchfork
samimi *adj* cordial, intimate, sincere, truthful, wholehearted

S

samimilik *n* intimacy
samimiyet *n* sincerity
samimiyetsiz *adj* insincere
sanat *n* art
sanat çalışması *n* artwork
sanatçı *n* artist
sancı *n* gripe
sandal *n* sandal
sandal kıçı *n* stern
sandalye *n* chair
sandık *n* chest, ark
sandviç *n* sandwich
sanık *n* defendant
saniye *n* second
sanrı *n* illusion
sanrılamak *v* hallucinate
sansasyon *n* sensation
sansür *n* censorship
santimetre *n* centimeter
sap *n* grip
sapık *n* pervert
sapık *adj* pervert
saplama *n* stab
saplamak *v* plunge
saplantı *n* obsession
sapma *n* aberration, deviation
sapmak *v* veer
saptırmak *v* pervert
sara *n* epilepsy
saray *n* court, palace
sardalya *n* sardine
sargı *n* dressing

sarhoş *adj* drunk
sarhoşluk *n* drunkenness
sarı *adj* yellow
sarılı birşeyi açmak *v* unwind
sarılmış *adj* convoluted
sarımsak *n* garlic
sarışın *adj* blond
sarkaç *n* pendulum
sarkık *adj* baggy
sarkmak *v* dangle
sarmak *v* curl, involved, wrap
sarmalamak *v* wrap up
sarnıç *n* cistern, reservoir
sarp *adj* steep
sarsılmak *v* jar
sarsılmış *adj* shaken
sarsıntı *n* convulsion
sarsmak *v* convulse, shake
satıcı *n* salesman, seller
satılıp biten *adj* sold-out
satın almak *v* buy
satış fişi *n* sale slip
satış yeri *n* outlet
satmak *v* market, sell
satranç *n* chess
savaş *n* battle, war
savaş gemisi *n* battleship, warship
savaşçı *n* warrior
savaşım *n* warfare
savaşmak *v* battle
savcı *n* prosecutor

S

savunma *n* defense
savunmak *v* advocate, champion, defend, fend
savunmasız *adj* defenseless, helpless, vulnerable
savunucu *n* defender
savurgan *adj* extravagant
sayaç *n* counter
saydam *adj* see-through, transparent
sayfa *n* page
saygı *n* respect
saygı duymak *v* respect, venerate
saygı göstermek *n* reverence
saygılar *n* regards
saygılı *adj* respectful
saygısız *adj* disrespectful
saygısızlık *n* disrespect
saygısızlık etmek *v* desecrate
sayı *n* issue, number
sayıca çok olmak *v* outnumber
sayısız *adj* countless, numerous
sayma *n* count
saymak *v* count, enumerate; regard, deem
saz *n* reed
sebebiyle *pre* because of
sebep *n* motive, reason
sebze *v* vegetable
seçenek *n* option
seçilebilir *adj* eligible

seçim *n* choice, election, selection
seçip ayırmak *v* sort out
seçme hakkı *n* pick
seçmek *v* choose, elect, select
sedye *n* stretcher
sefalet *n* gutter
seher *n* dawn
sekiz *adj* eight
sekizinci *adj* eighth
sekreter *n* secretary
seksen *adj* eighty
sel *v* flood
sel *n* torrent
sel basma *n* flooding
selam *e* hello
selam *n* hail
selamlama *n* greetings
selamlamak *v* greet, hail
semaver *n* urn
sembol *n* symbol
sembolik *adj* symbolic
semer *n* saddle
seminer *n* workshop
sempati *n* sympathy
sempatik *adj* congenial
semptom *n* symptom
semt *n* ward
sen *pro* you
senaryo *n* scenario
senato *n* senate
senatör *n* senator

S

senet *n* bond
senfoni *n* symphony
senin *adj* your
seninki *pro* yours
senkronize etmek *v* synchronize
sent *n* cent
sentez *n* synthesis
sepet *n* basket
sera *n* greenhouse
seramik *n* ceramic
serap *n* mirage
serbestlik *n* leisure
serçe *n* sparrow
seremoni *n* ceremony
serenat *n* serenade
sergen *n* shelf
sergi *n* display, exhibition
sergilemek *v* flaunt, exhibit
seri *n* string
serili *adj* tanned
serin *adj* chilly, cool
serinkanlı *adj* cool
sermaye *n* capital, funds
sermaye bulmak *v* fund
sermek *v* lay
serpilmek *v* flourish
sersem *adj* dazed, dizzy
sersemletmek *v* daze
serseri *n* bum, prowler
serseri *adj* slob
sert *adj* rigid, stark, strict, solid
sert bir biçimde *adv* sternly

sert rüzgar *n* gale
sert vurmak *v* smash
sertifika *n* certificate
sertleşmek *v* stiffen
sertleştirmek *v* harden, toughen
sertlik *n* hardness, rigor
serum *n* serum
servi *n* cypress
servis *n* service
ses *n* tone, voice, sound
sesli harf *n* vowel
sessiz *adj* mute, placid, quiet, silent
sessizlik *n* quietness, silence
set çekmek *v* foil
sevdirmek *v* ingratiate
sevecen *adj* loving
sevgi *n* love
sevgi dolu *adj* fond
sevgili *n* lover, sweetheart
sevgili *adj* darling, dear, beloved
sevimli *adj* amiable, cute, lovable
sevinç *n* pleasure
sevinçli *adj* elated
sevindirici *n* welcome
sevindirmek *v* delight
sevkiyat *n* consignment
sevmek *v* love
seyahat etmek *v* travel, commute
seyir *n* navigation
seyirci *n* audience, spectator

S

seyirci kalan *n* bystander

seyrek *adj* thin, infrequent, scarce, sparse

seyretmek *v* fleet, navigate

sezgi *n* intuition

sezon *n* session

sıcak *adj* hot

sıcak dalgası *n* heat wave

sıçan *n* rat

sıçrama *n* leap, skip

sıçramak *n* bounce, buck, pulsate, skip

sıçratmak *v* splash

sıçrayış *n* jump

sıfat *n* adjective, participle

sıfır *adj* null

sıfır *n* zero

sıfırlamak *v* nullify

sığ *adj* shallow

sığınak *n* haven, refuge, shelter, retreat

sığınmak *v* shelter

sığır *n* cattle

sığır eti *n* beef

sığır filetosu *n* sirloin

sık *adj* frequent

sık uğramak *v* haunt

sıkı *adj* firm, tight

sıkı tutunmak *v* hang on

sıkıcı *adj* boring, tedious

sıkılaştırmak *v* tighten

sıkılık *n* firmness

sıkıntı *n* gloom, hardship, bun

sıkıntılı dönem *n* downturn

sıkışık *adj* pressing

sıkışmak *v* huddle, squeeze up

sıkıştırmak *v* compact, compress, pressure, squeeze

sıkkın *adj* fed up

sıklık *n* frequency

sıklıkla *adv* often

sıkmak *v* clench

sımsıkı tutmak *v* grip

sınama *n* probing

sınamak *v* examine

sınav *n* examination, quiz

sınavda çakmak *v* flunk

sınıf *n* caste, type, classroom, class

sınıf arkadaşı *n* classmate

sınıflandırmak *v* classify

sınır *adj* borderline

sınırdışı *n* deportation

sınırdışı etmek *v* deport

sınırını aşmak *v* transcend

sınırlamak *v* bound, constrain

sınırlandırmak *v* limit

sınırsız *adj* boundless, unlimited

sıra *n* order, line, queue

sıradaki *adj* next

sıradan *adj* ordinary, unpopular

sırasında *c* while

sırasında *pre* during

sıraya girmek *v* line up

S

sırayla yapmak *v* alternate
sırdaş *n* confidant
sırıtma *n* grin
sırıtmak *v* grin
sırrını söylemek *v* confide
sırsıklam *adj* soggy
sırt çantası *n* backpack
sırtlan *n* hyena
sıska *adj* skinny
sıtma *n* malaria
sıva *n* plaster
sıva vurmak *v* plaster
sıvı *n* fluid, liquid
sıvılaştırma *n* liquidation
sıvılaştırmak *v* liquidate
sıyırmak *v* skim
sıyrık *n* graze
sızdırmak *v* extort
sızdırmazlık *n* leakage
sızma *n* infiltration
sızmak *v* exude, infiltrate, leak
sicile kaydetmek *n* enrollment
sicim *n* twist
sigara *n* cigarette
sigara içen *n* smoker
sigara içmek *v* smoke
sigara içmeyen *n* nonsmoker
sigara paketi *n* pack
sigorta *n* insurance
sigorta etmek *v* underwrite
sigorta olmak *v* insure
siğil *n* wart

sihir *n* magic
sihirbaz *n* magician, sorcerer
sihirli *adj* magical
siklon *n* cyclone
silah *n* arm, gun, weapon; cane
silahlanma *n* armaments
silahlanmak *v* arm
silahlı *adj* armed
silahsız *adj* unarmed
silahsızlandırmak *v* disarm
silahsızlanma *n* disarmament
silgi *n* eraser
silindir *n* cylinder
silmek *v* delete, erase; wipe
silüet *n* silhouette
simetri *n* symmetry
simge *n* token
simültane *adj* simultaneous
sinagog *n* synagogue
sincap *n* squirrel
sindirim *n* digestion
sindirmek *v* digest, suppress
sinema *n* cinema
sinir *n* anger, nerve, boundary, verge
sinir bozucu *adj* annoying
sinir bozukluğu *n* breakdown
sinirlendirmek *v* displease
sinirlenmek *v* anger
sinirli *adj* angry, edgy, furious, mad; uptight, nervous
sinirli bir şekilde *adv* furiously

S

sinmek *n* quail
sinod *n* synod
sinsice ilerlemek *v* sneak
sinyal *n* signal
sinyal vermek *v* signal
sipariş vermek *v* order
siper *n* screen, bulwark
siper etmek *n* shield
siren *n* siren
sirk *n* circus
sirke *n* vinegar
sis *n* fog, haze
sisli *adj* foggy
sistem *n* system
sistemli *adj* systematic
site *n* site
sivilce *n* pimple
sivri *adj* pointed
sivrisinek *n* mosquito
siyah *adj* black
siyanür *n* cyanide
siyasetçi *n* politician
siz suz eki *pre* without
sizin *adj* your
skandal *n* scandal
skandal çıkarmak *v* scandalize
skuter *n* scooter
slogan *n* catchword, slogan
soba *n* stove
sofra örtüsü *n* tablecloth
sofu *adj* ascetic
soğan *n* onion

soğuk *adj* aloof, cold, freezing
soğuk *n* chill
soğuk ısırması *n* frostbite
soğuk içecek *n* refreshment
soğukluk *n* coldness, coolness
soğumak *v* cool down
soğutmak *v* cool, refrigerate, chill
soğutucu *adj* cooling
sohbet etmek *v* chat
sokağa çıkma yasağı *n* curfew
sokak *n* street
sokak lambası *n* streetlight
sokmak *v* shove, sting
sokmamak *v* bar
sokuşturmak *v* squeeze in
sol *n* left
sola *adv* left
solmak *v* wither
solucan *n* worm
soluk *adj* pale
solukluk *n* paleness
solumak *v* gasp
solunum *n* respiration
som balığı *n* salmon
somun *n* loaf
somurtkan *adj* sullen
somut *adj* solid, concrete
somut *n* concrete
son *n* end
son *adj* final, last
son bulmak *v* culminate
son kısım *n* conclusion

S

son söz *n* envoy
son tarih *n* deadline
son zamanlarda *adv* lately
sona ermek *v* adjourn, last
sonbahar *n* fall, autumn
sonda *pre* beneath
sondaj yapmak *v* drill
sonek *v* affix
sonlandırmak *v* end, terminate
sonra *pre* after
sonraki *adj* latter, subsequent
sonraları *adv* later
sonsuz *adj* endless, everlasting, infinite, unending
sonuç *n* consequence, result, conclusion
sonuç çıkarmak *v* reason, conclude
sopa *n* bat, stick
sorgulamak *v* interrogate, question
sorgulanabilir *adj* questionable
sorguya çekmek *v* debrief
sormak *v* ask
soru *n* question
sorumlu *adj* accountable, liable, responsible
sorumluluk *n* responsibility
sorun *n* problem
sorunlu *adj* problematic
soruşturma *n* inquest, inquisition, investigation

soruşturmak *v* investigate
sos *n* sauce, gravy
sosis *n* sausage
sosyal *adj* sociable
sosyalist *adj* socialist
sosyalizm *n* socialism
sosyalleşmek *v* socialize
sovyet *adj* soviet
soy *n* ancestry
soyadı *n* last name
soygun *n* heist
soyguncu *n* robber
soyisim *n* surname
soykırım *n* genocide
soymak *v* peel, pillage, rob, shell, skin, strip
soysal *adj* generic
soyunma odası *n* locker room
soyunmak *v* undress
soyut *adj* abstract
söğüt *n* willow
sömestre *n* semester
sömürge *n* colony
sömürge kurmak *v* colonize
sömürgeci *adj* colonial
sömürgeleştirme *n* colonization
sömürmek *v* exploit
söndürmek *v* deflate, extinguish, put out
sönmek *v* fade
sönük *adj* faded, insipid
sörf yapmak *v* surf

S

söylemek _v_ say
söylendiğine göre _adv_ reportedly
söylenmek _v_ grouch
söylenti _n_ hearsay, rumor
söz vermek _v_ stipulate
söz vermiş _adj_ committed
sözcük _n_ word
sözde _adv_ allegedly, reputedly
sözde _adj_ dummy, so-called, would-be
sözle _adv_ verbally
sözleşme _n_ contract
sözleşmek _v_ contract
sözlük _n_ dictionary, glossary
sözünü kesmek _v_ heckle
spazm _n_ spasm
spekülasyon _n_ speculation
spekülasyon yapmak _v_ speculate
sperm _n_ sperm
sponsor _n_ sponsor
spontane _adj_ spontaneous
spor _n_ fitness, sport
spor salonu _n_ gymnasium
sporcu _n_ sportsman
sportmen _adj_ sporty
staj yapmak _v_ intern
stajyer _n_ trainee
stand _n_ stall
standart _n_ standard
standart duruma getirmek _v_ standardize

steno _n_ shorthand
steril _adj_ sterile
sterilize etmek _v_ sterilize
stok _n_ inventory
stok yığını _n_ stockpile
stoklama _n_ stocking
strateji _n_ strategy
stres _n_ stress
stres verici _adj_ stressful
su _n_ water
su basmak _n_ flood
su basmak _v_ inundate
su çiçeği _n_ chicken pox
su geçirmez _adj_ waterproof, watertight
su götürmez _adj_ indisputable
su hortumu _n_ hose
su kabuklusu _n_ shellfish
su kaybetmek _v_ dehydrate
su samuru _n_ otter
su üstünde durmak _v_ float
su yolu _n_ channel
suç _n_ crime, guilt
suç ortağı _n_ accomplice
suç ortaklığı _n_ complicity
suçlama _n_ accusation
suçlamak _v_ accuse, blame, incriminate
suçlu _adj_ criminal, delinquent, guilty
suçlu _n_ culprit, felon
suçluluk _n_ delinquency

S

suçsuz *adj* blameless
suda yaşayan *adj* aquatic
suikast *n* plot, assassination
suikastçı *n* assassin
suistimal *n* abuse
sukemeri *n* aqueduct
sulama *n* irrigation
sulamak *v* water, irrigate
sulandırmak *v* dilute, water down
sulu *adj* juicy, succulent, watery
sunak *n* altar
sunmak *v* present
sunucu *n* announcer
sunum *n* presentation
suret çıkarmak *v* reprint
susamak *v* thirst
susamış *adj* thirsty
susmak *v* silence
susturmak *v* gag, muffle, muzzle
suya bastırmak *v* soak
suya daldırmak *v* duck
sübvansiyon *n* subsidy
süğüne göndermek *v* exile
sükunet *n* tranquility
sülük *n* leech
sülün *n* pheasant
sünger *n* sponge
süngü *n* bayonet
sünnet *n* circumcision
sünnet etmek *v* circumcise
süper *adj* superb

süper güç *n* superpower
süpermarket *n* supermarket
süpürge *n* broom
süpürmek *v* sweep
sürahi *n* jug
sürat *n* velocity
sürdürmek *v* wage
süre *n* period, times, span
süreç *n* course, process
sürekli *adj* continuous
süreklilik *n* continuity
süren *adj* ongoing
sürenin dolması *n* expiration
süresi bitmek *v* expire
sürgü *n* bolt
sürgülemek *v* bolt
sürgün *n* banishment, exile
sürgüne yollamak *v* banish
sürmek *v* propel, ride, smear
sürpriz *n* surprise
sürpriz yapmak *v* surprise
sürşarj *n* surcharge
sürtünme *n* friction
sürü *n* flock, peck
sürücü *n* driver
sürüklemek *v* drag, drift
sürüklenmiş *adv* adrift
sürüm *n* edition, version
sürüngen *n* reptile
sürünmek *v* crawl
süs *n* embroidery
süslemek *v* adorn, embellish, embroider

S

süt *n* milk
sütlü *adj* milky
sütun *n* column
sütyen *n* bra
süvari *n* cavalry
süzgeç *n* strainer
süzülmek *v* glide

Ş

şahadet *n* testimony
şahane *adj* imperial, splendid
şahıs *n* person
şahin *n* buzzard
şahit *n* witness
şahlanmış *adj* rampant
şahsi *adj* personal
şair *n* poet
şaka *n* trick, gag, hoax, joke
şaka yapmak *v* joke, kid
şakayla *adv* jokingly
şakırdatmak *v* snap
şal *n* scarf
şalgam *n* rape
şamandıra *n* buoy
şamata *n* commotion
şampiyon *n* champ, champion

şan *n* glory
şanlı *adj* heroic
şans *n* luck, chance
şanslı *adj* fortunate, lucky
şanssız *adj* unlucky
şantaj *n* blackmail
şantaj yapmak *v* blackmail
şapel *n* chapel
şapka *n* hat
şaplak atma *n* spanking
şaplak atmak *v* spank
şarap *n* wine
şaraphane *n* winery
şarapnel *n* shrapnel
şarj *n* charge
şarj etmek *v* recharge, charge
şarjör *n* drum
şarkı *n* song
şarkı söylemek *v* sing
şarkı sözü *n* lyrics
şarkıcı *n* singer
şartıyla *c* providing that
şartlar *n* terms
şaşırtıcı *adj* amazing, astonishing, puzzling
şaşırtmak *v* amaze, astonish, baffle, bewilder, confound, stun
şef *n* chef, chief
şeffaf *adj* clear
şefkat *n* compassion, pity, tenderness
şefkatli *adj* compassionate

S
Ş

şeftali *n* peach
şehir *n* city
şehir dışı *n* suburb
şehirli *adj* civic
şehit *n* martyr
şehitlik *n* martyrdom
şehvet düşkünü *adj* prurient
şeker *n* sugar, sweets
şekerleme *n* candy
şekerleme yapmak *v* doze
şekerlemek *v* nap
şekil *n* form, shape, figure
şekillendirmek *v* shape
şekilsiz *adj* amorphous
şelale *n* waterfall, cataract
şempanze *n* chimpanzee
şemsiye *n* umbrella
şen *adj* festive
şenlik *n* festivity
şenlik ateşi *n* bonfire
şerefe *n* cheers
şerefli *adj* glorious
şeri *n* sherry
şerit *n* lace, strip, string
şevk *n* enthusiasm
şevk kırıcı *adj* discouraging
şey *n* thing
şeytan *n* demon, devil
şeytanca *adj* devious, satanic
şımartmak *v* pamper
şırınga *n* syringe
şiddet *n* violence

şiddetli *adj* drastic, fierce, intense
şiddetli sarsıntı *n* concussion
şifoniyer *n* dresser
şifre *n* password
şifre çözmek *v* decipher
şiir *n* poem, poetry
şikayet *n* complaint
şikayet etmek *v* complain
şilte *n* mattress
şimdi *adv* now
şimdiki *adj* present
şimdiye kadar *adv* hitherto
şimşek *n* lightning
şirket *n* firm, company
şiş *adj* bloated, swollen
şiş *n* bump
şişe *n* bottle
şişelemek *v* bottle
şişirmek *v* bloat, inflate
şişkinlik *n* lump
şişman *adj* corpulent, fat
şişmanlamak *v* fatten
şişmek *v* swell
şok *n* shock
şoke etmek *v* astound
şoke olmak *v* shock
şort *n* shorts
şort kilot *n* boxer
şömine *n* fireplace, hearth
şövalye *n* knight
şu anda *adv* currently
şu anki *adj* current

Şubat *n* February
şube *n* department, branch office
şurup *n* syrup
şüphe *n* doubt
şüphe uyandıran *adj* fishy
şüpheci *adj* skeptic
şüphelenmek *v* doubt
şüpheli *adl* doubtful, suspicious, uncertain
şüphesiz *adv* undoubtedly

T

taaffün *n* stench
taammüden *adv* willfully
tabak *n* plate
tabaka *n* coat
taban *n* sole
tabanca *n* handgun, pistol, revolver
tabiat *n* temper
tabla *n* ashtray
tablet *n* tablet
tablo *n* painting
tabur *n* battalion, troop; coffin, casket
taç *n* crown
taç giyme *n* crowning

taç giyme töreni *n* coronation
taç giymek *v* crown
taç yaprağı *n* petal
tadilat yapmak *v* remodel
tafra *n* pomposity
tahammül *n* tolerance
tahıl *n* grain
tahliye ettirmek *v* evict
tahmin *n* estimation, guess
tahmin *v* forecast
tahmin etmek *v* guess, expect
tahribat *n* devastation
tahrik *n* incitement
tahrip etmek *v* raze
taht *n* throne
tahta *n* wood, board
tahtadan *adj* wooden
takas etmek *v* exchange
takas yapmak *v* barter
takdir *n* admiration
takdir etmek *v* appreciate
takdir etmek *n* appreciation
takdire değer *adj* admirable
takım *n* platoon, team
takımyıldız *n* constellation
takibat *n* proceedings
takip etmek *v* follow, track
taklit *n* imitation
taklit *adj* counterfeit
taklit etmek *v* counterfeit, imitate
takma diş *n* dentures

takmak *v* insert
takoz *n* wedge
taksi *n* cab
taksit *n* installment
taktik *n* tactics
taktiksel *adj* tactical
takvim *n* calendar
takviye *n* reinforcements
takviye etmek *v* reinforce
talan edilmiş *adj* scrambled
talan etmek *v* plunder
talep *n* demand, claim
talep etmek *v* assess, demand, request, claim
talim *n* drill, practice, training
talim ettirmek *v* train
talimat *n* direction, prescription
talip olmak *v* aspire
tam *adj* absolute, complete, precise
tamahkar *adj* avaricious
tamam *adv* okay
tamamen *adv* completely, fully
tamamen *adj* total
tamamıyla *adv* entirely
tamamlama *n* completion, fulfillment
tamamlamak *v* complete, fulfill
tamı tamına *adj* exact
tamir etmek *v* rehabilitate
tamirat *n* reparation
tampon *n* bumper

tane *n* pellet
tanecik *n* particle
tanıdık *n* acquaintance
tanıdık *adj* familiar
tanıklık etmek *v* testify
tanım *n* definition
tanıma *n* recognition
tanımak *v* recognize, spot
tanımlamak *v* define
tanımlayıcı *adj* descriptive
tanıştırmak *v* introduce
tanıtım *n* advertising
tank *n* tank
Tanrı *n* God
tanrıça *n* goddess
tanrıtanımaz *adj* godless
tanrıya küfür *n* blasphemy
tapa *n* cork, tap
tapılası *adj* adorable
tapınak *n* sanctuary, shrine, temple
tapınma *n* adoration
tapmak *v* adore
tapmak *n* worship
taraça *n* slab
taraf *n* side
tarafsız *adj* impartial
tarafsızlık *n* candor
tarafsızlık *adj* disinterested
tarak *n* comb; rake
taramak *v* comb; scan
tarantula *n* tarantula**

taravet *n* tenderness

tarçın *n* cinnamon

tarım *n* agriculture, farming

tarım ilacı *n* pesticide

tarıma elverişli *adj* arable

tarımsal *adj* agricultural

tarif *n* description

tarif etmek *v* describe

tarife *n* tariff

tarifsiz *adj* unspeakable

tarih *n* history; date

tarih koymak *v* date

tarih öncesi *adj* prehistoric

tarihçi *n* historian

tart *n* pie

tartaklamak *v* manhandle

tartar *n* tartar

tartışılabilir *adj* debatable

tartışılmaz *adj* undisputed

tartışma *n* argument, controversy, debate, discussion

tartışmak *v* argue, debate, discuss, hassle

tartışmalı *adj* controversial

tartmak *v* weigh

tas *n* bowl

tasa *n* preoccupation

tasarım *n* design

tasarlamak *v* devise, premeditate

tasarruf etmek *v* economize

tasasız *adj* carefree

tasavvur etmek *v* envisage

tasdik *n* sanction

tasdik etmek *v* certify, sanction

tasdikli *adj* avowed

tasfiye *n* purge

taslak *n* framework, sketch, draft

taslak çizmek *v* outline, sketch, draft

tasma *n* leash

tasvip *n* approbation

taş *n* stone

taş ocağı *n* quarry

taşıma *n* transfer

taşımak *v* bear, carry, cart, transfer, transport, convey

taşınabilir *adj* portable

taşıyıcı *n* bearer

taşlamak *v* stone

taşma *n* outpouring

taşmak *v* boil over

taşralı *n* countryman

tat *n* delight, taste

tatil *n* holiday, vacation

tatlı *n* dessert

tatlı *adj* sweet

tatlılaştırmak *v* sweeten

tatlılık *n* sweetness

tatmin edici *adj* rewarding

tatmin etmek *v* quench, satisfy

tatmin olmamış *adj* dissatisfied

tatminkar *adj* gratifying

tatsız *adj* distasteful, tasteless

tava *n* frying pan, pan, saucepan
tavan *n* ceiling
tavanarası *n* attic
taverna *n* tavern
tavır *n* demeanor, manner
tavsiye *n* counsel
tavsiye etmek *v* advise, commend
tavşan *n* hare, rabbit
tavuk *n* chicken, hen
tavuskuşu *n* peacock
tay *n* colt
tayin *n* assignment
tayin etmek *v* appoint, assign, earmark
tayt *n* pantyhose
taze *adj* fresh
taze fasulye *n* green bean
tazelemek *v* brush up, freshen
tazeleyici *adj* refreshing
tazelik *n* freshness
tazı *n* greyhound, hound
tazminat *n* compensation, indemnity
tazminat vermek *v* pay off
teberru *n* gratuity
tebeşir *n* chalk
tebliğ *n* bulletin
tebrik etmek *v* congratulate
tebrikler *n* congratulations
tecavüz etmek *v* rape
tecavüzcü *n* rapist

tedarik etmek *v* supply, sustain
tedarikçi *n* supplier
tedavi *n* treatment
tedavi etmek *v* cure
tedavisi mümkün *adj* curable
tedbir *n* foresight
tedbirli *adj* discreet
tedirginlik *n* unrest
tefeci *n* pawnbroker
teftiş *n* inspection, supervision, review
teftiş etmek *v* supervise
teğet *n* tangent
teğmen *n* lieutenant
tehdit *n* threat
tehdit etmek *v* threaten
tehlike *n* pitfall, danger, hazard, peril
tehlikeli *adj* serious, dangerous, hazardous, perilous
tehlikeli girişim *n* venture
tehlikeye atmak *v* venture
tehlikeye sokmak *v* endanger
tek *adj* single, sole, unique
tek *n* single
tek elli *adj* singlehanded
tek eşlilik *n* monogamy
tek tük *adj* sporadic
tek yanlı *adj* unilateral
tekabül etmek *v* refer to
tekbiçimli *n* uniform
tekbiçimlilik *n* uniformity

T

tekelleştirmek *v* monopolize

tekerlek *n* rim, wheel

tekerlekli sandalye *n* wheelchair

tekerrür *n* recurrence

tekil *adj* singular

teklif *n* motion, offer, proposal

teklif etmek *v* offer, propose

teklif vermek *v* bid

teklifsiz *n* informality

tekmelemek *v* kick

tekne *n* vessel

teknik *adj* technical

teknik *n* technique

teknik detay *n* technicality

teknik ressam *n* draftsman

teknisyen *n* technician

teknoloji *n* technology

tekrar *adv* again

tekrar *n* repetition, replay

tekrar belirmek *v* reappear

tekrar doldurmak *v* refill

tekrar evlenmek *v* remarry

tekrar inşa etmek *v* rebuild

tekrar yapmak *v* redo, remake

tekrar yaşamak *v* relive

tekrarlamak *v* repeat, reproduce

tel *n* wire

telaffuz *n* articulation

telaffuz etmek *v* pronounce

telafi etmek *v* compensate, make up for, recoup

telaşlı *adj* bustling, frenetic

telefon *n* phone, telephone

telefon etmek *v* phone

telegram *n* telegram

telepati *n* telepathy

teleskop *n* telescope

televizyon *n* television

telgraf *n* wire

telif hakkı *n* copyright

telkin etmek *v* endorse

telkinde bulunmak *v* indoctrinate

tema *n* theme

temas *n* contact

temas etmek *v* contact

tembel *adj* lazy

tembellik *n* laziness

tembih *n* admonition

tembih etmek *v* admonish

temel *adj* basic, essential, fundamental, rudimentary, elementary

temel *n* base

temel bilgiler *n* basics

temelinde *adj* innate

temelsiz *adj* baseless, unfounded

temin etmek *v* assure

temiz *adj* clear, clean

temizlemek *v* clean, cleanse, clear, purge, wipe out

temizleyici madde *n* cleanser

temizlik *n* cleanliness, clearance

temizlikçi *n* cleaner

temkinli *adj* deliberate, wary
Temmuz *n* July
temsil etmek *v* represent
temyiz *n* appeal
temyiz etmek *v* appeal
ten rengi *n* complexion
teneke *n* tin
teneke kuru *n* canister
teneke kutu *n* can
tenezzül etmek *v* condescend, deign
tenha *adj* secluded
tenha yer *n* retreat
tenis *n* tennis
tenkit *n* criticism
tenör *n* tenor
tensel *adj* sensual
tente *n* awning
teori *n* theory
tepe *n* hill
tepe üstü *n* hilltop
tepeden bakma *n* disdain
tepeden bakmak *v* look down
tepelik *n* crest
tepelik *adj* hilly
tepki *n* reaction
tepki vermek *v* react
tepsi *n* tray
ter *n* perspiration, sweat
terapi *n* therapy
teras *n* terrace
terazi *n* scale

terbiye *n* upbringing
terbiyeci *n* trainer
terbiyesiz *adj* impertinent, rude
terbiyesizlik *n* rudeness
tercih *n* preference
tercih etmek *v* opt for, prefer
tercüman *n* interpreter, translator
tercüme *n* interpretation
tercüme etmek *v* interpret, translate
tereddüt *n* hesitation, quandary, scruples
tereddüt etmek *v* falter, hesitate, stagger
tereddütlü *adj* hesitant
tereyağı *n* butter
terfi *n* promotion
terfi ettirmek *v* promote
terim *n* term
terk *n* abandonment
terk etmek *v* resign
terkedilmiş *v* desert
terketmek *v* abandon, dump
terlemek *v* perspire, sweat
terlik *n* slipper
terminoloji *n* terminology
termit *n* termite
termometre *n* thermometer
termosifon *n* water heater
termostat *n* thermostat
terör *n* terror

T

terörist *n* terrorist
terörizm *n* terrorism
ters *adj* perverse
tersane *n* shipyard, dock
tersine *adv* conversely
tersine çevirme *n* reversal
tersten anlamak *v* misconstrue
tersyüz *adv* inside out
tertemiz *adj* immaculate
tertip *n* concoction
tertip etmek *v* concoct
terzi *n* tailor
tesadüf *n* coincidence
tesadüf etmek *v* coincide
tesadüfen *adj* casual,
  coincidental, incidentally
tesadüfi *adj* circumstantial
tesbih *n* rosary
teselli *n* consolation, solace
teselli etmek *v* console
tesir *n* touch
tesirli *adj* telling
tesirlilik *n* effectiveness
tesis *n* foundation
tesis etmek *v* institute
tesisatçı *n* plumber
teslim *n* concession
teslim etmek *v* concede, deliver,
  hand in, turn in
teslim olmak *v* capitulate,
  indulge, surrender, yield
teslimat *n* delivery

teslimiyet *n* surrender
tespit etmek *v* identify
test *n* test
test etmek *v* test
testere *n* saw
teşebbüs *n* attempt, proposition
teşebbüs etmek *v* attempt
teşekkür etmek *v* thank
teşekkürler *n* thanks
teşhis *n* diagnosis
teşhis koymak *v* diagnose
teşkil etmek *v* constitute
teşvik etmek *v* exhort
tetik *n* trigger
tetiklemek *v* trigger
teyp kaydedici *n* tape recorder
teyze *n* aunt
tez *n* thesis
tezahürat *n* ovation
tezahürat yapmak *v* cheer
tezgah *n* counter
tıkamak *v* clog, seal off
tıkanıklık *n* congestion
tıkanma *n* blockage
tıkırdamak *v* rattle
tıkıştırmak *v* cram, stuff
tıklamak *v* click
tıklım tıklım *adj* congested
tıknaz *adj* plump
tıpkısı *adv* very
tıpkısı *adj* identical
tırabzan *n* handrail

tırmalamak *v* claw
tırmanma *n* climbing
tırmanmak *v* climb, mount, scramble
tırmık *n* rake
tırnak *n* fingernail, nail
tırsmak *v* chicken out
tırtıl *n* caterpillar
tıslamak *v* hiss
ticaret *n* trade, commerce
ticaret yapmak *v* trade
ticareti yapmak *v* traffic
ticari *adj* commercial
ticari marka *n* trademark
tiksindirici *adj* detestable, heinous, repulsive, revolting, sickening
tiksindirmek *v* sicken
tiksinmek *v* loathe
tiksinti *n* revulsion
tilki *n* fox
timsah *n* alligator, crocodile
tipi *n* blizzard
tipik *adj* typical
tiroit *n* thyroid
titiz *adj* meticulous
titrek *adj* shaky
titremek *v* tremble
titreşim *n* vibration
titreşimli *adj* vibrant
titreşmek *v* flicker, vibrate
tiyatro *n* theater

tohum *n* seed
tohum ekmek *v* sow
toka *n* buckle
tokat *n* slap, smack
tokat atmak *v* smack
tokatlamak *v* slap
toksin *n* toxin
toksinli *adj* toxic
toleranssızlık *n* intolerance
tomar *n* scroll
tombul *adj* chubby
tomurcuk *n* bud
ton *n* ton
tonbalığı *n* tuna
tonik *n* tonic
top *n* web, roll, ball
top sürme *n* drive
topallamak *v* limp
toparlama *n* roundup
toplam *n* sum, totality
toplama *n* congregation
toplamak *v* aggregate, collect, congregate, gather, sum up
toplamda *adv* overall
toplanmak *v* convene, assemble
toplantı *n* party, convention, gathering, meeting, assembly
toplantı salonu *n* auditorium
toplu silah *n* cannon
topluluk *n* crowd, society
toplum *n* community
toprak *n* soil, earth

toprak duvar *n* dike
toptan satış *n* wholesale
topuk *n* heel
tornacı *n* lather
tornavida *n* screwdriver
torun *n* descendant, grandchild
tosbağa *n* tortoise
tost makinesi *n* toaster
totaliter *adj* totalitarian
toynak *n* hoof
toz *n* powder, dust
tozlu *adj* dusty
tökezlemek *v* stumble
tören *n* rite
törpü *n* file
tövbekar *n* penitent
trafik *n* traffic
trajedi *n* tragedy
trajik *adj* tragic
traktör *n* tractor
tramplen *n* springboard
tramvay *n* streetcar, tram
transit *n* transit
transplantasyon *v* transplant
traş olmak *v* shave
travma geçirmek *v* traumatize
travmatik *adj* traumatic
tren *n* train
tribün *n* grandstand
tripod *n* tripod
tromboz *n* thrombosis
tropik *n* tropic

tropik *adj* tropical
tufan *n* cataclysm, deluge
tugay *n* brigade
tuğ *n* tail
tuğla *n* brick
tuhaf *adj* cranky
tur *n* tour
tura *n* reel
turfanda *adj* precocious
turist *n* tourist
turizm *n* tourism
turnuva *n* tournament
turp *n* radish
turta *n* tart
tuş *n* key
tutam *n* pinch
tutarlı *adj* consistent
tutarlılık *n* consistency
tutarsız *adj* inconsistent
tutkal *n* glue
tutkallamak *v* glue
tutku *n* passion
tutkulu *adj* passionate
tutmak *v* hold
tutsak *n* captive, prisoner
tutsak etmek *v* captivate
tutsaklık *n* captivity
tutucu *adj* conservative
tutuklama *n* arrest
tutuklamak *v* arrest
tutum *n* attitude
tutumlu *adj* frugal, thrifty

tutumlu bir şekilde *adv* sparingly
tutumluluk *n* frugality
tutunmak *v* cling, hold on to
tutuşma *n* combustion
tuval *n* canvas
tuvalet *n* rest room, toilet
tuz *n* salt
tuzağa düşürmek *v* snare
tuzak *n* trap, noose, snare, pitfall
tuzak kurmak *v* trap
tuzlu *adj* salty
tüberküloz *n* tuberculosis
tüccar *n* merchant, trader
tüfeğin gezi *n* hindsight
tüfek *n* rifle
tüfekçi *n* gunman
tükenmeyen *adj* lasting
tüketici *n* consumer
tüketim *n* consumption
tüketmek *v* consume, deplete, sap, exhaust
tükürmek *v* spit
tümen *n* legion
tümleyici *n* complement
tümör *n* tumor
tümsekli *adj* bumpy
tünel *n* subway, tunnel
tünik *n* tunic
türbin *n* turbine
türetmek *v* derive
türev *adj* derivative
Türk *adj* Turk

Türkiye *n* Turkey
türlü *adj* various
tütsü *n* incense
tütün *n* tobacco
tüy *n* feather
tüyler ürpertici *adj* horrendous
tüyleri kabarık *adj* furry
tüylü *adj* fuzzy

U

ucuz *adj* cheap, inexpensive
ucuzlatmak *v* depreciate
uç *n* edge, tip
uç nokta *n* extremities
uçağın konması *v* land
uçak *n* flier, aircraft, airplane, plane
uçak kaçırmak *v* hijack
uçak pisti *n* airstrip
uçak postası *n* airmail
uçmak *v* fly
uçucu *adj* volatile
uçurtma *n* kite
uçurum *n* abyss, precipice, cliff
uçuş *n* fly, flight
uçuş ücreti *n* airfare
ufacık *adj* tiny

T
U

ufak çivi *n* tack
ufak ev *n* lodging
ufalamak *v* crumble
ufuk *n* horizon
uğramak *v* call on, drop in, stop by
uğraş *n* occupation, profession
uğraşıp başarmak *v* thrive
uğraşmak *v* bother, cope, molest
uğraşmak *n* plague
uğraştırıcı *adj* bothersome
uğursuz *adj* evil, ominous
ulaç *n* gerund
ulaşılır *adj* attainable
ulaşma *n* attainment
ulaşmak *v* attain, border on, come over
ulu *adj* almighty, supreme
uluma *n* howl
ulumak *v* howl
ulus *n* nation
ulusal *adj* national
ummak *v* anticipate
umrunda olmak *v* care
umudunu kırmak *v* dishearten
umursamaz *adj* reckless
umursamazca *adv* lightly
umut *n* expectancy, hope, prospect
umut etmek *v* hope
umut kırıcı *adj* disappointing
umutlu *adj* hopeful

umutsuz *adj* desperate
umutsuzluk *n* despair, dismay, qualm
un *n* flour
unutma *n* oblivion
unutmak *v* forget, get over
unutulmaz *adj* memorable, unforgettable
unvan *n* title
usanç *n* harassment
usandırmak *v* bore
usta *n* master
ustabaşı *n* foreman
ustalık *n* ingenuity
ustalık isteyen *adj* tricky
usulüne uygun *adv* duly
uşak *n* page
utanç *n* chagrin, shame
utanç verici *adj* disgraceful, shameful
utandırmak *v* embarrass, offend
utangaç *adj* bashful, self-conscious, shy
utanmak *v* shame
utanmaz *adj* shameless
uyandırmak *v* awake, evoke
uyanık *adj* awake, watchful
uyanış *n* awakening
uyanmak *v* wake up
uyarı *n* alert, attention, caution, warning
uyarıcı *n* stimulant

uyarıcı unsur *n* stimulus
uyarlamak *v* adapt
uyarlanabilen *adj* adaptable
uyarmak *v* alert, forewarn, stimulate, warn
uydu *n* satellite
uydurma *adj* untrue
uydurmak *v* fabricate, fake
uygulama *n* application
uygulamak *v* carry out, enforce, implement, apply
uygulanabilir *adj* applicable
uygun *adj* proper, agreeable, appropriate, expedient, fitting, pertinent, suitable
uygun *n* compatibility
uygun adım yürümek *v* march
uygun davranış *n* decorum
uygun olmayan *adj* unfit
uygun şekilde *adv* properly
uygunluk *n* conformity
uygunsuz *adj* awkward, inappropriate, inept, unsuitable
uygunsuz davranmak *v* misbehave
uyku *n* sleep
uykuda *adj* asleep
uykulu *adj* drowsy
uykusuzluk *n* insomnia
uyluk *n* thigh
uymak *v* obey
uymamak *v* counter

uysal *adj* amenable, compliant, docile, submissive
uysallık *n* docility
uyuklamak *v* snooze
uyum *n* adaptation, cohesion, harmony
uyumak *v* sleep
uyumlu *adj* compatible, low-key
uyumsuz *adj* discordant, misfit
uyuşmak *v* concur
uyuşmamak *v* conflict
uyuşmaz *adj* incompatible
uyuşmazlık *n* conflict, discord, discrepancy
uyuşturucu vermek *v* dope
uyuşuk *adj* numb
uyuşukluk *n* numbness
uyuyakalmak *v* drop off
uzağa *adv* far
uzak *adj* distant, remote
uzak durmak *v* shun
uzaklaşmak *v* go away, pull out
uzaklık *n* distance
uzakta *adv* afar, away
uzanmak *v* lie, lounge
uzanmış *adj* outstretched
uzatılmış *adj* protracted
uzatma *n* extension
uzatmak *v* extend, lengthen, prolong, protract, reach
uzay *n* space
uzlaşma *n* compromise**

U

üstün

uzlaşmak *v* compromise
uzlaştırmak *v* reconcile
uzman *adj* expert
uzmanlaşmak *v* master
uzmanlık alanı *n* specialty
uzun *adj* long
uzun bank *n* pew
uzun boylu *adj* tall
uzun süreli *adj* long-term
uzunca *adj* oblong
uzunluk *n* length

ücret *n* fee, wage
üç *adj* three
üç ayda bir *adj* quarterly
üç aylık *n* trimester
üçgen *n* triangle
üçlü *adj* triple
üçüncü *adj* third
üflemek *v* blow
üfleyip söndürmek *v* blow out
üfürük *n* puff
üfürükçü *n* exorcist
ülke *n* country
ülkenin iç kısmı *adj* inland
ülkesine iade etmek *v* repatriate

ülser *n* ulcer
ültimatom *n* ultimatum
ültrason *n* ultrasound
ümitle *adv* hopefully
ümitsiz *adj* hopeless
ün *n* fame, reputation
üniversite *n* university
ünlem *n* exclamation
ünlü *n* celebrity
ünlü *adj* famous, illustrious
ünsüz *n* consonant
üremek *v* breed
üretim *n* production
üretken *adj* productive
üretmek *v* generate, produce
ürkek *adj* timid
ürkeklik *n* timidity
ürkütücü *adj* dreadful, eerie, grisly, spooky
ürperme *n* tremor
ürpermek *v* quiver, shiver, shudder
ürperti *n* chill, shiver, shudder
ürün *n* produce, product; offspring
üs *n* base
üslup *n* wording
üst *adj* upper
üst giyecek *n* top
üstelemek *v* persist
üstü kapalı *n* insinuation
üstün *n* distinction

üstün *adj* exquisite, superior
üstün olmak *v* predominate, excel
üstünde *pre* above, on, over
üstünlük *n* primacy, superiority, supremacy
üstünü çizmek *v* cross out
üstünü örtmek *v* cover up
üstüste binmek *v* overlap
üşüşmek *v* mob
ütülemek *v* iron
üvey *adj* adoptive
üvey anne *n* stepmother
üvey baba *n* stepfather
üvey erkek kardeş *n* stepbrother
üvey kız *n* stepdaughter
üvey kız kardeş *n* stepsister
üvey oğul *n* stepson
üye *n* member
üyelik *n* membership
üzerine *pre* upon
üzerine titremek *v* cherish
üzgün *adj* sad, sorry
üzmek *v* sadden
üzücü *adj* regrettable, worrisome
üzülmek *v* worry
üzüm *n* grape
üzüntü *n* distress, worry

vaat *n* commitment, promise, preaching, sermon
vaaz vermek *v* preach
vadi *n* valley
vaftiz *n* baptism, christening
vaftiz etmek *v* baptize, christen
vagon *n* wagon
vaha *n* oasis
vahim *adj* fateful
vahişilik *n* ferocity
vahşet *n* atrocity
vahşi *adj* ferocious, savage, wild
vahşi doğa *n* wilderness
vahşi hayat *n* wildlife
vahşilik *n* savagery
vaiz *n* chaplain, preacher
vaka *n* happening
vakıf *n* foundation
vakit *n* time
vali *n* governor
valiz *n* suitcase
vals *n* waltz
vampir *n* vampire
van *n* van
vana *n* valve
vandal *n* vandal
vandalizm *n* vandalism
var olmak *v* exist
varış *n* arrival, coming

varis *n* successor

varlık *n* bud, being, existence, presence

varlıklı *adj* well-to-do

varmak *v* arrive

varsayılan *n* presupposition

varsayım *n* assumption, conjecture, hypothesis

varsaymak *v* assume, presuppose

vasıf *v* attribute

vasiyet etmek *v* bequeath

vat *n* watt

vatan haini *n* traitor

vatana ihanet *n* treason

vatandaş *n* citizen, compatriot

vatandaşlık *n* citizenship, nationality

vatansever *n* patriot

vazgeçmek *v* desist, forsake, give up, let go, remit, renounce

vazo *n* vase

ve *c* and

vefa *n* constancy

vefasız *adj* disloyal, fickle

vefasızlık *n* disloyalty

vefat *n* demise

vejetaryen *v* vegetarian

vekaletname *n* proxy

veranda *n* porch

vergi *n* tax

veri *n* data

verimli *adj* efficient; fertile, fruitful

verimlilik *n* fertility

veritabanı *n* database

vermek *v* give

vernik *n* varnish

verniklemek *v* varnish

veteriner *n* veterinarian

veto etmek *v* veto

veya *c* or

veznedar *n* teller

vızıldamak *v* buzz

vızıldayan alet *n* buzzer

vızıltı *n* buzz

vicdan *n* conscience

vicdan azabı *n* remorse

vicdanlı *adj* conscious, scrupulous

vida *n* screw

vidalamak *v* screw

vilayet *n* province

vinç *n* crane, hoist

virajlı *adj* crooked

virgül *n* comma

virüs *n* virus

vitamin *n* vitamin

vites *n* gear

viyadük *n* viaduct

voleybol *n* volleyball

voltaj *n* voltage

vuku bulmak *v* occur

vurgu *n* emphasis

vurgulamak *v* emphasize

V

vurgun *n* killing
vurmak *v* bang, hit, pound, strike, zap
vuruş *n* throb, impact, strike, beat

yaban domuzu *n* boar, wild boar
yabancı *n* alien, foreigner, stranger
yabancı *adj* extraneous, foreign
yadsımak *v* disclaim, disown
yağ *n* fat, oil
yağ çekmek *v* flatter
yağlamak *v* anoint, grease, lubricate
yağlı *adj* fatty, greasy
yağmur *n* rain
yağmur yağmak *v* rain
yağmurlu *adj* rainy
yağmurluk *n* raincoat
yaka *n* collar
yakacak *n* firewood
yakalama *n* grasp
yakalamak *n* capture
yakalamak *v* catch
yakın *pre* by, close to, near
yakın *adj* imminent, impending

yakın ilişki *n* affiliation
yakında *adv* soon
yakından *adv* closely
yakınlarda *adj* nearby
yakınlaşma *n* approach
yakınlaşmak *v* approach
yakınlık *n* rapport, proximity
yakınma *n* grievance
yakınmak *v* beef up
yakınsamak *v* converge
yakışıklı *adj* good-looking, handsome
yakıt *n* fuel
yakıt almak *v* fuel, refuel
yaklaşık *adj* approximate
yaklaşılabilir *adj* approachable
yakmak *v* scorch
yakut *n* ruby
yalamak *v* lick
yalan *n* falsehood, lie
yalan *adj* trumped-up
yalan söylemek *v* lie
yalancı *adj* liar
yalancı şahit *n* perjury
yalanlamak *v* refute
yalıtım *n* insulation
yalıtmak *v* insulate
yalnız *adj* alone, solitary
yalnız *n* loner
yalnız *adv* only
yalnız başına *adv* lonely
yalnızca *adv* solely

yalnızlık *n* loneliness, solitude
yaltaklanmak *v* pander
yalvarmak *v* beg, beseech, entreat, plead
yama *n* graft, patch
yamaç *n* hillside, slope
yamalamak *v* graft, patch
yamamak *v* darn
yamultmak *v* dent
yamyam *n* cannibal
yan *n* side
yan çizmek *v* shirk, sidestep
yan kapı *adj* next door
yan tümce *n* clause
yan ürün *n* by-product
yanak *n* cheek
yanan *adv* alight
yanardağ *n* volcano
yanaşmak *v* coast, dock
yandan *adv* sideways
yandaş *n* follower
yanıcı *n* combustible
yanıcı *adj* flammable
yanık *n* burn
yanılmak *v* err
yanılmaz *adj* infallible, unfailing
yanıltıcı *adj* deceptive
yanıltılmış *adj* misguided
yanıltmaca *n* fallacy
yanında *pre* alongside, beside, by
yanıt *n* answer
yani *adv* namely

yankesicilik *n* pickpocket
yankı *n* echo
yanlış *adj* inaccurate, incorrect, mistaken, wrong
yanlış anlamak *v* misinterpret, misunderstand
yanlış değerlendirmek *v* misjudge
yanlış hesaplamak *v* miscalculate
yanlışlık yapmak *n* miscarriage
yanlışlıkla *adj* accidental
yanmak *v* burn
yansıma *v* bounce
yansımak *v* rebound
yansıtma *n* reflection
yansıtmak *v* reflect
yanyana *adv* abreast
yanyana *adj* adjoining
yapabilmek *v* can
yapar görünmek *v* pretend
yapay *adj* artificial
yapayalnız *adj* lonesome
yapboz *n* jigsaw
yapı *n* constitution, structure
yapı içi *adv* indoor
yapıcı *adj* constructive
yapım *n* make
yapışkan *adj* adhesive, sticky
yapıştırmak *v* paste, stick
yapmacık *n* sham
yapmak *v* make, do
yaprak *n* sheet, leaf, leaves
yara *n* wound

yara izi *n* scar
yaralamak *v* hurt
yaralanmak *v* wound
yaralı *adj* hurt
yaramaz *adj* naughty
yaramaz kimse *n* rascal
yararlı *adj* beneficial
yararsız *adj* useless
yarasa *n* bat
yaratıcı *adj* creative
yaratıcı *n* creator
yaratıcılık *n* creativity
yaratık *n* creature
yaratım *n* creation
yaratmak *v* create
yarda *n* yard
yardım *n* aid, assistance, help, need
yardım etmek *v* assist, help
yardım istemek *v* invoke
yardıma muhtaç *adj* needy
yardımcı *n* aide, helper, contributor
yardımcı *adj* auxiliary, conducive, cooperative, subsidiary
yardımcı ders almak *v* minor
yardımcı olmak *v* aid
yardımsever *adj* caring, helpful
yargıç *n* magistrate
yargılamak *v* judge
yarı *adj* half
yarı yarıya *adv* fifty-fifty

yarıçap *n* radius
yarıda kesmek *v* interrupt
yarık *n* breach, cleft, crevice, rift, split
yarıküre *n* hemisphere
yarım *n* half
yarım yamalak *adj* sloppy
yarımada *n* peninsula
yarın *adv* tomorrow
yarış *n* race
yarışma *n* match
yarışmacı *n* competitor, contender, contestant
yarışmak *v* race
yarıya bölmek *v* halve
yarmak *v* hack, slit
yarşıma *n* competition
yas *n* mourning
yas tutmak *v* mourn
yasa dışı *adj* illegal, illicit
yasadışı *n* backdoor
yasak *n* ban, prohibition
yasaklama *n* restraint
yasaklamak *v* ban, forbid
yasal *adj* legal, legitimate
yasallaştırmak *v* legalize
yasallık *n* legality
yasama *n* legislation
yasama meclisi *n* legislature
yasaya uyan *adj* law-abiding
yasemin *n* jasmine
yaslanmak *v* lean on

yastık *n* padding, pillow
yastık kılıfı *n* pillowcase
yaş *n* age
yaşam *n* life
yaşam stili *n* lifestyle
yaşam süreci *adj* lifetime
yaşamak *v* live
yaşlı *n* elder
yaşlı *adj* old
yaşlıca *adj* elderly
yaşlılık *n* old age
yat *n* yacht
yatak *n* bed
yatak odası *n* bedroom
yatak örtüsü *n* bedspread
yatak takımı *n* bedding
yatakhane *n* dormitory
yatay *adj* horizontal
yatırım *n* investment
yatırım yapmak *v* invest
yatırımcı *n* investor
yatıştırıcı *adj* conciliatory
yatıştırılmaz *adj* implacable
yatıştırma *n* appeasement, sedation
yatıştırmak *v* appease, defuse, pacify, placate, sedate
yatmak *v* repose
yavaş *adj* slow
yavaş yavaş *adv* piecemeal
yavaşça *adv* slowly
yavaşlamak *v* slow down

yavaşlatmak *v* slacken
yavuz *adj* stern
yay *n* bow, arc, spring
yaya *n* pedestrian
yaya geçidi *n* crosswalk
yaygara *v* clamor
yaygara *n* fuss
yaygaracı *adj* fussy
yaygın *adj* frequent, prevalent, widespread
yayılıp yatmak *v* sprawl
yayılmak *v* emanate, span
yayımcı *n* broadcaster, publisher
yayımlamak *v* broadcast, release
yayın *n* broadcast, publication
yayınlamak *v* televise
yayla *n* prairie, plateau
yaymak *v* lay, propagate, spread
yaz *n* summer
yaz ortası *n* midsummer
yazar *n* author, novelist, writer
yazdırmak *v* dictate
yazı *n* writing, letter
yazıcı *n* printer
yazıcıya ait *adj* clerical
yazılı *adj* written
yazmak *v* write
yedek *n* backup, substitute
yedek *adj* spare
yedek parça *n* spare part
yedi *adj* seven
yedinci *adj* seventh

yeğen *n* niece, nephew
yel değirmeni *n* windmill
yelek *n* vest
yelken *n* sail
yelken açmak *v* sail
yelken iskotası *n* sheets
yelkenli *n* sailboat
yelpaze *n* fan
yem *n* bait
yeme *n* intake
yemek *v* eat, ingest
yemek *n* food, meal, dish
yemek borusu *n* esophagus
yemek odası *n* dining room
yemek tabağı *n* dish
yemek tarifi *n* recipe
yemek vermek *v* board
yemek yapma *n* cooking
yemin *n* oath
yemin etmek *v* vow
yemlik *n* crib; manger
yengeç *n* crab
yeni *adj* incoming, new
yeni *adv* newly
yeni baskı *n* reprint
yeni doğmuş *n* newborn
yeni evli *adj* newlywed
yeni gelen *n* newcomer
yeniden *adv* afresh, anew
yeniden cilalamak *v* refurbish
yeniden doğuş *n* rebirth
yeniden düşünmek *v* reconsider

yeniden ele geçirmek *v* recapture
yeniden finanse etmek *v* refinance
yeniden girme *n* reentry
yeniden inşa etmek *v* reconstruct
yeniden katılmak *v* rejoin
yeniden sahneleme *n* reenactment
yeniden seçmek *v* reelect
yenilebilir *adj* edible
yenileme *n* renewal, renovation
yenilemek *v* refresh, renovate
yenilenmiş *adj* renowned
yenileştirmek *v* renew
yenilgi *n* defeat, beating
yenilik *n* innovation
yenilmez *adj* invincible, unbeatable
yenmek *v* beat, defeat, prevail
yepyeni *adj* brand-new
yer *n* room, place
yer çekimi *n* gravity
yer değiştirmek *v* relocate
yer gösterici *n* usher
yeraltı *adj* underground
yeraltı sığınağı *n* bunker
yerel *adj* domestic, local, parochial
yerfıstığı *n* peanut
yerinde *adj* relevant
yerinden çıkarmak *v* dislocate
yerinden oynatmak *v* dislodge
yerine *adv* instead
yerine koymak *v* replace, substitute
yerini almak *v* supersede
yerini belirlemek *v* locate, plot

yerini değiştirmek *v* displace
yerleşik *adj* built-in
yerleşim *n* settlement
yerleşim bölgesi *n* enclave
yerleşme *n* relocation
yerleşmek *v* inhabit, settle
yerleştirilmiş *adj* located
yerleştirmek *v* place, accommodate
yerli *adj* native
yeşil *adj* green
yetenek *n* ability, capability, talent
yetenekli *adj* capable, gifted
yeteri kadar *adv* enough
yeterli *adj* competent, adequate, sufficient
yetersiz *adj* inadequate, insufficient
yetersiz beslenme *n* malnutrition
yetişkin *n* adult, grown-up
yetişmek *v* catch up
yetiştirmek *v* bring up, cultivate, rear, grow
yetki *n* authorization
yetki aktarmak *v* delegate
yetkilendirmek *v* authorize
yetmiş *adj* seventy
yığın *n* batch, heap, pile, bulk
yığışmak *v* agglomerate
yığmak *v* amass, pile, pile up

yıkamak *v* wash
yıkanabilir *adj* washable
yıkıcı *adj* destructive, shattering
yıkılış *n* downfall
yıkılmak *v* collapse
yıkım *n* demolition, destruction, ravage
yıkıp dökmek *v* vandalize
yıkmak *v* demolish, pull down, spoil
yıl *n* year
yıl boyu süren *adj* perennial
yılan *n* serpent, snake
yıldırım *n* thunderbolt
yıldırmak *v* daunt, terrorize
yıldız *n* star
yıldız imi *n* asterisk
yıldönümü *n* anniversary
yıllık *adj* annual
yıllık *adv* yearly
yılmaz *adj* intrepid
yıpranma payı *n* depreciation
yıpranmış *adj* decrepit
yırtık pırtık *adj* ragged
yırtmak *v* tear
yiğit *adj* daring, valiant
yiğitlik *n* bravery
yine de *adv* still, nevertheless
yine de *c* nonetheless
yinelemek *v* reiterate, replicate
yirmi *adj* twenty
yirminci *adj* twentieth

yiyecek *n* foodstuff
yiyip yutmak *v* devour
yobaz *adj* bigot
yobazlık *n* bigotry
yoğun *adj* intensive, dense
yoğunlaşmak *v* intensify
yoğunlaştırmak *v* condense, redouble
yoğunluk *n* density, intensity
yok edici *n* destroyer
yok etmek *v* eradicate, exterminate
yoklamak *v* ransack
yoksul *adj* destitute, impoverished
yoksulluk *n* poverty
yoksun *adj* deprived
yoksun bırakmak *v* deprive
yokuş *adv* uphill
yokuş aşağı *adv* downhill
yol *n* path, road, way
yol açmak *v* breed, cause
yol almak *v* head for
yol parası *n* fare
yol sayacı *n* odometer
yol şeridi *n* lane
yola çıkmak *v* depart, set off
yolcu *n* passenger, traveler
yolcu rehberi *n* itinerary
yolcu uçağı *n* airliner
yolculuk *n* journey
yolda kalmış *adj* stranded

yoldan çıkmak *v* stray
yoldan geçen *n* passer-by
yoldaş *n* companion
yoldaşlık *n* companionship
yonga *n* chip
yonga plakası *n* wafer
yontmak *v* whittle
yorgan *n* quilt, comforter
yorgun *adj* tired, weary
yorgunluk *n* exhaustion, fatigue, tiredness
yormak *v* wear out
yorucu *adj* exhausting, grueling, strenuous, tiresome
yorulmak *v* tire
yorulmak bilmez *adj* tireless
yorum *n* comment
yorum yapmak *v* comment
yosun *n* moss
yoz *adj* corrupt
yozlaşma *n* corruption
yozlaşmak *v* degenerate
yozlaşmış *v* corrupt
yön *n* direction
yön değiştirmek *v* avert
yönelmek *v* gravitate
yöneltmek *v* point
yönetici *n* director
yönetilir *adj* manageable
yönetim *n* executive, management, rule
yönetim kurulu *n* board

yönetmek *v* administer, govern, manage, mastermind, rule
yönlendirmek *v* channel, divert
yönlü *adj* oriented
yörünge *n* orbit
yudum *n* gulp, sip
yudumlamak *v* sip
yukarda *adv* upstairs
yukarı çekmek *v* hoist
yukarı çıkmak *v* ascend
yukarı kaldırmak *v* hold up, uphold
yukarı taşımak *v* move up
yukarıya doğru *adv* upwards
yulaf ezmesi *n* oatmeal
yumruk *n* fist
yumruklamak *v* punch
yumurta *n* egg
yumurta akı *n* egg white
yumurta sarısı *n* yolk
yumurtalık *n* ovary
yumuşak *adj* soft, balmy
yumuşakça *adv* softly
yumuşaklık *n* softness, leniency
yumuşamak *v* relent
yumuşatıcı *adj* laxative
yumuşatmak *v* soften
Yunan *adj* Greek
Yunanistan *n* Greece
yunus *n* dolphin
yurt *n* homeland
yurtdışında *adv* abroad

yurtsever *adj* patriotic
yutmak *v* gulp down, swallow
yuva *n* nest
yuvarlak *n* circle
yuvarlak *adj* circular, round
yuvarlanmak *v* tumble
yüce *adj* sublime
yüceltmek *v* exalt, glorify
yük *n* burden, load
yüklemek *v* burden, load
yüklenmek *v* undertake
yüklü *adj* burdensome, laden
yüksek *adj* high, lofty
yüksek ses *adv* aloud
yükseklik *n* altitude
yüksekten atmak *v* brag
yükselip alçalmak *v* fluctuate
yükseliş *n* upturn
yükselmek *v* go up, rise
yükselteç *n* amplifier
yükselti *n* elevation
yükseltmek *v* amplify, elevate, escalate, heighten, upgrade
yükü boşaltmak *v* unload
yün *n* fleece, wool
yün ipliği *n* yam, yarn
yünden *adj* woolen
yürek *n* guts
yüreklendirmek *v* hearten
yürekli *adj* audacious
yürekten *adj* hearty
yürümek *v* pace, walk

Y Z

yürütmek *v* rip off, execute
yürüyüş *n* hike, walk
yürüyüş yapmak *v* hike
yüz *n* face
yüz *adj* hundred
yüz ekşitme *n* grimace
yüz veren *adj* indulgent
yüz yüze *pre* facing
yüz yüze gelmek *v* confront
yüzde *adv* percent
yüzdelik *n* percentage
yüzen *adv* afloat
yüzey *n* surface, facet
yüzgeç *n* fin
yüzkarası *n* disgrace
yüzleşme *n* confrontation
yüzme *n* swimming
yüzmek *v* swim
yüzsüz *adj* cheeky
yüzü kızarmak *v* blush
yüzücü *n* swimmer
yüzük *n* ring
yüzüncü *adj* hundredth
yüzüncü yıl dönümü *n* centenary
yüzyıl *n* century

zaaf *n* frailty
zafer *n* triumph, victory
zahmet *n* trouble
zahmet çekmek *v* toil
zahmetli *adj* inconvenient
zahmetsiz *adj* painless
zalim *adj* atrocious, diabolical
zalim *n* tyrant
zamanında *adj* timely
zamanlamak *v* time
zamansız *adj* untimely
zamir *n* pronoun
zamk *n* paste
zan *n* presumption, supposition
zanaat *n* craft
zanaatkar *n* craftsman
zannetmek *v* presume
zarafet *n* grace
zarar *n* damage, deficit, harm
zarar veren *adj* damaging
zarar vermek *v* damage, injure,
harm
zararlı *adj* detrimental, harmful,
injurious, pernicious
zararsız *adj* harmless
zarf *n* adverb; envelope
zarif *adj* elegant, graceful, petite
zaten *adv* already
zatürree *n* pneumonia

zavallı *adj* miserable
zavallı *n* loser
zayıf *adj* weak, faint, slim
zayıflatmak *v* weaken
zayıflık *n* weakness
zebra *n* zebra
zehir *n* poison
zehirlemek *v* poison
zehirleyen *n* poisoning
zehirli *adj* poisonous
zeka *n* sense, mind
zeki *adj* clever, bright, intelligent
zemin *n* basement, floor, ground
zemin kat *n* ground floor
zencefil *n* ginger
zengin *adj* affluent, rich, wealthy
zenginleştirmek *v* enrich
zenginlik *n* wealth
zerafet *n* elegance
zeval *n* decadence
zevk *n* gusto, zest
zevk almak *v* savor
zevk sahibi *adj* tasteful
zeytin *n* olive
zımba *n* staple, stapler, punch
zımbalamak *v* staple
zımpara kağıdı *n* sandpaper
zıpkın *n* harpoon
zıplamak *v* hop, jump, leap
zırh *n* armor
zırhlı gemi *n* turret
zırva *adj* crappy

zihninde tartmak *v* ponder
zihniyet *n* mentality
zil *n* bell
zimmetine geçirmek *v* embezzle
zina *n* adultery
zincir *n* chain
zincirlemek *v* chain
zincirli testere *n* chainsaw
zindan *n* dungeon
zirve *n* apex, climax, summit
ziyafet *n* banquet, feast
ziyan *n* detriment
ziyaret *n* visit
ziyaret etmek *v* visit
ziyaretçi *n* visitor
zonklamak *v* throb
zooloji *n* zoology
zor *adj* difficult, hard, tough
zoraki *adj* strained
zorba *adj* brutal, bully
zorbalık *n* brutality
zorbalık etmek *v* brutalize
zorla *adv* forcibly, hardly
zorla girme *n* intrusion
zorla girmek *v* intrude
zorlama *n* coercion
zorlamak *v* coerce, compel, force, oblige, urge
zorlaştırmak *v* complicate
zorlayıcı *adj* compelling, binding
zorlu *adj* stringent, violent
zorluk *n* adversity, difficulty, hassle, severity

Z

zorunlu *adj* indispensable,
mandatory, obligatory
zulmetmek *v* persecute
zulüm *n* tyranny
züccaciye *n* glassware

zümre *n* class
zümrüt *n* emerald
zürafa *n* giraffe
zürriyet *n* posterity

Word to Word® Bilingual Dictionary Series

Language - Item # ISBN #

Albanian - 500X
ISBN - 978-0-933146-49-5

Amharic - 820X
ISBN - 978-0-933146-59-4

Arabic - 650X
ISBN - 978-0-933146-41-9

Bengali - 700X
ISBN - 978-0-933146-30-3

Burmese - 705X
ISBN - 978-0-933146-50-1

Cambodian - 710X
ISBN - 978-0-933146-40-2

Chinese - 715X
ISBN - 978-0-933146-22-8

Czech - 520X
ISBN - 978-0-933146-62-4

Farsi - 660X
ISBN - 978-0-933146-33-4

French - 530X
ISBN - 978-0-933146-36-5

German - 535X
ISBN - 978-0-933146-93-8

Greek - 540X
ISBN - 978-0-933146-60-0

Gujarati - 720X
ISBN - 978-0-933146-98-3

Haitian-Creole - 545X
ISBN - 978-0-933146-23-5

Hebrew - 665X
ISBN - 978-0-933146-58-7

Hindi - 725X
ISBN - 978-0-933146-31-0

Hmong - 728X
ISBN - 978-0-933146-31-0

Italian - 555X
ISBN - 978-0-933146-51-8

Japanese - 730X
ISBN - 978-0-933146-42-6

Korean - 735X
ISBN - 978-0-933146-97-6

Lao - 740X
ISBN - 978-0-933146-54-9

Nepali - 755X
ISBN - 978-0-933146-61-7

Pashto - 760X
ISBN - 978-0-933146-34-1

Polish - 575X
ISBN - 978-0-933146-64-8

Portuguese - 580X
ISBN - 978-0-933146-94-5

Punjabi - 765X
ISBN - 978-0-933146-32-7

Romanian - 585X
ISBN - 978-0-933146-91-4

Russian - 590X
ISBN - 978-0-933146-92-1

Somali - 830X
ISBN- 978-0-933146-52-5

Spanish - 600X
ISBN - 978-0-933146-99-0

Swahili - 835X
ISBN - 978-0-933146-55-6

Tagalog - 770X
ISBN - 978-0-933146-37-2

Thai - 780X
ISBN - 978-0-933146-35-8

Turkish - 615X
ISBN - 978-0-933146-95-2

Ukrainian - 620X
ISBN - 978-0-933146-25-9

Urdu - 790X
ISBN - 978-0-933146-39-6

Vietnamese - 795X
ISBN - 978-0-933146-96-9

All languages are two-way:
English-Language / Language-English.
More languages in planning and production.

Order Information

To order our Word to Word® bilingual dictionaries or any other products from Bilingual Dictionaries, Inc., please contact us at (951) 296-2445 or visit us at **www.BilingualDictionaries.com**. Visit our website to download our current catalog/order form, view our products, and find information regarding Bilingual Dictionaries, Inc.

 **Bilingual Dictionaries, Inc.**

PO Box 1154 • Murrieta, CA 92564 • Tel: (951) 296-2445 • Fax: (951) 296-9911
www.BilingualDictionaries.com

Special Dedication & Thanks

Bilingual Dicitonaries, Inc. would like to thank all the teachers from various districts accross the country for their useful input and great suggestions in creating a Word to Word® standard. We encourage all students and teachers using our bilingual learning materials to give us feedback. Please send your questions or comments via email to **support@bilingualdictionaries.**